Latin American Christian Democratic Parties

Latin American Christian Democratic Parties

EDWARD J. WILLIAMS
MARQUETTE UNIVERSITY

THE UNIVERSITY OF TENNESSEE PRESS
KNOXVILLE

Library of Congress Catalog Card Number 67–13159
Manufactured in the United States of America

To my wife, Grace

Preface

This book has a very simple purpose: to describe and analyze the Latin American Christian Democratic parties. Nine descriptive chapters attempt to set out what the Christian Democrats are about in Latin America—where they came from, what they are thinking, what they have done, and what they hope to do. The analysis should be construed as only a beginning; it is a modest effort, not a *fait accompli.*

Nevertheless, the subject of the book is crucially important in the development of Latin America. The Christian movement has been of primary significance in Europe over the last twenty years, and there seems to be every indication that it is rapidly assuming a similar position in Latin America. Much Latin American Christian Democratic literature has oversimplified the political future of the continent as an inevitable clash between democratic Christians and totalitarian Communists. The situation is much more complex than that. Still, there is little doubt that the movement has emerged as one of the strongest democratic forces in Latin America, and it behooves us to know what it is and where it is going.

The book is a result of the happy convergence of three major interests which I have developed over the last decade or so—these being Christian Democratic thought, political parties, and Latin American politics. The opportunity to combine all of one's interests is rare indeed. Even rarer for a North American political science student is the experience of working with an international political movement, and the study has certainly been enriched as a result of my association with the Center of Christian Democratic Action in New York during much of 1965.

Traditional Christian theory on man and society quite correctly emphasizes the essential interconnection of the human person and society. Man as a social being is realized in association with his fellows. If this proposition be true of man in the wider sense, it is equally so with reference to the scholar and his efforts; any accomplishment reflects the labors and ideas of many. It is, of course, beyond the ken of these short paragraphs to acknowledge all who have contributed. Debts of gratitude are obviously owed to numerous friends and colleagues whose names will not appear below. I am honor bound, however, to mention at least a few.

To my wife, Grace E. Williams, above all, I must render profound homage for having been a constant source of inspiration, a critical analyst, a reader (and re-reader), a typist at several stages of the work, and a booster of flagging spirits. It is, indeed, her work as much as my own.

Numerous scholars and politicians in both Americas offered inestimable assistance during the research and writing of the study. Gottfried Dietze, friend and mentor, presided at the launching. Valmore Acevedo Amaya, friend and colleague at the Center of Christian Democratic Action, counseled me through much of the research and writing. His analytic mind and wide-ranging experience in the Christian Democratic movement provided much of what is good in the book. The same debt of gratitude is owed to Edward Cohen, of the International Development Foundation; Enrique Pérez Olivares and Arnold van Niekerk, both of the *Instituto de Formación Demócrata Cristiana* (IFEDEC) in Caracas; and the officers and staff of the Christian-Democratic Research Center at the University of Notre Dame. All read most of the manuscript, and all contributed to its improvement. For ideas, inspiration, and information, I am also indebted to the many Christian Democrats whom I met and talked with at the Center and to my instructors and *compañeros* at the Sixth General Course on Christian Democratic Theory and Practice at IFEDEC in Caracas during April-May, 1965.

In a more practical vein, my thanks also go to the Marquette University Committee on Research for financial assistance in the final typing of the study, to Mrs. Marie Ziesch and Miss Joann DeWitt, who assisted at various stages in typing and revising the manuscript, and to Emil Stanislawski, who worked with me during the final stages of the endeavor and who assisted in the compilation of the index.

In keeping with long-standing custom, I finally note that none of the above named should be considered responsible for any weaknesses of this study. That burden, alas, is mine to bear.

February 3, 1967 EDWARD J. WILLIAMS
Milwaukee, Wisconsin

Contents

The Backdrop for Latin American Christian Democracy

1 INTRODUCTION 3
Latin American Political Parties, 4. Catholic Parties and Christian Democratic Parties, 9.

2 ORIGINS AND GROWTH OF THE MOVEMENT 13
Catalysts of Foundation and Growth, 17. Strength and Experience, 23. Roots of the Latin American Movement, 26.

3 THEORETICAL FOUNDATIONS 36
Tenets and Directions, 36. Nature of Man and Society, 51. The State, 60.

Latin American Christian Democratic Parties

4 CHARACTERISTICS AND ORGANIZATION 69
Ideological Parties, 69. Christian but Non-Confessional Base, 72. Democratic and Popular Emphasis, 75. Internal Party Structure, 81. Affiliated Organizations, 88.

5 DOMESTIC POLICIES AND PROGRAMS 94
Family Affairs and Local Government, 94. Education, 100. Labor Policies and Labor Unions, 102. Agrarian Reform, 105. Governmental Reform, 108.

6 ECONOMIC POLICIES AND PROGRAMS 112
Economic Humanism, 112. *La Reforma de la Empresa*, 116. Communitarianism, 118. The State and Economic Development, 123. The Private Sector, 127.

7 INTERNATIONAL ORGANIZATION AND POLICIES 133
Latin American Integration, 138. Intervention and Non-Intervention, 143. Attitudes Toward the United States, 146. Christian Democrats and the Soviet Bloc, 154. Rejection of Colonialism, 156. Attitudes Toward Cuba, 158.

8 RELATIONS WITH MILITARY FORCES AND THE CATHOLIC CHURCH 161
The Military, 161. Christian Democrats and the Church, 167. The Catholic Church in Latin America, 169. The New Church and the New Catholicism, 171. Latin American Catholic Tradition, 176. The Church and the Parties, 178. Christian Democrats and the Catholic Right, 182.

9 RELATIONS WITH OTHER POLITICAL FORCES 187
Christian Democracy—A Center Movement, 187. Coalition and Cooperation, 190. Christian Democrats and Communists, 193. Christian Democrats and the Peronistas, 201. The Venezuelan Social Christian—COPEI and Acción Democrática, 204. The Peruvian Christian Democrats and Acción Popular, 209. Relations with the Socialists, 214. Relations with the Radicals, 219. Christian Democrats and the Right, 222.

Latin American Christian Democracy: An Assessment

10 HANDICAPS TO THE MOVEMENT 229
The Messianic Bent, 229. Ideological Lacunae, 232. Internal Problems, 240. The Revolution, 251. The Christian Electorate, 258. Nationalism, 261.

11 ASSETS OF THE MOVEMENT 264
Ideology and Non-Traditionalism, 264. Heritage of the Parties, 266. Reputation of the Parties, 271. Organization and Training, 273. Electoral Appeal and Support, 275. Anti-Communist Bent, 279. The Future, 281.

BIBLIOGRAPHY 283

INDEX 297

The Backdrop for Latin American Christian Democracy

Introduction 1

The dramatic election of Eduardo Frei Montalva to the Chilean presidency in September of 1964 signaled the first full-fledged victory of a Latin American Christian Democratic party.[1] The beginning could not have been more propitious. The election pitted Christian Democrat Frei against Salvador Allende Gossens, the candidate of the left-wing coalition, Frente Acción Popular. The confrontation bore a striking resemblance to the crucial Italian election of 1948 in which the Christian Democratic victory was interpreted as the dawn of a new era of European democracy. The popular press was quick to apply similar predictions to the Latin American scene, and a spate of articles appeared hailing the newly emerged Latin American Christian Democratic movement as the savior of that troubled continent: the alternative to Peronista-type Jacobin nationalism or Castro-style Communist totalitarianism had suddenly appeared; the much-discussed Third Force of Latin American politics had evolved; the Democratic Left had found new allies.

Indeed, there was more than a grain of truth in these proposals. The Christian Democrats do ally with the Democratic Left; they do see themselves as a third force and, most surprising, the movement has literally burst upon the Latin American political scene unknown except to the most careful student. Before 1946, only two parties of Christian Democratic persuasion had achieved uninterrupted existence in Latin America: the National Falange of Chile, precursor of Frei's Christian Democratic party, and the Unión Cívica of Uruguay, which preceded the Christian Democratic party of that country. Today the Christian Democratic parties are of major significance in

[1] The subsequent Christian Democratic sweep of the March, 1965, legislative elections overcame the doubts of many who had seen Frei's victory as a personal triumph.

Chile, Venezuela, Peru, and El Salvador; they are important in Argentina, Guatemala, the Dominican Republic, and Uruguay; and they exist in every nation except Honduras and Haiti.

Despite its rapidly growing importance to the future of Latin American politics, little is known of the Latin American Christian Democratic movement. Only a few scholarly English-language articles have analyzed the movement; general works on Latin American parties pay little heed to it, and even textbook publications barely acknowledge its existence. Indeed, the entire range of Latin American political parties has been abysmally neglected by students of the area. The Latin American Aprista and Peronista movements have merited some attention, and some investigation has been undertaken on the Argentine Radical party, but this can be called only the smallest beginning.

LATIN AMERICAN POLITICAL PARTIES

Perhaps the fundamental reason for lack of interest in Latin American party development has been the widely held view that the so-called parties of that continent hardly merited the name. The early Conservatives and Liberals were little more than pressure groups roughly identified with the rural aristocracy and the newly developing commercial sectors. Politics, and political parties, was reserved for the rich and well born; party organization was shallow and usually involved only personal and family attachment. The parties were organized for elections; no ongoing structure was maintained.

Some evolution, however, was evident by the beginning of this century. Liberal parties had developed into fairly consistent, conscious representatives of the urban elite, and Conservatives had emerged as representatives of landed interests. Moreover, new forces had been nurtured within the womb of Latin American politics; pressures to broaden the base of political participation and power became increasingly vocal. Middle-class parties emerged soon after the turn of the century. The Radicals of Argentina and Chile, the Uruguayan Colorados, and the Colombian and Ecuadorian Liberals served as the power vehicles for the political aspirations of the middle class. Finally, after the Great Depression, and more dramatically following World War II, labor-oriented parties developed rapidly and exercised profound influence in numerous Latin American nations.

Lest this short chronology give the impression of infallible unilateral progression, it must be emphasized that much that is fundamental to political maturity is still lacking. As late as the early forties, a Bolivian noted: "in the incipient democracies of America, there are no more than two parties in conflict; one which enjoys the use of the fruits of power, and the other which mourns the nostalgia of them."[2] A Peruvian student is more specific. In a long list of handicaps to the formation of really effective parties, he has included "public indifference," "egoism and cowardliness of the ruling class and wealthy sectors," "skepticism with reference to the sincerity of party programs," "lack of faith in the office holders because they have often displayed treachery and demonstrated their incapacity and lack of scruples," and "the Peruvian tradition of *caudillismo*."[3] Federico Gil presents other reasons why the proper "climate" is lacking:

> Limitations of franchise, if not of a constitutional, of a practical order; lack of availability of political information; social-economic patterns which tend to prevent free expression of opinion; defects of the systems of electoral administration as well as of party organization; and lack of a sense of fair play or sportsmanship.[4]

These factors, however, are only surface reflections of a more fundamental malady that includes such indigenous complaints as "illiteracy, the low living standards, the ethnic and socio-economic tensions, the encumbrances of geography, and the meager means of communications and transportation encountered in much of Latin America."[5] Moreover, as the Latin Americans and Spaniards themselves are fond of saying, the so-called Spanish character—that perennial whipping boy—may be the cause of the political cancer. Salvador de Madariaga berates the Spanish propensity for "devouring their institutions with the acid of their corrosive individualities."[6]

[2] Luís Terán Goméz, *Los Partidos Políticos y su Acción Democrática* (La Paz: Editorial "La Paz," 1942), p. 3.

[3] Carlos Miró-Quesada Láos, *Autopsia de los Partidos Políticos* (Lima: Ediciones "Paginas Peruanas," 1961), p. 488.

[4] Federico G. Gil, "Responsible Parties in Latin America," *Journal of Politics*, XV (Aug., 1953), 334–35.

[5] Harold Eugene Davis (ed.), *Government and Politics in Latin America* (New York: The Ronald Press, 1958), p. 191.

[6] Salvador de Madariaga, *The Rise of the Spanish American Empire* (New York: The Macmillan Company, 1949), p. 283. For other examples of this oft-quoted theme, see Madariaga, *The Fall of the Spanish American Empire* (New York: The Macmillan Company, 1948), p. 16; Allison Williams Bunkley, *The*

The pessimism of this literature seems to preclude any rational study of Latin American political party theory and practice. Nevertheless, factors favoring the development of ideological parties that are firmly rooted in the society are multiplying rapidly. The time is ripe to launch a series of studies promising more order and understanding than has been possible previously; the maturity of the animal now permits a worthwhile examination. In short, the argument is that "Latin America is growing up politically."[7] It is a growth in sophistication that is a reflection of basic economic and social changes.

These changes account for the fact that the new political parties differ fundamentally from the "parties" of the first century of independence. They now represent fairly unified interests and promulgate coherent philosophies. Numerous groups have organized a hard core of militants within their organizations; and the distinctions among ideological positions are becoming clearer. The positions are represented by such groups as the Aprista Social Democrats, Communists, Radicals, some homogeneous Liberals and Conservatives, and Christian Democrats; each offers distinct programs and each sinks its roots deeper and deeper into the several national societies.[8] In Chile, for example, all parties with congressional representation are founded on relatively clear ideological bases. Peru is in the transition period between primitive personalist groupings, which center on one man, and mature parties, which focus on organization and program.[9] The major Venezuelan parties are ideological.

Moreover, these parties have also developed more comprehensive and permanent organizations, another crucial characteristic of a modern political system. One of the pathological conditions of traditional Latin American parties has been their lack of organized

---

Life of Sarmiento (Princeton, N. J.: Princeton University Press, 1952), pp. 172–73; W. W. Pierson (ed.), "Pathology of Democracy in Latin America: A Symposium," *American Political Science Review*, XLIV (March, 1950), 119.

[7] Robert J. Alexander, "The Emergence of Modern Political Parties in Latin America," *The Politics of Change in Latin America*, ed. Joseph Maier and Richard W. Weatherhead (New York: Frederick A. Praeger, 1964), p. 101.

[8] See, for example, Miró-Quesada, *Autopsia*, p. 490; Karl M. Schmitt and David B. Burks, *Evolution or Chaos? Dynamics of Latin American Government and Politics* (New York: Frederick A. Praeger, 1963), p. 24; Russell H. Fitzgibbon, "The Party Potpourri in Latin America," *Western Political Quarterly*, X (March, 1957), 6. For a refutation of this analysis, see, Antonio Díaz, "Los Partidos Políticos del Ecuador," *Política* (Caracas), III (Nov., 1963) and Frank Tannenbaum, *Ten Keys to Latin America* (New York: Alfred A. Knopf, 1962).

[9] Miró-Quesada, *Autopsia*, p. 490.

structures. This condition, however, is rapidly giving way to more mature organization.

> The new political party in Latin America also has a much more intensive internal life than did the older kind. It has local organizations throughout the country conducting activities of their own most of the year and not merely on the eve of an election or in the morning after a coup d'etat. They hold periodic membership meetings. They gather for regular local, regional and national conventions, and they do so even when no election or other change in government is in the offing.
>
> These parties involve relatively large numbers of citizens drawn from various classes. They often carry on organized activities within the ranks of labor unions, professional associations and other non-political groups. Many support a variety of periodicals and publish pamphlets and even books. Some have organized groups within them to carry on a continuous study of the economic and social problems of their countries—regardless of whether they are, at the moment, in the government or in the opposition. These studies may form the basis for policy and be published. Sometimes, though by no means always, the parties collect dues from their members and issue membership cards or other means of identifying those who belong.[10]

One final development merits attention. The growth of modern political parties in Latin America has been accompanied by a weakening of personalism, the Latin version of the European "decline of the notables." Personalist organizations still proliferate at election time but with less frequency and less intensity. Gilberto Freyre, while admitting that personalism still plays an important role in Brazil, suggests, nevertheless, that "none of Brazil's prominent political personalities stands completely aloof from their parties."[11] Others see "evidence that personalist parties are currently declining in number and influence."[12] A now-classic work on the emergence of the middle class in the new Latin American society states that "the *caudillos* and the colonels who shoot their way into the presidential chair are no longer the effective agents of all political change."[13]

[10] Alexander, "The Emergence of Modern Political Parties," pp. 103, 104.

[11] Gilberto Freyre, "Personalities versus Parties for the Presidency of Brazil," *Reporter*, XXI (July 23, 1959). 28.

[12] George I. Blanksten, "Political Groups in Latin America," *American Political Science Review*, LIII (March, 1959), 112.

[13] John J. Johnson, *Political Change in Latin America: The Emergence of the Middle Sectors* (Stanford, Cal.: Stanford University Press, 1958), p. viii.

Traditional methods of analyzing Latin American politics must undergo radical revision; the situation is no longer characterized solely by clashing personalities and ambitions involving demagogic appeals and brute force; parties, as defined by Western students, are now a part of the political landscape. In sum, the most correct analysis of the situation may be that of Duverger, who proposes the multiparty system of Latin America as a stage of the development of the political system. This "intermediate category" is characterized by "authentic parties possessing a minimum of organization and stability in juxtaposition to inorganic and unstable groups, . . . vestiges of inorganic groups subsist inside many countries that have organized parties."[14]

The fundamental premise of this study, then, is that Latin American political development now makes possible an analysis of the various nations' political parties. That much-neglected area of Latin American politics is ready for exploitation, and the Latin American Christian Democratic parties—as one example of this new phenomenon—are an appropriate subject for thorough examination. Hence, this study attempts to cover the Latin American Christian Democratic political party movement in its entirety, from its historical and theoretical origins to its present position in the continent's politics. The study is primarily descriptive, although the last two chapters review and analyze some of the movement's strengths and weaknesses—factors which have and will influence and condition its future effectiveness. Policy pronouncements from all of the Christian Democratic parties are included in an effort to highlight the common theory and practice which characterize the Latin American movement.

The various Christian Democratic parties are basically very similar, but some variations, both accidental and intentional, do exist. Latin Americanists are wont to point out, and correctly so, that Latin America is not the homogeneous unit that textbooks often imply. The twenty nations are similar, but separate and distinct. Generalizations are, alas, only generally valid, and this fundamental warning is certainly applicable to an analysis of the area's political parties. For example, a party, per se, is more effective in Chile than in Ecuador, more intelligible in Peru than in Paraguay. Christian Democratic parties, reflecting these differences, operate within par-

[14] Maurice Duverger, *Political Parties: Their Organization and Activity in the Modern State*, trans. Barbara and Robert North (New York: John Wiley and Sons, Inc., 1963), p. 228.

ticular environments and must be examined with reference to specific time and place. It seems quite impossible to present a frame of reference for each point made in this study. The reader, however, should be alerted to the differing circumstances which condition the activity of the several parties.

Two more points merit attention. The sources utilized and examples noted are usually of recent origin. The situation demands primary reliance on contemporary material, simply because the Latin American Christian Democratic parties are relatively new to the political scene. Nevertheless, this volume should not be interpreted as merely a modern history of the movement. By describing the philosophical and political positions of the parties, the author hopes to outline their characteristics and to provide the bases for further analysis of Latin American politics. Furthermore, specific parties have occasionally altered their positions on specific problems. This fact should not impair the value of the study, for it still offers a valid description of the tenor and direction of Latin American Christian Democracy. Second, the investigation has been limited to the political parties. Christian Democracy includes more: labor groups, social action organizations, and youth affiliates, for example. These groups are analyzed only when they impinge upon or condition the Christian Democratic parties themselves. University students, for instance, have been of real importance for several of the parties, and the feminine vote promises to be a key factor in the future success of the movement. Naturally, the activities and programs of the parties are influenced by these factors.

CATHOLIC PARTIES AND CHRISTIAN DEMOCRATIC PARTIES

Despite the sudden growth of the contemporary institutional parties, Latin American history reveals numerous examples of incipient movements of Christian Democratic predilection, as well as many individuals whose activity approximated the modern theory and practice of Christian Democracy. Ambrosio Romero Carranza, in a chapter entitled "Christian Democratic Antecedents in the Argentine Republic," traces the history of political thinkers and practitioners. "In our country," he notes, "there always existed Christian Democrats in all the political parties."[15] Although it may be gratuitous to call these

[15] Ambrosio Romero Carranza, *¿Qué es la Democracia Cristiana?* (Buenos Aires: Ediciones del Atlántico, 1956), p. 192.

thinkers Christian Democrats in the modern sense of that term, they were assuredly Christians and Democrats and they certainly anticipated many stances of the modern-day Christian Democratic movement. Reference might also be made to the early Latin American patriots, cited by Víctor Andrés Belaúnde, who were both ardent Catholics and equally fervent Republicans and Democrats.[16] Moreover, the traditional Conservative parties historically sheltered Social Christian factions. Notwithstanding these isolated examples of embryonic Christian Democracy, no authentic movement developed until the second decade of the present century.

Indeed, much confusion results from Christian Democratic literature in its fruitless attempt to establish an identity between traditional Catholic parties and modern Christian Democratic parties. Although an historical connection often exists, the differences are profound, and intelligent analysis necessarily demands a clear distinction. It is absurd, for instance, to equate the modern German Christian Democratic Union and the old Center party;[17] they differ as do the son and the father. To extend the metaphor, the modern Christian Democratic party is more often the bastard of the traditional Catholic party—a bastard, furthermore, which is sometimes not recognized and often vehemently repudiated; a bastard which not only bears a different name but also a different constitution.

The crux of this distinction is found in the shift from a negative stance to one of militant positive activity.[18] The original European Catholic parties and their counterparts in Latin America, the tra-

[16] Víctor Andrés Belaúnde, *Bolívar and the Political Thought of the Spanish American Revolution* (Baltimore: The Johns Hopkins Press, 1938), pp. 38–63.

[17] See Michael P. Fogarty, *Christian Democracy in Western Europe, 1820–1953* (Notre Dame, Ind.: University of Notre Dame Press, 1957), who recognizes this distinction when he says that the Center Party "resembled" the modern Christian Democratic party (p. 304). Luigi Sturzo also implicitly alludes to the difference, "The Philosophic Background of Christian Democracy," *Review of Politics*, IX (Jan., 1947), 5. Also Arnold J. Heidenheimer, *Adenauer and the CDU* (The Hague: Martinus Nijoff, 1960), notes: "One sign of this trend can be seen in the drastic decline of clerics within the leadership of the parties. Before World War I clerics were extremely numerous in the Zentrum; in the Weimar period they were still apparent and influential, whereas in the CDU the clerical collar has virtually disappeared from amongst the party's parliamentary representatives" (p. 131).

[18] Fogarty proposes that the "shift from defense to attack is the hallmark of the rising generation of Christian militants." *Christian Democracy in Western Europe*, p. 378.

ditional Conservative parties, were political because necessity demanded political organization. It was the best way to defend the interests of the Church and Catholicism. Rather comprehensive programs were developed, but only as a means of achieving the primary goals. Essentially, these political groupings were organizations of Catholics fighting to preserve their religious, and often their cultural and economic, identity in an overtly hostile atmosphere invoked by militant liberal national governments. Only after the religious conflict had been won, as in Germany, or subsided in intensity, as in many of the Latin American countries, could a positive, comprehensive, socially oriented political movement evolve. Only then was it possible "to restore to the political sphere criteria of action and values that [had] been discarded because of the conflict."[19]

The very use of the name "Christian Democracy" bears witness to this change. The term has been utilized in different ways. Initially, it served to outline an approving attitude with reference to liberal democratic political systems, later, to designate Catholic social action, and only recently, to apply to a full-blown socio-economic, political, philosophic system.[20] Before 1948, political parties founded upon Catholic social principles did not usually employ the name "Christian Democrat."[21] After 1948, however, all newly founded political parties have utilized the designation, and some older parties have adopted it.

The Uruguayan experience exemplifies the distinction between Catholic and Christian Democratic parties. Many Latin American parties, unlike some of their European cousins, are newly established organizations and have not evolved from traditional Catholic political groups. The Uruguayan party, however, was founded in a militantly secular political age to protect the Church and the faith, and only in the last several years has it demonstrated clear-cut Christian Democratic activity.[22]

The foundation of the party spanned the last part of the previous

[19] Mario Einaudi and François Goguel, *Christian Democracy in Italy and France* (Notre Dame, Ind.: University of Notre Dame Press, 1952), p. 1.

[20] Américo Plá Rodríguez, *Los Principios de la Democracia Cristiana* (Bogotá: Ediciones del Caribe, 1962), p. 7.

[21] See, for example, Sturzo's Popular Party, the French Mouvement Republicain Populaire, Chile's National Falange and Venezuela's COPEI.

[22] It may be interpreted as symbolic that the index for the first seven volumes of the *Hispanic American Report* lists not, "Unión Cívica," the correct name of the organization, but "Catholic Party."

century and the first part of the present century, an age marked by the progressive strengthening of anti-clerical liberal governments in Latin America generally and Uruguay specifically. In Uruguay, these militant reformist groups attained clear supremacy under the presidency of the renowned José Batlle y Ordóñez (1903–1907, 1911–1915). Discussing the formation period of the party, a history of the Unión Cívica declares that "the Jacobin epoch had begun, initiated under the Presidency of Batlle, against all which implied the predominance—not even the predominance, the simple conservation—of religious interests in the country."[23] The first program of the party, promulgated in 1912, declares that "its activity will respond naturally to the defense of Catholic interest. . . ." The document proceeds to point out that "its activities will not concentrate only on this end, but an integral development will have to encourage all initiatives and multiply all the improvements which procure the general well-being of the inhabitants of the Republic."[24]

Despite this claim to wider competence, there is little doubt that the primary rationale of the organization was the "defense of Catholic interests." Furthermore, political activity had been "approved and consecrated" by the prelates of the nation. Describing the Uruguayan situation in 1946, the party historian applauds the fact that the political environment "offers an agreeable calm, under the rule of a happy liberty." Now, he says, it is possible to attack "other problems, equally fundamental for the society, like those which refer to the social order."[25] This improvement was to result in the gradual evolution of the party into an authentic Social Christian political organization which adopted the name Christian Democratic party in 1962.

[23] Joaquín Secco-Illa, *Historia de la Unión Cívica* (Montevideo: Impresora Zorrilla de San Martín, 1946), p. 51.

[24] *Ibid.*, p. 133.

[25] *Ibid.*, p. 143.

Origins and Growth of the Movement 2

In the twentieth century, the full-blown Christian Democratic doctrine began to emerge in Latin America. As is true of so much Latin American social, economic, and political theory, the movement lagged about two decades behind its European counterpart and did not develop strong roots until the second decade of the century. One of the pioneer publications expounding this doctrine was Enrique Concha Subercaseaux's *Cuestiones obreras* (Worker's Questions) published in 1899,[1] and the earliest organization was the Democratic Christian Union of Argentina, founded in 1916. Although the Argentine party was short-lived, it was the first example of an institutional party based on Christian Democratic principles. During World War I, the movement became more widespread as a result of the social work and the study groups which developed in Argentina, Uruguay, and Chile. These three southern nations were the most industrially advanced in Latin America, and they received waves of European immigrants. Modern social problems intrinsic to the development process emerged. An outstanding Argentine of this period was Bishop Miguel de Andrea, who attempted to apply European solutions to the Argentine situation.[2] In neighboring Uruguay the Catholic Unión Cívica party was founded in August, 1912; it evidenced some characteristics of the later movements, including a concern for the redemption of the proletariat and an interest in social problems. The Uruguayan group was organized before the publication of Pope Leo XIII's revolutionary encyclical, *Rerum Novarum*, and developed over a period of twenty-five years from a strictly clerical undertaking into a type of early Catholic social-action organization and finally

[1] Harold Eugene Davis (ed.), *Government and Politics in Latin America* (New York: The Ronald Press, 1958), p. 87.

[2] Roberto Marchant, "Christian Democracy in Latin America," *Christian Democratic Review*, XI (June, 1961), 4, 5.

into a political party.[3] In Chile, several attempts at political organization were made by social Catholics before their efforts were finally successful in the mid-thirties. In 1922, they formed the Partido Popular, which was copied from Luigi Sturzo's Italian party of the same name. Ten years later the Partido Corporativo Popular was established; it too failed, and most of its members eventually joined the Falange Nacional,[4] successfully organized several years later.

Alceu Amoroso Lima, one of the most important ideologues of the Latin American movement, dates the emergence of Brazilian Christian Democracy from the foundation of the Catholic Electoral League in 1934, which was established as a maneuver to check the prevailing "totalitarian or neo-regalist spirit."[5] Two years later, two groups emerged in Paraguay. One of them founded the newspaper *Tiempo* and became known as the Tiempistas. Representatives of the group participated in the government beginning in 1942. Subsequently, the movement was suppressed by the dictator, Federico Chávez, and its previous leaders are now inactive.[6] A new group, the Movimiento Social Demócrata Cristiano (after 1965, the Partido Demócrata Cristiano) has emerged in Paraguay. In Peru, the most illustrious of the early Christian Democrats, the scholar-statesman, Víctor Andrés Belaúnde, was preaching Christian Democratic ideals as early as 1930. In Mexico, the right-wing, clerical Partido de Acción Nacional was organized in 1939. Although this opposition party never evolved into a mature Christian Democratic movement, it nurtured elements that provided the nucleus for the formation of an authentic Christian Democratic movement in 1964.

The 1940's witnessed the increasing development of the parties; this period saw the original efforts of many organizations that were to blossom in the late 1950's and early 1960's. In 1947, the Peruvian Agrupación Demócrata Cristiana was constituted, and a year later this seminal group joined with several other organizations to form the Movimiento Democrático, which espoused Social Christian ideals. In that period, Héctor Cornejo Chávez, later to become the

[3] Joaquín Secco-Illa, *Historia de la Unión Cívica* (Montevideo: Impresora Zorrilla de San Martín, 1946), especially the first two chapters.

[4] Bartolomé Palacios Silva, *Por los Fueros de la Verdad Tradicionalistas y Social-Cristianos* (Santiago de Chile: "Gutenberg" Impresores, 1948), pp. 18–24.

[5] Alceu Amoroso Lima, "An Interpretation of Brazilian Politics," *Social Science*, XXVI (Oct., 1951), 210.

[6] *Christian Democratic Review*, II (Oct. 31, 1952), 3.

standard-bearer of the party, was secretary to the then president, José Luis Bustamante y Rivero, who himself exhibited Christian Democratic tendencies. The party, however, was paralyzed after the *golpe de estado* of 1948 and did not re-emerge until the surrender of power by Manuel Odría in 1956.[7]

Various Christian Democratic nuclei operated in Argentina during the 1940's. Among them was the Movimiento Demócrata Cristiano de Tucumán and the Unión Demócrata Cristiana de Córdoba. These two convened in February, 1948, when the Movimiento Social Republicano was founded.[8] But Peronista tyranny suppressed the party, and not until the fall of Perón were several Catholic and Christian Democratic movements to organize.

The Venezuelan Social Christian party was started as a student movement in opposition to the semi-democratic regimes that followed the demise of Juan Vicente Gómez. It organized the Acción Nacional during the regime of General Isaías Medina Angarita (1941–1945). One of the party's two deputies in the national parliament was Rafael Caldera, one of the most significant figures in the contemporary Latin American Christian Democratic movement. The present Social Christian-COPEI party[9] was founded by Caldera in 1946.

The Cubans date the Christian Democratic initiatives from the decade of the 1940's. The best known of the several nuclei formed during this period was the Democracia Social Cristiana, directed by the Jesuit priest, Manuel Foyaca. Democracia Social Cristiana, a social movement, sponsored a forum on agrarian reform as early as 1950. Other Social Christian organizations formed in Cuba during that decade include Acción Cubana, a political movement, and Convivió, a youth group. Convivió counted among its membership José Rasco, one of the leaders of the present Cuban Movimiento Demócrata Cristiano, and Fidel Castro.[10]

In Nicaragua, the anti-Somoza youth established the Unión Na-

[7] *Congresos Internacionales Demócrata-Cristianos* (Santiago de Chile: Editorial del Pacífico, 1957), p. 166.

[8] "El Movimiento Social Republicano en Argentina," *Política y Espíritu*, III (July-Aug., 1948), 226.

[9] The official name of the party is now Social Christian-COPEI (Comité de Organización Política Electoral Independiente). "COPEI" is maintained as evidence of the party's historical continuity and because it is even more well-known than the "Social Christian" half of the name.

[10] Movimiento Demócrata Cristiano de Cuba, *Movimiento Demócrata Cristiano de Cuba* (Miami, 1961), pp. 38, 39.

cional de Acción Popular in 1948. The organization was officially defined as Christian Democratic, and was the first in Nicaragua.[11] This group was later to join the Conservative party in an attempt to remold its stance. Failure to achieve this end resulted in the rejuvenation of the Partido Social Cristiano in 1963. Costa Rican Christian Democracy was first personified by Rafael Angel Calderón Guardia, who assumed the presidency in 1940.[12] Later, José Figueres' National Liberation party approximated many Christian Democratic positions, although a Christian Democratic party did not emerge in Costa Rica until the 1960's.[13] In Bolivia, Christian Democrats operated in the Social Democratic party before the Paz Estenssoro Revolution in 1952. Study groups were founded in Bolivia as early as 1948, and the Partido Social Cristiano was formed after the Bolivian Revolution of 1952; in 1965, the group changed its name to Partido Demócrata Cristiano. The Colombian efforts at Christian Democratic organization date from the late 1940's. At that time, Manuel Mosquera Garces and Hernán Vergara founded the journal, *Testimonio*, a name which also came to designate the movement. Testimonio maintained a strictly non-political character, and not until 1960 was a political party established in Colombia. The Ecuadorian Movimiento Social Cristiano, which exhibited some Christian Democratic qualities, was founded by a group of Catholic intellectuals and university professors in 1951. Still very closely allied to the Conservative party, the coalition elected self-styled Social Christian Camilo Ponce Enríquez to the presidency in 1956. In 1964, a new Ecuadorian Partido Demócrata Cristiano was established by progressive youth, many of whom belonged to the Movimiento's youth affiliate.[14]

[11] Reinaldo Antonio Téfel Vélez, *Socialización en la Libertad* (Managua: Editorial Nicaragüense, 1964), p. 58.

[12] Germán Arciniegas, *The State of Latin America* (New York: Alfred A. Knopf, 1952), p. 286.

[13] Indeed, the policies of Christian Democratic parties and Figueres' Liberación Nacional are often similar. See, for instance, the closeness of the policies outlined in this endeavor and those of Figueres in Charles W. Anderson, "Politics and Development Policy in Central America," *Midwest Journal of Political Science*, V (Nov., 1961), 332–50.

[14] Neither the Ecuadorian Movimiento Social Cristiano nor the Partido Demócrata Cristiano is officially recognized by the international organ of Latin American Christian Democracy, the Organización Demócrata Cristiana de América. The Movimiento has sought admission but has been rejected. It seems probable that the Partido will eventually achieve official recognition.

The Partido Democracia Cristiano Guatemalteca was formed after the overthrow of the Arbenz Guzmán regime in 1954. In Panama, the party traces its origins to 1956 when important Christian Democratic study groups were launched. That same year, the Acción Social Demócrata was established; the group later changed its name to Unión Cívica Nacional and finally registered as the Partido Demócrata Cristiano in 1960. The Salvadorian Christian Democratic party, the strongest Christian Democratic political organization in Central America, was also founded in 1960.

The overthrow of the tyrant, Trujillo, produced three different Christian Democratic groups in the Dominican Republic, the strongest and most orthodox being the Partido Revolucionario Social Cristiano.

CATALYSTS OF FOUNDATION AND GROWTH

Three major factors or activities have served as catalysts in the formation of contemporary Latin American Christian Democratic parties. Helping explain the ideological directions of the parties, they also underlie the present-day strength and leadership. Important among these factors has been the growth of progressive youth and student groups. Another form of ferment has developed from the ideological splits within the Conservative ranks—traditional harbors of Social Christian tendencies. Third, the increasing opposition to authoritarian and dictatorial regimes has created additional support for the movement. These catalysts have often worked in tandem; indeed, in some instances, all three have been present.

Youth movements, of course, have often served as the foundations for new political groups in Latin America and elsewhere.[15] The importance of university students in Latin American politics is well known; they played a significant role in the organization of almost all the Latin American parties and in several instances were directly responsible for the founding of a party.

The powerful Chilean party originated with a group of Catholic University students who had been nurtured on the social doctrines of

[15] See Michael P. Fogarty, *Christian Democracy in Western Europe, 1820–1953* (Notre Dame, Ind.: University of Notre Dame Press, 1957), pp. 267–68, for the importance of university movements in the foundation of European Christian Democratic parties.

the popes and found the Conservative party, the natural home of Chilean Catholics, wanting. "The matter was clear as water," notes an historian of the movement. "The pontifical university taught the doctrines of the Popes, and the Popes were not in accord with the Conservative Party."[16] In *Chile Desconocido*, published in 1937, Frei Montalva outlines the changes which had overtaken the nation during the first Carlos Ibáñez del Campo dictatorship (1925–1931). A new class had emerged triumphant; government had become positive. It was impossible, he said, for the youth to be reconciled to old policies and programs. The Social Christian-oriented Movimiento de Estudiantes Conservadores had been established in 1933. The students entered the Conservative party in 1935 but retained organizational independence under the guise of the National Young Conservative Movement. Three years later, the group bolted the party to form the Falange Nacional. The split was certainly ideological, but it was intensified by the confrontation of youth and age within the Conservative party. Indeed, with the exception of Rafael L. Gumucio, a prestigious Conservative statesman, the membership of the party was almost entirely made up of the former students.

The origins of the Venezuelan party may be traced to a student movement led by Caldera during the López Contreras regime. The Social Christians broke away from the Venezuelan Students' Federation and founded the National Students Union in 1936.[17] The Peruvian party owes much of its modern impetus to student activity in the University of San Agustín in Arequipa. In 1950 and 1951, Arequipa Apristas and Communists sponsored a series of anti-Catholic demonstrations. The Catholic students resisted the militancy of their opponents and in 1955 assisted in the formal re-organization of the Peruvian Christian Democratic party. Students also initiated the movement in Nicaragua. Reinaldo Antonio Téfel Vélez, an important leader of the Christian Democrats of that beleaguered nation, writes:

> In 1944 there erupted in the University a new generation, the vanguard of the struggle against the Dictatorship. This generation fought in the streets, suffered persecution, tortures and exile. . . .

[16] Ricardo Boizard, *La Democracia Cristiana en Chile* (3rd ed.; Santiago de Chile: Editorial Orbe, 1963), p. 150.

[17] "The History of Social Christianity in Venezuela," *Christian Democratic Review*, II (July-Aug., 1961), 12.

> From it was born a group of young men who founded in 1948 a movement which was called the National Union of Popular Action. It sustained a revolutionary program which was officially designated as christian democratic. . . .[18]

The Mexican Movimiento Social Demócrata Cristiano has also benefited from student defections from the conservative Catholic Partido de Acción Nacional, as has the Ecuadorian Partido Demócrata Cristiano, which is composed of youthful dissidents of the conservative Movimiento Social Cristiano.

The second major impetus to formation of modern Christian Democratic parties—the ideological splits within the old Conservative parties—can be seen in the Chilean experience described above. The break with the Conservatives came in two steps. First, a semi-autonomous group was formed within the party. Relations between the young Social Christians and the older element were always strained, and in 1938, when the Conservatives nominated a presidential candidate who was unacceptable to the progressive younger faction, the split became irreconcilable. The revolting group founded the Falange Nacional.[19] In the period immediately following the defection, the Falange grew very slowly and received little electoral support. It was not until a second split had developed within the Conservative party that the Chilean Social Christian movement was to attain importance. In 1949, the old Conservative party divided into the Tradicionalistas and the Social Cristianos, the latter group led by the influential Eduardo Cruz Coke. Compared to the National Falange, according to Cruz Coke, the Social Cristianos were merely more cautious than their younger brethren in the Falange. Many in the Social Cristiano files, however, were markedly more conservative than their leader.[20] Later, the two Christian Democratic groups frequently cooperated in parliament and during elections as the Social Christian Federation. Finally, in the late 1950's

[18] *Socialización en la Libertad*, p. 58.

[19] Fredrick B. Pike, *Chile and the United States* (Notre Dame, Ind.: University of Notre Dame Press, 1963) points out the bitter conflict which developed between the two parties after the split. Some examples of the anti-Falange literature include: Carlos Aldunate Errázuriz, *División de los Católicos: Refuta una Carta de don Rafael Luís Gumucio*, no date; *Intervención de la Iglesia en Cuestiones Sociales* (1940), and *Polémica sobre Maritain* (1940).

[20] Roger S. Abbott, "The Role of Contemporary Political Parties in Chile," *American Political Science Review*, XLV (June, 1951), 453.

the Social Christians were dissolved and many of the party regulars and most of the electoral strength were absorbed by the Falange Nacional, which officially became the Christian Democratic party.

The present Argentine Partido Demócrata Cristiano also is rooted in traditional Conservative politics. As early as World War I, strong Christian Democratic factions were active in Conservative political circles. Later, the Democratic party assumed the mantle of political Catholicism in Argentina, and that party nurtured, before and during the Perón regime, the leaders who eventually founded the Christian Democratic party in 1954. The Argentine Christian party has also successfully recruited in the ranks of the two Radical parties and has campaigned diligently within the Peronista sectors.

The Nicaraguan experience is a novel variation on the Chilean theme. The movement was initiated by a group of aggressive university students who functioned independently as the Unión Nacional de Acción Popular (UNAP). In 1957, the UNAP majority faction decided to join the Conservatives with the object of converting that much stronger party into a vehicle for the Social Christians. The effort failed, however, and in 1963 an important group of Conservative leaders, comprising 20 percent of the party's national strength, bolted the party and joined the small Partido Social Cristiano Nicaragüense, which was composed of the adamant rump of the old UNAP.[21] The numbers and prestige of the new members transformed the revived Nicaraguan party into a considerable force in the struggle against the Somozas.

The Ecuadorian political scene provides another illustration of the Social Christian-Conservative relationship. The Movimiento Social Cristiano, least progressive of the Latin American groups, maintains a close alliance with the Conservatives, and Social Cristiano leader Ponce Enríquez was elected president with active Conservative support and coalescence. Indeed, one observer of the Ecuadorian scene notes that "the Movimiento Social Cristiano is nothing but a modernized branch of the old Ecuadorian Conservative Party."[22]

The opposition to authoritarian and dictatorial regimes, which has served as a third catalytic force, has often influenced the tone and ideological bent of Christian Democratic parties in Latin America. As in Europe, where the parties' opposition to Fascist regimes drove

[21] *Hispanic American Report*, XVI (Sept., 1963), 665.

[22] Antonio Díaz, "Los Partidos Políticos del Ecuador," *Política*, III (Nov., 1963), 113.

them to the Left and cooperation with Socialists and Communists, the anti-dictatorial position of the Latin American Christian Democrats has resulted in open and underground opposition, both singularly and in coalition, with Aprista, traditional Socialist, and even Communist movements. Opposition was mounted, for example, against the regimes of Perón, Odría, and Pérez Jiménez.[23]

During the long years of Perón's dictatorship, various Social Christian organizations appeared in the form of study groups or social-action clubs. As the Peronista movement became more arbitrary, dictatorial, and anti-Church, the various Christian Democratic groups assumed an anti-government stance and suspended their own disagreements to form a united front. In 1955, the National Promoting Committee was organized in Rosario. The aim of the Junta Promotora Nacional was to fight the dictatorship. The formation of this group touched off an anti-Church campaign by Perón, a tactical error which proved to be one of the fundamental causes of his downfall. The initial success of the Argentine party after the fall of Perón seemed to be a direct outgrowth of its activity during the waning days of the Peronista tyranny.

Opposition contributed significantly to the ideological bent of the party in the Venezuelan experience. Early supporters of the party included a group of Conservatives associated with Andean oligarchs and the Spanish Falange. After the fall of the Medina Angarita regime, the party emerged as the chief opposition to the Betancourt government, dominated as it was by the Acción Democrática. In 1946, Social Christian COPEI leader, Rafael Caldera, resigned from his cabinet post in protest against violence done to his party. "As the Government tended to become an exclusive Acción Democrática preserve, COPEI began to absorb landowner and Church elements, thus becoming increasingly rightist in character and increasingly antagonistic towards the regime."[24] During the repressive dictatorship of Pérez Jiménez (1948–1958), however, the Venezuelan party was forced to operate clandestinely, and it joined the more progressive Acción Democrática, Unión Republicana Democrática, and Communist parties in a struggle against Pérez. The party lost many of its Conservative elements and by the end of the dictatorial period

[23] Martin C. Needler, *Latin American Politics in Perspective* (Princeton, N. J.: D. Van Nostrand Company, 1963), p. 96.

[24] Edwin Lieuwen, *Venezuela* (New York: Oxford University Press, 1961), p. 87.

had become a strong advocate of basic social reform. It retained this progressive posture during its cooperation with the Betancourt government from 1958 to 1963 and following its decision to resume opposition to the Acción Democrática government of Raúl Leoni in 1964. The party had grown rapidly. Further growth seemed to demand an independent militancy in order to take advantage of what the party leaders interpreted as the decreasing popularity of the traditional Acción Democrática party. Indeed, the new "autonomy of action" of the Social Christian party is looked upon as the possible prelude to its assumption of power in 1969.

The clearest recent example of a Christian Democratic party's benefiting from its role as the major opposition is found in El Salvador. The 1964 elections gave the opposition parties representation in the Legislative Assembly for the first time since 1952. Since the number of opposition parties was limited, the newly formed Salvadorian Christian Democrats became the medium for opposition sentiment. The party elected 14 members in a 52-seat house and became the leader of the opposition.

The remaining dictatorships of the hemisphere offer three instances of Christian Democratic parties serving as opposition to the ruling government. The Cuban Christian Democratic Movement was specifically organized as a response to the incipient totalitarianism of the Castro regime. It had a short-lived experience on the island. Following initiation of the movement in 1959, its leader publicly criticized the government on television in January, 1960. As a result, persecution increased and the movement organized as a formal party in May of that year. It went into exile within five months. Although its size is difficult to estimate, the party became one of the five important counter-revolutionary groups that formed the Democratic Revolutionary Front in Miami. In Nicaragua, the Social Christians have a long history of active opposition to the Somoza regime. In Paraguay, the party was formed in 1959 as a nucleus for Christian opposition to the Stroessner dictatorship and today suffers harassment and persecution. "To be a Christian Democrat in Paraguay," offers a Brazilian party periodical, "means to be excluded from public office and to be confronted with imprisonment, torture or exile."[25] The organization has made periodic pleas

[25] *CINDEC: Boletin de Informações,* II (Dec., 1964), 7.

for a return to representative government. The movement stresses passive resistance, but its leaders have conceded that in extreme cases, rebellion may be the only acceptable course of action.[26]

STRENGTH AND EXPERIENCE

Although the election of Frei Montalva was the first example of a full-fledged victory for a Latin American Christian Democratic party, the parties as well as individual Social Christians have held numerous official positions in various Latin American governments. Moreover, many of the parties exert considerable influence in Latin America.

The Chilean National Falange participated in governments as early as the 1940's. In addition to holding occasional posts at the national level, the party slowly built up its local strength and in the municipal elections of early 1964 emerged as the most powerful party in the country, with 314 municipal council seats. This power was dramatically illustrated by Christian Democracy's triumph during the subsequent 1965 legislative elections.

The Venezuelan party has been represented in the National Congress since the party's formation in 1946. Its founder, Rafael Caldera, held the post of attorney general for a short time following the 1945 revolution. The Social Christian-COPEI formed part of the Betancourt coalition from 1958 to 1963, and party members held various posts during that period. Perhaps the most important office was that of the Ministry of Agriculture, occupied by Víctor Giménez Landínez, who was largely responsible for the Venezuelan land-reform program. As speaker of the lower house, party leader Caldera headed the coalition forces in the National Congress. The party's strength lies in western Venezuela, particularly in the three Andean states of Táchira, Mérida, and Trujillo.

The Peruvian government is a coalition of President Fernando Belaúnde Terry's Acción Popular and the Christian Democratic party. It is generally thought that the "small, but influential" Peruvian party provided Belaúnde Terry with the necessary margin of victory in 1963. Moreover, the highly capable Christian Democratic group is credited with "contributing, from within and without the govern-

[26] *Hispanic American Report,* XIII (June, 1960), 416.

ment, assurance of coherence of vision and doctrine."[27] In addition to directing the ministries of Justice and Agriculture, the Christian party counts 14 deputies and 5 senators in the Peruvian congress. The coalition's mayor of Lima is Christian Democrat Luis Bedoya Reyes. The electoral strength of the Peruvian organization is drawn from the cities of Arequipa and Lima.

The Brazilian Christian Democratic party has had representatives in the national and several state legislatures since its inception. The party received its original popular impetus from the dynamic Jânio Quadros, who began his spectacular political career in 1945 when he was elected a city councilman from a working-class suburb of São Paulo on the Christian Democratic ticket. Three years later he was elected a state deputy, again by the Christian Democrats. Though Quadros later split with the party, one writer refers to him as "the first leader of social christian persuasion to achieve supreme political power in Latin America."[28] The party has remained strong in São Paulo and other southern states; party stalwart Andrés Franco Montoro has held the post of president of the São Paulo House of Representatives. The party has controlled the last two administrations in the important state of Paraná. Ney Braga, governor in the first Christian Democratic administration of that state and later Castello Branco's minister of agriculture, is emerging as an influential Brazilian political personality.[29] The movement is also strong in the northeastern states of Pernambuco, Bahía, and Paraíba. On the national level, representatives of the Christian party have held important ministerial posts under Presidents Quadros, Goulart, and Castello Branco.

The confusion of the Argentine political arena has been mirrored in the Christian Democratic record in that volatile nation. The party made a surprisingly strong showing in its initial electoral test in 1957, but its performance has shown no clear pattern of growth or decline since that time. Internal splits and frequent cooperation with the Peronistas and other parties have made analysis

[27] *Perú*, Estudios de Actualidad, Primera Serie, No. 2 (Montevideo: Instituto de Estudios Políticos para América Latina, 1964), p. 20.

[28] Marchant, "Christian Democracy in Latin America," p. 3.

[29] Jordan M. Young, "Some Permanent Political Characteristics of Contemporary Brazil," *Journal of Inter-American Studies*, VI (July, 1964), 299. For a laudatory description of the Christian Democratic administrations in Paraná, see Don C. Trenary, "Brazil's Curitiba Has Big Plans For Future," *Milwaukee Journal*, March 17, 1966, Pt. I, p. 26.

difficult. In 1957, it was the third-ranking party in 7 of 23 provinces. It was one of only three parties to run candidates in all provinces and shared with the Intransigent Radicals the distinction of receiving votes in all of the electoral districts.[30] In 1963, the party doubled its 1962 percentage of the votes by winning 4.6 percent.[31] Yet the pendulum seemed to be swinging back in the March, 1965, elections as the party slipped to seventh place and lost three lower-house seats. The clash which polarized the Peronistas and President Arturo Illia's Peoples Radicals in that election, however, prohibits any valid conclusions. The party is strongest in the north and has elected a governor in the province of Jujuy. It is represented in both the Chamber and the Senate of the national government.

In Uruguay, the Unión Cívica, oldest of the Christian Democratic groups in Latin America, had consistently drawn about 5 percent of the votes. Its representation in the national legislature has usually numbered one or two senators and about five deputies. The 1962 re-naming and re-alignment of the organization into a more modern Christian Democratic party apparently did not affect its electoral strength. In the past the party has had outstanding militants called to take governmental ministries.

The conservative Ecuadorian Movimiento Social Cristiano had elected its founder, Camilo Ponce Enríquez, to the presidency in 1956 and many of his ministers were drawn from Social Christian ranks.[32] Party members, moreover, have served in ministerial posts with the military junta which assumed power in July, 1963. Party leader Francisco Acosta Yépez has served as foreign minister of Ecuador. In El Salvador, in addition to leading the opposition in the national legislature, the party controls a number of local government positions, the most important being the mayoralty of the capital city.

In the Dominican Republic, two of the parties that have shown

[30] Eduardo Zolvendo, *Geografía Electoral de la Argentina* (Buenos Aires: Ediciones Ancora, 1958), pp. 35, 29.

[31] James W. Rowe, "Argentina: An Election Retrospect," *American Universities Field Staff: Reports Service*, East Coast South American Series, Vol. 11, No. 1 (New York [1964]), p. 6.

[32] The authenticity of the Ecuadorian Movimiento Social Cristiano as a Christian Democratic party has always caused much anguish among Latin American Christian Democrats. One publication questions its credentials and notes its "conservative attitudes and positions" as well as the "innate aristocratic" predilections of its leader, Ponce Enríquez. *Ecuador*, Estudios de Actualidad, Primero Serie, No. 3 (Montevideo: Instituto de Estudios Políticos para América Latina, 1964), p. 6.

Christian Democratic leanings held numerous cabinet positions under the military junta which overthrew Juan Bosch. The Partido Revolucionario Social Cristiano, the strongest of the three Dominican groups and the third-ranking party during the short-lived Bosch regime, however, maintained a strict opposition policy during both the tenure of Bosch and the subsequent military government.

ROOTS OF THE LATIN AMERICAN MOVEMENT

No source of the Latin American Christian Democratic movement has been more influential than that of the Church. Primarily through the papal encyclicals, the Church has formed and molded the traditional Christian Democratic thought on which the movement is based. Party documents invariably note the pervasive influence of the Church's social teachings. The Panamanian party's program is typical. It states that the "fundamental inspiration of the party came from the social encyclicals. . . ."[33] The first encyclical is *Rerum Novarum* of Leo XIII, issued in 1891. In fact, it might be said that the entire Christian Democratic movement dates from the publication of that revolutionary document, although three subsequent encyclicals have also made major contributions to the movement. The first of the three—Pius XI's *Quadragesimo Anno*, published in 1931—not only revived the teachings of Leo XIII but also re-interpreted and introduced new elements. It condemned anew traditional Liberal thought and criticized those who had stood against proletarian organization. The document, according to historians of Chilean political parties, "accentuated and complemented" the developing Social Christian inclinations in that country and "opened new perspectives"[34] to the movement. The other two encyclicals—*Mater et Magistra* and *Pacem in Terris* of John XXIII—are quoted increasingly in the literature of the movement. The pontificate of John XXIII made a spiritual and practical contribution to Catholicism and Christian Democracy in Latin America, and the beloved "Peasant Pope" with his saintly warmth has served as an inspiration to Social Christians everywhere.

Much Christian Democratic ink has been expended in a heated denial of the proposition that Christian Democracy is essentially a

[33] Partido Demócrata Cristiano de Panamá, *El Partido Demócrata Cristiano de Panamá: Historia, Principios, Programa, Estructura* (Panamá, 1964), p. 7.

[34] Alberto Edwards Vives and Eduardo Frei Montalva, *Historia de los Partidos Políticos Chilenos* (Santiago de Chile: Editorial del Pacífico, 1949), p. 242.

negative response to the growth of the Socialist movement. One of the leading Latin American proponents states that "social christianity began to form itself in the middle of the nineteenth century—almost paralleled to the development of socialist ideas and not as a tardy response to them, as many believe. . . ."[35] Many Social Christian apologists like to point out that a full quarter of a century before 1848, Christian Democratic militants were active in France and other European countries. "When Marxism was scarcely initiated with the publication of the *Communist Manifesto,* there already existed in Europe writers like Villeneuva, Lacordaire and Montalembert, who had confronted social problems by means of Christian ideas and had proposed labor legislation which agitated the social environment of their time."[36] While these claims are historically accurate, they nevertheless miss the point by implying that these early Social Christian precursors initiate a straight line of progressive theoretical and practical growth. They seem to propose that a tightly organized group of activists and thinkers have slowly, but quite surely, extended the influence of Christian Democratic programs over the last century and a half. The implication, moreover, is that these intrepid warriors were nurtured in the womb of the Catholic Church. This, sadly enough, was not the case. Many of these early departures were condemned by the Church. These erratic ideologies often met with recalcitrant opposition in the Catholic community. Most were little known, disorganized, and of scant influence. Only when the Church, more than 50 years later, changed its position and bestowed its blessing upon the Social Christian movement was it able to blossom and achieve widespread acceptance and diffusion. Only then did the Christian Democratic movement begin its ascent to the place of power, influence, and significance which it holds in the contemporary world.

Jaime Castillo Velasco, a Chilean Christian, suggests much more realistically that the Church, as *magisterium,* was moved in 1891 because of the "threat of socialism. Moreover, the struggle against the penetration of socialism continued to be the essential preoccupation of the Encyclicals."[37] It is, assuredly, equally false to assert that

[35] *Una Tercera Posición. Selección de discursos demócrata cristianos pronunciados entre 1956 y 1960* (Lima: Editorial Universitaria, 1960), p. 4.

[36] Partido Social Cristiano de Nicaragua, *¿Que es el Partido Social-Cristiano Nicaragüense?* (Managua, 1961), p. 16.

[37] *Las Fuentes de la Democracia Cristiana* (Santiago de Chile: Editorial del Pacífico, 1963), p. 89.

the entire *raison d'être* of the movement has been the Socialist threat; this was certainly not true in the inception of the movement, nor is it true now. The affirmative drive of Catholic clerical and lay forces has always been evident. Socialism or no, there has been and probably would be a politically and socially progressive Christian movement. Still, though the evaluation of the Christian Democrats as a negative reaction may be insufficient, it, nevertheless, has some validity which should not be disregarded.

Contemporary Latin American Christian Democrats offer ample evidence of this continuing negative stance. Christian Democracy, says an Argentine, was obligated to transform itself into a political movement "to impede the bloody class struggle propitiated by Marxism."[38] It is not too far from the mark to propose that the fundamental rationale for the movement lies in the statement of Leo XIII that "the major scandal of the times is the apostasy of the masses." A leading clerical figure of the Latin American movement seems to endorse this interpretation when he states: "Social reform will be made with or without us, and, in this second case, it will be against us."[39]

The second important influence on Latin American Christian Democracy has emanated from modern European political thought and practice. The most prominent contribution has been the philosophy of contemporary French Catholic thinkers led by Jacques Maritain, Yves Simon, and Etienne Gilson. Modern European Social Democracy, especially that of Scandinavia, has also been a contributing factor. The practical impetus has been provided by the marked success of the European Christian Democratic parties in the post-war period. Latin America historically has been influenced by European cultural, economic, social, and political developments. The place of Voltaire, Rousseau, Montesquieu, and others is well documented, as is the role of the Positivist movement. The continent has traditionally looked to Europe.

Clearly the primary source of the contemporary movement is found in the "New Catholicism" of the French school and, more specifically, in its foremost teacher, Jacques Maritain. French thought holds a superior position in Latin American Christian Democracy.

[38] Ambrosio Romero Carranza, *¿Qué es la Democracia Cristiana?* (Buenos Aires: Ediciones del Atlántico, 1956), p. 43.

[39] Manuel Larraín Errázuriz, *La Hora de la Acción Católica* (Santiago de Chile: Editorial del Pacífico, 1956), p. 38.

In a chapter on Christian Democratic movements, a Colombian writer notes that "we have extended the historical facts about Christian Democracy in France because of its importance and influence in the world movement."[40] In the over-all picture of Christianity, "France continues to occupy a place of privilege."[41] Even the institutionalized Chilean Catholic Church is markedly influenced by clergy from France and the Low Countries.[42]

Maritain was known in Latin America as early as the 1930's. He gained wider recognition after the Spanish Civil War and dominated the Latin American Catholic intellectual community after World War II. Frei, himself important in the development of Latin American Christian Democracy, sees the New Catholicism as the instrument appropriate for dealing with the problems of the industrial age. "In this picture Jacques Maritain occupies a central position. Renovator of scholasticism, he has made operable and intelligible the fundamental philosophy. . . . He has proportioned an organic and systematic vision of Christian thought."[43] An Uruguayan Christian Democrat refers to the French thinker as "the unequaled master of philosophy."[44] An Argentine asserts that Catholic critics of Maritain were among those who supported the Peronista tyranny in its early days; conversely, "those who approved of Maritain never fell into totalitarianism nor were they attracted by Peronismo."[45]

Next to Maritain, the most important European in the development of the contemporary movement is the Italian, Luigi Sturzo, the founder and apologist of the Christian Democratic Popular party

[40] Francisco de Paula Jaramillo, *La Democracia Cristiana: Una Nueva Perspectiva para Colombia* (Bogotá: Ediciones del Caribe, 1962), p. 62.

[41] Eduardo Frei Montalva, *Pensamiento y Acción* (Santiago de Chile: Editorial del Pacífico, 1956), p. 52.

[42] Kalmet H. Silvert, "Some Propositions on Chile," *American Universities Field Staff: Reports Service*, West Coast South America Series, Vol. 11, No. 1 (New York, 1964), pp. 2, 3.

[43] Frei Montalva, *Pensamiento*, p. 52. For a more comprehensive discussion of the "New Catholicism," see pp. 171–176.

[44] *Congresos Internacionales Demócrata-Cristianos*, p. 117. Maritain, of course, has not completely captured the Latin American Catholic community. As examples of anti-Maritain literature, see, Jorge Ivan Hübner Gallo, "Catholic Social Justice, Authoritarianism and Class Stratification," in *The Conflict Between Church and State in Latin America*, ed. Fredrick B. Pike (New York: Alfred A. Knopf, 1964), pp. 197–207 and Francisco Ribadeneira Miranda, *Política Cristiana* (Quito: Editorial Fray Jodoco Ricke, 1955).

[45] Romero Carranza, *¿Qué es la Democracia Cristiana?*, p. 46.

organized following World War I.[46] The program of this party, which stood for administrative decentralization, educational autonomy in pursuit of greater recognition of Catholic schools, freedom of Christian syndical organization, and land reform, is reproduced in the programs of the Latin American parties. Upon the death of the Italian Social Christian, the Fifth International Congress of Latin American Christian Democracy expressed its profound sadness at the loss of the "Precursor of World Christian Democracy." Other Europeans who have been important to the movement include the Belgian, Cardinal Mercier; principal editor of the *Social Catechism of Malinas*, the French Social Christian thinker, Emmanuel Mounier; and the contemporary French Dominican, Louis Lebret.

The rival Social Democratic, or Socialist,[47] movement has also influenced the Latin American Christian Democratic position. Indeed, Social Christians have always recognized the ethical and eschatological appeal of the Socialist cause. The Christian movement rejects the materialistic basis taught by Social Democracy, and offers the alternative of peaceful progress seeking the development of man's total nature, both physical and spiritual. Still, the immediate goals and stances of the two ideologies are often similar. Both groups lean toward a third position; both place emphasis on the redemption of the proletariat. Party organization is consciously copied from the Socialist parties, though Christian Democrats are quick to add that they have developed certain forms which are their own.

Scandinavian Social Democracy seems to have a strong attraction for the Latin American movement. Frei, who is especially partial to Scandinavian economic thought and practice, has traveled widely in the northern countries and has often praised the cooperative system so successfully developed in those nations. He has also called attention to the public housing projects initiated by Social Democratic governments in Scandinavia.

Cooperatives are not new to Latin America. Numerous indigenous populations historically have operated within a cooperative eco-

[46] For a tribute to Sturzo, see Rafael Caldera, "Lo Político y lo Religioso dentro de lo Social," in *Moldes para la Fragua* (Buenos Aires: Librería "El Ateneo" Editorial, 1962), pp. 229–45.

[47] Socialist groups frequently may be called Social Democratic, Democratic Socialist, or simply Socialist. Hence, these terms are used interchangeably in this chapter, and especially in chap. ix. Similarly, the Christian movement may be known as Christian, Christian Democratic, and Social Christian.

nomic and social system. The Bolivian Christian Democratic leader proposes that the Latin American Christian Democratic ideal should include a large dose of cooperativism. The Christian Democratic system, he says, "will necessarily be complemented with cooperativism on a grand scale. Private business, in many of its forms, will be replaced by consumer cooperatives. Sweden, Denmark and Canada show magnificent cooperative experiences worthy of being assimilated in the new order."[48] Not to be discounted in the theoretical organization of industrial concerns, moreover, is the influence of Yugoslav Socialism. Left-wing Christian Democrats have been especially enamored with the much-publicized workers councils which characterize the Yugoslav system and which rather closely parallel traditional Christian thinking in this area.

Finally, the successes of European Christian Democratic parties have made important moral, ideological, and material contributions to their brethren in Latin America. Although one or two of the Latin American groups date from before World War II, only in the post-war period have they achieved electoral importance. Substantial growth was attained only in the 1950's when the European experience was already well established and recognizable. The parties' attraction to progressive elements after World War II was undoubtedly influenced by the power and prestige of their European counterparts. The parties are affiliated with the European movements; frequent meetings in formal congresses as well as encounters on a personal basis attest to considerable cross-fertilization.

Although Christian Democratic theory and practice was developed mainly in Europe and imported to Latin America after having achieved maturity, the Latin Americans have quickly adjusted the credo to Latin American needs. Not only have they molded their own doctrine, they have developed their own set of influential ideologues. Although the literature and congresses of the Latin American parties list scores of important precursors, the foremost Christian Democratic thinkers have appeared only within the last two or three decades.

The increasing impact of Neo-Thomistic thought in the universities has paralleled the rise of political Christian Democracy. A commentator on the Latin American intellectual scene cites rising

[48] Remo Di Natale, *América Latina Hoy: Esquemas Populares Demócrata Cristianos* (Caracas: Editorial Nuevo Orden, 1964), p. 76.

Neo-Thomism as one of the major trends in modern Latin American philosophical development.[49] Leading representatives of the intellectual movement include Jackson de Figueiredo and Alceu Amoroso Lima of Brazil, Clarence Finlayson and Frei Montalva of Chile, Nicolás Derisi of Argentina and Oswaldo Robles of Mexico. Their philosophical efforts are widely recognized. "Whether these neo-Thomists and neo-Aristotelians really restore God and theology to the heart of philosophy as they claim, or whether they merely create an illusion to that effect, their influence has been great, if for no other reason than the emphasis they give to social voluntarism and their consistent opposition to Marxism."[50] Amoroso Lima and Frei Montalva have been major political adapters of the more general philosophic stance. Among the earlier Christian Democrats perhaps none has been more influential than Alceu Amoroso Lima, who has written under the pseudonym of Tristan de Athayde. Since 1917, when he published his massive *O problema de trabalho*,[51] he has been a vigorous advocate of Social Christian ideas and activity. He was a founder of the Catholic student movement in Brazil and from its inception has participated in the Brazilian Christian Democratic party. Amoroso Lima was one of the originators of the Latin American Christian Democratic international movement established in Montevideo in 1947.

Another early figure important in the movement's international activities was Dardo Regules of Uruguay, the primary initiator of the historic Montevideo gathering. In his own country of Uruguay, he was the long-time leader of the old Unión Cívica and was the impulse behind that party's transition to a more progressive Christian Democratic stance. Under his tutelage, the organization dropped its conservative Catholic approach and moved toward the social and political philosophy of Maritain. He broadened the party's working-class support and laid the ground work for the re-orientation that the party is yet undergoing. Regules was one of those leaders peculiar to Uruguayan politics who, though he represented only a small minority party, managed to achieve immense prestige.

Of the contemporary political personalities, clearly the outstand-

[49] Harold Eugene Davis, "Trends in Social Thought in Twentieth Century Latin America," *Journal of Inter-American Studies*, I (Jan., 1959), 63–64.

[50] *Ibid.*, p. 63.

[51] See a selection from this work translated in Harold Eugene Davis, *Latin American Social Thought* (Washington: The University Press, 1961), pp. 520–29.

ing representatives of Latin American Christian Democracy are Frei and the Venezuelan leader, Rafael Caldera.[52] Of the two, first place must be awarded to the Chilean President. Beginning with the publication of *El Regimen del Salarido y su Posible Abolición* in 1933, Frei's works have received widespread distribution among Social Christian militants in Latin America. He was foremost among the founders of the young, progressive faction within the Chilean Conservative party in 1933 and led the way to the independent establishment of the Social Christian National Falange three years later. He taught labor law at the Chilean national university and the Chilean Catholic University. In 1945, at age thirty-four, he accepted the Public Works portfolio in the Ríos government. In 1949, Frei became the first Falangist senator, winning his seat from a northern left-leaning constituency. In his second senatorial term he represented one of the populous Santiago constituencies. He also worked with the influential United Nations Economic Commission for Latin America.

Equal to and at least partly the result of Frei's personal impact on the Latin American movement has been the dramatically successful growth of the Chilean party which culminated in the 1964 presidential victory and the Christian Democratic success in the legislative election in March, 1965. The presidential triumph was interpreted as the turning point of Latin American Christian Democratic fortunes; a new era had dawned and the movement was confident that Frei's victory was the first of a series that would sweep the continent. A Nicaraguan declared that "the triumph of the Christian Democratic Party of Chile has had profound impact on Nicaraguan public opinion and will undoubtedly benefit the local party."[53] The foundation of the newly organized Mexican Movimiento Social Demócrata Cristiano turned on whether or not Frei was elected in Chile.[54] *Pueblo y Libertad*, the Colombian party organ, pointed out that Frei had undertaken "a very grave responsibility because [his victory] . . . refers not only to the Chilean people who have elected him, but to all of Latin America. The future of the Latin American

[52] See, for example, the closing speech at the Fifth Latin American Christian Democratic Congress which singles out these two for special mention. *Congresos Internacionales Demócrata Cristianos*, p. 256.

[53] Reinaldo Antonio Téfel Vélez, *El Partido Social Cristiano de Nicaragua* (mimeographed), p. 3.

[54] *Hispanic American Report*, XVII (Oct., 1964), 691.

nations depends in good part on the successes which Frei is able to obtain through his program of '*Revolución en Libertad.*'"[55] *DECE*, the continental Christian Democratic organ, asserted that Frei's victory signaled the beginning of the struggle between the two approaches to social and political change offered by Frei and Fidel Castro—a revolutionary program in liberty as proposed by Christian Democrat Frei or a revolution in tyranny as dictated by totalitarian Castro.[56] Although the statement that the political fate of the Latin American continent depends on the achievements of the Frei government may be too facile for the careful observer to fully accept, it is nevertheless reasonable to conclude that Frei's record in office will be fundamentally important to the continued growth of the Latin American Christian Democratic movement. Victory in the elections was validly interpreted as being a crucial departure.

The second most eminent Latin American Christian Democrat is the Venezuelan Rafael Caldera. Caldera has been the leader of the strong Venezuelan COPEI-Social Christian party since he founded it in 1946. Caldera is important, of course, as the leader of one of the largest parties, but also because his concept of international social justice[57] has become an integral part of the movement's theory of international politics and the relationship of more-developed to less-developed areas. In his capacity as president of the Venezuelan Chamber of Deputies from 1958 to 1962, he spoke to the legislatures of many nations and had the opportunity to carry his pan-Latin-American philosophy throughout the continent.

The Argentine Christian Democrats have also been important in the continental movement because of the traditional role of that nation as a leader in Latin American intellectual movements and the wide distribution of works published in Argentina. The Chilean party has produced numerous ideologues of varying skill and significance. The three most heralded contemporaries are the economist, Fernando González Ruiz, Ismael Bustos, and Jaime Castillo Velasco. Mention should also be made of Héctor Cornejo Chávez, co-founder, twice presidential candidate, and recognized leader of the Peruvian party, Lino Rodríguez-Arias of Panama, and Fernando Avila Bastos of Brazil.

[55] "Frei Inicia la Revolución Demócrata Cristiano en América Latina," *Pueblo y Libertad*, III (Nov. 3, 1964), 1.

[56] "Grandioso Triunfo de Frei en Chile," *DECE*, I (Sept., 1964), 1.

[57] See pages 146–147 for a discussion of international social justice.

In the general area of economic thought and programs the Social Christian movement, like practically all of the progressive forces of Latin America, has been greatly influenced by the astonishingly successful and widely known United Nations' Comisión Económica para América Latina (CEPAL). A number of Latin American Christian Democrats have been associated with the commission, and Cepalista planks such as economic integration, industrialism, and state activity in the economy have been readily accepted by Christian Democrats throughout the continent.

Theoretical Foundations 3

TENETS AND DIRECTIONS

Newness is a key word in the movement. Christian Democrats see the world as advancing into a new era that is founded upon and fashioned by the ongoing social revolution. In their view, the establishment of a separate, third ideological position to meet new social, economic, and political needs has defined the era as Christian Democratic.[1]

An aura of messianic mystique surrounds the movement. Its literature and programs abound with allusions to the coming of the new age of Social Christianity. The Costa Rican party program states, for instance, that "Christian Democracy represents the concept of a new Society in which there is a new hope and a new faith. . . ."[2] An historian of Chilean social Catholicism points to World War I as the beginning of the new era; "we are able to point to the World War of 1914 as the beginning of a new anti-liberal epoch, an epoch in which new generations seek other routes and do not continue to operate under individualistic modes which began by erecting the edifice of material civilization and ended by bringing it to ruins. . . ."[3] Frei Montalva depicts the "central tenet of Christian Democracy" as the "belief that we are witness to the crisis of a world exhausted, to the death of paternalism, and to the birth of a

[1] Latin Americans have traditionally been receptive to this position. The most recent example of this predilection was Perón's proposal of Justicialism as the modern synthesis.

[2] Partido Demócrata Cristiano de Costa Rica, *1) Toma de posiciones del Partido Demócrata Cristiano—frente al Comunismo, frente al Capitalismo y frente a los regimenes políticos del pais. 2) Declaración de principios del Partido Demócrata Cristiano* (San José, n. d.), p. 2.

[3] Ricardo Boizard, *La Democracia Cristiana en Chile* (3rd ed.; Santiago de Chile: Editorial Orbe, 1963), p. 7.

civilization of work and solidarity *with man as its center*, rather than the pursuit of monetary gain that has pervaded the bourgeois society."[4] A Peruvian Christian Democrat equates the new age with those ushered in by the fall of the Roman Empire, the discovery of America, and the French Revolution.[5] Another Chilean approves of Maritain's proposition that the contemporary world is witnessing the "liquidation of four centuries of anthropocentric humanism."[6] The most important ingredient of this present world dilemma is defined as a "crisis of the spirit."

The new era has two major characteristics: it is the age of social justice and the age of the people. Writing in 1942, Frei proposed, "the idea of liberty was the political conquest of the nineteenth century. Justice is the foremost goal of our century."[7] In *Sentido y Forma*, the Chilean President named the second major characteristic when he referred to the new epoch as the age of the common man, "or what we call the age of the worker."[8] The ascension of the people constitutes the essence of this historical period. It is useless for the representatives of privilege to resist "because historical processes will not be detained by the use of force."[9] "New men with new ideas" are called for. The message of Latin American Christian Democracy, in sum, is "a new response to the inquietudes of our epoch."[10]

The central feature of this new response to the demands of the modern age is a revolutionary posture. The parties loudly proclaim that they are revolutionary, advocating revolutionary measures in pursuit of revolutionary goals. According to the organ of the newly founded Colombian Social Christian Democratic party, that party is motivated by "an undeniable revolutionary mystique."[11] The Para-

[4] Eduardo Frei Montalva, "The Aims of Christian Democracy," *Commonweal*, LXXXI (Oct. 9, 1964), 65.

[5] Héctor Cornejo Chávez, *Que se Propone la Democracia Cristiana* (Lima: Ediciones del Sol, 1962), p. 3.

[6] Quoted in Jaime Castillo Velasco, *Las Fuentes de la Democracia Cristiana* (Santiago de Chile: Editorial del Pacífico, 1963), p. 41.

[7] Eduardo Frei Montalva, *Aun es el Tiempo . . .* (Santiago de Chile: Talleres Gráficos "El Chileno," 1942), p. 89.

[8] Eduardo Frei Montalva, *Sentido y Forma de una Política* (Santiago de Chile: Editorial del Pacífico, 1951), p. 114.

[9] *Ibid.*, p. 57.

[10] Américo Plá Rodríguez, *Los Principios de la Democracia Cristiana* (Bogotá: Ediciones del Caribe, 1962), p. 3.

[11] "Editorial," *Pueblo y Libertad*, III (Aug., 1964), 4.

guayan Movimiento Demócrata Social Cristiano declares that its "program of personalization implies a basic revolution in the present scheme of Paraguayan life."[12] The goal of this revolution will be to replace present liberal democratic structures and forms with those of a social and organic democracy. This revolutionary character, in fact, is one of the fundamental differences between the Latin American movement and its European counterpart. The "high standards of living and effective liberty" extant in Europe permit the European parties to be less "advanced"; the "completely different situation" in Latin America, however, compels the parties to be "necessarily revolutionary."[13]

Christian Democrats castigate those who would retain the present inequitable system; such groups hold an "erroneous" position. Those who attempt to conserve liberal democratic regimes, however, are not always directly responsible for the injustices perpetrated within the system; rather the system itself invites injustices. Contemporary structures encourage unjust distribution of goods and services and the continuance of the oligarchical political system. Change, however, is immanent as well as imminent. The mission of the Christian movement is to stimulate this change, direct it, and collaborate with others in effecting it, seeking always the conditions that will unshackle and elevate the people.

The Christian Democrats believe that revolution is the only means by which the Latin American people can fulfill their historic role. Christianity's emphasis on the essential equality of all men and the Christian stricture that governments must create an environment in which man can develop his personality imply support of the revolution, they say; to assert otherwise would present an "horrendous caricature" of the Christian position. The Christian Democrats see the revolution as inevitable. Their task is to channel this force toward constructive maturation and to keep it from falling under Communist influence and leadership. Writing as early as 1947, Dardo Regules warned that the revolution is "like a cyclone which propels and envelops us." He cautioned his co-religionists of the "enormous impatience of the great masses."[14]

[12] *Mensaje de Navidad del Movimiento Social Demócrata Cristiano al Pueblo del Paraguay* (Asunción, Dec. 25, 1961), p. 2.

[13] Tomás Reyes Vicuña quoted in Lino Rodríguez-Arias Bustamante, *La Democracia Cristiana y América Latina* (Lima: Editorial Universitaria, 1961), p. 93.

[14] "Nuestro Movimiento," *Política y Espíritu*, II (May, 1947), 156, 157.

Christian Democrats deny that violence is necessary. Theirs is a "*Revolución en Libertad*," the essence of which is profound change in the present system. Their concept calls for a social revolution, the establishment of a new order. Caldera says that the word "revolution," which has often been "synonymous with bloodshed and chaos, must be understood as the acceleration of history . . . , as the rupture with that part of the past which retards the accomplishments of social aims, and the adoption of those measures and systems which can bring about the realization of the Christian concept of man."[15] The emphasis—indeed, the Christian message stresses this—is on legal methods which can and must be employed to achieve revolutionary goals. A Nicaraguan party publication defines the Social Christian concept of revolution in these terms:

> It is a deliberately produced change; it responds to an ideology and a plan; it is rapid and profound and it refers to all basic structures (political, juridical, social, economic). The change of the present structures, consequently, is rapid, profound and all-encompassing. In the revolution we ought to distinguish two moments and two rhythms: a) the moment of the radical rupture with the present structures, b) the moment of the elaboration of the new order. The rupture is always rapid; it is almost a cut in history; a crossing out of the past and a new beginning. The elaboration of the new order can be only relatively rapid. The important thing is that the period of preparation for the new order is not transformed into a permanent reality. In this case the revolution has collapsed as a *revolution*. Because the revolution is a "change," it logically terminates with the establishment of a new order.[16]

Cornejo Chávez further explains the Christian Democratic interpretation of revolution. The term "revolution" is most correctly understood, he says, not as the violent means to effect a political change, but as the end result of a change that affects the very heart of the socio-economic system. Given this definition, the Latin American Christian Democratic parties are revolutionary.[17] Comparing the

[15] Rafael Caldera, "Crucial Test for Christian Civilization," *The Alliance for Progress: A Critical Appraisal*, ed. William Manger (Washington: Public Affairs Press, 1963), p. 24.

[16] "ABC de la Democracia Cristiana o Social-Cristianismo," *Combate* (Organo del Partido Social Cristiano Nicaragüense), April, 1964, p. 9.

[17] Héctor Cornejo Chávez, *Nuevos Principios para un Nuevo Peru* (Lima: Publicaciones de la Juventud Demócrata Cristiano, 1960), p. 198.

Christian and Communist concepts of the revolution, Reinaldo Antonio Téfel Vélez asserts: "Communism is apparently revolutionary in its methods, but really reactionary in its goals. On the other hand, Christian Democracy is apparently evolutionary in its methods, but really revolutionary in its goals because it is concerned with a vitally profound and intense revolutionary change in sentiment and content even though this change is gradually and voluntarily provoked, encouraged and guided."[18]

Still other factors help define the Latin American Christian Democratic concept of the revolution. First, despite its fundamental nature, the revolution must not be construed as a total break with the past. The best of the past is retained while other elements are rejected. Frei warns that the goal is not to reject the past in all of its content, but only to tear from the historical "skeleton" the "accidents and errors, the fatty material."[19]

Second, the revolution is to be undertaken *with* the people as well as *for* them. The messianic idealism demands an earth-shattering, comprehensive effort on the part of the people to lift themselves, and the nation, by their bootstraps. The "unknown reserves" of man must be mobilized. Frei criticizes the "mystic hope" that a change of those in power is enough. "What is really needed," he says, "is a great effort toward change among all the people in common." This motivating force he refers to as the "psychology of creation."[20] The aim is to make a revolution, not impose one. It is to be an effort of "the poor, the humble, the peasant, the disinherited, the illiterate, the exploited, the persecuted and the hungry." It will "transform the dispossessed proletariat into a responsible and free property owner."[21]

Finally, the revolution is to be Christian, not only in principle, but in leadership and ultimate goal. It will be accomplished by Christian Democrats and will usher in a new age of Christianity. The very success of the revolution will connote the fundamental reestablishment of a Christian society. Following the first international conference of Latin American Christian Democrats, Amoroso Lima saw the possibility of a new step in Latin American civilization. The

[18] Reinaldo Antonio Téfel Vélez, *Socialización en la Libertad* (Managua: Editorial Nicaragüense, 1964), p. 20.

[19] Eduardo Frei Montalva, *La Política y el Espíritu* (Santiago de Chile: Ediciones Ercilla, 1940), p. 119.

[20] Frei Montalva, "The Aims of Christian Democracy," p. 64.

[21] Téfel Vélez, *Socialización*, pp. 14, 23.

historical periods of "Official Christianity" and "Official Agnosticism" had been transcended; on the horizon was an era of "Free Christianity" led by a "non-confessional apostolate" and founded on the principles of "Christian Humanism"; it would claim "neither official establishment nor privilege."[22] The aim is not a "simple repetition of another Christian Age." The "New Christianity" has to be constituted "under the sign of political tolerance, of interior religious commitment and fraternal and egalitarian sentiment."[23] Christianity, for the Latin American militants, is intrinsically and historically the friend of the dignity of man, liberty, and, by direct implication, political, social, and economic democracy. There can be no conflict between Christianity and democracy; those which have been recorded historically are viewed as aberrations not to be found in the modern Christian Democratic movement. Christianity acts as a ferment of liberty, justice, and fraternity, and it inspires practical solutions to difficult contemporary problems. Moreover, the opposition of Christianity and Socialism no longer exists. The new synthesis of Social Christianity, of Christian Democracy, transcends and envelops both concepts.

The new era and the social revolution are vitalized for Christian Democrats in the movement's unique political stance—a third position to take its place in opposition to Communism and capitalism. The position finds its major expression in the Latin American Christian Democrat's violent denunciation of East and West, communistic and capitalistic economics, and totalitarian and liberal democratic political systems. This is not merely the middle path between the two dominant contemporary systems. Indeed, Christians repudiate the supposed dichotomy of Soviet Communism and American capitalism. The Mexican movement calls this a "false and immoral dilemma." Both systems are unjust; the first, politically unjust, the second, economically unjust. "The real dilemma is Christianity or materialism, be it capitalistic or communistic materialism."[24]

As if to emphasize the break with the Western as well as the Eastern materialism, and, undoubtedly, to avoid the epithet of "im-

[22] Alceu Amoroso Lima, "La Reunión de Montevideo," *Política y Espíritu*, II (May, 1947), 153.

[23] Jaime Castillo Velasco, "¿Que es un Partido Demócrata Cristiano?" *Política y Espíritu*, XIII (Aug. 15, 1957), 12.

[24] Movimiento Social Demócrata Cristiano de México, *Bases Ideológicas*, Folleto Número 1 (México, D.F.: March 28, 1963), p. 12.

perialistic lackey," the critique of American capitalism is more voluminous and, perhaps, more vehement than is the condemnation of Communism and the Soviet Union. Moreover, it seems that the Christian Democrats make a conscious effort to overcome the popular opinion that their movement exists merely to combat atheistic Socialism and Soviet Communism. Their credentials as enemies of that system are not challenged, and the case need not be proved. At the other extreme the long record of cooperation between Conservative forces and Catholicism is well known, and an effort is underway to reject this historical tie.

There is little doubt that Christian social thought is cogently acute, often devastating, in its estimation of the consequences of the liberal democratic capitalist era. The atomism and depersonalization of modern society invite constant attack by Christian critics. The Latin American movement, then, cannot be construed as a new departure, although the scope and intensity of the critique may be more profound than that of its precursors. It is asserted for example, that the structure of the moral, social, and economic universe forged under liberal capitalist regimes is the very contradiction of the human essence.[25] Two ideologues of the Chilean movement have gone so far as to interpret private capital as the supreme evil and agree with Marx that all private ownership, except of consumer goods, should be abolished.[26] Capitalists are accused of "taking the lion's share" of the results of the product and monopolizing social privileges and political power. The system reduces the worker to a number "as if the dignity of man were not superior to the dignity of a machine." All economic activity turns on the idea of profit and not on the satisfaction of needs; "technology enslaves man rather than serves him." The fruits of the society are enjoyed by a relative few "at the cost of the frustration of millions of men."[27]

The capitalist economic system breeds a situation in which owners and management manifest no interest in the conditions of labor, nor concern for the laboring class. Moreover, the system imposes upon the workers a continual "state of misery" because the attempt to improve their lot threatens the rights of the proprietors. All of these

[25] Jaime Castillo, *Las Fuentes de la Democracia Cristiana*, p. 86.

[26] Fredrick B. Pike, *Chile and the United States . . .* (Notre Dame, Ind.: University of Notre Dame Press, 1963), p. 261.

[27] Cornejo Chávez, *Nuevos Principios para un Nuevo Peru*, p. 207.

conditions are the result of the "spirit of capitalism."[28] The crude lust for profits, an intrinsic ingredient of liberal capitalism, is repeatedly condemned. The system vitiates the possibility for Christian brotherhood and replaces it with omnipresent and comprehensive competition.

Additionally, because the system, per se, is in error, modifications, even if well intended and progressive, will not suffice. A Nicaraguan party pronouncement rejects the modern reforms of "popular capitalism," which attempt to incorporate the worker into the enterprise by means of profit-sharing and ownership of stock. These schemes are merely "a means of diminishing the effects of capitalism without abandoning the system."[29] The Mexican Movimiento charges "popular capitalism" with merely "diluting" the system even if the immediate gains are acceptable. "It is useful for the workers to have shares in the enterprize in which they work, but only as an important step toward the conquest of the ownership of the means of production. This system is not the ultimate goal of Christian Democracy, but only the first stage in the long process of transforming the enterprize."[30]

Liberal capitalism also stands accused of creating, maintaining, and encouraging the proletarianization of the masses, of alienating man from his work, his community, his spirit and his soul. The concept of labor as a commodity degrades and exploits the workers. Economic exploitation has profound ramifications in the social sphere: it promotes completely different modes of living and thinking and stratifies the society into caste-like classes. The system is capable of creating wealth but is incapable of distributing it; on the contrary, Christian Democrats agree with Marx that this wealth is increasingly concentrated into fewer hands.

The Christian Democratic critique further declares that the capitalistic system has sown the seeds of its own destruction and is now at the point of extinction. It has demonstrated that it is incapable of resolving economic and social problems. The capitalistic system has completed its mission. "The experiences of all Europe and Asia as well as the changes in many other countries including the nordic na-

[28] Jaime Castillo, *Las Fuentes de la Democracia Cristiana*, p. 71.

[29] "ABC de la Democracia Cristiana o Social Cristianismo," p. 7.

[30] Movimiento Social Demócrata Cristiano de México, *Bases Ideológicas*, pp. 10, 11.

tions, demonstrate that humanity now seeks another road in which human labor advances to its full expression in a regime of more comprehensive justice, in which the goods of production serve man instead of being instruments of profit."[31]

Although the economic aspect of Western theory has borne the brunt of the Christian Democratic attack, the political and social implications of liberal democratic ideology have also been censured. Social Christian literature condemns the atomistic character of individualistic liberalism in which man is described as an isolated individual, without organic or communal ties. The declaration of principles established by the Latin American Christian Democratic parties in international congress opposes "individualistic liberalism which fails to recognize the existence of a common good superior to merely private interests."[32] The position also rejects "exaggerated and irreligious liberalism which has directly engendered individualism, jacobinism, individualistic capitalism and anarchy, and, in reaction, has engendered Marxist collectivism."[33] Christian Democratic thinkers consider the "hidden hand" of classical liberal theory as absurd. They sustain, conversely, that "great moral and social effort is necessary to combat egoism which implies materialism and the exploitation of the weak."[34] Extrapolated to the socio-politico sphere, Christians charge that individualistic liberalism is neutral before the problem of truth because it refuses to set out moral norms on the naive assumption that the only measure of truth is the marketplace.

Traditional liberal thought has not been concerned with the socio-economic ramifications of its credo, whereas the Christian Democratic concept of democracy incorporates an awareness of, indeed, a concentration on, these factors. The Dominican Social Christian party stated baldly: "the great problem of the so-called Democracies, is precisely that they have not realized democracy."[35] Noting the emergence of various political parties in the closing days of the Perón re-

[31] Frei Montalva, *Sentido y Forma de una Política*, p. 57.

[32] *Congresos Internacionales Demócrata Cristianos* (Santiago de Chile: Editorial del Pacífico, 1957), p. 219.

[33] Ambrosio Romero Carranza, *¿Qué es la Democracia Cristiana?* (Buenos Aires: Ediciones del Atlántico, 1956), p. 161.

[34] Marcelo Martínez Candia, *Ni Marxismo ni Liberalismo: Social Cristianismo* (Santiago de Chile: Editorial del Pacífico, 1952), p. 19.

[35] Partido Revolucionario Social Cristiano de la República Dominicana, *Democracia Cristiana: Principios e Ideas Fundamentales* (mimeographed), p. 3.

gime, Gustavo Franceschi observed that many of the parties featured purely political planks in their platforms. These groups missed the fundamental point that the age of narrow political democracy had passed. The contemporary period evokes, and the populace demands, he asserts, the inclusion of socio-economic proposals in the programs of political organizations.[36] The Colombian Christian party, while admitting that the Colombian National Front has made valuable contributions to the stability of the nation, states: "We are not in accord with the social policy of the National Front. . . . There persists in the circles of government a bourgeois mentality which is surely incapable of supporting the social transformation demanded by justice."[37] The liberal bourgeois tenor of the newly developing Central American common market is also critized by Social Christians. A Nicaraguan proposes that the "social dimension" is "absent in letter and spirit from the Treaty of Economic Integration," and he points to the comparable document of the European Common Market, written under the aegis of Christian Democrats, which devotes an important chapter to the social question.[38] Criticizing the Prado government in Peru, Cornejo Chávez outlined the Social Christian position. "A democracy which grants only liberty, but not economic security and social justice," he said, "is not a democracy in the modern sense of that word."[39]

Finally, economic imperialism, the handmaiden of the liberal capitalist era, draws vitriolic criticism from the Latin American movement. Imperialism "threatens the liberty" of the Latin American peoples, warns Frei Montalva, and "it will be our duty to combat it."[40] Among other accusations, capitalistic imperialism is blamed for the War of the Pacific and the fall of Jânio Quadros of Brazil.[41]

These charges point up vividly the nature of the Latin American critique. In their analysis of capitalism, Latin Americans generally,

36 Gustavo Juan Franceschi, *La Democracia Cristiana* (Buenos Aires: Ediciones Criterio, 1955), p. 11.

37 Francisco de Paula Jaramillo, *La Democracia Cristiana: Una Nueva Perspectiva para Colombia* (Bogotá: Ediciones del Caribe, 1962), p. 83.

38 Téfel Vélez, *Socialización*, p. 70.

39 *Nuevos Principios para un Nuevo Peru*, p. 99.

40 Frei Montalva, *Sentido y Forma de una Política*, p. 78.

41 Remo di Natale, *América Latina Hoy: Esquemas Populares Demócrata Cristianos* (Caracas: Editorial Nuevo Orden, 1964), p. 44; *Congresos Internacionales Demócrata Cristianos*, p. 114.

including Social Christians, paint a caricature of the system. There are, of course, exceptions to this representation,[42] but the caricature is common enough to provide an excellent foil for the Christian Democratic theory.[43] In response to the charge that their description of capitalism is distorted, at least insofar as modern states are concerned, the Latin American Christian Democrats react with a three-fold counter-charge. First, the essence of capitalism does not change despite reforms. Second, North American capitalism has had no effective check in Latin America; neither governments nor other social forces were sufficiently powerful, wilful, or well developed to counteract the dynamic forces of foreign capitalism. Hence, the practices of North American capitalism in Latin America have not been a reflection of its practices in the United States where government and labor act as counter-forces. Third, say the Latin American Christian Democrats, the practices of indigenous capitalism have been such as to validate their critique.

Even so, the Latin American Christian Democratic evaluation is not totally negative. In the economic sphere, Social Christians are quick to admit the "enormous technical progress" achieved by liberal capitalism; mankind has advanced to higher levels of existence. This "creative effort" merits accolades.[44] Christian Democrats agree that liberal governments are capable of significant political progress. Their nature may prohibit them from undertaking the social revolution, but many reforms are within their ken. Describing the liberal democratic Colombian National Front, Francisco De Paula Jaramillo confesses, "no one can deny there has been a sincere return to an ambiance of liberty and of respect for human rights, which includes wide opportunity for the opposition to organize, to formulate its criticism and to undertake vast electoral campaigns."[45] Another admission is that liberal capitalist nations have achieved social progress. Note, however, that this progress is attained *in spite of* capitalism and not

[42] See, for instance, "President Frei on U. S. Capitalism," *America*, Sept., 1964, p. 285.

[43] One of the outstanding examples of this characteristic is the Dominican Social Christian publication, *ABC* . . . , pp. 13, 16, which calls North American capitalism "anti-christian" and postulates that "Liberal Capitalism recognizes no limitations on private property." See also Pike, *Chile and the United States*, p. 261.

[44] See Rodríguez-Arias, *La Democracia Cristiana y América Latina*, p. 57 and Romero Carranza, *¿Qué es la Democracia Cristiana?*, p. 111.

[45] *La Democracia Cristiana: Una Nueva Perspectiva*, p. 83.

because of it. Strong social and political forces bred by the capitalistic system have been able to effect social progress. Furthermore, the more intelligent champions of capitalism have now realized that the maintenance of the system demands fundamental reform. Significant segments of European capitalism recognize the need "thanks especially to the oracular vision of the leaders of [European] Christian Democracy."[46] In sum, Latin American Christian Democrats envisage liberal democratic theory and practice as incomplete rather than basically in error. The principles of democracy must have social and economic, as well as political, implications and ramifications. Liberal democratic regimes have taken the first step; Christian Democratic governments will complete the task.

Christian Democratic thinkers may be more comprehensive in their critique of the liberal capitalist Western world, but their rejection of Marxist Socialism and Soviet Communism is no less intense or unequivocal. One Social Christian source sees Soviet Communism as the equally unacceptable mirror twin of its Western liberal democratic, capitalistic brother. Neither twin is acceptable.

> To absolute individualism, it opposes absolute socialism; to private property, socialized property; to private initiative, state mechanisms of promotion and state control of development; to the "Night Watchman" state, the simple regulator of private activity, the all powerful Totalitarian State; to a class society, a classless society; to the anarchic struggle for existence, the rigid establishment of enforced and pointless community.[47]

In the famous letter to President Eisenhower from the Christian Democratic-dominated Chilean student's federation, the students stated that there were "impassable barriers separating us from Communist ideology and methods."[48] As might be expected, the Cuban critique is particularly severe. It calls Communist doctrine "intrinsically perverse" and sees international Communism as the "gravest danger to Christian civilization and the security of our continent."[49]

[46] Rodríguez-Arias, *La Democracia Cristiana y América Latina*, p. 66.

[47] Mario Read Vitini, "Hacia un Economía Humana," *Eistín Diario* [Santo Domingo], Martes, Aug. 4, 1964.

[48] Quoted in Milton S. Eisenhower, *The Wine is Bitter: The United States and Latin America* (Garden City, N. Y.: Doubleday and Company, 1963), p. 246.

[49] Movimiento Demócrata Cristiano de Cuba, *Movimiento Demócrata Cristiano de Cuba* (Miami, 1961), p. 52.

Latin Americans generally, and Christian Democrats particularly, are repelled by the materialism and formal atheism of the Communist credo. The Panamanian party rejects all totalitarian regimes, but "especially atheistic communism." An Argentine party leader notes that "the basic difference" between doctrinaire Socialism and Social Christianity "is that Christian Democracy is spiritualistic while Marxist socialism is materialistic."[50] Latin Americans agree with their European brethren on the bases for the rejection of Communism:

> The grounds for the opposition to Communism, therefore, ranged from opposition to the materialistic conception of life which had spread among the masses, to the rejection of the centralizing techniques which Communism brings to governmental problems. Christian Democracy was against the Communist policy of leaving all primary education in the hands of the State; it was against what it felt to be the ultimate total transfer of all means of production to the State; it was against a class conception of the State, a conception which primarily considered economic interests and rights belonging to members of given economic groups to the neglect of the rights belonging to all as citizens of a political community.[51]

Latin American declarations are similar; in 1949, an international congress met at Montevideo and made the statement that

> [Christian Democracy] also rejects Marxist solutions which propose to replace, under the pretext of a temporary solution, the dictatorship of capital with the dictatorship of the State, giving to the State the ownership of the means of production, without liberating the workers nor substantially altering the spirit of the existing regime insofar as it lacks respect for the integral development of the human person.[52]

In comparing the differences in the economic sphere between Christian Democracy and Communism, a leading Latin American Social Christian journal lists four fundamental reasons for rejecting Communism. First, the proposition of an unselfish man who can possess things in common with others is absolutely erroneous; it is an "illusion." Second, state ownership of property destroys the values of

[50] Nathan Miller, "A New Force in Latin America? The Rise of Christian Democracy," *Baltimore Sun*, Sept. 9, 1963.

[51] Mario Einaudi and François Goguel, *Christian Democracy in Italy and France* (Notre Dame, Ind.: University of Notre Dame Press, 1952), p. 33.

[52] *Congresos Internacionales Demócrata Cristianos*, pp. 48, 49.

pluralism. Third, the Communist utopia presupposes a long period of collectivistic totalitarianism, and Christian Democracy cannot accept this subjection of means to ends. Last, the Marxist doctrine cannot be separated from the philosophy in which it is found, a system that seems to stress a society of mass producers characterized by drab depersonalization.[53]

However, the movement does acknowledge some contributions of Communist theory and practice. After having outlined the "irreconcilable incompatibility" between Marxism and Social Christianity, the Peruvian Cornejo Chávez cautions that this rejection "should not impede Christian Democracy from admitting the importance of economic phenomena in the life of the community or for the realization of each human being." Moreover, it must "accept the existence of the fact of the class struggle . . . and combat the unjust distribution of wealth and struggle for a more just distribution of goods among all."[54] In addition, an international congress has indicated that it is "indispensable" to acknowledge that the eastern European Soviet regimes have contributed to the "elimination of certain retarded forms in the social structure and at times have produced important reforms of a material order . . . which contribute to the stability of these regimes and of efficacious propaganda in their favor."[55]

Special and continuing emphasis is placed on the strength of the Communist message. An official pronouncement of the Latin American movement calls the attraction of Soviet Communism the "major danger" of the contemporary period. "It is more than a simple doctrine, it is a new faith, an international organization and a powerful social force. . . . Its influence has been even more profound when the Soviet propaganda machine has encountered social sectors which have suffered the effects of capitalism or the loss of religious faith."[56] The Chilean student's message warns that Christianity and democracy must provide the masses with "work and bread, dignity and security" within the next ten or fifteen years; if not, "the fiery breath of Communism will cover the entire earth."[57]

Faced with the threat of this all-encompassing ideology, the people

[53] "Principios del Comunitarismo" (Publicación del Departamento de Capacitación del PDC), *Política y Espíritu*, XVI (Aug., 1962), 44.

[54] Cornejo Chávez, *Nuevos Principios para un Nuevo Peru*, p. 206.

[55] *Congresos Internacionales Demócrata Cristianos*, p. 231.

[56] *Ibid.*, p. 222.

[57] Eisenhower, *The Wine is Bitter*, p. 246.

may find that hope for salvation lies in the equally comprehensive doctrine of Christian Democracy. This total philosophy covers all aspects of man's existence; it goes beyond the shallow efforts of neo-liberalism that seek to solve the modern dilemma with a shortening of the work week or a raise in salaries. A struggle against totalitarianism based upon the liberal ideology

> exhibits an innocence which borders on the absurd. To oppose them a [political movement] must also have a passionate faith which is multiplied in the thousand activities of man, which crops up in the smallest details of man's existence, which has a mystique to generate poets, martyrs, apostles, propagandists, and technicians; all possessed of a spirit and vision engendered by a final, unique and absorbing system.[58]

The dichotomy is not between Communism and democracy, but between Communism and capitalism; the Third Force, the new message of Christian Socialism, synthesizes the best of both systems.

Latin American Christian Democracy stands against the twin materialisms. As early as 1922, the Catholic Unión Cívica had proclaimed that the true concept of the mission of power was found "between individualism and absolute centralism, between liberalism and socialism."[59] The essence of the Social Christian credo is the conciliation of liberty and justice. The new synthesis harmonizes the substance of truth contained in the doctrines of East and West. The fundamental contribution of capitalism is the recognition of the need for a margin of liberty in economic relations; that of Communism is the inclination toward the foundation of a socio-economic order based on justice.

Although this philosophical and political Third Force results in a position near the center of the political spectrum and evidences many characteristics of both major movements, Christian Democrats firmly deny that it is merely a middle-of-the-road political compromise or an eclectic philosophy. Although some theses and positions seem to be close to those of the two opposing systems, Christian Democracy organizes its ideas and formulates its policies independently. It starts with and is dedicated to the principle of the immanent dignity of the human person, and any coincidence with other

[58] Frei Montalva, *La Política y el Espíritu*, p. 35.

[59] Ariosto Domingo González, *Los Partidos Tradicionales*, ed. José María Serrano (Montevideo: Librería Cervantes, 1922), p. 317.

systems is irrelevant. Moreover, neutralism is vehemently rejected. "The true Christian," writes a Dominican, "knows that Christianity cannot admit of neutrality in the permanent struggle between good and bad. . . . Christianity is a doctrine of responsibility. Neutralism is its negation."[60]

Christian Democrats also reject those centrist "floating groups" who, for the purposes of immediate gain, are willing to coalesce or remain independent. The militants of these organizations are, "with excessive frequency," dominated by personal interests. This position, exemplified by the Radical parties and advanced sections of the Liberal parties, is "uncreative," "anemic," and lacks a "vital core." This type of centrism has fallen into disrepute because it always hides other intentions.[61]

The authenticity of a completely unique stance is frequently affirmed by the Latin American movement. Any accusation of vapid centrism or eclecticism draws spirited denial from the Christian Democrats. Speaking at the Second National Congress of the Peruvian party, Jorge Bolaños Ramírez answered the critics:

> We are not accommodating democrats who mix a portion of Communism and another of Capitalism to obtain the flavorsome cocktail of Christian Democracy. No co-religionists, we have our own doctrine, as old as Christianity and as young as our powerful and progressive party. It is old because it is based on a message which has had two thousand years of existence and new because we shall apply it to the political, social, and economic reality of our time. It is evident, then, that we are able to exhibit our own doctrine, our own idea, which is neither an American cocktail nor a Russian salad.[62]

NATURE OF MAN AND SOCIETY

If the direction of the Latin American Christian Democratic movement is only generally indicated, the stance on the nature of man and society has been given more complete definition. Although Latin Americans have recently added emphasis to specific areas, Chris-

[60] Read Vitini, "Hacia un Economía Humana."

[61] Frei Montalva, *La Política y el Espíritu*, p. 116.

[62] *Una Tercera Posición* . . . (Lima: Editorial Universitaria, 1960), p. 54. For a discussion of the movement's place on the political spectrum, see pp. 187–190.

tian Democratic theory has been long developing and is a fairly unified and rational doctrine. Of all the recognized forces in the Latin American political spectrum, only the Marxists challenge the Christian Democrats in offering a well-constructed, all-encompassing theory of man and society. Christian Democrats insist upon the fundamental necessity of a total philosophy and deride those who attempt to operate in the political sphere without a concrete set of principles. One leading thinker submits that it is "absurd" to present a political program without the underpinning of a "conception of man, society and the State."[63]

The basic element of the Christian Democratic definition is the concept of man as a person. "Christian humanism," "integral humanism," and "economic humanism" or "communitarianism" are the terms usually employed to denote the philosophic position.[64] Personalism defines man as a being of spirit and matter, of body and soul. Man has a terrestrial role which he enacts in temporal history, but he also has a transcendent role. Society must provide a twofold response to this dual nature. Its ability to do so is the supreme measure of a socio-political order.

In addition, the person can be understood only as an integral part of society, for he is, by nature, social as well as spiritual. Catholic social theory and Christian Democratic doctrine have traditionally opposed the separation of man and society. The two concepts can only be understood as they relate to one another. Society is not the sum of isolated individuals; rather, it is the organization of human persons who must interact to achieve material, intellectual, and spiritual fruition. Personalism, therefore, implies a communitarian or solidarist organization of the society and stresses the need for responsibility to and for the community. This traditional doctrine forms the crux of the Latin American Christian Democratic position.

The Christian Democrats also distinguish between the human person, a concept which takes into account both matter and spirit, and the individual, a postulation of traditional Liberal thought. The individual is depicted as being purely physical, leading to the establishment of a society based on animal and inorganic foundations rather than on principles of community and fraternity. "The person

[63] Frei Montalva, *La Política y el Espíritu*, p. 34.

[64] The last two terms have a more pronounced economic connotation and will be discussed in the section dealing with the economic policies of Latin American Christian Democracy, pp. 112–123.

. . . is anterior and superior to the individual. . . ." The person, of course, has individuality because he is "intrinsically indivisible and distinct from all others. He is a reality which exists in itself."[65]

Based on this principle of personality, Latin American Social Christians espouse the credo of Christian or integral humanism. The movement admits of no practical conflict between the concepts of humanism and Christianity. On the contrary, there is an affinity between the two positions which has been hidden because humanist thinkers during the eighteenth century insisted that the ideas were in opposition. The dust of conflict has now cleared, however, and a synthesis has been undertaken. Christian Democracy, says an Argentine theoretician, complements the Christian humanist position.

> They both proceed from the Evangelic message, they both have an optimistic conception of life, they both seek to fortify the dignity and liberty of human persons, they both pursue the establishment of increasingly perfected human and christian social structures, they both center the life of human persons in God, in Christ and in the Church. Neither of the two immobilizes the Christian because they do not permit him to rest upon the truths which he possesses.[66]

This "Theocentrism" implies a "humanism of the spirit. It does not forget the material, which would also be a monstrous error, but it puts its accent on the specifically human."[67]

Integral humanism is fundamentally similar to Christian humanism but gives added emphasis to the multi-faceted nature of man. The simplistic Liberal and Marxist definitions are rejected; man is far too complex for these overly facile doctrines. They have fatally missed the forest of man's personality by concentrating on the trees of specific characteristics. Man is neither completely economic nor political; neither is he a completely religious being as so many conservative Latin American Catholics have assumed. The Cuban Movimiento Demócrata Cristiano stresses that he is not the representative of any one segment of the society alone. The person, cautions the movement,

> is not for the family, an error of many parents who destroy the personality of their children; nor for the race, the error of those who engender racial hatred; nor for labor, the error of those who sustain

[65] Partido Revolucionario Social Cristiano de la República Dominicana, *Democracia Cristiana: Principios e Ideas Fundamentales*, pp. 3, 4.

[66] Romero Carranza, *¿Qué es la Democracia Cristiana?*, p. 66.

[67] Frei Montalva, *La Política y el Espíritu*, p. 130.

> that there are men who were born exclusively to work; nor for capital, the error of those who have as their ideal the simple accumulation of wealth; nor is he for the state, the error of those who think that the only implication of personality is the community.[68]

Integral humanism sees man as both spiritual and temporal, both social and individual, and stresses the necessity of developing these various aspects of man's nature in an integral fashion. It seeks the realization of the entire man in all of his ramifications.

Other concepts enlarge these basic definitions of man in Latin American Christian Democratic literature. The concept of the "vertical" man is occasionally introduced. The vertical theory adds vitality to the definition of man as particular and unique; each man is a human personality made in the image of God. Horizontal man, conversely, conjures up the image of the mass society and the identity of man with class rather than with the whole of society in a community relationship.

There is little emphasis on differences among men and the resulting hierarchical nature of society, although this traditionally conservative Catholic view does occasionally appear. Indeed, the "progressive" stance of the movement seems to preclude any comprehensive discussion of this doctrine; it is found only in the most thorough treatises.[69] Equally remarkable is the infrequent mention of the doctrine of original sin, the imperfectability of man. The literature of the movement is generally optimistic and constantly stresses the ability of man to progress instead of emphasizing his limitations. Indeed, it seems reasonable to conclude that these conservative Catholic shibboleths are consciously avoided lest the positive contributions of Latin American Christian Democracy be lost in the quagmire of Jesuitical definition and qualification.[70]

A Peruvian thinker has summarized the fundamental views of Latin American Christian Democracy as follows: man is both material and spiritual; the religious values of Western society must be maintained; free will is an actuality; man's rights are prior to those of the state; all men are essentially equal.[71]

[68] Movimiento Demócrata Cristiano de Cuba, *Ideario* (Miami, n. d.), p. 8.

[69] See, for instance, Rodríguez-Arias, *La Democracia Cristiana y América Latina*, p. 12, and Frei Montalva, *Aun es el Tiempo . . .*, p. 100.

[70] For exceptions to this rule, see Frei's *Aun es el Tiempo . . .*, p. 89, and *La Política y el Espíritu*, p. 189.

[71] Cornejo Chávez, *Nuevos Principios para un Nuevo Peru*, p. 206.

The concept of the nature of society in Latin American Christian Democratic thought rests on the basic propositions that society is an instrument for the use and benefit of its members and that, in a well-ordered society, the good of the person is identified with the common good. The concept repudiates the totalitarian leanings of many solidaritists by emphasizing the instrumental nature of society; it has no existence apart from man, and its primary function is to provide the means by which man's temporal and transcendent nature may be perfected. Society, defined as a "social organization, has its origin in man and has as its end the creation of the conditions in which man realizes his ends."[72] Each individual, as person, is the concern of the societal structure. Perhaps in no other area of the Christian Democratic system is the adjective "Christian" so important. The rejection of totalitarianism is based on the article of faith which postulates the absolute and unique value of the human soul, a value which infinitely transcends the competence of any socio-political order.

The second element in the definition of society submits that the common good is achieved through the social integration of the rights and duties of the human person. Society must conform to the norm of the common good which, by definition, realizes the values of personality. The good of the social organization equals the common good of human persons. "Hence," in the words of Maritain, "there is nothing more illusory than to pose the problem of the person and the common good in terms of opposition. In reality, it is posed in terms of reciprocal subordination and mutual implication."[73] The common good, moreover, must not be construed as merely the accumulation of several particular goods. "In the same way that society is not the sum of individuals, the common good is not the sum of particular goods. Society is not the sum; it is the organization, that is, the order of relations among individuals. Moreover, the common good is not the sum, it is the general condition which permits the realization of individual goods."[74] The accent falls on the harmonious interaction of particular human persons and is another facet of the Christian Democratic abhorrence of the mass society. Caldera insists that "the people is no amorphous mass, but an aggregate of human

[72] Frei Montalva, *Sentido y Forma de una Política*, p. 83.

[73] Jacques Maritain, "The Person and the Common Good," *Review of Politics*, VIII (Oct., 1946), 444.

[74] Plá Rodríguez, *Los Principios*, p. 54.

beings, conscious of their dignity, conscious of their personality."[75]

Indeed, the concept of man and society is an example of the fundamental rejection of extremes so characteristic of contemporary Christian Democratic thought. For instance, Amoroso Lima, the "Jacques Maritain of South America," states that there are two kinds of freedom, "responsible and irresponsible." He identifies these with "freedom of the human person and freedom of the individual."[76] If atomistic, individualistic liberty is a danger to the foundation of the "true" common good, stifling authoritarian order is also recognized as detrimental to the integral development of the human person. An Uruguayan, citing examples of false concepts of the common good, criticizes the "conservative mentality which seeks order and exterior peace" even though this goal is often attained at the "sacrifice of justice which is a superior value."[77] In the last analysis, the practical organization of the common good encompasses the concepts of both liberty and justice in correctly measured proportions. Some doctrines have developed justice at the expense of liberty, and others have emphasized liberty to the extreme. Christian Democrats, however, seek a vibrant third position that falls into neither error in pursuing the common good.

The instrument for harmonizing the imperatives of liberty and justice is pluralism. The pluralistic concept of social organization has become a basic ingredient of Christian Democratic thought. Luigi Sturzo saw the concept as a method of "affirming the principle of liberty without falling into theoretical agnosticism and into practical individualism. . . ."[78] One scholar, describing the development of Catholic politics in Austria, asserts that "pluralism . . . should be the foundation of any social theory claiming the adjective 'Catholic.' "[79] Pluralism is derived from two opposite tendencies existing

[75] "[Speech] at the Closing Session," *Report of the Second Inter-American Congress of the Inter-American Association for Democracy and Freedom* (1961), p. 27.

[76] Amoroso Lima, "Discussion and Commentaries," on William S. Stokes' "Catholicism and Democracy in Latin America," *Responsible Freedom in the Americas*, ed. Angel del Rio (Garden City, N. Y.: Doubleday and Company, 1955), p. 381.

[77] Plá Rodríguez, *Los Principios*, p. 59.

[78] Luigi Sturzo, "The Philosophic Background of Christian Democracy," *Review of Politics*, IX (Jan., 1947), 13.

[79] Alfred Diamant, *Austrian Catholics and the First Republic* (Princeton, N. J.: Princeton University Press, 1960), p. 46.

in the nature of man and society; both should be taken into account in social organization. One is "the tendency of diversity which is manifested in the multiplicity of opinions, points of view, affections, vocations, preferences, etc. The other is the tendency of unity which is presented as a result of the existence of a series of common necessities and elements."[80]

Pluralism is manifested in the existence of numerous intermediate societies within the body politic. These intermediate structures develop between man and the state and are the outcome of natural communities based on economic, professional, religious, and cultural proclivities of man. The natural communities of man are as varied as the facets of his nature. They include the "family, trade unions, the region, the vast area of the economy, the multiplicity of the spirit, creations of man's genius, the expression of his culture, international relations, religious faith and . . . universal ideas which transcend the nation."[81] These intermediate communities are crucial, for they "permit the integration of men into the society, impede the atomization of the individual within the anarchic liberal society and the dehumanization of man in the totalitarian state and collectivistic regimes."[82]

The pluralistic concept also is seen as two-sided from another point of view. Pluralistic groups can be primarily vertical or horizontal. Vertical pluralism, for example, functions within a natural economic community and encompasses the entire scale of individuals from workers, to management, to stockholders. Horizontal pluralism cuts across economic endeavors and is founded upon the "co-existence of different opinions and ideologies and diverse initiatives which have their origin in the exercise of liberty."[83]

The intermediate societies are key instruments for the fulfillment of man's nature. Christian Democratic parties contemplate the encouragement of these groups through the legal and economic channels of the state. "In a true democracy which has substance and content," notes Frei Montalva, "Community life is necessarily intense. The community is part of the sentiment of the human group

[80] Plá Rodríguez, *Los Principios*, pp. 33, 34.

[81] Frei Montalva, *Sentido y Forma de una Política*, p. 112.

[82] Movimiento Demócrata Cristiano de Cuba, *Tesis Sindical* (mimeographed), p. 4.

[83] Movimiento Demócrata Cristiano del Paraguay, *Acta Fundacional y Declaración de Principios* (Asunción, 1960), pp. 6, 7.

and no central government is capable of being a substitute. There is measured the vital pulse of the nation, its culture, its sentiment of cooperation, its capacity to organize and to resolve the thousand problems which surge from reality. . . ."[84] Pluralism is recognized as another manifestation of the popular and progressive nature of Latin American Christian Democracy. It is described as an "optimistic philosophy, which believes that it is possible for men of the most distinct schools of thought and most diverse beliefs to march in common."[85]

The principle of subsidiarity, long nurtured by Catholic social theory, is an analog of social pluralism. It sets forth that each level of the socio-political structure should be left to complete the tasks that it can effectively undertake. Each group is able to perform its sphere of work for the good of society as a whole as well as for its particular members. This sphere ought to be reserved to the unit on the condition that it adequately performs its function. A higher authority may set guide lines for the subordinate unit and make recommendations and suggestions. Only as a last resort, however, may the higher agency assume the tasks of the lower. In political terms, this principle encourages the existence of vibrant intermediate bodies and guards against the unmerited growth of state machinery. One of the early Peruvian Christian Democrats warns against this bureaucratic growth. "The State ought not substitute itself . . . for the intermediate entities . . . , but complement their action by creating a juridical and institutional framework which guarantees their free . . . functioning. . . ."[86]

Finally, the Latin American Christian Democratic movement urges optimum individual participation. It is clearly the most efficient method of social and economic organization and provides the additional dividend of integrating man into his political environment; it encourages man to be a conscious member of the society. Participation enriches the human experience. The goal is to evoke a real and active participation of each citizen in the society. Involvement gives the individual a stake in the government and state and brings about

[84] Eduardo Frei Montalva, *La Verdad Tiene su Hora* (Santiago de Chile: Editorial del Pacífico, 1955), p. 112.

[85] Eduardo Frei Montalva, *Caminos de la Política: Un Enfoque de Cinco Doctrinos*, ed. Sergio Guilisasti Tagle (Santiago de Chile: Editorial Universitaria, 1960), pp. 115, 116.

[86] Víctor Andrés Belaúnde, *et al.*, *Política, Deber Cristiana* (Lima: Editorial Universitaria, 1963), p. 73.

an authentic stability, not a false, superficial order founded on force or hopeless ignorance.

The examples of pluralistic social organization envisaged and promoted by Christian Democrats encompass the entire hierarchical scale and horizontal plane of the society from the family to the national community. Surely no facet of Christian Democratic theory is as well known as its deep concern for the maintenance of the family unit. Frei Montalva has stated, "without the family there is no society."[87] According to the Cuban Christian group, "the family, conceived as a social, natural and primary nucleus, constitutes the vital unity of the entire society."[88] The family serves as the primary environment for the person, and it conditions his formation, his conduct, his success or his failure. The values and habits that it develops influence the entire social process, and it forms the basis of the human society and of the Christian Democratic creed. One manifesto, indeed, concludes that the family is "anterior to all human law."[89]

Perhaps not so well known is the concern of Christian Democrats for the development of other intermediate social and political bodies. The gamut of these intermediate bodies presents communities with the potential for integral development into legally constituted structures. These groups are to be encouraged to establish their own governmental organization, write their own constitutions, and provide machinery to solve their own problems. Labor unions, for example, are seen as natural and not artificial entities. Their range of responsibility to the person is multi-faceted. "Labor Unions ought not only to be instruments of the economic struggle but communities preoccupied with technical, moral and spiritual perfection; with the professional preparation of its members; with the betterment of their living conditions; and with the formation and development of a professional ethic. . . ."[90]

A comprehensive summary of the practical significance of the movement's pluralism is outlined by Américo Plá Rodríguez. In the social order, Christian pluralism demands the recognition of the existence and legitimacy of distinct types of communities from the

[87] Eduardo Frei Montalva, *Chile Desconocido* (Santiago de Chile: Ediciones Ercilla, 1937), p. 53.

[88] Movimiento Demócrata Cristiano de Cuba, *Ideario*, p. 12.

[89] Movimiento Social Cristiano del Ecuador, *Manifiesto del 13 de Noviembre y Declaración de Principios* (Quito: Editorial Chimborazo, 1951), p. 9.

[90] *Congresos Internacionales Demócrata Cristianos*, p. 337.

family to the state. Each one of these groups ought to have its own "organization, development . . . full autonomy and . . . maximum liberty compatible with the public order." In the administrative order, Plá continues, the theory calls for separate and autonomous groups directed by governors chosen from within the community. He gives the university as an example of this kind of organization; university affairs should be in the hands of representatives chosen from the three interested groups—students, professors, and alumni. In the local order, he demands "authentic recognition of municipal autonomy." This can only be effected when each "department, each region or each zone has its own local authorities who are vigilant in the defense and progress of their charges." Next, Plá endorses economic autonomy and discusses the possible dangers of such a plan. He recognizes the chaotic implications of complete independence in the economic sphere and offers the "primacy of the political over the economic" as the ultimate solution to the problem. In the order of labor relations, pluralism imposes regulations emanating from labor and professional groups and emphasizes the importance of collective bargaining. Central government may have to formulate general guide lines, but the stress should be on self-regulation. "From the sociological point of view," he notes, "the situation will be much more peaceful and fecund as a result of norms approved by the interested parties themselves than it would be as a result of rules imposed by means of authoritative enactments."[91]

THE STATE

The state in Latin American Christian Democratic theory is a positive agent actively seeking the common good but, at the same time, limited by theo-philosophic principles and organic social structures. The movement rejects the neutral liberal state. The first paragraph of Frei's *Política y Espíritu* declares unequivocally that "the State is the expression of an ideology and follows it in the organization of society." The state, he continues, impinges on man's existence in numerous ways. It "organizes" man, it "controls" him, it "creates the press which he reads," it "censors and orders his radio programs, it educates his children impressing upon them a determined character and it especially controls his economic life. . . . These facts are produced in diverse gradations," Frei concludes, "but there is

[91] Plá Rodríguez, *Los Principios*, pp. 39–42.

almost no modern nation which is not submitted to this system."[92] The 1949 Montevideo Congress repeated and expanded this position when it passed a lengthy resolution outlining the "essential contradiction" of liberal democratic states. These entities, charged the Congress, were founded on the principle that effective liberty obviated the possibility of an ideological state; but the consequences proved the principle invalid. The very liberty to which the state was consecrated permitted a dominant group to exercise socio-economic license that denied, for the mass of the people, the possibility of really fulfilling their human personality.[93]

Latin American Christian Democrats affirm that the principle of authority, with this implied right to exercise political power, has its origin in God. The divine origin of political authority, however, is only a part of the position. Modern Catholic thinkers adhere to one of two doctrines to explain the nature of authority within the political community—the translation theory or the designation theory. Latin American Social Christians prefer the translation theory, the older and more democratic of the two. It is the basis of Thomistic thought and is another indication of the influence of Neo-Scholasticism. The translation theory holds that political authority is vested by God in the community as a whole; with the establishment of a body politic comes a simultaneous bestowal of authority, the natural property of political organization. Ultimate sovereignty rests with the people who translate it to a legal sovereign. Governmental legitimacy is based on a free and rational delegation from the people.[94]

The second international conclave of the Latin American movement, held in Montevideo in 1949, resolved, "the principle of authority has its origin in God, although the nominal holder of that authority ought to be elected by the consent of the people."[95] A Peruvian party platform reiterates the same idea and adds that the people must "determine the form of government" and "directly designate the governors."[96] The state in Latin American Christian Dem-

[92] Frei Montalva, *La Política y el Espíritu*, p. 33.

[93] "El Congreso Demócrata Cristiano de Montevideo de 1949," *Política y Espíritu*, IV (Aug.-Dec., 1949), 27, 28.

[94] For a short discussion of the two theories, see Henry J. Schmandt and Paul G. Steinbicker, *Fundamentals of Government* (Milwaukee: Bruce Publishing Company, 1954), pp. 121–24.

[95] *Congresos Internacionales Demócrata Cristianos*, p. 43.

[96] *Manual del Elector* (Lima: Editorial Juan Mejia Baca, 1962), p. 173.

ocratic thought, in sum, is democratic and is based on a conscious ideological foundation.

The movement proposes an active policy that assumes comprehensive responsibility for the well-being of individual citizens and for the growth and stability of the economy. The state is a dynamic welfare state, though it falls far short of totalitarianism. In practice, the competence of the state is somewhere between the two poles of the traditional liberal democratic state and the totalitarian Soviet Communist state, reflecting the movement's penchant for the third solution. "We do not believe," notes a foremost Peruvian ideologue, "in a State . . . which suffocates private initiative, which is converted into industrial, commercial and administrative omnipotence and which reduces the individual to a simple cog in a tyrannical and unmerciful machine. But," he continues, "if we are enemies of the totalitarian State, we are equally enemies of the gendarme State because . . . the policy of 'laissez-faire, laissez-passer' envelops a concept . . . in good part responsible for the injustices of capitalism. . . ."[97] As early as the second decade of this century, the Catholic Unión Cívica's official program pronounced: "The State is . . . not able to reduce its mission to merely negative functions . . . by simply maintaining internal and external security."[98]

The state must exercise wide authority in originating, fostering, and even enforcing reforms in the society. Indeed, this task has a special urgency in a developing continent where neither private resources nor expertise is adequate to the task. The Latin American Christian Democratic state cannot be satisfied with the status quo. Order "is the most torpid of concepts. Authority is an active element . . . , and if it ceases to be, the society corrupts and degenerates."[99]

Major facets of the doctrine are readily evident in party policy pronouncements. First, the state must be the vehicle of rapid and dynamic change; slow evolution is not good enough. The present continental crisis demands planned governmental revolution.[100] Moreover, the middle and proletarian classes look to the state to bring about new conditions of life and to modify the structures on

[97] Cornejo Chávez, *Nuevos Principios para un Nuevo Peru*, p. 106.

[98] Ariosto Domingo González, in *Los Partidos Tradicionales*, p. 317.

[99] Frei Montalva, *Aun es el Tiempo* . . . , p. 15.

[100] Frank Tannenbaum sees this penchant for "centralized control and guidance" as "well-nigh universal" in Latin America. "The tradition . . . antedates Independence and . . . all political credos take it for granted. The idea of plan-

which the old ruling classes were founded. Javier Correa Elias, speaking as president of the Fifth International Congress of Latin American Christian Democrats, summarized the position of the movement when he declared: "The economic phenomenon is closely tied to the moral . . . and the State must intervene . . . to orient economic activity to the common good to impede the illicit enrichment of the economically powerful and to make impossible . . . the servitude and suffering of the economically weak."[101]

Such a policy means that the state must assume the major responsibility for the planning and direction of the national economy. Christian Democrats feel that both industrial and agricultural production can be significantly increased under the guidance and encouragement of the state. Beyond this fundamental task, the state must also undertake the diversification and re-orientation of the several national economies as well as make a start in the development of international economic cooperation. Finally, the doctrine emphasizes the primacy of the political in its concept of the state. Economic planning serves the political ends of the society and technicians serve statesmen.

The several parties differ slightly on the subject of Church and state, although all clearly stand for religious liberty. Significant progress has been achieved in this knotty area of Latin American politics, but the problem still remains in many of the nations, and an early solution seems doubtful. One recent publication warns that the Church-state problem "is too firmly implanted in the inheritance of the area to be eliminated in a generation or two. . . . It is difficult, if not impossible to envisage any arrangements that will isolate church and state one from the other."[102] Indeed, public worship by non-Catholics has been limited in Peru and Colombia in recent years. Moreover, the Peronista tyranny even imposed restrictions on the activities of the Catholic church.

Three positions are evident in the movement. The most widely accepted is exemplified in the statement of a Nicaraguan party leader who opposes the recognition of any "official," "legitimate," or

---

ning, seemingly so new and revolutionary, is congenial to even the most conservative Latin Americans. . . . The notion is old and inevitable." "The Future of Democracy in Latin America," *Foreign Affairs*, XXXIII (April, 1955), 444.

[101] *Congreso Internacional de la Democracia Cristiana: Anales del quinto . . .* (Lima: Editorial Universitaria, 1960), p. 44.

[102] John J. TePaske and Sydney Nettleton Fisher (eds.), *Explosive Forces in Latin America* (Columbus: Ohio State University Press, 1964), p. 50.

"majority" religion.[103] The second is expressed by the Colombian Partido Social Demócrata Cristiano, which finds "the separation between Church and State as a necessity for the free completion of their respective missions," although "this does not impede mutual collaboration in areas of the common wellbeing."[104] An early Argentine pronouncement called for the union of Church and state. "This union," the writer explains, "has always existed in our country conducing to grandeur, peace and prosperity and never bringing inconveniences of any species to any government or to any inhabitant of the Republic."[105]

If the state in Latin American Christian Democratic thought is charged with a positive mission and armed with the authority to undertake a radical transformation of the society, its competence is limited by equally efficacious and intransigent principles. Institutionalized pluralism is a formidable check on state omnipotence. The comprehensive autonomy of the family, the local community, regional subdivisions, syndical organizations, and the Church all limit the activity of the state. Subsidiarity also guards against unnecessary and deleterious growth of state apparatus. The constant stress on decentralization affords additional limits. Moreover, the belief in the inviolable nature of the human personality is a bulwark against totalitarian political authority. The Paraguayan movement sees God as the "foundation of all power, and only He has absolute power. Authority, therefore, does not govern without limitations and the liberty of man supersedes the excesses of human power. . . ."[106] Among three essential ideas which inform the action of Christian Democratic parties is listed "the dignity of the human person, and respect for his liberties and natural rights . . . and the subordination of both public and private social life to the moral values of Christianity."[107]

In the last analysis Latin American Christian Democrats admit the right of active resistance to, and the violent overthrow of, tyrannical governments. The Declaration of Principles of the Panamanian

[103] Téfel Vélez, *Socialización*, p. 29.

[104] "Conclusiones de la Comisión Ideológica," *Pueblo y Libertad*, III (Aug., 1964), 6.

[105] Romero Carranza, *¿Qué es la Democracia Cristiana?*, pp. 97, 98.

[106] Movimiento Social Demócrata Cristiano del Paraguay, *Acta Fundacional y Declaración de Principios*, pp. 7, 8.

[107] Alberto Edwards Vives and Eduardo Frei Montalva, *Historia de los Partidos Políticos Chilenos* (Santiago de Chile: Editorial del Pacífico, 1949), p. 244.

party observes that all pacific measures must be expended before other recourse is justified, but, "among the natural rights of man, we recognize the right of revolution."[108] The Ecuadorian Movimiento Social Cristiano hedges its statement. "Authority is a natural institution. It ought to be defended and respected. The right of rebellion is only justified when all legal means to correct the flagrant violation have been exhausted. . . ."[109] A Peruvian, however, is both bolder and more specific: "Christian social philosophy since St. Thomas has taught the doctrine of a just rebellion against tyranny; and that philosophy teaches that tyranny is not only aggression against fundamental human rights, but it is also a tyranny when inveterate incapacity impedes social reforms without which the normal exercise of those rights is an illusion." After setting down this rather liberal interpretation of the right of revolution, Ernesto Alayza Grundy warns against the promiscuous utilization of the doctrine. "The moralists are strict," he says "in pointing out the objective conditions which ought to be satisfied in order to justify a revolutionary attitude and the use of violence." These conditions include a "serene and objective" analysis of the situation, the exhaustion of peaceful means, a complete understanding and measurement of the consequences of the revolution to ascertain that the good achieved is not exceeded by the evil of violence, some assurance of success, and elimination of intrinsically evil means.[110]

Some specific examples of justified revolutions include the Latin American independence movement, the Argentine Revolution of 1955, the Venezuelan of 1958, and the Cuban of 1959.[111] Furthermore, a congress of Caribbean Christian Democrats recognized "as licit the active resistance against the dictatorships of Trujillo, Somoza and Duvalier in the Caribbean Zone and of Stroessner in Paraguay."[112]

[108] Partido Demócrata Cristiano de Panamá, *El Partido Demócrata Cristiano de Panamá: Historia, Principios, Programa, Estructura* (Panamá, 1964), p. 26.

[109] Movimiento Social Cristiano del Ecuador, *Manifiesto*, p. 10.

[110] Belaúnde, *Política, Deber Cristiana*, p. 81.

[111] Plá Rodríguez, *Los Principios*, p. 27, and Romero Carranza, *¿Qué es la Democracia Cristiana?*, pp. 178–81.

[112] "El Congreso del Caribe," *Política y Espíritu*, XV (May, 1961), 54; the Paraguayan party admits the right of revolution, but notes that "passive resistance ought to be the method of struggling for the channeling of the Republic"; Movimiento Social Demócrata Cristiano del Paraguay, *Manifesto de Movimiento* . . . (Asunción: May 31, 1960), p. 2.

Latin American Christian Democratic Parties

Characteristics and Organization 4

IDEOLOGICAL PARTIES

The development of ideologically coherent and organizationally unified parties has significantly modified the tenor of Latin American politics. The bases of the Christian Democratic ideology are, most simply, Christian social, political, and economic theories combined with democratic principles. Of equal importance to the content of this position, however, is the fact that the Christian Democratic parties—and other Latin American political parties—emphasize goals and purposes which transcend mere political power and enjoyment of the spoils of government. The movement cannot be fully understood without an appreciation of this fact; this is one of its most distinctive characteristics.

The growth of ideologically inclined parties has two major ramifications. First, political phenomena become more predictable. In spite of the constant discrepancy between theory and practice, some general courses of action are outlined in advance and then pursued. "Ideologies," says Sigmund Neumann, "are the key to an understanding of the long range strategy behind the day-to-day tactics of political movements."[1] Second, the development of ideology usually connotes the formation of popularly based parties that seek to include the masses in the political process.[2] This is not an entirely one-way process; often, a feedback is evident. Parties that hope to enlist mass support must develop a complex set of policies, often based on principles that are minimally coherent. Conversely, mass

[1] Sigmund Neumann (ed.), *Modern Political Parties* (Chicago: University of Chicago Press, 1956), p. 417.

[2] Maurice Duverger, *Political Parties: Their Organization and Activity in the Modern State*, trans. Barbara and Robert North (New York: John Wiley and Sons, 1963), p. vii.

awareness of the political process demands that political organizations evolve working programs designed to meet a wide range of needs, and these programs in turn, intentionally or not, result in the expression of fairly unified ideological principles. Although Latin American parties differ in many respects, many of them give evidence of this ideological base. Christian Democrats are proud of their success in developing an ideology and, indeed, must be placed near the top in any ranking of parties that have attempted to do so.

On the whole, the rapid growth and maturation of contemporary Latin American political parties are directly attributable to the development by each party of an ideological stance. Indeed, a Panamanian party manifesto, recognizing this fact, proclaims that it is a "different party"; "it is different because it is neither traditionalist nor personalist. It is authentically ideological."[3] The ideological position of the Peruvian party has been called an "exceptional thing in Peruvian political life. It is the only group founded on a common vision and the elaboration of solutions based on political design. The other formations are of the more traditional Latin American type, allied around a polarizing personality."[4] A history of the Uruguayan Unión Cívica boasts that the party has the "glory" of being the first in that country to "write and publish" its program and principles.[5] Throughout Latin America, "the parties are characterized by the primacy of the ideological over the political. This connotes permanent activity, more intense during electoral campaigns, but regularly manifested in inter-electoral periods. The dynamic factor of the party is not politics, but ideology."[6] Another spokesman, Américo Plá Rodríguez, also notes specifically their ideological bent; they are "parties of ideas." They possess "vital and exclusive principles which inspire permanent party action." These basic principles, moreover, provide "fundamental unity to the trajectory and activity of the party in spite of various directors, representatives and militants. . . ."[7]

[3] Partido Demócrata Cristiano de Panamá, *El Partido Demócrata Cristiano de Panamá: Historia, Principios, Programa, Estructura* (Panamá, 1964), p. 30.

[4] *Perú*, Estudios de Actualidad, Primera Serie, No. 2 (Montevideo: Instituto de Estudios Políticos para América Latina, 1964), p. 21.

[5] Joaquín Secco Illa, *Historia de la Unión Cívica* (Montevideo: Impresora Zorrilla de San Martín, 1946), p. 132.

[6] Pedro Pablo Aguilar, *Los Partidos Demócrata Cristianos*, Lecture prepared for El Instituto de Formación Demócrata Cristiana (Caracas: mimeographed, n.d.), p. 5.

[7] *Los Principios de la Democracia Cristiana* (Bogotá: Ediciones del Caribe, 1962), p. 16.

Latin American Christian Democrats regard proper ideological formation as essential to the success of the movement. Panamanian leaders postponed official inscription of the party because they "considered that it [was] necessary, before proceeding with a quantitative inscription, to be sure that the popular sectors had a better knowledge of the fundamental principles which inspire the Movement." The same party rejects electoral or governmental coalition with other forces on the grounds that its message would be "diluted." Coalition would be "traitorous to the Panamanian people who want a new alternative of liberty, social justice and progress."[8]

Furthermore, Christian Democrats assert that the times, and especially the struggle against Marxism, demands ideological orientation. A negative, anti-communist stand is not enough. "The multitudes have never been moved by defensive negation, but by the positive pronouncement of an affirmation." "When Marxism operates on all levels and presents in detail 'its' solution which is the product of 'its' thought, petty bourgeois reformism is not even a provisional dike. The experience of the last years is too clear to dispute." Any "serious" political movement must inculcate "a response to each inquietude and each human expression; only thusly will it have vigor and profundity in political action."[9]

In the last analysis, then, Latin American Christian Democracy espouses a messianic, all-encompassing philosophical system, a "universal current of ideas . . . projected and developed on the sociopolitical and economic planes of human life."[10] The parties are, of course, political agents operating in the purely public sphere, but they also embrace certain spiritual and moral values and place as much emphasis on these as they do upon purely instrumental political goals. Speaking at an international conference of the continental movement, Frei Montalva contended that Christian Democracy is "more than a political party. It is an interpretation of human life, it is a sense of the human person with his immortal soul, with his sacred rights. . . ."[11] The Cubans call Christian Democracy a "posture

[8] Partido Demócrata Cristiano de Panamá, *El Partido Demócrata Cristiano de Panamá*, pp. 11, 31.

[9] Eduardo Frei Montalva, *La Política y el Espíritu* (Santiago de Chile: Ediciones Ercilla, 1940), pp. 41, 36.

[10] Partido Revolucionario Social Cristiano de la República Dominicana, *Democracia Cristiana: Principios e Ideas Fundamentales* (mimeographed), p. 1.

[11] *Congreso Internacional de la Democracia Cristiana: Anales del quinto . . .* (Lima: Editorial Universitaria, 1960), p. 244.

before life and history which is more than a simple ideological, political and social movement."[12]

CHRISTIAN BUT NON-CONFESSIONAL BASE

Regardless of differing interpretations, the word "Christian" is basic to the Christian Democratic movement. "It is possible," notes one militant, "that the name Christian Democrat induces misunderstanding. It does not imply an exclusive democracy only for Christians nor even a democracy under the control of Christians."[13] The term must be interpreted in its broadest sense, implying an historical, cultural tradition, as well as a theological commitment. The Dominican Partido Revolucionario Social Cristiano, for example, acknowledges the "value of the christian roots of the Dominican people. Without entering the religious area, it bases its principles and solutions on the moral teachings of the Gospel as the inspiration of social justice."[14] The Venezuelan Partido Social Cristiano-COPEI rejects specific religious definitions but "sustains the Christian ideal and proclaims it as the integrating element of the nationality and as a source of obligations of social justice, of human action and of public service."[15] The stress is on Christian duty rather than on special truth or a particular Christian competence.

The Cuban exile organization warns that Christian Democracy is not an "exclusive and arrogant" position, although it does think that a "fertilely christian terrain" is the best foundation for democracy. Nor is Christian Democracy a "sacred chair which intolerantly dogmatizes"; rather, it is a "tribune for a continuous dialog between the people and the government." Last, the Cubans forswear any "permanent crusade which predicates a holy war . . ." and call their movement a "civic and moral legion which preaches by example and believes in persuasion."[16] The Latin Americans are not unaware of the dangers of the Christian label. In one of the closing

[12] Movimiento Demócrata Cristiano de Cuba, *Ideario* (Miami, n.d.), p. 6.

[13] Eduardo Frei Montalva, *Caminos de la Política: Un Enfoque de Cinco Doctrinos,* ed. Sergio Guilisasti Tagle (Santiago de Chile: Editorial Universitaria, 1960), p. 111.

[14] Partido Revolucionario Social Cristiano de la República Dominicana, *Programa del Partido Revolucionario Social Cristiano* (mimeographed), p. 1.

[15] Partido Social Cristiano-COPEI, *Programa* (3rd ed.; Caracas, 1961), p. 5.

[16] Movimiento Demócrata Cristiano de Cuba, *Ideario,* p. 7.

speeches at the Lima Congress, Caldera warned: "We well know that the people have had and conserve, in great part, doubts about us. They have heard us talk of justice, they have heard us talk of charity, they have heard us talk of Christianity, and they cannot forget that many have played with and exploited and abused the name of Christianity to implant and perpetuate injustice."[17]

The social and political obligations of the religion demand a response by Christians. An ideologist of the movement berates the early Christians for seeking the contemplative solitude of the Egyptian desert. Christianity, he asserts, must realize itself as an active social doctrine.[18] The present leader of the Argentine party has noted that "we should not tremble because we are called socialists who pray."[19] To those who argue that Christianity should rightly be a doctrine of individual salvation and not a political philosophy, Social Christians respond that man lives in this world, and his salvation must be worked out, in no small part, through the structures and institutions of the temporal order.

The direct implication of this definition of Christian politics is the unequivocal repudiation of confessionality. The manifesto of the Salvadorian party is typical of the pronouncements on this issue. It declares that the Christian Democratic party "categorically denies that it is in any way directed by the Catholic Church or any other religious body, believing that politics and religion should not be mixed."[20] Francisco de Paula Jaramillo states that the movement is "not a religious confraternity, nor is it a beneficiary or charity center or association, nor is it a movement to spiritually reform men; in fine, it is not an institution with confessional characteristics or ends."[21] The first international conference of the incipient Christian Democratic movement in 1947 listed among its "bases" that "the

[17] *Congreso Internacional de la Democracia Cristiana: Anales del quinto . . .*, p. 250. Elsewhere, it has been noted that "the masses are cautious about the party because of their previous and regrettable experiences with clerical political organizations." See *CIF Reports*, V (Feb., 1966), 23.

[18] Ambrosio Romero Carranza, *¿Qué es la Democracia Cristiana?* (Buenos Aires: Ediciones del Atlántico, 1956), pp. 13, 14.

[19] Quoted in Nathan Miller, "A New Force in Latin America? The Rise of Christian Democracy," *Baltimore Sun*, Sept. 9, 1963.

[20] "Foundation of the Christian Democratic Party of Salvador," *Christian Democratic Review*, II (May, 1961), 10.

[21] *La Democracia Cristiana: Una Nueva Perspectiva para Colombia* (Bogotá: Ediciones del Caribe, 1962), p. 9.

movement will not have a confessional character and all who accept these principles are able to participate."[22]

To exclude non-Christians would be "a sin against democracy [and] against the nature of the political party which is concerned with attaining and maintaining the Common Good, not the salvation of souls."[23] The Latin Americans have given practical significance to this position, and Protestants, Jews, and agnostics are active party militants. Moreover, a North American student asserts that many Chilean Falangistas see the official religious stand of the party as an "embarrassment, and they vociferously deny that there is any issue at all. For them the Falange is a kind of Radical party which is not anti-Clerical."[24] The selection of party names has been an indication of this deliberate attempt to avoid confessional overtones. Luigi Sturzo's Partido Popolare, perhaps the first modern Christian party, set the tone, and the early Latin American parties followed the Italian lead.

The position is that the Church and political parties are separate entities and can have no organic tie. The 1912 program of the Unión Cívica noted that the party would defend the Church's interest. Nevertheless, "it would be an error to believe that the Unión Cívica is a Catholic party . . . , because this concept is not exact. Catholicism is represented in the world by the Church which is not definitively or exclusively affiliated with any political party."[25] "No party has the right to call itself a Catholic Party, to undertake the representation of the Church or to believe that it is the only 'orthodox' channel for Catholics who operate in political life."[26] One author insists that a Catholic party would, by definition, be submitted to episcopate authority, but Christian Democratic organizations are most correctly called "parties of Christian inspiration" and are completely independent of Church influence.[27]

If the party cannot aspire to represent the Church, neither can

[22] "Acta Final de la Reunión de Montevideo," *Política y Espíritu*, II (May, 1947), 149.

[23] Benjamín Miguel H., "The Word 'Christian' as Designation of a Political Party," *Christian Democratic Review*, IX (Nov., 1959), 4.

[24] Kalman H. Silvert, "Elections, Parties and the Law," *American Universities Field Staff: Reports Service*, West Coast South America Series, Vol. 4, No. 4 (New York, March 10, 1957), p. 15.

[25] Joaquín Secco Illa, *Historia de la Unión Cívica*, pp. 133, 134.

[26] Frei Montalva, in *Caminos de la Política*, p. 111.

[27] Gustavo Juan Franceschi, *La Democracia Cristiana* (Buenos Aires: Ediciones Criterio, 1955), p. 8.

the Church interfere in political affairs; the Church's business is not politics. "The authorities of the Church do not determine how a Christian should vote on a law like the Defense of Democracy. The decision corresponds to a political judgment pronounced by men who have charge of public matters in view of determined circumstances and guided by the doctrine."[28]

DEMOCRATIC AND POPULAR EMPHASIS

If the Latin American Christian Democratic parties sometimes are embarrassed by the Christian label, the democratic designation is constantly emphasized. The two terms have not always been complementary in Latin America, and the modern movement stresses the importance of democratic methods. The Brazilian, Andrés Franco Montoro, bases the democratic credo of the movement on its belief in the human person: "Because we believe in the human person, we believe in the people; therefore, we are democrats."[29] Dardo Regules has defined democracy as "a mode of living which founds power on consent and which organizes the state by means of universal suffrage. It has two characteristics and two ends; as characteristics, publicity about the government and responsibility of the governors; as ends, the protection of the human person and the realization of the common good."[30]

Héctor Cornejo Chávez notes that the movement could well arrive at the necessity for a democratic politic by an argument *ad absurdum.* No other system works. An amplification of this same point proposes that "Jesus Christ did not outline any particular form of government," and yet: "Christians have begun to understand that in our epoch dignity and liberty can only be advanced to their maximum guarantee . . . by means of a democratic regime. Historical experiences teach that imperial states, monarchies and dictatorship always concluded by propagating despotism. . . . "[31]

Despite the difficulties which beset democratic regimes in less-developed nations, the movement argues that free government is necessary; it is the best method of educating the masses to assume

[28] Jaime Castillo Velasco, *El Problema Comunista* (Santiago de Chile: Editorial del Pacífico, 1955), p. 167.

[29] De Paula Jaramillo, *La Democracia Cristiana*, p. 103.

[30] *Congresos Internacionales Demócrata-Cristianos* (Santiago de Chile: Editorial del Pacífico, 1957), p. 120.

[31] Romero Carranza, *¿Qué es la Democracia Cristiana?*, p. 52.

responsible citizenship. The fact that the party doctrine so strongly favors self-government reflects the omnipresent Latin American faith in the power of education. Caldera teaches the efficacy of enlightened leadership and berates those governments that have not guided the people along the road to ordered liberty.[32] The current Peruvian party president reiterates this point and adds that the beleaguered nation has survived the treachery and evil of dictatorships; it can surely "support, for some years, the inexperience of its people."[33] Although Christian Democracy recognizes that liberties cannot be absolute and foresees regulation, in doubtful areas it prefers to make concessions to liberty. Christian Democrats further argue that the concept of order has been prostituted in Latin America; it has been used to "annul . . . public liberties," it has "destroyed constitutionalism," and it has been the tool of "reactionary forces."[34]

On the whole, the record of Latin American Christian Democrats in protecting constitutional and democratic government and actively fighting despotism has been good. The Venezuelan Social Christian-COPEI actively opposed Pérez Jiménez and assisted in his eventual political demise. It was a major prop in the shaky democracy of the Betancourt regime, and even in its stance of "autonomy of action," beginning in 1964, the party refused to oppose democratic government blindly. Although selectively opposing some governmental programs, it maintained its loyalty to the basic principles of the democratic system. The Guatemalan Social Christians opposed the leftist Arbenz Guzmán and the rightist Miguel Ydígoras Fuentes governments and actively fought the Enrique Peralta military dictatorship. The Dominican Partido Revolucionario Social Cristiano, the internationally recognized Christian Democratic party on that island, was formed clandestinely during the Trujillo tyranny. It constantly expressed vociferous opposition to the extra-constitutional regime that developed after the overthrow of Juan Bosch in 1963, stating that those who had undertaken the coup were acting purely on personal, and not patriotic, motives. Opposition to the overthrow also came from the Social Christian student group, the Bloque Revolucionario Universitario Cristiano.[35] In the 1965 civil

[32] Rafael Caldera, *El Bloque Latinoamericano* (Santiago de Chile: Editorial del Pacífico, 1961), p. 61.

[33] Héctor Cornejo Chávez, *Nuevos Principios para un Nuevo Perú* (Lima: Publicaciones de la Juventud Demócrata Cristiana, 1960), p. 12.

[34] *Una Tercera Posición* . . . (Lima: Editorial Universitaria, 1960), p. 38.

[35] *Hispanic American Report*, XVI (Dec., 1963), 968.

war, Social Christians took to the streets to fight with the constitutionalist side against the military junta.

More specific examples are legion. The Paraguayan Movimiento Social Demócrata Cristiano has joined other parties in demanding the end of the Stroessner regime. The Argentine party was a significant factor in the opposition to Perón and was instrumental in his eventual ouster. In July, 1955, a manifesto issued by the newly founded party berated the Peronista government for its "personalism and contempt for constitutional rights. . . . "[36] The party later stood for amnesty for all political prisoners and abrogation of measures that had forced some into exile. After the fatal triumph of the Peronistas in the March, 1962, elections, the Christian Democrats were the only major party to promise coalition aid to President Arturo Frondizi in an attempt to save the floundering Argentine constitutional system. In Chile the party stood against the Defense of Democracy measure, which outlawed the Communist party, and has repeatedly voted down attempts by over-zealous administrations to impose a state of siege. On one such occasion, Frei countered the government's proposal: "In this country which lacks portions of tea, of milk and of houses, we should not also suppress liberty."[37]

Complementing their emphasis on democratic principles, the Christian Democratic parties also claim, with varying degrees of validity, to be popular organizations, based on and concerned with the masses. The ex-president of the Peruvian party believes that the Christian parties have an

> Unavoidable popular vocation and the directors have the obligation of . . . penetrating resolutely into labor files, not to subjugate the syndicates nor to convert them into instruments of our party, but so that [Christian] social thought is known in its entirety and the working classes know that beyond communism, socialism and Aprismo, there are other national movements which know and defend their points of view. . . .[38]

Among the recommendations to the Social Christian movements passed by the second international congress was the exhortation to participate in labor organizations. Indeed, the statutes of the Pana-

[36] Carlos Hamilton, "The Future of Argentina and Christian Democracy," *Christian Democratic Review*, V (Sept., 1955), 4.

[37] Eduardo Frei Montalva, *Pensamiento y Acción* (Santiago de Chile: Editorial del Pacífico, 1956), p. 76.

[38] Partido Demócrata Cristiano del Peru, *Partido Demócrata Cristiano: IV Asamblea Nacional Arequipa, 1959* (Lima: Editorial Ausonía, 1959), p. 18.

manian party list among the obligations of the militants the duty of "demonstrating social sensitivity in the defense of the interests of the workers and of the needy sectors. . . ."[39] An Argentine, after stating that Christian Democracy is concerned with all classes and all men, adds:

> Being a movement not only profoundly democratic, but also profoundly christian, it seeks especially to protect the weak, the poor, the oppressed, and as the worker is frequently found in a situation of weakness, poverty and oppression, it has always demonstrated a manifest predilection to defend the working class. Besides, although love of neighbor implies to Christian Democrats the equal love for all men and women of all social sectors, they profess a special love for those who integrate the sector to which Jesus Christ belonged during his life on earth. Therefore, this conduces them to demonstrate a special preoccupation for the workers.[40]

Although the urban proletariat is most often courted by the various parties, the rural peasantry is also sought and the parties are often more successful with the *campesino* (peasant) than with his city cousin. The Chilean party has wide support among all sectors but has made a viable agrarian reform program its major goal and has appealed to the rural proletariat to organize along labor union lines. The Venezuelan Social Christian-COPEI has most of its strength among the rural voters and actively pursues an extension of an already well-received agrarian reform bill, a measure popularly associated with COPEI minister of Agriculture Víctor Giménez Landínez. The Uruguayan party devotes special attention to the rural sectors, and its predecessor, the Catholic Unión Cívica, "has made concrete legislative contributions to the comparatively few sound policies which have been adopted in the field."[41]

The movement's trenchant criticism of the traditional oligarchy confirms its association with the popular element. The small Bolivian

[39] Partido Demócrata Cristiano de Panamá, *El Partido Demócrata Cristiano de Panamá*, p. 49.

[40] Romero Carranza, *¿Qué es la Democracia Cristiana?*, p. 105; for a discussion by a leading Social Christian of the dignity of labor, see Rafael Caldera, *Moldes para la Fragua* (Buenos Aires: Librería "El Ateneo" Editorial, 1962), pp. 293–96, "Que Obrero Que Llamamos Cristo."

[41] Philip B. Taylor, Jr., *Government and Politics of Uruguay*, Tulane Studies in Political Science, Vol. VII (New Orleans: Tulane University Press, 1960), p. 52.

party had been in continuous opposition to the Paz Estenssoro National Revolutionary Movement, but it stood even more adamantly against the return of the oligarchs who had ruled the nation before the 1952 revolution. The Colombian party has praised some accomplishments of the National Front in that nation but rejects the continuation of the National Front because it is the tool of the oligarchy. Indeed, the anti-oligarchic stand of the party is so strong as to prompt the organ of the Colombian party, *Pueblo y Libertad*, to apologize for the "upper-class" accent of the party leader, Rivera Concha. He could be mistaken for one of the oligarchy, says the paper, "but when one begins to talk with him, it is instantly evident that he is a true christian revolutionary."[42]

None has been so comprehensive in criticism as the Peruvian Héctor Cornejo Chávez, who has constantly harangued the oligarchy. "The oligarchy not only exists," he proposes, "but has determined and determines the orientation of almost all our governments and is able to distort the future of our country."[43] The oligarchy is a "small circle of those who prosper unlimitedly at the expense of the misery of all the rest."[44]

> Among all those causes of our backwardness, among all of those responsible for the situations of the misery and the ignorance of our people, there is one responsible group which we cannot fail to mention and that group is the oligarchy which has controlled the political power from behind the throne by means of financial power. It has managed and continues to manage the country as if it were a hacienda and tries to manage Peruvians as if they were peons of that hacienda.[45]

The very parlance of the Christian Democratic movement indicates a conscious attempt to assume the popular mantle. The term "revolution" is omnipresent. Marxist catchwords, such as "capitalist exploitation" and "imperialist lackey," are frequently heard. Indeed, many Latin American Christian Democratic militants refer to one another as "comrade."

Though the movement is characterized most importantly by its

[42] "Habla Alvaro Rivera Concha Para 'Pueblo y Libertad,'" *Pueblo y Libertad*, III (Aug., 1964), 8.

[43] Cornejo Chávez, *Nuevos Principios para un Nuevo Perú*, p. 199.

[44] *Ibid.*, p. 127.

[45] Cornejo Chávez, *Que se Propone la Democracia Cristiana* (Lima: Ediciones del Sol, 1962), pp. 109, 110.

Christian-aconfessional and democratic-popular nature, there are several other aspects that merit mention. First, despite the existence of an international organization, the national parties vociferously deny any international domination similar to that of Moscow over other Communist parties. A Dominican publication affirms that the party "does not form part of any international political party nor does it obey any signs, orders or insinuations from any foreign entity. It is a political institution of Dominicans for Dominicans."[46] Each one of the Christian Democratic national groups constitutes a different party. Because of their common philosophical foundations, however, there is an affinity among the diverse parties that permits them to take advantage of common experiences, to work together on doctrinal investigations or in the preparation of practical initiatives. "Nevertheless, Christian Democrats are not able to issue the same rules for all nations. In economic matters the circumstances of time and place vary so differently that determined technical solutions would be apt for some nations and catastrophic for others."[47]

The Latin American Christian Democratic movement also stresses the essentially political nature of the party and its separation from groups with purely economic, cultural, or religious goals. The Christian Democrats believe that the university groups, labor unions, and professional organizations ought to be independent of each other because they serve different purposes. This independence does not prohibit cooperation between organizations, of course, and very close ties usually exist between Christian parties and other groups founded upon Christian social principles. The political party is considered the integrating agent of the various efforts just as the Christians see the state as the overseer and director of the commonweal. A labor union, for instance, is depicted as the defensive organ of a class, but the political party is responsible for the common good; it is the arbiter of various classes and interests. "Political parties primarily exercise civic functions; they order different tendencies of opinion, they examine the political vocations and aptitudes of the citizenry and they organize popular cooperation in the function of government."[48]

Politics is not only the integrating force of society, but it is the key to reform. The Panamanian Partido Demócrata Cristiano, in a dis-

[46] *El ABC de Movimiento Revolucionario Social Cristiano* [Dominican Republic] (Imp. de L. H. Cruz, 1964), p. 22.

[47] Romero Carranza, *¿Qué es la Democracia Cristiana?*, p. 118.

[48] *Ibid.*, p. 157.

cussion of economic and social development, notes that "substantial changes" in the "political organization" of the nation are required as a basis for subsequent reform of secondary structures.[49] The Paraguayans "have insisted and insist that the political problem is the most acute because its lack of solution implies general and immediate uneasiness and the aggravation of the other fundamental problems of the country. . . . It is absurd to attempt the solution of socio-economic problems without laying down firm bases for the solution of the political crises."[50]

Because politics is the agent of reform, the movement absolutely rejects the timeworn shibboleths of Christian charity to work the necessary changes and demands the use of revolutionary methods. Really intransigent problems "are unable to be solved on the bases of particular work of certain persons undertaken with a Christian spirit. These works are laudable and can help . . . ," but, in the last analysis, Christians must "utilize the abundant and powerful mechanisms of authority for the promotion of the common good."[51]

INTERNAL PARTY STRUCTURE

Despite the relative youth of most of the Latin American parties, they exhibit a deep concern for effective political organization and at their best display rather mature structures. The organization of Catholic and Christian Democratic parties has traditionally been rather comprehensive and effective, second only to that of Communist and some Socialist groups. The Latin American movement has, on the whole, reflected this concern for organization despite the fact that political groups in Latin America are less unified than their European counterparts.

The Latin American Christian Democratic parties are complex organizations. They are federally, and sometimes confederally, structured bodies encompassing a large number of groups on both the vertical and horizontal scale. Vertically, the party federation reaches all levels, from the neighborhood through the provincial or state or-

[49] Partido Demócrata Cristiano de Panamá, *El Partido Demócrata Cristiano de Panamá*, pp. 30, 31.

[50] Movimiento Social Demócrata Cristiano del Paraguay, *Mensaje del Movimiento Social Demócrata Cristiano al Pueblo del Paraguay* (Asunción, Dec. 25, 1960).

[51] De Paula Jaramillo, *La Democracia Cristiana*, p. 51.

ganization to the national organization. Horizontally, the party is affiliated with functional and special interest groups such as women's associations, professional associations, labor sections, and student groups.

Communist and particularly Socialist influence upon Christian Democratic organization is marked, although certain unique aspects bear the clear stamp of Catholic corporative theory, which focuses on group autonomy. Duverger explains that modern militancy demands that democratic parties imitate the methods and structure of their enemies.[52] On the whole, the Christian parties have not been quite so effective as their Marxist opponents but have, nevertheless, achieved significant results. The most intransigent problem seems to be the heterogeneous nature of Social Christian organizations. Christian Democratic parties take in almost the entire socio-economic scale and integrate disparate cultural, and sometimes national, communities.

In the techniques of party organization and political militancy, the movement has been profoundly affected by recent developments in North America. The 1960 Kennedy campaign has been closely studied in Christian Democratic ranks, and the movement has made several attempts at sophisticated political analysis. One public opinion center has been established in Venezuela, and several of the other parties have taken the initial steps to establish similar organizations.

Most of the Latin American Christian parties have drafted comprehensive statutes governing party organization and regulation. Rules governing membership in the several parties vary slightly but are fundamentally based on an individual's acceptance of the party's principles and program. The Chilean party sets a minimal age of eighteen, whereas the Cuban exile movement has a lower age limit of sixteen. Besides the age requirement, the Cuban party demands that the potential member be "interested in the moral, political, economic and social problems of the Cuban people."[53] In addition to these general stipulations, all of the parties require the neophyte to make formal application for membership; many issue membership cards to dramatize the ties which bind party and member. The Chilean party *Estatutos* make the Communal Council of the party

[52] Duverger, *Political Parties*, p. x.

[53] Movimiento Demócrata Cristiano de Cuba, *Reglamento* (Miami: mimeographed, 1964), p. 1.

the official inscription agency, and the Venezuelan COPEI demands that the new applicant be sponsored by two members of the party.

The several parties set forth long lists of rights and obligations of members. Among the privileges of the members the Panamanian group includes the right "to criticize, within the party, the acts of the leadership . . . while always observing in public a strict party discipline."[54] The *Estatutos* of COPEI permit the individual to "intervene in the elaboration of the strategy of the party and in the fixing of a position with reference to national problems." The member presents his opinion before his local party unit, and theoretically this opinion is relayed upward to the national decision-making units. The party stresses that the "principles of internal democracy" must always prevail. The Social Christian-COPEI militant, moreover, has the right of seeking the revision of instructions and tasks assigned to him, but, if his plea fails, he must give the directing agency his "full and strict" support. His appeal must be transmitted through regular party channels.[55] The privileges of the Chilean Social Christian militant include the right to be elected to party and public posts on the Christian Democratic ticket, but the party sets out various seniority requirements ranging from six months for public or party offices on the communal level to five years for the national office of senator or party post of similar stature.[56]

Obligations to the parties range from practical loyalty to those affecting modes of behavior. The Cuban movement requires that its members contribute financially to the party in accord with regulations drafted by the corresponding Executive Committee. The Venezuelan party excuses the unemployed from paying dues but requires office-holders to remit part of their salary, usually 20 percent, to the party coffers.[57] The Cuban member may "not censure before a stranger the political line" of the organization, and he must "faithfully guard the secrets of the organization."[58] The COPEI office-holder is required to follow the line of the party in his public functions. Moreover, the Copeyano, or member of the COPEI, is obligated to accept public posts at the request of the party; conversely,

[54] Partido Demócrata Cristiano de Panamá, *El Partido Demócrata Cristiano de Panamá*, p. 50.

[55] Partido Social Cristiano-COPEI, *Estatutos* (Caracas, 1961), pp. 7, 8.

[56] Partido Demócrata Cristiano de Chile, *Estatutos* (Santiago de Chile: Editorial del Pacífico, 1962), p. 8.

[57] Partido Social Cristiano-COPEI, *Estatutos*, p. 44.

[58] Movimiento Demócrata Cristiano de Cuba, *Reglamento*, p. 1.

he may not accept any without party concurrence.[59] Chilean party and public office-holders are required to make a yearly written report of their activities, and party support depends upon the approval of these reports as well as on other information. In addition to these traditional duties, several of the parties outline general norms of activity. The Dominican Partido Revolucionario Social Cristiano demands "honesty" and "morality," especially in matters of "national economy." The Cuban movement requires "public conduct which edifies and promotes in the society a christian democratic conscience."[60] The Chilean oath includes a section in which the neophyte promises, before God and country, to struggle for "truth, liberty," and the "redemption of the proletariat."[61]

The parties have established judicial procedures to handle infringements of party discipline or failure to fulfill the duties of the movements. Disciplinary actions range from private admonishment to expulsion from the party and include public admonishment, temporary suspension, and exclusion from the privilege of holding public or party office. The disciplinary agencies and their competence are closely defined, and appeal from one level of party hierarchy to another is permitted. Procedural regulations are spelled out and include the usual rights of defense. Expulsion is usually administered only by the highest disciplinary tribunal of the party. The Cuban movement permits ultimate appeal before the General Assembly of the party.

On the national level, the various Latin American Christian Democratic parties are markedly similar in their institutional structures and in the manner in which they subdivide the party geographically. The parties are divided into village, town, province, state, and regional groups. These are, of course, complemented by functional, horizontal groups.

The supreme component of the party structures is the national convention, usually held yearly or biennially. The Chilean party's statutes, for instance, demand a national convention at least once every three years. The Cuban Movimiento defines its National Congress as "the maximum authority of the Movimiento Demócrata Cristiano, where its sovereignty is found, and where, in the last instance, its

[59] Partido Social Cristiano-COPEI, *Estatutos*, p. 7.

[60] Movimiento Demócrata Cristiano de Cuba, *Reglamento*, p. 1.

[61] Partido Demócrata Cristiano de Chile, *Estatutos*, pp. 6, 7.

general policy is defined and oriented."[62] The various national conventions usually include delegates from regional and functional organizations, other executive organs of the party, all national office-holders, and very often all provincial or state office-holders. The convention sets general policy, revises the statutes of the party, nominates the party's candidate for presidential elections and, perhaps most importantly, elects the party executive committee variously called the National Directorate, National Executive Committee, National Council, or National Committee.

The national executive committees usually number from ten to thirty members. They are the most powerful and influential bodies in the party structure. Their competence covers the gamut of day-to-day matters of policy as well as important executive and administrative affairs. The Venezuelan National Committee, for instance, has the authority to dissolve the leadership of regional or functional organizations and to assume temporary command.[63] The groups also have the power to appoint and remove other party officials, propose and sometimes appoint the party's candidates for public office and often for party posts. They also have charge of the party's publication and are responsible for the convoking and organization of the national congresses or conventions. The Cuban National Executive Committee has the additional task of assisting and coordinating the anti-Castro struggle both within and without Cuba. The president or secretary-general, the titular head of the party structure, officially heads the national executive committee.

In addition to the executive committees, most of the Latin American Christian Democratic parties maintain a slightly larger group charged with counseling the executive and other special functions. Some examples of these organs are the Chilean National Junta, the Cuban Policy Commission, and the Venezuelan National Council. Finally, the national party structure almost always includes a tribunal, the court of last resort for party disciplinary matters.

Generally, the territorial subdivisions of each party follow the national pattern of organization. The regions or states have their own convention, executive committee, counseling and policy group, and disciplinary tribunal. Moreover, when membership permits, the parties maintain a third level of similar organization on the district,

[62] Movimiento Demócrata Cristiano de Cuba, *Reglamento*, p. 2.

[63] Partido Social Cristiano-COPEI, *Estatutos*, p. 20.

city, town, or rural scale. When lack of sufficient members prohibits a complete organization at the lowest level, the parties try to establish basic groups wherever party members exist. These organs "meet periodically to study the doctrine of the party, maintain the spirit and action of the movement and fortify the sense of solidarity and service in their militancy."[64]

Furthermore, all of the parties attempt to publish newspapers, reviews, and other periodicals. The publications vary in quality and regularity of appearance, but a genuine effort is made to capitalize on this important aspect of modern political militancy. The oldest of the Social Christian journals in continuous operation is *Política y Espíritu*, which began publication immediately following World War II. The message is also spread by a series of books issued through publishing houses in Santiago, Caracas, Bogotá, and Montevideo.

The several parties also sponsor and have working agreements with institutes and schools throughout the continent. The best known of these is the international movement's Instituto de Formación Demócrata Cristiana in Caracas, which trains middle-level party leaders from the entire continent. Many of the national parties sponsor projects for the study and analysis of the political, economic, and social problems of their respective nations. The Chilean party was one of the first Latin American political parties to undertake such a program. In 1964, a study noted that more than one hundred Chileans were at work preparing a governmental program for the expected Christian Democratic victory at the polls.[65] The Social Christian-COPEI sponsors the Luigi Sturzo Institute and cooperates with the National Institute of Trade Union Research. The Argentine, Brazilian, Uruguayan, Guatemalan, Peruvian, and Panamanian parties have functioning schools or research institutes, and others are in the process of establishing similar facilities.

The various levels of the party structure are organized on a democratic basis, but the relationship of lower to higher body is one of inferior to superior and is based on the principles of indirect election and control. The lowest officials of the party are directly elected, but the national leaders are chosen by the system of indirect election. The delegates to the Venezuelan Social Christian-COPEI national

[64] *Ibid.*, p. 39.

[65] *Chile,* Estudios de Actualidad, Primera Serie, No. 1 (Montevideo: Instituto de Estudios Políticos para América Latina, 1964), p. 15.

convention, for example, are designated indirectly. The municipal party members directly elect the delegates to the district convention, which in turn elects delegates to the state convention and, finally, this organ selects the delegates to the national convention, which chooses the national executive officers of the party.[66]

To escape the dangers of entrenched and stagnant leadership, however, the parties make an effort to change periodically the national and lower-level leadership. Often the president or secretary-general may not succeed himself; in some instances the same stipulation applies to other posts within the party hierarchy.

The degree to which the party controls its members who hold public office is difficult to ascertain. As a rule, the party exercises less power over its representatives in government than it claims. Nevertheless, the Christian Democratic parties do hold greater power over their representatives than do most other Latin American parties. The crux of the question in specific cases is: exactly who makes up the party leadership? The problem is irrelevant when the same persons are both party leaders and office-holders. This is usually the case among Christian Democratic parties in Latin America as in Europe. And even when the party leadership does not coincide with political representation, the office-holders enjoy considerable freedom of action.[67]

In theory the parties maintain strict control over their militants. Several of the parties collect a fixed percentage of their representatives' public salary, indicating at least minimal party control. The Chilean party statutes note that the National Council of the party must give permission before members may accept ministerial, diplomatic, or "any other political or administrative post within the exclusive confidence of the President of the Republic." Moreover, the deputies and senators must be granted special permission to absent themselves from their posts or the country during legislative sessions.[68] The party leaders also set the general policy of the party within the legislature. They set the terms and judge the desirability of entering into electoral pacts or government coalitions. Moreover, the party oversees the daily activity of public officials. On two separate occasions COPEI has expelled important party members for breaking with the party line. In 1952, it expelled all of its delegates

[66] Aguilar, *Los Partidos Demócrata Cristianos*, p. 22.
[67] Duverger, *Political Parties*, p. 190.
[68] Partido Demócrata Cristiano de Chile, *Estatutos*, pp. 17, 18.

who had cooperated with Pérez Jiménez by attending the constitutional convention following a fraudulent election. In 1961, COPEI ousted those who had supported an attempted military coup. In Chile in 1966 the party discharged one of its deputies, Patricio Hurtado, for having openly sympathized with Fidel Castro in Castro's dispute with President Frei.

AFFILIATED ORGANIZATIONS

In addition to the formal party structure, the Latin American Christian Democratic parties maintain, sponsor, or have relations with, a complex group of affiliated organizations. The Guatemalan party, for example, has organized or has cooperated with four separate organizations, including labor (Frente Cristiana de Trabajadores de Guatemala), peasants (Federación Campesina Social Cristiana), students (Frente Estudiantil Social Cristiana), and women (Movimiento de Promoción Femenina). This type of affiliation is typical of modern mass parties, but it is a distinctive quality of Christian Democratic parties. There seem to be two basic reasons for this. One is the strong influence of corporative theory. The other is the socio-economic heterogeneity of the parties, which invites this solution to a difficult problem; auxiliary organizations help to introduce a modicum of structure and manageability. Ancillary groups and activities, furthermore, furnish an additional attraction to militancy and provide a way to hold half-hearted members or to increase the loyalty of the already committed. A Venezuelan Social Christian deputy elaborates upon this theme:

> If the party promotes the constitution of peasant leagues to struggle for agrarian reform, many campesinos who are not social christians or who simply sympathize with the idea will be disposed to join these leagues and operate in a form coincident with the objectives of the party. That is, the party has succeeded in broadening popular participation in the struggle for one of its ends.[69]

"The idea," the Copeyano continues, "is to augment the strength of the party which is a community with general ends by promoting and orienting satellite communities which have special coinciding ends."[70] Moreover, the system elucidates the general lines of eco-

[69] Aguilar, *Los Partidos Demócrata Cristianos*, p. 18.
[70] *Ibid.*, p. 17.

nomic problems by focusing attention on the major economic segments of the community, although it sometimes has the deleterious effect of encouraging a division of interests within the party.

Latin American Christian Democrats look upon their youth affiliates as supremely important. Indeed, the message has been eagerly received by university and other youth, and Social Christian youth is a generally well-organized, vibrant force throughout the continent. The youth affiliates include both university students and young workers; they encourage social and sports clubs for young people and political training in secondary schools. Christian Democrats are fond of emphasizing that theirs is the "Party of Youth." Their claim is valid and their approach is wise, for it is difficult to over-emphasize the importance of youth in politics in Latin America.[71]

The Chilean Christian Democratic youth affiliate has been the longest developing and is the strongest entity of its kind in Latin America. The Social Christan students have controlled the Federación Estudiantil de Chile since 1954; in the 1964 elections they placed eight of eleven students on the federation's executive committee. The group controlled student associations in eight of the nine Chilean universities in the same year.

The Venezuelan Juventud Revolucionaria Copeyana is probably the second most powerful movement on the continent and may have more influence within the party itself than any other Latin American Christian Democratic youth affiliate. One observer notes that the COPEI youth "has become a sort of engine for the party, driving it forward, while at the same time exerting a strong influence on its doctrine."[72] The group, of course, adheres to the same basic program as its parent, but its activity is generally more progressive and militant. Indeed, the students have occasionally taken to the streets to clash with the Communists and the Castro-aligned Movimiento de Izquierda Revolucionaria. In the universities the COPEI youth is generally recognized as the first force, but it has been continually

[71] See, for instance, Walter S. Washington, "Student Politics in Latin America: The Venezuelan Example," *Foreign Affairs*, XXXVII (April, 1959), 463, who sees "three conditions [which] give special weight and direction to student political activity: (1) Latin Americans have respect for the educated; (2) an increasing number of students come from the poorer classes and are impatient for social reform; and (3) Latin American populations are young—over 70% of Venezuelans, for instance, being under 30 years of age."

[72] Franklin Tugwell, "The Christian Democrats of Venezuela," *Journal of Inter-American Studies*, VII (April, 1965), 257.

frustrated in its attempts to control the Central University by coalitions of the other Venezuelan student political forces.

Although not nearly so long in development, Christian Democratic student groups have also exerted considerable strength and influence in the Dominican Republic and Nicaragua. In the Dominican Republic the Social Christian Bloque Revolucionario Universitario Cristiano has run a close second to the pro-Communist leaders. In the 1964 elections at the University of Santo Domingo, the Christian Democrats garnered only 300 votes less than the first group and placed 21 members of a total of 50 in the student assembly. In Nicaragua, the Christian affiliate now controls the Catholic university in Managua and has made great strides in the national university.

One of the most unusual Catholic or Christian Democratic student groups in Latin America is the Brazilian Acção Popular (AP), a coalition between Communists and left-wing Catholics. The group has been encouraged by the controversial Christian Democrat Paulo de Tarso Santos and is "the most radical of any Christian Democratic movement in Latin America."[73] Acção Popular has controlled the Brazilian National Student Union for years. AP should not be confused with the regular Christian Democratic youth affiliate in Brazil, a group neither so radical nor so strong.

Other national student movements of significance are found in Peru, where the Christian Democrats have usually been represented in the student government, and Panama, where the student effort, as a reflection of the entire Social Christian movement, has been making notable progress.

On the international plane the several youth groups are organized as the Juventud Demócrata Cristiana de América. The international had its first congress in Lima in 1959 and has its headquarters in Santiago de Chile. The Latin American federation is in turn a member of the world-wide International Union of Christian Democratic Youth. The Social Christian youth of Central America and Panama formed a regional organization in 1965. The Federación de Estudiantes Social Cristianos de Centro América y Panamá (FESCAP) maintains its headquarters in Guatemala.

If the Christian Democratic labor movement has not had the same outstanding success as its youth movement, there is little doubt that

[73] Timothy F. Harding, "Revolution Tomorrow: The Failure of the Left in Brazil," *Studies on the Left*, IV (Fall, 1964), 52.

it wields considerable power in some nations and is beginning to exert its influence in others. In some Latin American nations the Christian forces have chosen to work within the already-existing labor unions; in others they have established separate groups. Some countries have a unified labor movement, others have multiple, competing units.

The Chilean National Falange began to organize within the laboring sectors in the early forties. The Social Christians decided at the outset to infiltrate the existing Central Unica de Trabajadores de Chile rather than follow the customary practice of founding rival bodies. The Chilean body has made steady progress and is now a very close second to the Communists in the executive committee of the unified labor union. Indeed, the victory of Frei at the polls may provide the opportunity for the union forces to finally cap their long drive for predominance.[74]

The Venezuelan Social Christian-COPEI has only recently developed strength within that nation's labor union movement. At first, the party's rather conservative bent precluded any significant concentration on the laboring masses. Then COPEI followed the traditional pattern and sought to establish a rival Christian labor-union movement. The success of the venture was limited, however, and in 1959 the party leadership forsook this gambit. Its following began to infiltrate the national Confederación de Trabajadores de Venezuela. The party has displayed increasing interest in broadening its working-class support and has achieved considerable success.

Other nations with important Christian syndical organizations include the Dominican Republic, Ecuador, Colombia, Costa Rica, and Nicaragua. The Dominican Republic, along with British Honduras, is one of the two American countries where the Christian Democratic international, Confederación Latino Americana de Sindicalistas Cristianos (CLASC), claims to control a majority. The Christian union, the Confederación Autónoma de Sindicatos Cristianos (CASC), represents some 80,000 workers in 168 organizations.[75] In Ecuador, the Confederación Nacional de Trabajadores Católicos, not associated with the Christian international, was founded in 1933 and is a potent force among that nation's labor unions. The Colombian Unión de Trabajadores de Colombia was founded in 1946. Some of the found-

[74] Donald D. Ranstead, "Chile Turns Left," *Commonweal*, LXXX (Sept. 4, 1964), 596.

[75] *Hispanic American Report*, XVII (Oct., 1964), 713.

ers were members of the Testimonio Christian Democratic social-action group that exercised influence in Colombia following World War II. The Costa Rican Movimiento Sindical Rerum Novarum claims to be the oldest trade-union movement in Latin America and rivals a communist-leaning group for the support of that country's laboring classes. The Nicaraguan Movimiento Sindical Autónomo de Nicaragua (MOSAN), established in 1962, has grown very rapidly.

The international organization of the Social Christian trade-union groups is less coherent than that of the party and the youth affiliates. The Confederación Latino Americana de Sindicalistas Cristianos has existed since 1954 and claims five million adherents in Latin America. Indeed, the CLASC has been careful in calling itself an organization of *sindicalistas* (unionists) rather than a confederation of *sindicatos* (unions). The distinction is important because many of the most influential Christian trade unions are not affiliated with CLASC but with the rival Organización Regional Interamericana de Trabajadores (ORIT), which is assisted by the AFL-CIO. CLASC and ORIT are respectively affiliated with the International Federation of Christian Trade Unions and the International Confederation of Free Trade Unions. The Social Christians control none of the unified national labor associations. The influential Colombian and Ecuadorian labor movements, moreover, are affiliated with ORIT, as are the unified labor groups of Chile and Venezuela, which contain strong Social Christian minorities. In many countries, however, Christian labor militants do hold dual membership in their own movement and in CLASC.

If the youth movements have generally exerted a "progressive" influence upon the Christian Democratic movement, the same is probably more true of the militant and dynamic CLASC. Although its influence is not so widespread as the strong youth groups, the intense fervor and pugnaciousness of the syndical organization have made its significance felt in Social Christian circles throughout the continent.[76]

[76] A comprehensive discussion of the CLASC is not within the purview of this study. Little beyond the official publications of the organization has been written about this fascinating and controversial group. CLASC's cutting criticism of both ORIT and North American policy in Latin America has ruffled the feathers of many in the United States. The ex-president of CLASC has correctly noted that: "Unfortunately, over the years CLASC has made a number of enemies as a consequence of its statements and positions on political events in Latin America or

Last, the Latin American Christian Democrats have also actively organized women and peasant groups. The attraction of the Christian Democratic message to women is well known,[77] and the parties have not been remiss in organizing in this area. All of the parties maintain women's affiliates. The Latin American Christian Democratic women are also organized internationally; they held their first congress in Lima in 1959.

The *campesino* groups are also important in the Christian Democratic scheme, and the parties have achieved marked success in this area. In both Chile and Venezuela, peasant groups contribute greatly to party strength. In Chile the affiliated groups are the Asociación Nacional de Obreros Campesinos and the Unión de Campesinos Cristianos, and in Venezuela, the Frente Campesino. Generally, however, the peasant groups do not exercise an influence commensurate with their numbers within the party.

---

relations between the United States and the various Latin American nations." For discussions pro and con, respectively, concerning CLASC, see José Goldsack, "Why a Christian Democratic Labor Organization," *America*, CXVI (Jan. 28, 1967), 154–56; and Gladys Delmas, "Latin Labor's Alarming Christians," *The Reporter*, XXXII (Feb. 25, 1965), 27–30.

[77] See pp. 275–277 for a discussion of the importance of the feminine vote for Latin American Christian Democratic parties.

Domestic Policies and Programs 5

FAMILY AFFAIRS AND LOCAL GOVERNMENT

Latin American Christian Democratic experience in government has been limited. Most of the parties are relatively young. Nevertheless, for the most part they have worked out rather complete programs and policy statements. These, coupled with the general theory and the history of other Christian Democratic movements and parties, give a clear idea of the movement's primary legislative and administrative goals.

Perhaps the fundamental goal of Christian Democrats is the strengthening of the family. Indeed, in the eyes of Social Christians, it is the family and not the individual that is the basic unit of society. In Europe the Christian parties were responsible for many innovations to assist the family, and several countries established departments or ministries of family affairs under Christian Democratic governments. Among the many ways that the family can be assisted through governmental programs, one of the most basic and most commonly used is the family allowance, a system under which a worker is paid according to the size of his family or according to the number of people he supports. The Uruguayan Unión Cívica was the originator of a family allotments law enacted in that nation in 1943. In Brazil the small Christian Democratic party was mainly responsible for a similar innovation in 1963; the law is popularly called the Franco Montoro Law after the leader of the Social Christian party. The Venezuelan Social Christian-COPEI has been responsible for introducing family subsidy legislation in that nation.

A direct result of this concentration on the family is the equally comprehensive Social Christian concern for women. The attention to the rights of women covers the entire field from family to political life. COPEI's program calls for legislation governing maternity protection, including both pre-natal and post-natal care.[1] Several of the parties demand aid for the unwed mother. The Dominican Partido Revolucionario Social Cristiano requests governmental assistance for the widows of the victims of the Trujillo tyranny.[2] The Unión Cívica Nacional, precursor of Panama's present Christian party, put forth a series of legislative demands for greater protection of married women; among them were measures concerning the wife's rights of inheritance and ownership of property. Indeed, the young Colombian party goes so far as to suggest the "creation of obligatory social service" as a means of stimulating the participation of women in the national life.[3]

More sensitive areas of Christian Democratic programs and policies include those of marriage, divorce, and birth control. There seems to be a strong effort to avoid restrictive pronouncements that might open unnecessary wounds. The issue of divorce is controversial throughout the continent. The Argentine party, one of the most "advanced" in the Latin American movement, has opposed the legalization of divorce. The Paraguayan Movimiento reflects the general position; it pronounces matrimony as "indissoluble when it is contracted in the presence of a representative of the religious community to which the parties belong."[4] A part of the constitutional reform suggested by the conservative Ecuadorian Movimiento Social Cristiano says that "Catholic marriage . . . does not admit of legal dissolution."[5]

The stand on birth control is even more unequivocal. The rationale for the opposition to birth control is not that traditional theology dictates it, however, but that Latin America is under-populated, and full exploitation of the continent's resources calls for larger numbers of people. Moreover, Christian Democrats point out that Latin Amer-

[1] Partido Social Cristiano-COPEI, *Programa* (3rd ed.; Caracas: Secretaría Nacional de Propaganda, 1961), p. 15.

[2] Partido Revolucionario Social Cristiano de la República Dominicana, *Declaración de Principios y el Programa de Gobierno de Partido Revolucionario Social Cristiano* (mimeographed), p. 4.

[3] Partido Social Demócrata Cristiano de Colombia, *Partido Social Demócrata Cristiano* (Bogotá: Ediciones del Caribe, 1964), p. 21.

[4] Movimiento Social Demócrata Cristiano del Paraguay, *Acta Fundacional y Declaración de Principios* (Asunción, 1960), p. 9.

[5] Movimiento Social Cristiano del Ecuador, *Planteamiento de Reformas Constitucionales Bajo el Signo de la Democracia Cristiana* (Quito: Editorial "Fray Jodoco Ricke," 1963), p. 68.

ica's real problem is centered in the political and economic spheres, and not in that of population. Caldera admits that the spectacular increase in population presents great problems but maintains that birth control is not a fitting response. According to him, birth control usually results in a process of "reverse selectivity." The rate of growth diminishes among the more privileged groups but continues to increase among the lower socio-economic groups. Furthermore:

> A tendency toward restriction of the birth rate seems particularly strange in a continent with a population that scarcely occupies half of its territory, where vast and promising areas wait to be colonized and where methods that permit the most productive use of nature and of labor, and which have been employed so successfully in densely populated regions, have not yet been tried out on a large scale.

"The problem," he concludes, "is not to limit life but to conquer the means of making existence possible."[6] Remo Di Natale, the Bolivian party leader, echoes Caldera. He rejects the solutions of those "quacks" who would cure the Latin American malady with the "magic herb of birth control." These "charlatans" miss the fundamental truth that Latin America's problem involves economic and political structures, not the remote threat of overpopulation. Paraguay is one-fourth larger than Italy but counts less than two million in population, whereas Italy has over fifty million. If Argentina had the density of Israel, it would have more than three hundred million; its actual population is about twenty-three million. Di Natale further states that Latin America ought to "jubilantly salute" the population explosion because "the horizon presents sparks of hope only for very large countries and the first requisite . . . is to have an enormous population."[7]

In hesitant opposition to this stand, the Frei government has supported the formation of the autonomous Committee for Family Protection, which, among other activities, distributes birth-control

[6] Rafael Caldera, "Crucial Test for Christian Civilization," *The Alliance for Progress: A Critical Appraisal*, ed. William Manger (Washington: Public Affairs Press, 1963), pp. 29, 30.

[7] Remo Di Natale, *America Latina Hoy: Esquemas Populares Demócrata Cristianos* (Caracas: Editorial Nuevo Orden, 1964), pp. 23, 24. Indeed, this opposition to birth control is perfectly consistent with traditional Latin American political thought. Almost all thinkers have seen the lack of a sufficiently large population as one of the crucial weaknesses of the Latin American body politic.

information. Moreover, the 1967 Conference of the Planned Parenthood Federation was set for Santiago de Chile, with Frei scheduled to take part in the opening ceremonies.

For Latin American Christian Democrats, one of the most important steps in the promotion and support of the family has been a widespread housing program. As early as 1937 Frei called housing the "greatest of the national necessities." The family is best encouraged by a rich home life, but, as Frei has noted, "no home is possible without a house." Caldera also sees the necessity for a housing program. "When we talk of the redemption of the family," he warns, "we know that it is a false and deceitful word if we are not able to make man the dweller of a decorous and commodious home where the family can live in dignity."[8]

In a lengthy report on housing at the Lima international congress of the Organización Demócrata Cristiana de América, it was noted that the primary support for any housing program in Latin America must come from the private sectors of the economy. The proportion will vary from country to country, but usually a nation can devote no more than about 5 percent of the public budget to a housing program. Private funds must at least equal this amount and, hopefully, double or even triple it. Public monies will complement these private funds with services, institutions, and incentives, as well as provide the backing for the actual construction of housing or the granting of indirect subsidies for lower socio-economic groups.[9] Caldera, in his 1963 election campaign in Venezuela, illustrated the policy when he called a technical conference of Social Christians and independents to outline a plan for the construction of 100,000 houses per year. The conference devised a sophisticated plan to be financed through both private and public contributions.[10] In Chile a campaign promise of Frei's was realized when he established in late 1965 a cabinet-level Ministry of Housing to coordinate all services in the field. The plan was to construct 360,000 homes in a six-year period by utilizing the government housing agency already in existence,

[8] *Congreso Internacional de la Democracia Cristiana: Anales del quinto . . .* (Lima: Editorial Universitaria, 1960), p. 250.

[9] *Ibid.*, pp. 203–10.

[10] See I Congreso Nacional de Profesionales y Técnicos de COPEI y Independientes Socialcristianos, *100,000 Viviendas por Año para Venezuela (Plan Caldera)* (Caracas: Publicación de la Secretaría Nacional de Organismos Profesionales del Partido Socialcristiano-COPEI, No. 1, 1963).

Corporación de la Vivienda, increasing participation of public but semi-autonomous savings and loan associations, and instituting a system of Promoción Popular in which the government would supply land and materials and the future occupant would furnish the labor and construction skills.[11]

The revamping of the physical and social environment requires the direct involvement of local government; indeed, local government is the key to the solution. This, of course, requires that regional and municipal governments be themselves revitalized and strengthened. And since this area has been one of the traditional weak spots of political organization in Latin America, it is not surprising that Latin American parties have developed this facet of their program into one of the most important planks in their platforms.

The party's plan to revitalize the *municipio*, or local government, demonstrates this preoccupation with the organization of strong intermediate governmental structures. An early Peruvian party manifesto declared that the "*municipio* is the organic and natural expression of the local community. . . ."[12] The infant Colombian Partido Social Demócrata Cristiano devotes a lengthy and comprehensive article of its platform to this problem, promising

> To struggle for the fiscal vigorization of the *municipios* so that they do not have to depend on the disorganized and sporadic auxiliary assistance granted by the Congress. It is necessary to modify the taxing system and the distribution of the taxes so that they are received directly by the *municipio*, which, besides investing them in the satisfaction of their own necessities, ought to contribute to the expenditures of the department or the nation in conformity with regulations. Or to study a constitutional formula which would guarantee a fixed quota to be distributed among the distinct municipal administrations in accord with plans previously agreed upon by technical organizations. To struggle, lastly, for the socio-economic re-vigorization of the *municipio* by means of administrative measures which

[11] *Hispanic American Report*, XVII (Oct., 1964), 647. "El Programa de Gobierno de Frei," DECE, I (July, 1964), 5; Eduardo Frei Montalva, *360,000 Nuevos Habitaciones se Construirán en el Gobierno de Frei* (Santiago de Chile: Sopech Impresores, 1964). Writing in late 1965, a Chilean noted the marked increase in housing construction and proposed that the 1966 goals would be easily met providing that a cement strike was not prolonged. See Manuel Corvanlán Vera, "Un Año de Lucha Contra la Inflación," *Ercilla*, Miercoles, Dec. 29, 1965, No. 1595, p. 17.

[12] *Manual del Elector* (Lima: Editorial Juan Mejía Baca, 1962), p. 175.

> will transfer to the *municipio* permissions, titles, etc., which are necessary for the citizens to normally develop their professional or economic activities.[13]

The movement favors a large dose of municipal planning and has long been critical of its dearth in Latin American cities. As early as 1943, the Unión Cívica was decrying the "absence of the most elemental technical direction" in municipal policy. The results were "anti-hygienic, anti-economic and anti-esthetic. . . . It is a principle of urban hygiene and of social justice that urban growth, as this law foresees, ought to be decided by the city and not by the private property owner."[14] An international congress noted that city governments must be granted "faculties for local planning, intervention in the urbanization of lands and inspection of rural and urban housing."[15] The 1962 platform of the Peruvian party called for "state and community action against the monopolization of urban lands and those apt for urban expansion and against speculation in these lands."[16]

The same platform strongly emphasized the need for popular election of local officers. In Peru this was achieved under the coalition government of President Fernando Belaúnde Terry. In December, 1963, the Alianza Acción Popular-Demócrata Cristiano sponsored the first local elections in forty years and garnered over 51 percent of the votes.

The parties also attempt to assist the growth of vibrant local government by recommending policies and programs of decentralization. The manifesto of the Bolivian Partido Social Cristiano declared, "popular government must be decentralized. The concentration of all power, in the communist style, is anti-popular and, consequently, retrogressive."[17] Writing as early as 1937, Frei Montalva decried the unchecked growth of the city of Santiago and foresaw the necessity

[13] Partido Social Demócrata Cristiano de Colombia, *Partido Social Demócrata Cristiano*, p. 22.

[14] Tomás G. Brena, *Democracia Cristiana en el Uruguay* (Montevideo: Impresora Zorilla de San Martín, 1946), pp. 108, 109.

[15] *Congreso Internacional de la Democracia Cristiana: Anales del quinto . . .*, p. 189.

[16] Partido Demócrata Cristiano del Perú, *Programa de Gobierno* (Lima: Imp. "El Condor," 1962), p. 33.

[17] "Manifiesto del Partido Social Cristiano de Bolivia," *Política y Espíritu*, X (May 15, 1954), 31.

of a policy of administrative and economic decentralization.[18] The Frei government hopes to overcome the population imbalance of Chile by offering tax incentives and other inducements to industries willing to locate in areas other than the overgrown capital. The party also proposes a similar movement of governmental agencies away from the capital to take some of the pressure off the areas of highly concentrated population.

EDUCATION

Education occupies a special place in all developing areas, and nowhere is this more dramatically evident than in Latin America. One student has observed that "the political leaders of Spanish America have almost universally associated working democracy with education."[19] The position of figures like Domingo Sarmiento, Andrés Bello, José Vasconcelos, and José Varela in the continent's folklore attests to the adulation and esteem that Latin Americans hold for education. Latin American Christian Democrats mirror the intense concern for the rapid and comprehensive improvement of the educational structure. President Frei, for example, launched a crash program almost immediately upon assuming office. New enrollments during his first year numbered 186,000—up a full 146,000 from the average of recent years.[20]

If all Latin Americans agree on the importance of education, they do not always agree on matters of educational form or content. The Christian Democrats, for example, oppose the concept of purely secular education, insisting that a moral emphasis, like that found in private Catholic schools, is essential to a viable educational system. The Paraguayan movement declares that "all true education necessarily possesses a spiritual, moral, and religious content. Therefore, the pretended neutrality of secularism is a contradiction and, as such, unrealizable."[21] This view of education is not limited to the more

[18] Eduardo Frei Montalva, *Chile Desconocido* (Santiago de Chile: Ediciones Ercilla, 1937), pp. 130–35.

[19] John J. Johnson, *The Military and Society in Latin America* (Stanford, Cal.: Stanford University Press, 1964), p. 134.

[20] Cole Blasier, *Chile in Transition* (Washington: Public Affairs Press, 1966), p. 10.

[21] Movimiento Social Demócrata Cristiano del Paraguay, *Acta Fundacional y Declaración de Principios*, p. 16.

conservative segments of the Latin American movement. Writing in 1937, Frei deplored the fact that religion was not taught in the Chilean school system. Moral education, he cautioned, is necessary to inculcate ethical action and healthy idealism.[22]

Christian Democrats believe that the best method of assuring a solid moral education is to promote the continued efficacy of a private school system. To further this goal, Argentine Christian Democracy sought to establish a pluralistic school system of private and confessional institutions subsidized by the state. The state would be permitted some control over these schools, but it must be kept to an absolute minimum. The principle would even apply to institutions of higher learning.[23] If groups are unable to finance their own schools, then the state is obliged to provide the material assistance necessary for maintenance of a system.

Latin American Christian Democrats believe that the establishment of a school system under the exclusive control of the secular state is totalitarian. This belief is based on the Christian Democratic insistence on the primacy of freedom of instruction and the rights of the family. The Costa Rican party says, "the State . . . ought to respect the right of the family to orient the education of the children, assuring it by a proportional distribution of its resources. . . ."[24] Freedom of instruction implies that each group in a pluralistic society has the right to pattern the form and content of its education according to its own norms with as little governmental supervision as possible.

Although the emphasis is still on traditional humanistic education, the Latin American movement also stresses other facets and goals of education. One goal should be to inculcate nationalistic and democratic values. Frei has noted that Chile is unknown (*Chile Desconocido*) because the teaching of Chilean history is so weak. As a result of this shortcoming, the people have not developed a sense of national identity and pride. Emphasis in these areas, including formal programs, is more necessary in a new, incoherent nation like

22 Frei Montalva, *Chile Desconocido*, pp. 107, 108.

23 Ambrosio Romero Carranza, *¿Qué es la Democracia Cristiana?* (Buenos Aires: Ediciones del Atlántico, 1956), pp. 140–46.

24 Partido Demócrata Cristiano de Costa Rica, *1) Toma de posiciones del Partido Demócrata Cristiano—frente al Comunismo, frente al Capitalismo y frente a los regimenes políticos del país. 2) Declaración de principios del Partido Demócrata Cristiano* (San José, n.d.), p. 6.

Chile than it may be in Europe or the United States where a sense of national consciousness is strongly entrenched.[25] Additionally, the educational systems should be making a special effort to prepare the workers for the eventual responsibility of administrative posts within the newly structured economic framework that Christian Democrats foresee. The Fifth International Congress of Latin American Christian Democracy held at Lima in 1959 passed this resolution:

> The Latin American Christian Democratic parliamentary groups will promote in their respective countries the establishment by the State of schools and courses for the workers in order to give them the basic cultural and technical means so that they can gradually assume responsibility in the fundamental decisions of the enterprise as well as the direction of it. . . .[26]

Finally, there is a growing concern with technical education to provide the "necessary knowledge in a world which is living in a scientific revolution of incalculable projections." Christian Democrats are realizing more and more how crucial technicians are in an industrial society. Caldera proposes that "large-scale programs of technical education . . . should form an essential part of any general plan for educational development."[27] As if in response to his fellow leader's charge, President Frei included a plan to increase technical training in his educational reform proposals of 1965.

LABOR POLICIES AND LABOR UNIONS

The general goals of Christian Democratic labor policy are to strengthen the institutionalized labor movement and to improve the economic, political, and social lot of the working man. With the proletarian masses gaining power rapidly, any Latin American political force has no choice but to devise policies and methods for dealing with that undeniable phenomenon. Thus, the policy is not only an end in itself, but also the only conceivable way to introduce a modicum of social and political stability into the restless nation-states of the continent. Furthermore, the result of increased labor strength and freedom will be the inexorable, steady growth of proletarian responsibility in the economic life of each nation.

[25] See Frei Montalva, *Chile Desconocido*, pp. 97–124.

[26] *Congreso Internacional de la Democracia Cristiana: Anales del quinto . . .*, p. 172.

[27] Caldera, "Crucial Test for Christian Civilization," p. 30.

The basic tenet of Christian Democracy *vis à vis* labor unions was contained in *Rerum Novarum*: the right to organize unions is a natural right that cannot be infringed upon by the state. The labor union theoretically is similar to the family, in that both are natural communities. The Cuban movement has postulated: "the right of association is a natural right. Consequently the right to organize labor unions is inherent in the human nature of the workers as human persons and closely tied to the vital interests of the worker and his family."[28] The same natural law sanctions the right of workers to organize in any convenient form, pluralistic or unified, ideological or neutral. Freedom of organization, then, implies that the unions are free from state control and that the workers are free to form multiple, or separate Christian Democratic, unions.

Labor unions are depicted as more than agencies solely devoted to the economic improvement of the laboring classes. They are instruments for the realization of social justice; they will contribute to the change of the economic structures. Their role, in short, is revolutionary. Social Christianity envisages four major functions of the labor-union movement. First, it has a defensive and redemptory mission within the class struggle; it must defend the interest of the proletariat and attempt to improve the lot of the laboring man economically and socially. Second, in pursuit of this goal, it has an educative and constructive obligation to prepare the working man for better times. Third, it must organize the people into labor-union groups, and last, it has the revolutionary task of helping to create the just society within the Christian Democratic program.

Latin American Christian Democracy defends the right to strike as the most potent weapon of organized labor. Just strikes must be defended, moreover, whether they are legal or not, for "it is evident that something can be just, although not legal through the defect of some positive requisite."[29] Going beyond the mere support of the just strike, however, the movement asserts the reality of the class struggle and, in many cases, sees it as the most effective means for the achievement of social justice. According to the theory, a Christian Democratic government must assist the masses to attain a voice in politics so as to force the upper classes to conform to the dictates

[28] Movimiento Demócrata Cristiano de Cuba, *Movimiento Demócrata Cristiano de Cuba* (Miami, 1961), p. 54.

[29] "ABC de la Democracia Cristiana o Social-Cristianismo," *Combate* (Organo del Partido Social Cristiano Nicaragüense), April, 1964, p. 4.

of social justice. A party publication admits that labor unions ideally ought not to be the instruments of the class struggle. Nevertheless, unions are compelled to organize to defend their interests, inasmuch as class conflict is inevitable in a liberal capitalistic era. The union should be the force behind the transformation of the capitalist enterprise into a Social Christian enterprise.[30] The class struggle, however, is not permanent and will be transcended in the Christian Democratic society; amicable cooperation will reign. Class conflict will end when all men are made property owners. In such a society there would be no strikes. "In the Christian Democratic regime, the interests of the workers will be the interests of the entire nation. The means of production will be owned by those who work. It would be absurd to suppose that the owners themselves are going to undertake strikes against their direct interests."[31]

The immediate aim of the program is to depoliticize the labor union movement; it should be independent and not a tool of the government or of political parties. The political party offers the working man the opportunity to exercise his influence in the political sphere, whereas the syndical movements represent his interests in social and economic areas; the two functions must not be confused. Indeed, the Mexican movement sees strikes motivated by "political or sectarian" interests as being unjust.[32] Although all Latin American political movements have been guilty to some extent of using labor unions to promote their own political ends, the criticism is particularly directed to the Communists who have made blatant use of syndical organizations.

The exact amount of state regulation of labor unions proposed by Latin American Christian Democrats is unclear. Nevertheless, it seems obvious that some regulation would be required by Social Christians. Syndical organizations are more than merely private groups because they perform important public functions. The state will recognize and assist them, but it will also impose certain rules and regulations. Frei's program foresaw the need for governmental

[30] *Ibid.*, p. 3.

[31] Movimiento Social Demócrata Cristiano de México, *Bases Ideológicas,* Folleto Número 1 (México, D.F., March 28, 1963), pp. 3, 4.

[32] *Ibid.*, p. 3. Frei has echoed this charge with specific reference to the Chilean Left. In 1965, he termed a serious copper strike as a "political conspiracy." See, *News From Chile*, No. 22, Dec. 1, 1965 (Chilean Embassy, Washington, D. C.).

checks in the area of finances. "This wide right of labor union organization and activity ought to suppose a correlative growth in syndical responsibility. Syndical activity must submit to a law for the management of social funds. It must submit accountability and be subject to fiscal investigation by state agencies. It must publish its monetary reports."[33] A similar set of stipulations already exists in the Venezuelan labor law, which was prepared by Caldera in 1938.

The practical measures that the Latin American movement has proposed in the field of internal social legislation are legion. The first program of the Catholic Unión Cívica included a long list of social goals. The proposed legislation included the limitation of the work day, the prohibition of Sunday work, the end to the employment of children and women with minor children, the responsibility of the enterprise in case of accidents, official recognition of labor unions, the right to strike, the formation of a conciliation and arbitration service, the creation of consumers cooperatives, etc.[34] The present Argentine Christian Democratic party has sponsored legislation to attain full employment, halt the cost-of-living spiral, provide low-cost housing units, and increase expenditures for cultural, public health, and social-assistance programs.[35] In Venezuela, Social Christian Arístides Calvani authored a bill to compel the oil companies to maintain employment through "tough days" so as to alleviate the problem of unemployment.

AGRARIAN REFORM

The necessity for agrarian reform in Latin America is universally recognized. Indeed, the words "agrarian reform" have become a shibboleth on the continent's political scene; one and all pledge their support of the concept. The difficulty of describing this reform, of course, lies in the definition of the concept, which differs with each movement's interpretation of the problem, and in the many technical issues involved. It is possible, however, despite the complex nature of the subject, to obtain a fairly clear, general picture of the Christian Democratic programs.

[33] "El Programa de Gobierno de Frei," p. 6.

[34] Joaquín Secco Illa, *Historia de la Unión Cívica* (Montevideo: Impresora Zorrilla de San Martín, 1946), p. 141.

[35] *Hispanic American Report,* XVII (March, 1964), 75.

The starting point of Christian Democratic policy is the unequivocal and realistic repudiation of simplistic schemes. The multi-faceted nature of an effective agrarian reform program is constantly emphasized. Agrarian reform is not merely the re-apportionment of land expropriated from the previous oligarchic owners. Christian Democrats advocate an integral land reform program that calls for an entire socio-economic and political overhaul of the prevailing system. They reject the demagogic appeals of those who reduce the problem to one of its aspects, the formal change of ownership.

The Christian Democratic program is based on several fundamental propositions. First, agrarian reform is a social and human problem as well as an economic one; the special character of Latin American rural life and customs must be taken into account at all points. Second, the land ought to belong to those who work it, either personally or, in some cases where historical custom or other circumstances merit it, in cooperative form. The democratization of private property, not its elimination, is the goal. Third, "the agrarian problem is preferably resolved in the place where it presents itself." "The right of the man who works the land cannot be transferred to any chosen piece of land, to another continent, to another nation or to economically undeveloped or unexploitable virgin lands. On the contrary, he has a concrete right to the land that he works."[36] This does not imply that Christian Democrats eschew colonization projects, which award lands to peasants in newly developed areas far from their homes. For reasons of social interests of the individual or the commonweal, the peasant often cannot be allotted the land that he has worked. In these cases, the movement agrees that colonization is a viable alternative, although forced migration is never justified.

A host of specific programs have been devised for the application of these general rules. The Peruvian party, for instance, wants to limit the maximum and minimum amount of land to be owned by one group or one person. Expropriation would progress from non-cultivated lands, to those under-cultivated, to those owned by absentee landlords.[37] The Christian Democrats also have stressed the need for an organized market to assure the peasants the security of a predictable demand for their products at stable prices. They list

[36] Víctor Giménez Landínez, "Reforma Agraria Integral: Bases Jurídicas de su Planificación," *Política,* III (Dec., 1963), 19.

[37] Partido Demócrata Cristiano del Perú, *Programa de Gobierno,* p. 27.

the development of road systems, railroads, ports, and other infrastructural improvements as being the direct concern of an integrated and comprehensive agrarian reform project. Attention must also be given to irrigation, mechanization, and rural electrification. Giménez Landínez calls for special credit facilities and technical assistance. Among the countless problems of successful agrarian reform, Giménez singles out the maintenance of a stable price program and the organization of the market. He notes that only in a very few instances have satisfactory results been achieved in these areas, and to illustrate his warning he points to contemporary difficulties of the European Common Market.[38]

An important facet of Christian Democratic agrarian reform programs stresses the application of reform measures to the numerous indigenous Indian communities of Central America and the Andean states. The integration of the Indian into the national society is clearly a problem of the first magnitude. Christian Democrats see education as the ultimate answer but also think that traditional Indian cultural patterns demand a special response in the area of agrarian reform. Of central importance in the Christian Democratic program is the preservation of the old forms of common property through the establishment of cooperatives. The traditional agricultural collectivism of the Indians seems eminently adaptable to the system.[39] Moreover, cooperativism fits clearly into the Christian scheme for developing pluralistic, intermediate communities. Finally, the cooperative system has the advantage of overcoming the evils of *minifundia* land-holdings; it is a workable compromise between the twin scourges of *latifundia* and *minifundia.*

The practical influence of the Christian Democratic movement in agrarian reform has been limited, but not totally absent. The old Catholic Civic Union of Uruguay has traditionally been solicitous of the agrarian sectors and has sponsored much legislation in this general area, including programs of technical assistance, cooperatives, and colonization.[40] Christian Democrats have exercised influence in the formation and administration of the Peruvian agrarian reform promulgated by the Acción Popular-Demócrata Cristiano

[38] Giménez Landínez, "Reforma Agraria Integral," p. 28.

[39] R. J. Owens notes that a similar Aprista emphasis "won it a wide popular following throughout the country." *Peru* (New York: Oxford University Press, 1963), p. 65.

[40] Brena, *Democracia Cristiana en el Uruguay*, pp. 106–8, 130.

coalition. Christian Democrat Enrique Torres Llosa, ex-minister of agriculture and presently general director of the National Office of Agrarian Reform, was one of the drafters of the legislation. The present agricultural minister is the Christian Democrat, Javier Silva Ruete. Perhaps the best-known example of the Christian Democratic initiative in agrarian reform can be found in Venezuela, where Agricultural Minister Víctor Giménez Landínez was one of the chief drafters and administrators of the successful Betancourt agrarian reform program.

GOVERNMENTAL REFORM

Although most of the Christian Democratic critique is devoted to an examination on the theoretical level of the fundamental political structure of Latin America as a whole, it has also been concerned with more specific reforms of existing governmental institutions. Almost all of the parties, for instance, specifically spell out the necessity of establishing a career civil service. COPEI's program is characteristic; it demands that admission to governmental employment be based on criteria that verify competency and that advancement be founded upon merit.[41]

The pattern of Latin American Christian Democratic thought on executive and presidential power is not completely clear, but there seems to be a consensus that the times demand strong, vigorous presidential leadership. In two debates concerning the feasibility of a plural rather than a single executive, the parties have favored the latter. In Uruguay, the Uníon Cívica strongly opposed the re-institution of the plural executive in 1952. Even after the system had been established, the party criticized its weakness and called for constitutional reform to permit the majority faction of the council complete control of the executive branch. The Civic Union pointed to an inability, under the system, to make important decisions to rectify the economic problems of the country. In Venezuela before the 1958 elections, there seemed to be general agreement between Betancourt's Acción Democrática and the Unión Republicana Democrática that a government by council patterned after that of Uruguay should be established. The council would be composed of representatives of all political parties and the armed forces. COPEI adamantly opposed the proposition, however, on the grounds that a

[41] Partido Social Cristiano-COPEI, *Programa* (Caracas, 1958), p. 24.

major constitutional overhaul would be necessary, and that effective government demanded a single executive.

Frei Montalva has noted that a president must be "efficacious," and have "wide powers," to respond to the "vertiginous and complex conditions of our times which demand authority, very rapid measures, total responsibility, and, therefore, considerable freedom of action."[42] In conjunction with these proposals, Frei campaigned for the right of plebiscite in Chile. He held that this was the only method for the executive to know the opinion of the people on fundamental problems.

> The Parliament is renewed only periodically and in the meantime problems arise which the Government did not consider, which were not foreseen at the time of the election and which may modify its decision. The only form of knowing with certainty what the people think and want, in any given moment, on matters of great national importance is direct consultation with them by means of a referendum or a plebiscite.
>
> This is especially important in a time when profound changes are required in the social and economic order.[43]

The Latin American movement states unequivocally that judicial power must be enhanced and strengthened. Frei has asked for administrative tribunals that would have the "competence to annul illegal acts of the administration, issue sanctions against arbitrary activity and insure the responsibility of governmental functionaries."[44] The Peruvian party has outlined the reforms necessary to transform the judicial power. It proposes a "radical modification" of the system of naming judges to the highest courts by replacing the present appointive procedures with a system of election by a national council of justice. It also calls for the right of judicial review for the Supreme Court, the right of the courts to invalidate administrative decrees and resolutions, and the right of *amparo* to protect individual and collective liberties that the constitution has already established.[45]

[42] Eduardo Frei Montalva, *Aún es el Tiempo . . .* (Santiago de Chile: Talleres Gráficos "El Chileno," 1942), pp. 68, 69.

[43] Eduardo Frei Montalva, *Soy Categoricamente Partidario de Reforma de la Constitución: Posición del Senador don Eduardo Frei ante las ideas de la reforma de la Constitución* (Santiago de Chile: Editorial del Pacífico, 1964), p. 10.

[44] *Ibid.*, p. 12.

[45] Partido Demócrata Cristiano del Perú, *Programa del Gobierno*, pp. 14, 15.

Although seeking numerous reforms in all areas of the government, the movement has particularly emphasized the necessity of strengthening the legislative branch. The Dominican Partido Revolucionario Social Cristiano has voiced a typical complaint when it has demanded an end to "rhetorical and verbalistic parliamentarianism" that functions merely as an "archives" for unsuccessful legislative proposals. One improvement would be to increase minority representation in parliament and, at the same time, afford institutionalized means for the opposition to criticize the government. Frei Montalva has outlined several internal reforms to improve the efficiency of the Chilean chamber: the deputies ought to have more staff assistance, and investigatory power and facilities of the chamber should be widened and strengthened to permit closer scrutiny of executive and administrative acts and policy. Frei also wants to establish a "conflict of interests" regulation by which a legislator's election renders his direction of a private business "absolutely" incompatible with his duty as a public servant.[46]

The most important of the legislative reforms envisaged by the Latin American Christian Democratic movement involves the introduction or broadening of functional representation in the governing process. Formally, none of the parties or movements support the idea of the totally corporative state. Nevertheless, although the whole may be repudiated, many of its parts are still retained. Most of the parties propose some form of functional representation either within political bodies or as separate council. Often the parties or leaders call for a mixed system with some functional or corporative attributes. The Peruvian Christian Democratic party, for example, favors a functional senate which would be "predominantly technical."[47] A constitutional reform program offered by the Ecuadorian Movimiento Social Cristiano includes the establishment of more corporative representation in the Senate. The groups represented would include workers, commerce, industry, the armed forces, the national police, private banks, white-collar workers, and others.[48] The Panamanian Rodríguez-Arias also prefers a combination of political and corporative representation, with one chamber of a bi-

[46] Frei Montalva, *Soy Categoricamente Partidario . . .*, pp. 5–7.

[47] Partido Demócrata Cristiano del Perú, *Programa del Gobierno*, p. 8.

[48] Movimiento Social Cristiano del Ecuador, *Planteamiento de Reformas Constitutionales . . .*, p. 35.

cameral legislature elected by "communities and institutions" and the other representing political interests.[49]

The Christian Democrats envision two results from the introduction of functional representation. The nation will be more fairly and comprehensively represented in the legislature. Politico-territorial criteria alone do not adequately reflect the complexity of the national community. Second, representation of unions and popularly based organs would help bind the alienated masses to the state and society. A feeling of integration and, hopefully, responsibility would be evoked, as the lower classes become a part of the decision-making process of the nation.

Further evidence of concern for the masses is exemplified by the movement's call for reform of the electoral system. All the parties stand for universal suffrage and the rejection of literacy requirements, the latter a much-debated and intensely contested political issue in Latin America. A Social Christian has explained his criteria for rejecting literacy tests. "It constitutes a manifest injustice that the governments which have the obligation of educating the people and which have been incapable of satisfactorily fulfilling that duty, invoke or take advantage of its own fault to deny the right to vote to the illiterate population."[50] He notes further that it is a "manifest absurdity" to "punish those who have not had the opportunity to learn. They are obliged to obey the laws, to pay taxes and to serve in the military, but are not permitted to vote."[51] In addition to universal suffrage, the Panamanian and Colombian parties propose to lower the age limit to eighteen, and the Dominican party has proposed the establishment of obligatory voting.

[49] Lino Rodríguez-Arias Bustamante, *La Democracia Cristiana y América Latina* (Lima: Editorial Universitaria, 1961), p. 106.

[50] Frei Montalva, *Soy Categoricamente Partidario . . .*, p. 9.

[51] "El Programa de Govierno de Frei," p. 7.

Economic Policies and Programs 6

ECONOMIC HUMANISM

Latin American Christian Democrats have devoted considerable energy to the critique of both capitalistic and socialistic economic systems, but their own economic program is not minutely detailed. Its general direction, however, despite the lack of comprehensiveness, is sufficiently clear.

At the first international meeting of Christian Democrats at Montevideo in 1947, it was asserted that economic humanism would supersede both state and individual capitalism. Economic humanism will supply the material and social necessities of the community by following five basic principles: the precedence of moral over material gain, the precedence of consumption over production, the precedence of labor over capital, replacement of patronage by co-ownership, and the replacement of salary by profit-sharing.[1] Economic humanism sees man as the center of the world economy. "Man is the end because the world economy has as its reason for being the production of goods and services to satisfy his necessities; wealth, whatever its form or quantity, has its causal determination and its quantitative and qualitative measure in the consumer."[2]

A corollary of these basic principles, which is a direct response to the comparative lack of Latin American economic wealth, is that great emphasis is placed on the importance of providing the necessities for all, even if it must be at the expense of the affluent or wealthy few. "No one," writes a leader of the Colombian party, "ought to

[1] "Acta Final de la Reunión de Montevideo," *Política y Espíritu*, II (May, 1947), 149.

[2] Américo Plá Rodríguez, *Los Principios de la Democracia Cristiana* (Bogotá: Ediciones del Caribe, 1962), p. 82.

possess more than he needs to maintain a decent life and guarantee the future of his loved ones; at least while there are others who . . . are suffering misery."[3] The vital necessities are primary, and secondary needs must be postponed. Such goals will invariably demand "limiting powers . . . and restricting liberty . . . , because it will be necessary for those who have arrived at levels of sufficiency of abundance to detain their rhythm of progress to provide to the more backward participation in this wealth."[4] The newly established Frei government seemed ready to pursue this principle. The first figures issued late in 1965 showed a decrease in purchasing power among the upper classes as a result of new taxes and improved collection techniques.

The Christian Democratic program foresees the establishment of a mixed economy. Private ownership is an integral part, indeed, the key ingredient, of the program; private property is the base of the new responsibility in the new era. The Nicaraguan party insists that "before the communist practice of 'no proprietors' and the capitalist of 'few proprietors,' we sustain the social christian theme of 'all proprietors.' "[5] The Salvadorians offer "to those who own nothing, the introduction of a system whereby they will gradually come to own something, agricultural or urban, industrial or commercial."[6] Téfel Vélez looks to "a republic of proprietors," in which man will be the "owner of his house, the owner of his land, the owner of his agricultural implements, co-owner of industrial and commercial enterprises, and communal owner of communitarian and cooperative enterprises."[7]

Christian Democrats favor the retention and encouragement of a system of private property for two basic reasons: Property stimulates development of the human personality and allows the personality to express itself in the socio-economic order. Individuality is made

[3] Francisco De Paula Jaramillo, *La Democracia Cristiana: Una Nueva Perspectiva para Colombia* (Bogotá: Ediciones del Caribe, 1962), p. 32.

[4] Víctor Andrés Belaúnde, *et al., Política, Deber Cristiano* (Lima: Editorial Universitaria, 1963), p. 74.

[5] Partido Social Cristiano de Nicaragua, *¿Que es el Partido Social-Cristiano Nicaragüense* (Managua, 1961), p. 12.

[6] "Foundation of the Christian Democratic Party of Salvador," *Christian Democratic Review*, XII (May, 1961), 10.

[7] Reinaldo Antonio Téfel Vélez, *Socialización en la Libertad* (Managua: Editorial Nicaragüense, 1964), p. 39.

manifest in the things a man owns, creates, produces, and builds. Thus, private property is viewed as a natural right, intrinsic to personality. Collective or total state ownership, conversely, vitiates the human personality; it is a threat to liberty, which is an integral part of the total concept of social justice. Second, the practical result of a system based upon private property is advantageous; the common good is promoted more efficiently, and more effectively, than it would be under a system of collective ownership.

Although the right of private property holds a central position in the economic thought of the movement, it is not considered an absolute right. Contributing to the human personality as well as serving the commonweal, property has a double function. Therefore, the defense of private property should not be confused with the defense of an individualistic, capitalistic regime. Both the Church and the Social Christian movement have condemned this system. Private property, though a natural right, is secondary, derived from the right to life, and therefore instrumental, not primary. "The qualitative value of the right to property bases its legitimacy on the measure in which it serves to assure the life of the person, the family and the society. Therefore, the right to property is a right of men, complemented by social experience."[8]

The limiting factor, then, is the common good. Private property may be an essential right of man, but it is not inalienable, for it has a social function that can be legally established according to time and place; it can, therefore, vary in its specifics according to time and place. The Argentine party has succinctly captured the doctrine when it proposes to defend "publicly disciplined" private property and to utilize "socially controlled" private initiative. The principle is quite clear. This does not mean, of course, that the application of the principle is simple; Frei candidly admits that it is "extraordinarily difficult to point out adequate institutions and formulas so that this social function can be realized in a determined time and place."[9] Nevertheless, the fundamental proposition is one which all Christian thinkers agree upon. Communism, notes a spokesman, is not the only force that renounces the "liberal concept of unlimited private

[8] Caonabo Javier Castillo, "El Socialcristianismo y La Propiedad Privada," *Eistín Diario* [Santo Domingo], Aug. 4, 1964.

[9] Eduardo Frei Montalva, *Pensamiento y Acción* (Santiago de Chile: Editorial del Pacífico, 1956), p. 29.

property." To think so is "so absurd that it can only be contained in minds fevered by an irrational anticommunism."[10] Last, the support of the right to private property should not be construed to mean that other forms of ownership, such as collective ownership in cooperatives or communitarian enterprises, are illegitimate.

Although the goals of economic humanism may be revolutionary, even messianic, the movement's spokesmen are conscious of the long-range nature of the undertaking. A gradual transition is foreseen. After all, it is not a simple re-distribution of property that is proposed, but a gargantuan effort to increase production. Even as an infant party, the Chilean Falange Nacional predicted a long period of labor; the many problems that faced the nation could not be solved immediately or simultaneously.[11] The Fifth International Congress of Latin American Christian Democracy expressed the same idea: "The low level of economic and political development, in both rural and urban sectors, the existing social stratification, the disparate levels of education and other factors show that it would be illusory to think of a rapid implantation of a new type of Communitarian Enterprise."[12]

Nor does the movement minimize the political problems involved in its program. The last statement of the economic chapter of the 1955 Santiago international congress admits the political risks intrinsic to a sophisticated plan that often stresses creation of more wealth rather than the distribution of existing wealth, while also recognizing the basic necessity of re-distribution. The program can be, indeed is, attacked from both Right and Left. The Right sees it as Communism, and the Left as a sell-out to free-enterprise capitalism. Nevertheless, the chapter urges that these risks must be chanced if the democratic system in Latin America is to be saved. Faced with the economic progress of the Communist nations, the fundamental reform proposed by Christian Democracy is the only hope for the preservation of a democratic politic.[13]

[10] Javier Castillo, "El Socialcristianismo y La Propiedad Privada."

[11] "Declaración de Principios de la Falange Nacional," *Política y Espíritu*, III (June, 1948), 146.

[12] *Congreso Internacional de la Democracia Cristiana: Anales del quinto . . .* (Lima: Editorial Universitaria, 1960), p. 167.

[13] *Congresos Internacionales Demócrata-Cristianos* (Santiago de Chile: Editorial del Pacífico, 1957), p. 298.

LA REFORMA DE LA EMPRESA

The methods of achieving the goal of economic humanism and the environmental system in which it is to mature are fully outlined in Latin American Christian Democratic literature. The first and most important objective is *la reforma de la empresa*, the reform of the enterprise. Indeed, the translation is weak; the proposition calls for a revolutionary re-structuring of the present relationships of labor and management. The goal is to transcend the split between labor and management that prevails under the present system. The new synthesis will establish the communitarian society in which economic humanism will be attained.

The present system meets neither the economic nor the social requirements of the Christian Democrats. It is not constructed to serve the interests of the consumer and therefore does not adequately contribute to the common good. Moreover, it is incapable of resolving the class struggle or mitigating its deleterious effects. The worker is not a part of the enterprise; on the contrary, he is all too often its worst enemy. The movement aims to elevate the concept of work by encouraging its spiritual and human elements. *La reforma de la empresa* is central to such change.

> Christian Democracy seeks to transform the present enterprise into another in which there exists an authentic community of benefits, authority and property. It wants to transform the capitalist enterprise into a communitarian enterprise in which both labor and capital will jointly participate in the three fundamental aspects—ownership, direction and distribution of profit.[14]

Christian Democrats see this reform as a natural complement to developments in other political and social areas. The economic order, according to their interpretation, has not kept pace with these other areas. For example, the working man has achieved political power and influence which he exercises through the suffrage and political parties. It is incongruent that in the economic sphere he is still treated as an instrument, "without intervention, without responsibility, without any participation in direction."

Mere reform in the guise of "popular capitalism" is not enough. The ownership of stock is a step in the right direction, but these hesitant changes are only the beginning. The ultimate goal is essen-

[14] Plá Rodríguez, *Los Principios*, p. 78.

tial transformation. Indeed, the long-range goal is the complete elimination of the salary system, which would be supplanted by another more just system,[15] and the end to unfair distinctions between laborers and others which prevail under the present economic forms.

> In a system of communitarian property there is no discrimination in relation with those who collaborate in an enterprise. Since it conforms to a new concept within a Christian social order, workers are, without distinction, all those who contribute, in whatever manner, physical or intellectual efforts to the production of goods. Nor is anybody excluded from the right or obligation of working. Directors, administrators, workers, white collar men, technicians, etc., form part of the personnel of the enterprise and, as workers, part of the community participating in its benefits according to their true necessities and capacities. Communitarian property is, consequently, the establishment of economic and social democracy within economic enterprises.[16]

The reform of the present system is based on co-participation, co-determination, and co-ownership. The first step is the introduction of profit-sharing schemes, allowing the worker to participate in the profits of enterprise. Co-ownership and co-determination belong to more advanced stages of the development. Co-ownership, which a Peruvian calls "one of the most noble Christian Democratic ideals,"[17] can be achieved by issuing stock to the workers as part of their pay until all members of the endeavor become part-owners. In the last stage, co-determination, boards of directors with worker representation are established. The direction of the enterprise should not be the sole responsibility of any one of the groups within the community. There should be unity of control by the three major contributors to the productive process—capital, management, and labor.[18]

The purpose of *la reforma de la empresa* is, of course, to integrate the working man into the society, to overcome the split between labor and management, to re-unite the worker and his product, and

[15] See Eduardo Frei Montalva's *El Regime del Salarido y su Posible Abolición* (Santiago de Chile: Editorial del Pacífico, 1933).

[16] "ABC de la Democracia Cristiana o Social-Cristianismo," *Combate* (Organo del Partido Social Cristiano Nicaragüense), April, 1964, p. 8.

[17] *Una Tercera Posición . . .* (Lima: Editorial Universitaria, 1960), p. 56.

[18] Jorge Bolaños Ramírez, Juan Hurdano, and Enrique Arguedas Ibáñez, *El ABC de la Democracia Cristiana* (Lima: Editorial Universitaria, 1960), Pregunta 18; *Congresos Internacionales Demócrata-Cristianos,* p. 320.

to render the class struggle obsolete. Remo Di Natale, the Bolivian Social Christian leader, explains the reform.

> Each worker is definitively incorporated into the property of the goods of production. The enterprise is his; it all belongs to him as it does to his companions in a relationship of common ownership. The fruits of his labor belong to him and to no other. Therefore, he likes his work and is strongly tied to it. He has a voice and a vote in the policy of the enterprise; the initiatives which he proposes are democratically discussed. He is a human being and not a mere tool.[19]

Christian Democrats see workers' participation as leading to cooperation and collaboration; mutual interest replaces antagonism. It is a practical reform designed to improve the productive process as well as a social reform designed to elevate the worker's concept of himself.

COMMUNITARIANISM

The economic system proposed by Latin American Christian Democrats has various names, though the term most often employed is "communitarianism." It has also been called Christian Socialism or economic humanism and has been described as being fundamentally a system of communitarian property-holding. All of these labels may be valid, although each offers the opportunity for slightly different interpretations or emphases. However, the terms are often used interchangeably, and consistent distinctions are therefore difficult to ascertain. Moreover, "communitarianism" actually refers to two different things: it is used to describe the property relationships within the proposed economic order and also to describe the end result of the Christian Democratic revolution, i.e., the "communitarian society."

Despite these semantic obscurities, the central idea of Christian Democratic communitarianism is fairly clear. It is most frequently employed with regard to industrial property and to the relation of industrial workers to industrial management. The Mexican Movimiento has offered the simplest and most lucid definition: "The expression means ownership in common of several subjects over one thing. When Christian Democracy talks about communitarian prop-

19 *América Latina Hoy: Esquemas Populares Demócrata Cristianos* (Caracas: Editorial Nuevo Orden, 1964), p. 74.

erty, it refers especially to the ownership of the means of production by the workers."[20]

Ownership by the workers means the progressive elimination of the salary system. Private property remains a crucial part of the scheme but it is "socialized"—that is, more evenly and widely distributed—in the interest of the common good. Ownership is not limited to the industrial sphere alone but becomes universal; society is transformed into a comprehensive system of cooperatives, thus eliminating entirely the classic division of men into the haves and the have-nots.

Communitarianism is seen as a new step in man's social evolution, a new form of society that is characterized by what Frei has called the "communitarian sense"; "it represents a social structure where the community formed by the men who work in the same enterprise, whatever its nature, industrial or agrarian, acquire fundamental importance. This implies the supercession of class conflict inherent in our present organization."[21] Another Chilean, Ismael Bustos, sees the communitarian society as being one step beyond and superior to pluralism. Pluralism merely supplies society with an answer to present diversity of religious, social, and economic groups, whereas communitarianism, on the other hand, offers a humanistic and fraternal—and therefore cohesive and unifying—approach that improves upon Christian pluralism.[22]

It is clear that the movement espouses socialization, but with a consciously Christian orientation that is similar to that expressed in the *Mater et Magistra* of Pope John XXIII. The emphasis is on society as a community of individuals and not on the state. The people are not solely object, but subject *and* object of the socializing change. In short, socialization is pre-eminently both Christian and democratic. The people themselves and not the state are responsible for their own social redemption. The key point in the Christian Democratic proposal for revolution is that cooperative ownership be nurtured by the people themselves. Christian Democracy "rejects the

[20] Movimiento Social Demócrata Cristiano de México, *Bases Ideológicas*, Folleto Numero 1 (México, D.F., March 28, 1963), p. 9.

[21] Eduardo Frei Montalva, *Caminos de la Política: Una Enfoque de Cinco Doctrinos*, ed. Sergio Guilisasti Tagle (Santiago de Chile: Editorial Universitaria, 1960), p. 107.

[22] See Fredrick B. Pike, *Chile and the United States . . .* (Notre Dame, Ind.: University of Notre Dame Press, 1963), p. 432.

state corporatism protagonized by the totalitarian regimes and pronounces for social corporatism which signifies the organization of the society from the bottom up; that is, it proposes free men operating in free communities."[23] The corporations must emerge primarily from private initiative and grow through their own efforts. They should not be created by the state; and only after having attained relative maturity may they be recognized by the legal organs of the body politic. Membership in the various corporations must be voluntary. President Frei has called upon the Chilean peasantry to "construct large, responsible organizations, neither tutored by the State nor, much less, by political parties. Construct serious and responsible organizations which really represent and defend your interests. The government and the country will hear of them, and then you are going to have . . . power in your country."[24]

The movement denies emphatically that totalitarianism is intrinsic in corporative theory. "To try to establish an opposition between the corporative idea and the expression of political liberty is entirely absurd. Men who are grouped by functions in the economy are also grouped by political ideas in other organizations and even in the same union there are men of diverse ideologies."[25]

The Latin American movement emphasizes the necessity of maintaining the separation of the economic and political spheres. They must be independent of one another in the corporative scheme. However, in the last analysis, the political power is supreme. Corporative representation in the legislature means participation in the lawmaking process in an economic and social advisory capacity only. Such representation is political in only a formal, limited sense; corporate representatives function completely in the economic sphere.

Though the term "communitarianism" in its most limited sense (and therefore in its most familiar sense) is used in reference to the industrial sector of the economy, in its broadest sense—when the "communitarian society" is being discussed—it is used to refer to

[23] Lino Rodríguez-Arias Bustamente, *La Democracia Cristiana y América Latina* (Lima: Editorial Universitaria, 1961), p. 105.

[24] "Campesinos Con Frei," *Noticias de Chile* (Santiago de Chile), July, 1965, p. 12.

[25] Eduardo Frei Montalva, *La Política y el Espíritu* (Santiago de Chile: Ediciones Ercilla, 1940), p. 159.

all property relationships. When the agrarian sector is under discussion, the word "cooperativism" is most usually employed. Cooperativism is central to the movement's programs in the area of agrarian reform. The property relationships are essentially the same in urban communitarianism and rural cooperativism; both assume collective ownership and control of the means of production and collective guidance of the activity.

Communitarianism is clearly very close to traditional Catholic corporatism. Semantics, again, pose a problem; indeed, as one apologist of the movement frankly admits, "communitarianism or communalism is essentially corporative." Christian Democratic thought has always been significantly influenced by corporatism, and the Latin American branch is no exception.[26] The most crucial point of similarity between the two lies in their common emphasis on the idea that economic and social groups have a unity and vitality of their own; the concept is obviously fundamental in shaping the specific theories of both communitarianism and Catholic corporatism. For example, an international congress of Latin American Christian Democrats has declared that "the State ought to recognize the professional organization as a juridical institution with normative, executive, and jurisdictional powers."[27] The economic or social functions of each group are taken into account in the creation of the economic democracy of the future. It might be noted here that the very organization of the Christian Democratic party itself, with its horizontal structure of affiliated functional groups, is a fine illustration of the practical impact this idea has had on the party.

On the other hand, the communitarianism of Latin American Christian Democracy does not resemble corporatism as it has been applied in some nations. The Latin American movement, for instance, in response to the example of Fascist corporatism, simply states that the Italian experience was not authentic corporatism but an unfortunate corruption of an essentially valid doctrine. They say

[26] Rodríguez-Arias, *La Democracia Cristiana y América Latina*, p. 105. Corporate theory, of course, was not originally a Fascist contribution, but a Catholic one developed by French Catholic theorists. See John Clark Adams and Paolo Barile, *The Government of Republican Italy* (Boston: Houghton Mifflin Company, 1962), p. 46.

[27] "El Congreso Demócrata Cristiano de Montevideo de 1949," *Política y Espíritu*, IV (Aug.–Dec., 1949), 31.

that the system established in Italy, no matter what it called itself, was fundamentally opposed to any true form of corporatism. The distinction, say the Latin Americans, lies in the origin of the corporations. In the system's corrupted and totalitarian variety the corporations were created by and subject to the state. In Latin America, however, the corporations would mature on their own and would be recognized by the state only after they had reached maturity.

Latin American critics often point to the experiences of Mexico and Bolivia to demonstrate the weakness of the rural cooperative system. The Christian Democratic response is similar to that offered in defense of corporative organization. As was true of the false and degenerate corporativism of Mussolini's Italy, the Mexican and Bolivian experiences have not encompassed *true* cooperativism.

> If cooperativism has not hitherto been fruitful in the agrarian reform programs of Mexico and Bolivia, it is simply because it has been subject to obstacles and torpidity on the part of the agents of the governmental parties of those countries who are interested in maintaining vast sectors of the campesino population in a state of political submission which is incompatible with a liberal movement like free cooperativism.[28]

In short, though communitarianism has certain similarities to traditional corporatism, the Latin American movement nonetheless insists that its programs should not and cannot be confused with corporative experiences elsewhere.

If Latin American communitarianism looks like traditional, even Fascist, corporatism to its critics on the Left, it has just as frequently been called communistic by its critics on the Right. The movement is socialistic, but, as Christian Democrats are quick to point out, not in the Marxist sense of the term. The Social Christians insist that there are fundamental differences between the two positions; the property relationships characteristic of each of the two systems are absolutely distinct.

> In a communitarian regime the employees have full and direct access to the ownership of the means of production of the enterprises in which they work. They are the owners of the enterprise, in a corporative form, and they have direction over it.
>
> In a communistic regime, the State is the owner of the means of production and it is the employer of the workers. And as the State is

[28] Di Natale, *América Latina Hoy*, p. 79.

represented by the government, it is the employer of the workers by means of public functionaries and of the leaders of the Communist Party.[29]

THE STATE AND ECONOMIC DEVELOPMENT

The ultimate social objective of the Latin American Christian Democratic economic policy is the creation of an integrated, stable society based on independent economic communities. The prerequisites of this plan are a more equitable distribution of the continent's wealth and a general increase in the wealth and production of the several nations. Ultimately, of course, the problem is the economic development of the continent's resources, for the social and political underdevelopment makes full achievement of the long-range plans of the Christian Democratic movement impossible. Economic development is crucial. In one of the closing speeches at the fifth international congress of the Organización Demócrata Cristiana de América, Frei outlined the movement's fundamental interest in economic growth. "We know precisely not only what we want," he said, "but why we want it and how we are going to get it: economic development to realize social justice."[30] Mirroring this concern, the Seventh International Congress in 1966 chose as its general theme "Development and Solidarity."

The first goal the Christian Democrats seek is industrialization. They see this as the means of achieving the necessary wealth and establishing both economic and political independence. Nations that produce only raw materials cannot compete successfully in the modern world, and Latin America's position is becoming increasingly vulnerable. A nation that produces only raw materials is at the mercy of the industrialized world; it cannot be master of its own policies or economic situation.

The result of industrialization will be increased output in both industrial and agrarian sectors. More equitable distribution of wealth is, of course, a desirable end, but it must be founded on a more productive economy. Mere re-distribution will not suffice. It is argued that the various programs such as agrarian reform and *la reforma de*

[29] Movimiento Social Demócrata Cristiano de México, *Bases Ideológicas*, pp. 9, 10.

[30] *Congreso Internacional de la Democracia Cristiana: Anales del quinto . . .*, p. 243.

la empresa will result in more production. Nevertheless, these two programs must be accompanied by efforts to increase production in other areas, to create new industries, and to make better use of the established ones.

A major part of this effort will be undertaken by the state. Traditional Christian Democratic and traditional Latin American theory and practice converge in this proposition; both emphasize vigorous state activity. Christian Democrats have always granted a rather wide competence to the state, and contemporary Latin American thought holds that the state must assume a significant role in industrialization. A North American student of the continent sees a "direct link" in Latin American thought between industrialization and state intervention.

> State intervention in the economic sphere first came about as a result of the desire to hasten economic expansion. It is now justified on the basis of three widely held beliefs: (1) Industry cannot survive without protection from outside competition, and only the state can provide that protection; (2) since the accumulation of domestic private capital is slow, the state, with its ability to accumulate capital fairly rapidly through taxation and foreign loans, must intercede in the industrial sphere in order to maintain the highest possible rate of development; (3) solicitude for the working class requires that the state exercise some control over the prices of necessary commodities.[31]

Although the degree of intervention that is proposed may vary somewhat from party to party, all Latin American Social Christian political groups concur in these general conclusions. The movement in international congress has noted that the state should make general plans and point out the over-all lines of economic activity in order to create the conditions for development. It should avoid direct intervention when possible, but it would be justified in three defined circumstances: when the industry is a public service, when industries do not attract private capital and thus need the state to promote basic investment, and when private ownership may constitute a danger to the commonweal.[32] The early Argentine allowances for state intervention were more limited. They proposed state control over credit,

[31] John J. Johnson, *The Military and Society in Latin America* (Stanford, Cal.: Stanford University Press, 1964), pp. 139, 140.

[32] *Congresos Internacionales Demócrata Cristianos*, p. 319.

money, taxes, and tariffs. The party did, however, call for temporary measures to fix prices on necessities.[33] Frei seems to advocate rather comprehensive state authority, though he is careful to propose the encouragement and protection of the private sector as well.

> The planning of economic development, the problems of international commerce and its evident disequilibrium, basic investments which are the primary exigency of our life as a nation, the impulse to scientific investigation and technical formation and defense against monopolies are tasks which the state cannot renounce. . . . But [private business] must have the security that the wide field of economic life within this rationally defined area will be open to it and will not be uselessly invaded by the State, which, despite its organized strength, will encounter difficulty in completing the specific tasks which are urgently demanded of it. . . . It would be utopian and inconvenient for it to embark upon others which ought to be left to private initiative.[34]

Christian Democracy has also proposed more specific programs of state activity. A Peruvian, for example, charges the state with the obligation of establishing, or helping to establish, basic industries such as energy-producing complexes, steel works, petrochemical plants, fertilizer production, and the machinery industry.[35] The Cuban exile group would have the state furnish free transportation for agricultural goods, construct warehouses and refrigeration plants, and guarantee basic prices for agrarian products.[36] Another official declaration proposes the protection of the peasant by having the state watch over the contracts between the rural producer and large companies.[37]

Self-help programs that are sweeping the continent and go under

[33] "Que Piensan los Partidos en Materia Económica," *Camoatí*, XVII (May, 1957), 160, 161. See also, "Declaración de la Junta Nacional del Partido Demócrata Cristiano Argentino sobre Medidas Específicas que Contribuirán al Restablecimiento de la Situación . . . ," *Política y Espíritu*, XIII (June 15, 1947), 29.

[34] Eduardo Frei Montalva, *La Verdad Tiene su Hora* (Santiago de Chile: Editorial del Pacífico, 1955), p. 44.

[35] Héctor Cornejo Chávez, *Que se Propone la Democracia Cristiana* (Lima: Ediciones del Sol, 1962), pp. 47, 48.

[36] Movimiento Demócrata Cristiano de Cuba, *Movimiento Demócrata Cristiano de Cuba* (Miami, 1961), p. 14.

[37] *Congreso Internacional de la Democracia Cristiana: Anales del quinto . . .*, p. 132.

the general name of Promoción Popular (in Peru, Cooperación Popular) are encouraged by Christian Democrats. The program solicits the assistance of the populace of individual communities in developing the nation. The heart of the plan lies in cooperation between government and people; the government supplies materials, expertise, and technical assistance, and the people furnish the labor. The concept has been enthusiastically accepted throughout the continent.

The comprehensive programs of economic development and distribution will obviously require a great effort on the part of the Christian Democratic governments. Success would depend upon the use of general, scientific planning. A Chilean Social Christian economic expert points to the contemporary evolution of a "science and technology of economic development. On them we base our policy . . . in a rational manner to achieve an outlined objective."[38] Frei declares that "advanced technology tends to objectivize social and economic problems in almost mathematical terms . . . ; the problem of economic development has its own science which, in many aspects, goes beyond the quarrel between socialism and capitalism."[39] Modern technology is the key to advancing the economic revolution, which is the pre-condition of political and social revolution.

The forces of science and technology will be harnessed to and directed by a comprehensive economic plan. The movement seeks "rationality," "predictability," and "design." Priorities must be devised to encourage the intelligent use of scarce resources. The Christian Democrats decry the traditional methods which lacked rational design as being "indiscriminate" and "inoperative." An international congress has called for the creation of national productivity centers representing the state, labor, capital, and consumers to "study, promote, coordinate, and in certain cases, to execute" plans enveloping industrial, mining, and agricultural production as well as the public services.[40] Giménez Landínez also stresses the fundamental necessity of multi-interest planning. The state acting alone is not satisfactory. Interested public and private groups ought to participate in any wide-ranging project.[41] Speaking in 1956, one of the early Peruvian Social Christians looked to the already-existing National

[38] Juan de Dios Carmona, *Caminos de la Política . . .*, p. 128.

[39] Frei Montalva, *ibid.*, p. 123.

[40] *Congresos Internacionales Demócrata Cristianos*, p. 318.

[41] Víctor Giménez Landínez, "Reforma Agraria Integral: Bases Jurídicas de su Planificación," *Política*, III (Dec., 1963), 14, 15.

Economic Council as the integrating agency for economic planning.[42] The Peruvian party later suggested the creation of a national council of transportation to "discipline and hierarchize" public and private activity in that sector.[43] The Chilean party has proposed the establishment of a national agency to integrate and assist the Chilean mining industry.

THE PRIVATE SECTOR

Although the unrestrained private enterprise of traditional capitalism may be unacceptable to Social Christians, they do not advocate the total elimination of the private sector. Nor do they completely reject all of the characteristics of the liberal capitalistic system. The Christian Democratic emphasis on pluralism and social autonomy presupposes a wide use of competitive mechanisms. An early Argentine apologist stated that "totalitarian experiences have convinced the peoples of the Christian civilization that private initiative is necessary as a motor of economic activity."[44] The doctrine's aversion to the omnipotent state presages the retention of much of the present system of private property at least during the period of transformation. Moreover, the problem must be seen in the light of both immediate and ultimate goals. Even though the present concept of private property would be altered in the communitarian society, the pressures of the immediate problems in the modern world demand a slow transition from the present situation to a more desirable one.

If a choice had to be made between capitalism and communism, furthermore, there seems little doubt that Social Christians would favor the less evil liberal capitalistic organization. The Cuban party has noted that both philosophies disguise themselves behind false masks; both are actually materialistic, not humanistic, systems. "But there is a fundamental difference. Private monopolies can be obliged to evolve, through the democratic system, toward a more just situation, while socialism necessarily brings a dictatorship by putting into a single hand both economic and political power."[45] Even the strong-

[42] *Una Tercera Posición*, p. 14.

[43] Partido Demócrata Cristiano del Perú, *Programa de Gobierno* (Lima: Imp. "El Condor," 1962), p. 24.

[44] Ambrosio Romero Carranza, *¿Qué es la Democracia Cristiana?* (Buenos Aires: Ediciones del Atlántico, 1956), p. 117.

[45] Movimiento Demócrata Cristiano de Cuba, *Movimiento Demócrata Cristiano de Cuba*, p. 17.

ly anti-capitalistic Dominican party has conceded that a capitalistic system is able to be just in that it can pay a fair salary and respect the human dignity of the worker. However, the Dominican party does add that "individual egoism" makes this highly unlikely.[46]

At first, the Argentine party seemed to favor an emphasis on private enterprise, at least through the transition period. Indeed, at the Constitutional Convention in the mid-fifties, the Argentine delegation favored private capital in the exploitation of Argentine oil.[47] But the party, under new leadership, has since changed its policy. The Peruvian party has also taken a rather moderate stand on this issue.

In the new era the need for leaders in commerce and industry will still exist. Fundamental reforms will promote the over-all growth of the economy and expansion of domestic and international markets; thus, the opportunities for business will be enhanced. Industries will benefit from better trained and more responsible labor, credit facilities, technical advice, and a generally stable situation more inviting to private initiative. The Salvadorian party, for example, has offered the great proprietors: "The guarantee of their rights, conditioned to the common good, and the general development of the economy which, no doubt, will compensate them for the economic sacrifices which the implantation of true social justice implies."[48]

Nevertheless, most of the declarations still emphasize a reformed and restricted private sector as the means to communitarian ownership. This restricted private sector will replace the avaricious owners who have reigned for so long in Latin America. Ultimately, then, private enterprise is welcomed and encouraged, but only insofar as it is a communitarian organ that is integrated with all of the other forces of production in the society and is directed toward effective service of the community. In this form it will receive the blessing of the society and the active assistance of the state.

In the interim period Christian Democrats envision regulation and increased taxation of private enterprises for the purpose of improving the lot of the worker and financially assisting the government. The Latin American movement does not admit a contradiction be-

[46] *El ABC del Movimiento Revolucionario Social Cristiano* ([Dominican Republic] Imp. de L. H. Cruz, 1964), pp. 8, 9.

[47] Alfredo Galletti, *La Política y los Partidos* (México: Fondo de Cultura Económica, 1961), p. 243.

[48] Comité Organizador del Partido Demócrata Cristiano, "Manifiesto," *La Prensa Gráfica* [El Salvador], Dec. 5, 1960, p. 13.

tween the continued existence of private business and advanced social legislation. Rafael Caldera noted: "The Venezuelan experience with petroleum is rich in lessons. It makes liars of those wailing prophets according to whom the establishment of advanced laws in favor of the workers would imply the ruin of the industry. It has proved that business prosperity is also compatible with the Venezuelan aspiration of obtaining a more just participation."[49]

Though the movement's attitude toward the large industries may be suspicious, motivated by a desire to moderate possible abuses, its attitude toward small business is one of positive encouragement. The Cuban exile movement sees a great difference between the social obligations of large industries and the responsibilities of smaller operations "directed by their owners in close collaboration with the workers. . . . [These smaller centers] need the stimulus and the assistance of the society in order to develop and progress."[50] Frei's program promised to establish special credit facilities that would be accessible to the small and medium producers to "liberate them from usury interest . . . which inevitably leads them to ruin."[51]

Finally, Latin American Christian Democrats favor joint ownership by private concerns and the state of some large-scale undertakings. The Frei government, for instance, has pursued this policy with the North American copper companies in Chile. The state has bought into a number of the companies and has joined with private concerns in initiating other new ventures. The program was expected to be in full operation by August of 1966. The Peruvian party foresees a similar plan for the development of Peruvian oil holdings. In Brazil, Christian Democratic governor Ney Braga during his successful term levied a special 2 percent sales tax to assist the financing of joint government-private ventures in Paraná.

EXPROPRIATION AND NATIONALIZATION

The Latin American Christian Democratic movement sees nationalization and expropriation as both advisable and justifiable. The ultimate justification for these measures is the furtherance of the

[49] Rafael Caldera, "Contestación del Académico," in Arturo Uslar Pietri, *El Petróleo en Venezuela* (Caracas: Empresa el Cojo, 1955), p. 49.

[50] Movimiento Demócrata Cristiano de Cuba, *Movimiento Demócrata Cristiano de Cuba*, p. 8.

[51] "El Programa de Gobierno de Frei," *DECE*, I (July, 1964), 4.

commonweal. Three instances are cited in which state assumption of private property is warranted. First, key industries of primary national importance may be nationalized. Second, the state may nationalize in areas where private industries cannot or will not meet the demands of the commonweal. Third, uneconomically utilized property is liable to expropriation. The fundamental goal, however, is transformation, evolution, and modification and not nationalization or expropriation. Even when nationalization seems mandatory, the movement prefers the formation of communitarian cooperatives; direct control by the state, per se, is avoided.

Key or strategic industries compose much of the infra-structural sector of the economy. Most of the Latin American political parties agree that foreign and private investment should not be allowed in this area. There has been rather frequent nationalization of private holdings in such public utilities as gas, electricity, and transportation. Christian Democrats agree that these sectors are so intrinsically wedded to the national well-being that they ought not to be in private hands.

One example of expropriation for the commonweal is the acquisition of lands for housing projects. Even the conservative Ecuadorian Social Christian Movement has chosen to permit the state to seize property for housing programs; it bases its approval on "social interest."[52] Agrarian reform is another area where nationalization and expropriation are seen as being fully justified. An international congress of the movement has declared: "Christian Democrats affirm that the land is destined to feed all the people and that in this consists its end or social function. The right of private property is justified insofar as it is the best means of achieving this end. For that reason, the public authority is able, in the common interest, to regulate its use or to decree its expropriation."[53]

The movement, furthermore, asserts that because property has a social function, its misuse constitutes a social wrong and justifies

[52] Movimiento Social Cristiano del Ecuador, *Planteamiento de Reformas Constitucionales Bajo el Signo de la Democracia Cristiana* (Quito: Editorial "Fray Jodoco Ricke," 1963), p. 71. See also, I Congreso Nacional de Profesionales y Técnicos de COPEI y Independientes Socialcristianos, *100,000 Viviendas por Año para Venezuela (Plan Caldera)* (Caracas: Publicación de la Secretaría Nacional de Organismos Profesionales del Partido Socialcristiano-COPEI, 1963), p. 48.

[53] *Congresos Internacionales Demócrata Cristianos*, p. 323.

expropriation. Pressures exerted through taxation should be tried first to encourage the owner to use his property to the best social advantage, but if this sort of pressure fails, social justice demands seizure. "The land is a natural resource and its inadequate exploitation can provoke its ruin," notes an international congress. "For that reason, its ill-use not only constitutes a transgression against the present patrimony of humanity, but also against future generations."[54] The movement also foresees the expropriation and redistribution of lands where the state undertakes irrigation, railroad, or road-building projects.

Specific examples of nationalization or projected nationalization set forth by Christian Democrats may clarify the general principles. In Chile, all concede that the copper industry will ultimately be nationalized, though there is much disagreement about the timing of the move. Early in his regime, President Frei called for the nationalization of the United States-owned Chilean Telephone Company as well as an electric company, also U. S. owned. A number of Peruvian Social Christians have proposed the immediate nationalization of that nation's oil industry. Actions taken by the conservative Uruguayan movement supply two instructive examples. In 1948, the parliament was discussing the acquisition of the British-owned railroads, and the Unión Cívica approved the measure on the grounds that the public-service character of the railroads made it imperative for the state to take them out of foreign hands.[55] In that same year, the party also endorsed state ownership of the water industry.[56] Finally, both the Colombian and Peruvian parties have called for the nationalization of at least part of the banking system, both because the banks are of primary importance to the commonweal and because they have used their power and influence poorly.

Although the right of nationalization and expropriation is generally accepted in Latin American Social Christian circles, the adherence to strict procedures and indemnification is thought to be essential. Indeed, only one party has specifically pronounced that the state may assume control without payment.[57] The Panamanian party expresses the general attitude of the movement when it asserts that

[54] *Ibid.*

[55] *Democracia Cristiana en Acción: Cuenta Parlamentaria de la Unión Cívica 1946–1950* (Montevideo: Ediciones de la Unión Cívica, 1950), p. 115.

[56] *Ibid.*, p. 57.

[57] De Paula Jaramillo, *La Democracia Cristiana*, p. 34.

"expropriation is only undertaken for reasons of public utility or social interests defined by law, by means of judicial decision and previous indemnification."[58] Not all of the parties, however, follow the principle of previous payment. Frei Montalva has established a system of long-term payment for the state's copper holdings in Chile, and his agrarian reform legislation has provided for payment of 10 percent upon assumption of the property with the remainder to be paid over a period of 25 years. The Peruvian, Cornejo Chávez, also proposes long-range indemnification. He noted that he has no intention of "robbing," but "we are going to initiate the agrarian reform without waiting for the State to have beforehand all the money necessary to pay a just price for these expropriations."[59]

[58] Partido Demócrata Cristiano de Panamá, *El Partido Demócrata Cristiano de Panamá: Historia, Principios, Programa, Estructura* (Panamá, 1964), p. 25. See also Partido Revolucionario Social Cristiano de la República Dominicana, *Programa del Partido Revolucionario Social Cristiano* (mimeographed), p. 7, and "Foundation of the Christian Democratic Party of Salvador," p. 10.

[59] Cornejo Chávez, *Que Se Propone la Democracia Cristiana*, p. 120.

International Organization and Policies 7

International cooperation forms an important part of the Christian Democratic message, and the Latin American branch of the movement has adopted it as a major goal. It is little wonder that this interest finds concrete realization in an international organization of Latin American Christian Democratic parties. In fact, an international organization preceded the formation of most of the national political parties. The first international meeting took place in Montevideo in April, 1947, attracting delegates from Argentina, Brazil, Chile, and Uruguay, yet only the last two delegations represented full-fledged political parties. The initiative for this first conference had been taken by Senator Dardo Regules of Uruguay, who became the first permanent secretary of the movement.

The purpose of the meeting was to lay the foundation for an international organization founded on the Christian Democratic ideology. A second congress was convoked in the same city two years later, and at that meeting the Organización Demócrata Cristiano de América was born. The group was often referred to as the "Montevideo Movement" during its early years. The 1949 meeting was attended by representatives from Peru and Colombia in addition to the four nations that had been represented in 1947; since that time the organization has grown rapidly and now has affiliates in almost all nations of the Western Hemisphere.

The preamble of the constitution states that the purpose of the organization is "to promote the interchange of information and experiences among the groups of Christian Democratic tendency which exist in America." The affiliated Social Christian groups are "primarily, those of a political character."[1] The organization specif-

[1] *Congresos Internacionales Demócrata-Cristianos* (Santiago de Chile: Editorial del Pacífico, 1957), p. 212.

ically denies any "international" ambitions similar to those of Socialists or Communists. One Christian Democratic militant explains: "International cooperation of Christian Democratic parties does not mean the formation of some kind of tightly-linked international organization, but the creation of a free forum where Christian Democrats . . . can present and discuss their problems and look for their practical solution."[2] The international organization is not able to issue orders or resolutions that formally obligate the member parties; instead, the Latin Americans depict their organization as a sort of liaison among the continental affiliates.

It should be emphasized that in reality the resolutions of the various congresses carry considerable weight with the respective parties, and the organization, in point of fact, speaks for the continental movement. In addition to the congresses, the international movement maintains a president, secretary-general, and board of directors whose pronouncements carry at least semi-official, and often official, import. Moreover, the organization acts to define Latin American Christian Democracy in that it permits organizations to join the international movement and in so doing issues its official blessing to its members as "authentic" Christian Democratic movements. Admission is not automatic; many groups have been accepted only provisionally, others have waited for some years before gaining admission, and some have been left to wither on the vine. The Cuban movement, for instance, was kept waiting for more than five years before final acceptance, and the conservative Ecuadorian movement has never been granted official recognition. The organization acts in its official capacity when it permits approved groups to send their militants to the organization's leadership school in Caracas and to benefit from frequent technical and occasional indirect material assistance.[3]

[2] "Interview with Senator Eduardo Frei Montalva of Chile," *Christian Democratic Review*, VI (May, 1956), 3.

[3] The international propensities of the movement have occasionally provided problems for member parties. Many Latin American nations officially outlaw political movements based upon international organization. The aim of this legislation has been to ban Communist parties, but it has also worked to the detriment of the Christian Democratic groups. The original draft of the 1965 Brazilian party statute portended difficulties for the Christian Democrats, but the party was able to modify the language of the legislation. Moreover, the strong Salvadorian party has been unable to officially affiliate with ODCA because of legislation of this type. See, on the Salvadorian case, "Texto Oficial: Acuerdos Finales del VI Congreso Latinoamericano," *DECE*, I (July, 1964), 8.

The Latin American Christian Democrats have conducted seven international congresses since 1947.[4] In 1949, the attending groups founded the Organización Demócrata Cristiana de América (ODCA). Since then, the organization has held international conclaves in Santiago de Chile, 1955, São Paulo, 1957, Lima, 1959, Caracas, 1964, and Lima, 1966. In addition to these ODCA congresses, a special Caribbean Zone international meeting at Caracas was organized by the Venezuelan COPEI in 1961. Though not an official ODCA congress, the conclave had the backing of the international organization; its purpose was to assist the new parties of the Caribbean area in ideological and practical formation. In that same year the Third World Conference of Christian Democrats met in Santiago de Chile, the first intercontinental congress to be held in Latin America. The youth and feminine international congresses are held conjointly with the ODCA meetings.

From the seminal group of four nations that formed the "Montevideo Movement" in 1947, the Organización Demócrata Cristiana de América has matured into a fairly sophisticated international organization. At the sixth international congress at Caracas in 1964, the organization admitted three new members: the Christian Democratic Movement of Cuba, the Social Christian Democratic Movement of Mexico, and the Christian Action party of Puerto Rico. The three additions brought the total official membership to 16; the old members included parties and movements representing Argentina, Brazil, Bolivia, Colombia, Chile, Guatemala, Nicaragua, Panama, Paraguay, Peru, the Dominican Republic, Uruguay, and Venezuela. The congresses usually award observer status to representatives from other countries and territories in Latin America and Europe.

Membership is assiduously sought by embryonic parties in Latin America, but certain requirements must be met before membership will be considered. The constitution of the organization states that the applicant's doctrinal principles must agree with those of the or-

[4] For the first, second, and third international congresses, see *Congresos Internacionales Demócrata-Cristianos*; for the fourth, see *II Congreso Internacional de Democracia Cristã* (São Paulo: mimeographed, 1957). The Brazilians called this the second congress, apparently not recognizing the first two Montevidean meetings. For the fifth, see *Congreso Internacional de la Democracia Cristiana: Anales del quinto . . .* (Lima: Editorial Universitaria, 1960); for the sixth, Organización Demócrata Cristiana de América, *VI Congreso Latinoamericano de la Democracia Cristiana: Informe Final* (Caracas: May 15–18, 1964); for the Caribbean Congress, see "El Congreso del Caribe," *Política y Espíritu*, XV (May, 1961), 53–56.

ganization, the applicants must have demonstrated fidelity to these principles in their activity, and the party or movement must agree to "accept" the statutes and accords of the congresses.[5] The members are accepted by the congress by an absolute majority of the individual national delegations; each national body has one vote.

The congress, moreover, often makes recommendations to a new delegation once it has been accepted into the organization. The Cuban Movimiento was warned that it should "develop no activity of a military type" and that it should disassociate itself from any "groups or parties of a rightest tendency." The Mexican organization was urged to seek the unity of all Christian forces in a nation where disunity had been much in evidence.[6] In lieu of official recognition the organization often substitutes informal support and interest. Although the nascent Costa Rican party was not qualified for official acceptance, the "Congress opted to manifest its backing and solidarity with that movement and to instruct the Secretary General to maintain permanent relations with it to the end of contributing to its fortification, with a view to future official recognition." Curaçao's National party was rejected, but the secretary-general was instructed to maintain contacts with it to promote "better understanding and friendship."[7]

Official recognition has particular significance in countries that have more than one group parading the Christian Democratic banner. After the fall of Trujillo in the Dominican Republic, for instance, three parties assumed the mantle—the Partido Demócrata Cristiano, the Partido Progresista Demócrata Cristiano, and the Partido Revolucionario Social Cristiano. The first two of these groups were rather conservative, and the international body gave its official blessing to the third. Two groups exist in Ecuador, the conservative Movimiento Social Cristiano of ex-President Camilo Ponce and the newer Partido Demócrata Cristiano. ODCA has recognized neither, but indications are that the younger, more progressive group will be the one to gain eventual admission. Mexico, Argentina, and Uruguay have also had two or more so-called Christian groups. The outstanding example however, is Bolivia, which has spawned a great number of groups trying to take advantage of the increasing prestige of the Christian label. The rightest Falange party, although never offi-

[5] *Congresos Internacionales Demócrata-Cristianos*, p. 213.
[6] "Texto Oficial: Acuerdos Finales del VI Congreso . . . ," p. 8.
[7] *Ibid.*

cially assuming the Christian title, has advertised itself as a Christian Democratic party. When General René Barrientos came to power, in November, 1964, two more Christian groups emerged, the Movimiento Popular Cristiano and the Unión Popular Demócrata Cristiano. The ODCA-recognized party is the long-suffering Partido Demócrata Cristiano, previously called the Partido Social Cristiano.

The original constitution of the international organization was written in 1949 and has since been amended and modified. The congresses are to meet at least every three years, although special circumstances have sometimes prohibited this. The congresses divide their work among committees which then bring their conclusions to the floor. The committees give attention to such subjects as housing, Indian policy, international policy, and health and dietary problems. Commonly, resolutions of the congresses are adopted in plenary session by a majority of those present and voting; special resolutions, known as *acuerdos*, demand unanimity. The president of the organization is elected by the congress; men such as Dardo Regules, Caldera, and Frei have held the post. The organization also has a Council and a Directorate. The Council counts one delegate from each member nation and meets at least once each year. A new body, the Comité Directivo was formed at the sixth congress. It numbers seven members and will undoubtedly have greater influence than the old Council.[8] Originally, the secretariat was to move about the continent and be situated wherever the last congress had met. This idea was abandoned, however, and in 1955 a permanent secretariat was established in Santiago de Chile. The secretary-general, Chilean Senator Tomás Reyes Vicuña, was first elected in that same year and has held the position since.

The Organización Demócrata Cristiana de América is, in turn, an affiliate in the World Union of Christian Democracy, officially founded in 1964 in Caracas. The world union includes ODCA, the Nouvelles Equipes Internationales (NEI), which comprises the strong western European parties, and the Christian Democratic Union of Central Europe (CDUCE), which is composed of exile movements from Iron Curtain countries. The international spokesmen claim that Christian Democratic parties, or at least movements with similar doctrine, are found in both Asia and Africa. Examples of these parties are the Lebanese Falange, the Viet Namese Popular

[8] See "Nueva Estructura se Dió la D.C. en América Latina," *DECE*, I (June, 1964), 5.

Revolutionary Movement, Togo's Progressive party, and groups in the Philippines, the Camerouns, Kenya, Upper Volta, and the French Congo. Delegations from Kenya, Upper Volta, and the French Congo have attended a Latin American Christian Democratic Youth congress.

Although the official organization was formed in 1964, there had been cooperation and official intercourse among the various international federations before that time. The first formal meeting took place at ODCA's 1955 congress in Santiago de Chile; world conferences of Christian Democracy have been held in Paris in 1956, Brussels in 1958, Santiago in 1961, and Strausbourg in 1963. At the ODCA São Paulo congress in 1957, the first intercontinental unit was established to initiate cooperation among the several movements. The International Union of Christian Democratic Youth is an auxiliary of the World Union of Christian Democracy. Affiliated groups and offices of the international Christian Democratic movement are located in Santiago de Chile, Caracas, Paris, Bonn, Rome, and New York.

Relations are generally good between the continental movements, but there are occasional areas of strain. The Latin Americans are usually more "advanced" and theoretically inclined than their more moderate and practically-minded European brethren. Caldera has noted that the parties "naturally differ due to the disparity of circumstances between industrial and emerging nations."[9] The Chilean Radomiro Tomic has also observed that the two occasionally assume "discordant positions . . . on economic measures, in the rhythm of the social transformation process and even in specific decisions in the international field." Tomic makes clear, however, that these are only formal differences and do not affect the substantial agreement between the Christian Democratic groups.[10]

LATIN AMERICAN INTEGRATION

Latin American Christian Democratic foreign policy rests on two fundamental assertions: the integration of the nations of Latin

[9] Rafael Caldera, *The Growth of Christian Democracy and Its Influence on the Social Reality of Latin America*, Speech delivered to the second annual conference of the Catholic Inter-American Cooperation Program (New York: Center of Christian Democratic Action, 1965), p. 18.

[10] *Unidad y Diversidad de la Democracia Cristiana en el Mundo* (Santiago de Chile: Imprenta del Pacífico, 1962), p. 6. See also Eugene K. Culhane, "Congress in Caracas," *America*, CVII (June 9, 1962), 370.

America is an urgent necessity, and it is the duty of the rich nations to help the poor (demonstrating the concept of international social justice). The two assertions are not mutually exclusive, of course; each interacts with and conditions the other.

The Latin American branch of Christian Democracy, as well as its European cousin, emphasizes the internationalist stance of the movement. There is probably no other principle or deed of which the Christian Democrats are more proud than their unflagging support of international cooperation. The Latin Americans continually allude to the European Common Market; they point with obvious pride to Christian leadership in that accomplishment and constantly stress their resolve to achieve a similar success in Latin America. An Uruguayan sees Christian Democratic concern with international cooperation as being as fundamental in the definition of the movement's ideology as is its democratic bent, its Christian inspiration, and its pursuit of social justice. The author explains why.

> Although theoretically international cooperation does not seem to be, in its own right, a characteristic on the same level as the others, it is certain that it is an outstanding characteristic of Christian Democratic parties and that historically and experientially they have possessed it in the highest grade.
>
> So that to omit it under the pretext that it does not have the same hierarchy as the others would be to prescind a datum of reality which has enormous practical and political significance.[11]

Certainly, few modern movements or parties would ever completely repudiate international cooperation. Nevertheless, some groups are more internationally minded than others, and an objective analysis reveals that Christian Democrats are foremost among such groups. A North American writer has explained that Christian Democratic and Catholic politics have developed historically within a framework of dual loyalty to both national and international institutions. He sees the "Catholic heritage of ultramontanism" as providing the foundation for an internationalist policy.[12] Américo Plá Rodríguez believes that this policy has an even more profound origin, for it emanates from the very heart of the doctrine. Because the doctrine is based on the Christian concept of the human person

[11] Américo Plá Rodríguez, *Los Principios de la Democracia Cristiana* (Bogotá: Ediciones del Caribe, 1962), p. 91.

[12] Arnold J. Heidenheimer, *Adenauer and the CDU* (The Hague: Martinus Nijhoff, 1960), p. 19.

as the supreme political value, the claims of the individual supersede "prejudiced" and "egoistic" claims of nation states; hence, political organization, to further the human personality, must also transcend these secondary claims. Plá goes on to say that Social Christian pluralism evokes a view of nations as natural, but not essentially separate and hostile, groupings. Just as various groups are able to cooperate fruitfully within the boundaries of a country, nation-states are able to interact and cooperate for the good of the international community, which is but a macrocosm of the individual nation. "Each ought to contribute, without losing its personality and its peculiar life, to the benefit of the international community." Finally, says Plá, the Christian's preference for pacific and constructive means compels him to assume an internationalist stance.[13]

ECONOMIC AND POLITICAL INTEGRATION

Whether the international position finds its direct source in Social Christian theory or not, there is little doubt that the Latin American movement has been strongly in favor of continental and intercontinental cooperation and integration. The major emphasis, of course, is on Latin American integration, and most Christian Democrats see it as the first issue of the times. Radomiro Tomic may overstate the case, but he does, nevertheless, capture the spirit of the Christian Democratic position. "The fight for the integration of Latin America must 'make or break' Christian Democracy on this continent. There will be neither alphabets nor bread for our people if there is no integration. There will be no full cultural destiny for us . . . if there is no integration."[14] The movement sees economic and political integration as the answer to the problems which face Latin America. The policy is more than a voluntary choice, for the present historical epoch demands, not city-states like Uruguay or even nation-states like Mexico or Argentina, but continental designs like the United States, the Soviet Union, or a united western Europe. Amoroso Lima has predicted that "history will likely record the passage from nationalism to continentalism as one of the most characteristic signs of our times."[15]

[13] Plá Rodríguez, *Los Principios*, pp. 97, 98.

[14] "Latin America on the Threshold of a New World," *Christian Democratic Review*, VIII (May, 1958), 13.

[15] Alceu Amoroso Lima, "An Interpretation of Brazilian Politics," *Social Science*, XXVI (Oct., 1951), 202.

Frei has discussed the situation comprehensively. He teaches that alliances of large groups of nations are a prerequisite for the development of individual nations. Smaller nations cannot construct a solid economic platform.

> Even a most elementary understanding of today's happenings indicates that a modern economy requires vast markets and that it is of vital importance that separate economic systems be complemented to permit development. This constitutes the only way of defeating the obstacles created by insufficient output, a situation that presently impedes the establishment of conditions to improve the people's economic and social condition. One step in the right direction would be integration because of geographic necessity. The natural pooling of physical and human resources would permit Latin America to expand its economic and industrial power.[16]

Nor, in theory at least, do the Social Christians bemoan the consequent loss of sovereignty. "National sovereignty," notes a Panamanian, "is subordinate to the necessary interdependence of peoples."[17] An Argentine asserts that "the talk of absolute sovereignty is to satisfy pride, and at times interest, but not to respond to reality."[18] The goal, in sum, is to gradually substitute interdependence through integration for the present "fiction" of national sovereignty.

Christian Democrats have outlined specific programs in both economic and political spheres. The movement enthusiastically backs the Latin American Free Trade Association, which was organized in 1960, but hopes that ultimately the trade association will be superseded by a more unified and stronger common market. The idea of internal free trade and reduction of tariffs is a long step in the right direction, but a really effective program, according to the movement, must have the authority to establish a continent-wide tariff and production policy *vis à vis* foreign markets and suppliers. Only by this method can embryonic Latin American industry be effectively encouraged.

Christian Democrats believe that the promotion of regional pacts within Latin America is another important step in the direction of continental integration. The Venezuelan Social Christian-COPEI,

[16] Eduardo Frei Montalva, "Current Trends and Prospects in Latin America," *Journal of International Affairs*, XII (1958), 114–16.

[17] Lino Rodríguez-Arias Bustamante, *La Democracia Cristiana y América Latina* (Lima: Editorial Universitaria, 1961), p. 106.

[18] Gustavo Juan Franceschi, *La Democracia Cristiana* (Buenos Aires: Ediciones Criterio, 1955), p. 12.

for example, has begun to cooperate with the nations of Grand Colombia in order to establish a wider solidarity, and the sister Colombian party has reciprocated.[19] Christian Democratic President Frei negotiated the "Mendoza Agreement" with Argentine President Arturo Illia in October, 1965. The concord was agreed upon with the idea that the economic integration of the two nations would encourage wider Latin American cooperation. It calls for the complementary development of automobile, machinery, tool, and railroad-equipment industries and joint construction of air navigation aids. The two presidents also planned the construction of a high-speed road from Argentina's Mendoza to Chile's coastal Valparaiso. The Peruvians have favored the creation of a regional merchant marine. Christian Democrats have backed the common market in Central America and propose to make it stronger and more effective. A leading Nicaraguan Social Christian has suggested that Panama and British Honduras be encouraged to become part of the Central American Federation and that the Christian Democratic movement take the initiative by organizing a united Central American Christian Democratic Federation.[20] Social Christian labor union cooperation already exists in Central America, and a leadership school and research center are in the planning stages. There is also a Central American Social Christian student federation.

To achieve political integration, Christian Democrats have proposed a comprehensive structure of inter-Latin American participation. The Fourth International Congress at São Paulo in 1957 called for the formation of a continental parliamentary union "formed by members of parliaments, freely elected, to meet once a year to discuss, without national limitations, the problems of the American Community of Nations."[21] The Sixth International Congress of the Organización Demócrata Cristiana de América advanced a plan for even more Latin American supra-national entities which would "constitute the germ or prefiguration of what in the future will be the

[19] See Partido Social Cristiano-COPEI, *Programa* (Caracas: Secretaría Nacional de Propaganda, 1958), p. 7 and Partido Social Demócrata Cristiano de Colombia, *Partido Social Demócrata Cristiano* (Bogotá: Ediciones del Caribe, 1964), p. 29.

[20] See Reinaldo Antonio Téfel Vélez, *Socialización en la Libertad* (Managua: Editorial Nicaragüense, 1964), pp. 71–73.

[21] "Common Goals: Conclusions and Resolutions of the Congress," *Christian Democratic Review*, VII (Oct., 1957), 11.

executive, legislative and judicial powers of an integrated Latin America." Two executive agencies were proposed, a council of ministers for economic activity and a council of ministers for education. The plan for a Latin American legislature was also broadened. Initially, the delegates would be elected by the several national parliaments in proportion to the political parties represented in each parliament; later, however, they would be elected by universal suffrage. The parliament, in the first stage, would have the authority to debate and to approve legislative recommendations which would be submitted to the several national legislatures. The recommendations would be given preferential treatment within each nation. The Latin American parliament would meet twice each year and could be called into extraordinary session by an absolute majority of the participating nations.[22]

An inter-Latin American court has also been suggested by the Social Christian movement. The idea was first introduced at the Third International Congress in 1955, when an inter-American Tribunal for the Protection of Human Rights and an international court were outlined.[23] The fifth congress resolved to "revise the principle of non-intervention to make it compatible with the defense of human rights, creating to that effect an Inter-American Court of Justice. . . . "[24] Finally, the sixth conference amplified the proposal by suggesting that the court should be patterned after The Hague World Court. It should have one judge designated by each of the member states and should be especially concerned with the uniformity of Latin American legislation, particularly in matters connected with eventual integration.[25]

INTERVENTION AND NON-INTERVENTION

The Latin American Christian Democrats hold that any effective policy of cooperation and integration must be based on responsible, democratic government in each of the member states. No federation could hope to attain success if governments were free to undermine

[22] "Una Corte y un Parlamento Latinamericanos Propone la Democracia Cristiana," *DECE*, I (June, 1964), 8.

[23] *Congresos Internacionales Demócrata-Cristianos*, p. 229.

[24] *Congreso Internacional de la Democracia Cristiana: Anales del quinto . . .*, p. 123.

[25] "Una Corte y un Parlamento . . . ," p. 8.

it or repudiate its regulations on the basis of personal, dictatorial whim.[26] The Third International Congress declared that "the existence of dictatorships of Latin America is one of the worst obstacles in the task of achieving political and economic unity. . . . There will be no Latin American unity without true democracies throughout the continent."[27]

The Christian Democratic response to dictatorial governments ranges from verbal condemnation to actual intervention. Individual Social Christians, the parties, and the movement in official conclave have, at various times, condemned Duvalier, Somoza, Stroessner, Castro, Pérez Jiménez, and Perón, as well as the Mexican and Paz Estenssoro Bolivian regimes, for being overtly dictatorial or imposing undue restrictions upon democratic activity. The movement has also stated that those parliamentary groups not chosen in free and genuinely democratic elections ought not to be represented in the intercontinental legislature. Moreover, it has urged that international recognition should be withheld from governments that have been established by irregular methods.[28] In Venezuela, COPEI adhered to this resolution by tacitly accepting the "Betancourt Doctrine," which refused to recognize undemocratically chosen regimes. The Caracas Caribbean Congress pledged its "help" to Christian Democrats living under dictatorships in that area. The movement has asked the international secretariat to devise a system by which a party may obtain an immediate general agreement of assistance or defense of its members who are detained, persecuted, or have their liberty restricted. In one of the closing speeches of the Santiago congress, Manuel Ordóñez of Argentina intimated that the Chilean democracy, and especially the Christian Democratic National Falange, had been of assistance in overthrowing the Perón tyranny. He pledged the support of Argentine Christian Democracy in the unseating of other dictatorships.[29]

In extreme situations, moreover, Latin American Christian Democrats seem prepared to sanction direct, physical intervention. The literature is filled with cries for a "rethinking," or a "revision" of

[26] See K. C. Wheare, *Federal Government* (3rd ed.; New York: Oxford University Press, 1953), pp. 47, 48. Wheare proposes that democratic governments are a necessary prerequisite for successful federation.

[27] *Congresos Internacionales Demócrata-Cristianos*, p. 225.

[28] *Congreso Internacional de la Democracia Cristiana: Anales del quinto . . .*, p. 216.

[29] *Congresos Internacionales Demócrata-Cristianos*, p. 348.

the traditional doctrine of non-intervention. Dardo Regules, one of the most important early ideologues, expressed the general feeling of the movement. Speaking against the Pérez Jiménez regime in Venezuela, he noted, "The idea of non-intervention, which began as a defense of weak Latin America against Yankee imperialism, has now been transformed into a perfect guarantee for military dictatorships to the effect that it can convert the international protection of the rights of man into the international protection of the rights of tyrants."[30]

The intervention, however, should be multilateral, not unilateral North American action. The movement opposes the practice of the Yankee "Big Stick."[31] More specifically, intervention should be undertaken by an international organization; most agree that it should be the function of the Organization of American States. The secretary-general of the Organización Demócrata Cristiana de América has outlined the policy.

> For intervention to be possible, it is required that it be multilateral and the fruit of the organs of international organizations to which nations have freely adhered. In the measure in which a country has accepted a determined scheme of international organization and has inserted itself in it, in this measure it is subject to the agreements acquired, and it accepts that this organization is collectively able, in some measure, to rectify its own internal acts. This decision to participate in international determinations also represents a renunciation of part of the concept of sovereignty. Absolute sovereignty has ceased to exist. In fact, the concept of sovereignty is increasingly limited through international conduct prefixed in treaties. . . .[32]

Another leading Social Christian notes that the classic principle of non-intervention set down in Article 15 of the OAS charter should be interpreted only in relation with Article 5, paragraphs "d" and "j," which define the principle of representative democracy. Viewed in

[30] *Christian Democratic Review*, IV (March, 1954), 7.

[31] For the official ODCA pronouncements on the North American intervention in Santo Domingo in 1965, see "La Intervención Militar de Estados Unidos Constituye otro Hecho Negativo de Incalculcables Consecuencias," *La Verdad sobre la República Dominicana* (Caracas: Secretaría Ejecutiva CLASC Caribe, mimeographed, June, 1965), last page. See also *DECE*, I (May, 1965). The issue gives over much space to the Dominican intervention.

[32] Tomás Reyes Vicuña, *Planificación en la Libertad* . . . , lecture prepared for El Instituto de Formación Demócrata Cristiana (Caracas, mimeographed, n.d.), p. 29.

this light, intervention would not be confused with arbitrary exercise of power.[33] The Peruvian party has specifically urged that the OAS be given the facilities necessary to "impede" the establishment of "dictatorships of whatever type" in Latin America. Nevertheless, these theoretical pronouncements are rather questionable in view of Christian Democratic Chile's refusal to sanction the organization of an Inter-American Peace Force in 1965 on the grounds that it would tend to "destroy the basic principle of non-intervention and threaten to divide the American States into irreconcilable blocs."[34]

ATTITUDES TOWARD THE UNITED STATES

INTERNATIONAL SOCIAL JUSTICE

Although the concept of international social justice theoretically has wider application than Latin American-North American relations, practical considerations give urgency to the application of this concept in relations between the two Americas. The concept was originally authored by Caldera, who continues as its major apologist. It has now been accepted by the movement as one of its fundamental principles. The Fifth International Congress asserted that the "principles of social justice . . . obligate the economically strong countries with respect to the economically weak."[35]

The concept of social justice implies that each man should go beyond the mere fulfillment of his contractual obligations in order to contribute to the common good. Extrapolated to the international sphere, the principle holds that each people or nation, commensurate with its capacity, must do everything necessary for less fortunate

[33] Rafael Caldera, *El Bloque Latinoamericano* (Santiago de Chile: Editorial del Pacífico, 1961), p. 23.

[34] For the Peruvian position, see, Partido Demócrata Cristiano del Perú, *Programa de Gobierno* (Lima: Imp. "El Condor," 1962), p. 37. The Chilean position is outlined in *News From Chile* (Washington: Chilean Embassy), No. 19, Oct. 15, 1965.

[35] *Congreso Internacional de la Democracia Cristiana: Anales del quinto . . .*, p. 216. For another example of the acceptance of the doctrine, see Remo Di Natale, *América Latina Hoy: Esquemas Populares Demócrata Cristianos* (Caracas: Editorial Nuevo Orden, 1964), p. 100. Caldera claims that the principle had been accepted in the preparatory papers of the Punta del Este Conference; see *La Idea de Justicia Social Internacional y El Bloque Latinoamericano* (Caracas: Editorial Sucre, 1962), p. 11.

peoples or nations to achieve the international common good. Caldera has explained the fundamental duty as follows:

> There is a social justice which obligates the stronger with regard to the weaker; it demands from the richer an obligation with regard to the poorer; it demands duties which can neither be figured by machines nor the mathematics of communitive justice.
>
> There is a social justice which establishes inequality of duties to re-establish fundamental equality among men; that social justice, which exists in the name of human solidarity, imposes whatever is necessary for the common good.[36]

Caldera outlines the consequences of the doctrine of international social justice in *La Idea de Justicia Social Internacional y El Bloque Latinoamericano.* The doctrine implies that assistance is not a simple act of benevolence but the fulfillment of a duty. The nation should not make its responsibility to other nations subordinate to its own national self-interest. International social justice dictates that the customary bilateral economic treaties should be superseded by multilateral agreements that take into consideration the varying needs of the signatories. A nation that buys from a raw producer should not obligate that nation to open its internal markets to manufactured goods. International social justice also demands that raw-material producers must not be submitted to the law of supply and demand. The right to a minimal level of well-being implies that these nations should be guaranteed against catastrophic changes in prices. Lastly, the doctrine gives small nations the right to organize into regional common markets. These efforts must be encouraged by the wealthier nations. Caldera concludes his analysis with the claim that he is not expounding a "utopian or impractical" idea, for nations are beginning to realize that political problems often have their bases in economic and social problems, and they are becoming increasingly aware of their duty to resolve the fundamental injustices in these areas.[37]

ECONOMIC POLICIES

Latin American Christian Democratic attitudes toward the United States are schizophrenic. On the one hand, the party rejects and

[36] Caldera, *El Bloque Latinoamericano,* pp. 25, 26.
[37] Caldera, *La Idea de Justicia . . . ,* pp. 12–15.

often vehemently criticizes the liberal capitalism and economic imperialism of its northern neighbor. On the other, however, it recognizes the comparative superiority of the North American system over its Soviet opponent and grudgingly admits the occasional benevolence of the United States. Moreover, the Latin Americans are realistic enough to know that the accident of geography has inextricably tied them to the United States, and, if they are to survive, they must make the best of a difficult situation.

North American assistance is necessary for Latin American development and integration. Frei Montalva has noted that the cooperation of the United States is "fundamental" for the "economic development and future prosperity" of Latin America as well as for the "well-being of its peasant, industrial and mining masses." Those who encourage hatred between the two continents, he warns, are sacrificing the people.[38] The United States' assistance is the means of achieving the economic development and political integration that will ultimately permit the southern continent to assume a posture of independence or equality *vis à vis* the United States. As the Social Christians point out, moreover, cooperation would be mutually beneficial. A strong, stable Latin America would obviate the possibility of Soviet imperialism in the Western Hemisphere, and a wealthy Latin America would offer the United States a huge and rapidly growing market.

The most widely accepted and constantly stressed plank of the Christian Democratic platform is the one calling for the establishment of a system of commodity price stabilization among the Western nations, specifically to include the United States. Because prices of raw materials increase less rapidly than those of manufactured goods, the less-developed sectors suffer a comparative net loss in trading with the more developed. The unhappy result of this process is that the Latin American nations often lack the funds and always lack the stability requisite for industrialization. A Venezuelan Copeyano explains the Social Christian position:

> All long-range planning supposes a stable range of economic growth. The emerging nations get the resources for their economic development from primary exports and use them to pay for imports of capital goods from the industrial countries, to diversify their economies and to take appropriate measures for social reform. But

[38] Eduardo Frei Montalva, *Pensamiento y Acción* (Santiago de Chile: Editorial del Pacífico, 1956), p. 229.

when a country cannot get the resources it expected because of the decline of prices, or because of the discriminatory practices against its products in the markets of the industrial countries, the situation becomes very dramatic. . . .[39]

In sum, loans and other aid often do not adequately compensate for the loss engendered by the decrease of prices for raw materials on the international or North American market. The answer is price stabilization. A Bolivian declares that the "alternative is clear; either we receive just prices for our exports or the Alliance for Progress will become a tragicomedy undertaken to distract the masses of the Latin American continent."[40] Caldera has observed that a 20 percent increase in the price of export products would almost equal the total amount of aid promised by the Alliance for Progress.[41] Since the richer nations can take advantage of lower prices on necessary raw materials during good times, the movement charges these nations with the obligation of maintaining markets and prices during hard times. Social justice or no, however, the Christian Democrats have also acted to further their own cause by calling for marketing agreements among exporting nations.[42]

The Christian Democratic position on foreign investments reflects the general ambiguity of Latin American attitudes toward the United States. Obvious suspicion of private foreign capital is mixed with the realization that it is both necessary and beneficial. Caldera has observed that some representatives of North American private capital have shown:

Sensitivity, understanding and a spirit of justice . . . [and] their attitude has been changing progressively in favor of a new deal. But the truth also compels us to say that in many cases their desire for profit has been their only standard, and that this has frequently led them into pacts with reprehensible forces, and into actions that

[39] Valmore Acevedo Amaya, *Trade Rather Than Aid: An Approach to International Cooperation*, lecture at Corning Community College, Corning, N. Y., April 14, 1965 (mimeographed), p. 8.

[40] Di Natale, *América Latina Hoy*, p. 101.

[41] Rafael Caldera, "Crucial Test for Christian Civilization," *The Alliance for Progress: A Critical Appraisal*, ed. William Manger (Washington: Public Affairs Press, 1963), p. 28.

[42] See *Congreso Internacional de la Democracia Cristiana: Anales del quinto . . .*, p. 81. For the same analysis of the Latin American dilemma from a non-Christian Democrat, see José Figueres, "The Problems of Democracy in Latin America," *Journal of International Affairs*, IX (1955), 13–15, 20–23.

> have aggravated structural ills and increased the causes of ill-will between the continents.[43]

Private capital alone can never meet the needs of Latin America. By its very nature it is not attracted to many of the areas which must be developed to insure economic growth.

The aim of the policy is to utilize private investment for the development of the state. The movement generally favors the type of investment that encourages development, is employed for useful activities, re-invests a substantial part of its earnings for improving and expanding its facilities or implanting new ones, and finally, foreign investment that joins with native public or private capital in joint ventures. An example of this last type is to be found in Chile, where foreign investors and the Frei government together have invested in the copper companies in a project of joint ownership.

Frei has suggested that the state will welcome foreign investment, but only on the condition that it will be accepted on Chile's terms. The foreign investor should submit to Chilean laws, respect the interests of the Chilean nation, manifest justice in its treatment of Chilean workers, and be ready to associate with the Chilean state. At the same time, he continues, foreign investment must be granted guarantees for a just return and fair treatment.[44] The Dominican party would regulate the behavior of foreign investors in order to prevent imperialistic penetration.

> The party proposes to establish a series of measures by means of which foreign investment will be accepted in our country. Among them: foreign investors must scrupulously respect our laws and institutions, they must submit absolutely to Dominican tribunals and authorities, they should not displace national enterprise, they should undertake activities which contribute to national progress, which contribute to the diversification of our exports and to the equilibrium of our balance of payments. They must employ advanced technical methods, raise the standard of living of our workers, reinvest a reasonable proportion of profits, etc. We ought to be vigilant, besides, that foreign enterprises always respect the rights of the indigenous working man, especially his right to unionize.[45]

[43] Caldera, "Crucial Test . . . ," p. 36.

[44] See "El Programa de Gobierno de Frei," *DECE*, I (July, 1964), 4, and Frei Montalva, *Pensamiento y Acción*, pp. 166, 167.

[45] *El ABC del Movimiento Revolucionario Social Cristiano* ([Dominican Republic] Imp. L. H. Cruz, 1964), pp. 25, 26.

In order to implement these generally accepted goals on an international scale, the Fifth International Congress and several of the national parties have proposed the adoption of a continent-wide treaty to govern foreign investment.

POLITICAL POLICIES

The most important departure in inter-American policy in recent years has been the Alliance for Progress. The Latin American Christian Democratic response to President Kennedy and his Alliance was markedly enthusiastic. Indeed the entire continent, and especially the Social Christians, was extraordinarily sympathetic to Kennedy. A Bolivian noted, for example, that "Kennedy talks to the Latin Americans with a language very different from the brutal language of imperialism. . . . We are in the presence of a new development. For the first time in history the United States officially recognizes the right of her southern neighbors to realize structural reforms and it is putting its resources at the service of these reforms."[46] Even before the Alliance came into existence, the movement's spokesmen were heralding a new era of friendship and understanding in inter-American affairs. The Chilean party was the first apologist for the Alliance in that nation and has generally furthered the approval and implementation of the pact's conditions. In 1962 the Peruvian party specifically mentioned in its platform that it would seek the active participation of that nation in the Alliance and in the internal reforms it suggested.[47]

The original enthusiasm has receded somewhat, although the movement still adheres to the basic proposals of the Alliance. The secretary-general of ODCA holds that the movement must be "intransigent" in demanding that the Alliance support a "social transformation" and that if it does not, then there should be no Alliance. If the program is merely a guise to consolidate the traditional economic interests of both continents, the Alliance should be abandoned.[48]

Christian Democrats criticize the strict intergovernmental procedures that the Alliance imposes. They think that intermediate

[46] Di Natale, *América Latina Hoy*, p. 98.

[47] Partido Demócrata Cristiana del Perú, *Programa*, p. 19.

[48] Reyes Vicuña, *Planificación en la Libertad . . .*, p. 34.

non-governmental agencies should be permitted to submit proposals and solicit assistance directly. As now constituted, the Alliance too often becomes just another political tool for the ruling governmental party. Well-developed and deserving projects go unaided because their organizers or sponsors are not part of the government party. Finally, the movement is opposed to the allegedly frequent use of the Alliance as an instrument of North American foreign policy.

Nonetheless, despite numerous exceptions, there is yet a strong undercurrent of genuine friendship and sympathy for the United States among Latin American Christian Democrats. Frei has often been a critic of North American policy; nevertheless he has observed, "both Americas are heirs of Western and Christian Civilization. From that trunk was born two branches, so that they have the same profound origin and, in spite of many differences, a substantially common mind and a similar conception of man."[49] The goal for Latin American Social Christians is to form a common block, a common consensus, and a common spirit. This resolve has given birth to numerous concrete acts and statements of solidarity. During World War II, the Social Christians were sympathetic to, and supported, the Western effort.[50] The São Paulo international congress has recorded that "solidarity between the United States and the 20 countries of Latin America implies that they have a common destiny which binds all of them to unite in facing the grave problems of the contemporary world."[51]

This feeling of amity does not preclude areas of friction between the two Americas. The problem of intervention is, of course, still vibrant in Latin America, and Social Christians are as strong in their condemnations of North American intervention as are other political groups. No rebirth of the Monroe Doctrine would be tolerated by

[49] Eduardo Frei Montalva, *La Verdad Tiene su Hora* (Santiago de Chile: Editorial del Pacífico, 1955), p. 130. In a speech marking the completion of his first year in office, Frei alluded to Chile's "loyal and frank friendship with the United States" as well as the "understanding" and "economic cooperation" on the part of the U. S. "This is something," he concluded, "which we must duly recognize and acknowledge." See, *News From Chile* (Washington: Chilean Embassy), No. 21, Nov. 15, 1965.

[50] See, for example, Ricardo Boizard, *La Democracia Cristiana en Chile* (3rd ed.; Santiago de Chile: Editorial Orbe, 1963), p. 268 and Tomás G. Brena, *Democracia Cristiana en el Uruguay* (Montevideo: Impresora Zorilla de San Martín, 1946), p. 369.

[51] "Common Goals: Conclusions and Resolutions of the Congress," p. 10.

the movement.[52] The Panamanian Christian Democratic party was among the demonstrators against the United States for its control over the Panama Canal and has officially declared its support for eventual nationalization. As a first step to this goal, the party calls for the negotiation of a new juridical status for the Canal, which would include the neutralization and denuclearization of the area.[53]

The most virulent criticism is directed against North American assistance to dictatorial regimes and against its tendency to impose promiscuously the charge of Communism on genuinely progressive social and political movements. Social Christians decry the practice of dealing with, supporting, and, at least indirectly, encouraging the dictatorial governments that have tyrannized the Latin American people. According to Frei, the only thing worse than the degradation of having to ask a large country for aid in overthrowing a bad government is "the utilization by a great power of its influence in sustaining such a government, especially when it violates the most basic principles of human rights to do so."[54] Tomás Reyes Vicuña has lectured the United States on the same problem. "It is equally necessary for the United States to understand that Latin American dictatorships, even when they are condescending to its immediate commercial interest, lead to the destruction of good understanding between the two Americas, and, therefore, it commits a great error when it accords them its backing, or still worse, preferential treatment."[55]

Of equal intensity is Latin American Christian Democracy's response to North American insensitivity to the Communist question. The movement prides itself on being the most responsible answer to the Communist threat and derides the United States for failing to understand Communism as it exists in Latin America. The United States should provide moral and material assistance to the forces of revolutionary democracy and recognize it as the only valid alternative to Communism.[56] Just social revolution must not be confused

[52] See, for example, *Hispanic American Report*, XII (May, 1959), 338, 339; XVI (Sept., 1963), 714; and n. 31, above for examples of protest against North American intervention.

[53] Partido Demócrata Cristiano de Panamá, *El Partido Demócrata Cristiano de Panamá: Historia, Principios, Programa, Estructura* (Panamá, 1964), p. 43.

[54] Frei Montalva, "Current Trends . . . ," p. 113.

[55] *Congresos Internacionales Demócrata-Cristianos*, p. 392.

[56] For an example of this position, see "Congreso del Caribe," pp. 53–56, and Frei Montalva, *Pensamiento y Acción*, p. 231.

with Communist revolution. The United States has concentrated on gathering diplomatic support for useless condemnations of Communist subversion when it should be addressing itself to problems of structural change. Finally, the movement has condemned the North American practice of stressing military assistance to fight Communism; too often these arms go to bolster dictatorial regimes.[57]

CHRISTIAN DEMOCRATS AND THE SOVIET BLOC

Christian Democratic rejection of the Soviet Union betrays none of the ambiguity that is characteristic of its attitude toward the United States. The movement, of course, claims to be the Third Force and certainly repudiates both socio-economic systems. It also makes a distinction between Latin American Communism and Soviet Communism; the one is often interpreted as a disease within the Latin American body politic that can be adequately diagnosed and cured; the other, however, is an intrinsic part of an essentially different historical tradition.[58]

The basis of the condemnation of the Soviet Union is that it represents an essentially alien, non-Western, non-Christian civilization. The Western world, for all of its faults, is depicted as having attained an infinitely more advanced stage of historical evolution. The United States and other Western nations are frequently criticized, but there is little doubt as to where Christian Democratic sympathies actually lie. The Social Christian Caribbean Congress, for instance, declared that "neutralism cannot exist before the Soviet threat. Our peoples, because they belong to the Western World, have their most profound roots in the Christian civilization."[59] José Rasco, a Cuban exile leader, rejects "a fence-sitting position between the Western world, essentially Christian, despite its lapses, and the Eastern world, basically pagan. . . . If, in case of political conflict a choice must be made between Washington and Moscow, between Lincoln and Lenin, we must decide, despite risks, for the world where liberty does not perish."[60] As early as 1948, the Uruguayan Unión Cívica

[57] *Congresos Internacionales Demócrata-Cristianos*, p. 228.

[58] For a discussion of the Third Force concept, see pp. 41–51. For the policy *vis à vis* internal Communism, see pp. 193–201.

[59] "Congreso del Caribe," pp. 53–56.

[60] Quoted in Leslie Dewart, *Christianity and Revolution: The Lesson of Cuba* (New York: Herder and Herder, 1963), p. 151.

had taken the same position. It noted that if Washington and Moscow are understood as the two poles of world imperialism, then it rejected both. If, however, they are interpreted as exemplifying "two philosophies of life, one which permits man to live with decorum and dignity and the other which subjugates and crushes the human person—in that dilemma, we cannot be neutral."[61] Between North American democracy, with its manifest shortcomings, and Soviet Communism, the movement stands clearly with its northern neighbor as a representative of the Western, Christian concept of man and society. The Caribbean Congress alluded to this distinction when it denounced Soviet imperialism. "Being clearly anti-imperialistic, we denounce that Soviet imperialism constitutes an even greater threat than capitalist imperialism. . . . We denounce the hypocritical anti-imperialism of the Communists and their allies which . . . opens up the field for the penetration of Soviet imperialism, whose oppression is already exercised in an asphyxiating form over the satellite countries."[62]

This short description of Christian Democratic attitudes should not be misinterpreted; the movement has not embraced the North American system nor its foreign policy. Anti-Yankee feeling runs deep in Latin America, and Social Christians are substantially in accord with the reigning opinion. This analysis only recognizes that most thoughtful Christian Democrats see the United States as the lesser of the two evils.

Suspicion and rejection of the Soviet Union have taken several concrete forms. The movement has called unilateral disarmament by the West "antipatriotic and suicidal."[63] The Venezuelan COPEI was responsible for blocking the Betancourt government from assuming official relations with the Soviet Union,[64] and the Ecuadorian Movimiento Social Cristiano has endorsed that nation's severance of relations with Cuba, Czechoslovakia, and Poland.[65] The movement as a whole, and many of its members individually, vehemently condemned the Soviet Union for crushing the Hungarian revolution.

[61] Brena, *Democracia Cristiana en el Uruguay*, p. 66.

[62] "Congreso del Caribe," pp. 53–56.

[63] See *Congresos Internacionales Demócrata-Cristianos*, p. 234, and *Una Tercera Posición* . . . (Lima: Editorial Universitaria, 1960), p. 46.

[64] See *Hispanic American Report*, XIV (March, 1961), 48 and XIV (May, 1961), 230.

[65] *Ibid.*, XVI (May, 1963), 277.

Not all members of the movement have agreed with the policy of prohibiting relations with Soviet-bloc nations. Indeed, Frei has visited the Soviet Union as a guest of the government, and a representative of the Chilean party has visited Peking. A policy of maintaining commercial intercourse and political relations is generally accepted by the movement. The ODCA secretary-general explains:

> It is clear that relations are not maintained with the [Soviet] regimes but with the countries. If we were to maintain relations on the basis of regimes, we would be unable to have them with any dictator or any totalitarian regime whatever its tendency. In fact, relations on the world plane would be very limited. Relations do not imply, therefore, a compromise with the orientation of the governments of the countries.[66]

Both the international movement in continental conclave and the Frei government have taken a similar position. Frei sees commercial relations with the Soviet bloc as a method of reducing United States' influence in Chile, and the 1966 international conclave at Lima resolved that the parties should try to "open new markets in Europe and in the countries situated behind the Iron Curtain."[67]

REJECTION OF COLONIALISM

Although overt colonialism is rapidly disappearing in the world, there are still vestiges of the system in Latin America. The Christian Democratic movement, as might be expected, stands unequivocally against the perpetuation of colonies in the Western Hemisphere. The goal is to liberate all of the remaining peoples in Latin America. In the Caribbean where most of the remaining colonies are located, the Caribbean Congress of Social Christian movements deplored the situation, declaring the very presence of these colonies to be a "sin against the fundamental principles of democracy, liberty and self-determination of peoples." The congress called for the "liquidation" of these entities and suggested that ODCA establish a permanent committee to coordinate the activity of all the American nations to achieve this end.[68] The Fifth International Congress also took cog-

[66] Reyes Vicuña, *Planificación en la Libertad . . .*, p. 36.

[67] See *Congresos Internacionales Demócrata-Cristianos*, p. 235; "El Programa de Gobierno de Frei," p. 7 and *Hispanic American Report*, XVII (June, 1964), 354; "Reunión en Lima," *Visión*, XXX (May 13, 1966), 15.

[68] "Congreso del Caribe," p. 56.

nizance of the issue. It suggested two concrete measures: a program of scholarships for students of the colonial areas of the hemisphere to "promote the creation of spiritual ties" between these areas and the rest of the continent, and the initiation of a program of immigration for the excess populations of the Antilles.[69]

The "liberation" of the Caribbean zone, of course, also applies to Puerto Rico. Tomás Reyes Vicuña has declared that Puerto Rican "subordination" as an associated commonwealth of the United States does not square with Christian Democratic sentiments. "A country with its own characteristics, essentially Latin and especially Latin American, ought to be independent."[70]

Quite understandably, the movement has declared its solidarity with other under-developed and ex-colonial peoples. "We are sure," notes one Social Christian, "that more important than the strident division between Washington and Moscow is the division between highly industrialized and underdeveloped countries." The ex-president of the Latin American Christian labor union international organization develops the same point.

> We Latin Americans, however, find the world divided along a different axis. There is a bloc of rich, economically developed countries and a bloc of poor, underdeveloped countries. In the rich bloc we see the United States, the Soviet Union and other wealthy nations, all located in the world's Northern Hemisphere. (We, alas, are in the southern half.)
>
> Thus, in our view the significant division is not between East and West, but between North and South. We feel more identified with the African nations than with the United States. For we and they have common needs and a common future to work out together. It is becoming clearer to us that we are a "third world."[71]

Because of this basic affinity among nations with similar problems, the movement suggests a closer relationship with these groups, par-

[69] *Congreso Internacional de la Democracia Cristiana: Anales del quinto . . .*, p. 19.

[70] Reyes Vicuña, *Planificación en la Libertad . . .*, p. 19. See following for the movement's Cuba policy.

[71] Eduardo Frei Montalva, *Sentido y Forma de una Política* (Santiago de Chile: Editorial del Pacífico, 1951), p. 181. José Goldsack, "Why a Christian Democratic Labor Organization," *America*, CXVI (Jan. 28, 1967), p. 155. See also *Congresos Internacionales Demócrata-Cristianos*, p. 374, for a similar statement on this "basic contradiction" of the contemporary world.

ticularly, the Afro-Asian bloc. The Frei government has pursued this policy and has negotiated a long-term trade exchange with Algeria as well as a more comprehensive agreement with copper-producing Zambia covering exchange of information, consultation on copper marketing and investments, and Chilean scholarships for Zambian mining students and technicians. The parties also seek to promote cooperation among under-developed nations in the United Nations and other international bodies to find solutions to common problems, and, undoubtedly, to present a stronger united front against the "have" nations. It is believed that the developing nations should press for development funds and programs that would ease their common problems.

ATTITUDES TOWARD CUBA

The Latin American Social Christian attitude toward Cuba follows rather closely the attitude of most of the progressive forces in the Western Hemisphere. What began as positive approval became hesitant criticism and finally blossomed into rejection and repudiation. Even before the Castro movement had succeeded in ousting Batista on January 1, 1959, most Christian Democrats had declared their support. Later, in April of 1960, the moderate Caldera still supported the Cuban regime. "I am not afraid of speaking on the Cuban problem," he said, "because I agree, first with the principle of self-determination for our sister nation of Cuba; second, with the belief that the peoples of Latin America, as one, would defend Cuba's sovereignty, if it is menaced."[72] Indeed, the Chilean Christian Democrats had co-sponsored a rally with the Communists at which Castro was to have been the main speaker.

Even after the tide of approval for the Cuban revolution had receded, some positive attributes were still being recognized. The Cuban phenomenon had injected a dynamic quality into the Latin American politic. Both the Latin Americans and the North Americans now realized the importance of resolving the problems that crippled the continent. Previously, the United States had been indifferent to the revolutionary fervor which was mounting in Latin America. As

[72] Rafael Caldera, "[Speech] at the Closing Session," *Report of the Second Inter-American Congress of the Inter-American Association for Democracy and Freedom* (1961), p. 31.

for the indigenous oligarchy, it had assumed an Olympian attitude while continuing to rule in the same way that had proved so selfishly advantageous throughout the last century. "The arrival of Castro has penetrated the Latin American people because it has demonstrated how, in the winking of an eye, old institutions and men who had taken advantage of power for the exclusive benefit of their own circles can be rubbed out."[73] The experience of Cuba also permitted the Latin Americans to see the working of Soviet imperialism at first hand. The Soviet threat had always been distant, but now the people realize that it is a present and dangerous reality.[74]

It was the Communist and particularly the Russian intervention in the Cuban Revolution that finally led to a withdrawal of the Latin American Christian Democratic support. A movement that had aroused great hopes among the people had been delivered into the hands of the Communists and had become an instrument of Soviet imperialism. The Social Christians had been staunch supporters of the revolution, but they became increasingly disenchanted with Castro, his Communist administration, and his affinity for the Soviet Union. The Cuban government's executions, for instance, prompted the Argentine party to declare publicly its hostility to the regime. Christian Democratic elements were influential in Panama's break with Cuba. The Caribbean Congress denounced the Castro regime and expressed its support for the Cuban Social Christian movement. In 1966 the Lima Congress specifically condemned the Tri-Continental Congress held in Havana that same year.

The most comprehensive and authoritative pronouncement was issued by an ODCA council meeting in Buenos Aires in August, 1960. The group first noted that the Cuban Revolution was the "most serious single example of disruption in American politics." It then addressed a series of "considerations" to the continent's Christian Democratic parties. The revolution, noted the Council, had been hailed and welcomed by the entire world. It had compromised its basic ideals, however, and had threatened its own internal development and its role in Latin America because of its growing connection with the Communist system. The Council blamed this "deviation" on the following factors: the failure of the United States to recognize the value of the revolution for Cuba and Latin America, and its

[73] Rodríguez-Arias, *La Democracia Cristiana y América Latina*, p. 27.
[74] Reyes Vicuña, *Planificación en la Libertad . . .*, p. 35.

policy of backing the interests of private North American capital; the infiltration of the Cuban Communist party, and the large-scale offers of markets and financial and technical assistance by Russia and other countries of the Soviet bloc; and the general hostility of the ruling groups in Latin America, and the apathy of the genuinely democratic Latin American political sector *vis à vis* the revolutionary program. The Council then specified three points of disagreement with the behavior of the Cuban leaders: the seemingly indefinite deferment of elections and the substitution of so-called "direct democracy, the practical application of which would deliver men and nations everywhere into the arbitrary hands of those who hold power"; the "speed and magnitude" of the relations being undertaken with the Communist world; and the opening of the continent to Soviet penetration, a move which would thrust Latin America even more seriously into the Cold War and the struggle for world domination.[75]

[75] "Declaration on Cuba," *Christian Democratic Review*, X (Aug.-Sept., 1960), 12, 13.

Relations with Military Forces and the Catholic Church

8

THE MILITARY

Because the traditional Latin American ruling class was an interlocking directorate, association with one faction often implied affiliation with all three branches of that unholy trinity, the military, the Church, and the oligarchy. Needless to say, Christian Democratic parties are accused of sympathies for and association with the Church.[1] By a process of extrapolation, they are also charged with an affiliation with the military. The Christian Democratic response to this charge is, of course, much more complex than the accusation. It includes, on the one hand, frequent anti-military pronouncements and legislative acts. On the other hand, the anti-military stance of the party is somewhat mitigated by the facts that strong Catholic attitudes continue to predominate in the military sectors, that centers of leadership recruitment often overlap, and that the military and the party often share the same areas of geographical and socio-economic support. Lack of sufficient material makes concrete conclusions difficult, but some valid propositions of a general nature are, nevertheless, possible.

As a preface, it should be noted that the military plays a major role in almost all of the Latin American nations. If need be, the military's almost absolute control of the means of violence makes it the final arbiter of the body politic. More subtle than overt force, of course, is the military's power in social and economic affairs, power which utilizes the ingrained habits of Latin American custom and tradition, the much-trumpeted threat of Communist subversion, and the immense economic influence of the military establishments. Civil-military relationships are changing profoundly, but this fact

[1] For a discussion of the Christian Democratic parties and the Church, see below.

should not becloud the fundamentally important role which the military still plays in Latin American politics.

Perhaps the most dramatic of these changes is the internal evolution of the military establishments. One recent study of the Latin American military has noted that the struggle "between the old and the new, between farm and city, between vested interests and newly-organized labor [has resulted] in institutional upheavals in the armed forces as far-reaching and profound" as those in civilian society.[2] This would seem to forecast the development of young, dynamic, socially motivated groups within the Latin American military establishment.[3]

Viewed in this light, the newly emerging factions within the military and the developing political parties are rivals. The parties are a challenge to the traditional position of the military as the final word in national politics. Moreover, they present a special threat to the ambitious, socially inclined, "Nasseristic" factions, because their influence can often be used to check military political power. The parties have been able to present opposition to military ambitions and power moves. "In recent decades," notes a study, "the political parties have displayed a healthy vigor in the face of persecution by dictatorships. The rank and file have remained loyal, and tens of thousands have risked death, jail or exile to struggle against dictatorial oppression."[4]

The position of Christian Democratic parties is ambiguous. The seemingly positive affinity between the movement's Catholicism and the traditional military sectors may be contrasted with numerous examples of the parties' anti-militarism. The Conservative Catholic bent of the traditional Latin American military establishment is well known. In the Argentine military, for example, there is an "unwritten requirement" that all officers be at least nominal Catholics.[5] The explanation of the connection among the military and Catholicism, if not the Church specifically, may be explained by social environ-

[2] Edwin Lieuwen, *Arms and Politics in Latin America* (New York: Published for the Council on Foreign Relations by Frederick A. Praeger, Inc., 1960), p. 126.

[3] See L. N. McAlister, "Civil-Military Relations in Latin America," *Journal of Inter-America Studies*, III (July, 1961), 345.

[4] Robert J. Alexander, "The Emergence of Modern Political Parties in Latin America," *The Politics of Change in Latin America*, ed. Joseph Maier and Richard W. Weatherhead (New York: Frederick A. Praeger, 1964), p. 123.

[5] John J. Johnson, *The Military and Society in Latin America* (Stanford, Cal.: Stanford University Press, 1964), p. 113.

ment. An important segment of the officer corps comes from recent immigrants and from small-town, intensely Catholic backgrounds. These groups are the "hard core, Catholic elements in the republics."[6] Whatever the explanation, military governments have frequently looked benignly upon the activities of the Church and Catholics.[7]

There are, moreover, specific examples of either accidental or intentional interaction or assistance between military groups and Christian Democratic parties. The Frei candidacy, for instance, was supported by the Movimiento Nacional y Popular, which was composed of retired military men and policemen of the Frente Nacional de las Fuerzas Armadas y Carabineros. In early 1965, the young Colombian Partido Social Demócrata Cristiano threw its enthusiastic support to a military adventurer, Ruiz Novoa. Despite warnings from sister parties, the group persevered in its support and suffered a loss of prestige when the mercurial General forsook the party to form his own group and later to ally with the Liberal party. In that same year the small Bolivian party suffered a minor internal split when a faction bolted to support the self-proclaimed Social Christian, General René Barrientos. The group and others formed the Movimiento Popular Cristiano to back the policies and the presidential ambitions of the military man. In Peru, furthermore, there seems to be little doubt that the military looked with favor upon the 1963 victory of the coalition which included the Christian Democrats. The military had previously blocked the assumption of power by the coalition's chief opposition, Haya de la Torre's APRA party. In this case it appears to have been the younger, progressive faction of the military, and not the traditional Catholic sector, which was the chief supporter of Belaúnde Terry's coalition.[8]

Perhaps Venezuela provides the most striking historical example of military support of a Social Christian party. During the short-lived democratic experiment between 1945 and 1948, the military showed a marked preference for the COPEI party over Betancourt's Acción Democrática. They sought COPEI participation in the government and, after the military coup in 1948, COPEI was permitted to continue functioning. It is true, of course, that this incipient co-

[6] *Ibid.*, p. 137.

[7] Increasingly, the more progressive attitude of the Church has modified this traditional relationship. See pp. 171–176.

[8] See *Hispanic-American Report*, XVI (July, 1963), 485.

operation soon ended because of COPEI's rejection of the brutal military dictatorship, but even after the fall of the Pérez Jiménez regime, there was some doubt that the military would permit any party but COPEI to govern.[9] The basis for this historical affinity seems to be two-fold. The COPEI was considerably more conservative and Catholic than the other two major political forces; and there was, and continues to be, though to a lesser extent, an amazing coincidence between COPEI and the military in its socio-economic and geographic areas of recruitment and strength. Both were, and are, based in the western Andean states of the republic.[10]

Although these examples and considerations do point up general and specific amity between the Social Christians and the military, the contrary evidence is perhaps even more impressive, and, it seems, belies any fundamental concordance between the Christian Democratic movement and the military tradition or establishment. Perhaps the most striking evidence of this fact is the success of Christian Democracy in Chile, one of the most demilitarized nations on the continent. The Chilean military has seldom played a significant role in that nation's politics. The Chilean society is markedly non-militaristic, and the Chilean Christian Democratic party is the oldest, most influential, and strongest in Latin America. Perhaps even more important, however, are the programs and activities of the parties *vis à vis* the military. If this be the basis for conclusions, then there is little doubt that the movement stands four-square against militarism and the traditional role of the military in Latin American politics.

The programs, manifestos, and pronouncements of the parties are studded with proposals for the demilitarization and professionalization of the armed forces. The message of the Paraguayan movement is typical. "The Movimiento Social Demócrata Cristiano desires the rational ordering of the Armed Forces. There can be no true democracy if the military power is converted into a partisan political instrument, denaturalizing its specific function and delivering its best human reserves to the corruption of privileges achieved by force. Neither can a true democracy be constructed with a military structure which goes beyond and destroys the economic capacity of the

[9] *Ibid.*, XI (May, 1958), 151. This period marks the time when COPEI evolved from the rather conservative party which it had been into a much more progressive Social Christian party.

[10] For the concentration of military officers originating from this area, see Johnson, *The Military and Society*, p. 107.

Nation."[11] A Nicaraguan, representing a nation that has suffered much under a politically inclined military, sees the "nationalization and democratization" of the army as the solution. "The Army," he says, "is the people. The people armed to defend the people unarmed. The conception of the army as an armed party . . . is an affront to the army itself and to its national nature and ends."[12]

One of the most interesting Social Christian documents with regard to the military is a long open letter that the Argentine party addressed to the nation's armed forces in 1962. The party prefaced its message by noting that it did not seek the destruction of the armed forces but rather its security within the total picture of the Argentine nation. The party then set out to lecture the military on exactly how it was to achieve this "security." The letter observed that the nation undertakes an "enormous economic effort and great social sacrifice" to sustain the armed forces. Moreover, year in and year out, it confers upon them "the moral and physical health of the new juvenile broods. It has the right, consequently, to expect that this money is not ill-spent and this youth is not jeopardized."

The party then notes that the modern conception of the armed forces transcends mere internal security and external protection. The military must be a predominant force in the nation's progress. There ought to be constant interchange of technical and scientific capacity between the military and civilian sectors. Cooperation has resulted in "astonishing progress in the most powerful countries of the modern world." Not only persons, but also institutions must learn to live in harmony in an authentic democracy. The letter ends with a paragraph warning the military of the dangers inherent in its activity.

> For many years as a result of their own will and historical circumstance, the Armed Forces of the nation have increasingly forsaken their own tasks and their own specific ends. From organs based on rigid principles of order and hierarchical authority, indispensable for its nature, little by little the Armed Forces have been transformed

[11] Movimiento Social Demócrata Cristiano del Paraguay, *Mensaje de Navidad del Movimiento Social Demócrata Cristiano al Pueblo del Paraguay* (Asunción: Dec. 25, 1960), p. 4. For other examples, see Movimiento Social Cristiano del Ecuador, *Manifiesto del 13 de Noviembre y Declaración de Principios* (Quito: Editorial Chimborazo, 1951), p. 16 and Partido Social Cristiano-COPEI, *Programa* (Caracas: Secretaría Nacional de Propaganda, 1958), p. 10.

[12] Reinaldo Antonio Téfel Vélez, *Socialización en la Libertad* (Managua: Editorial Nicaragüense, 1964), p. 52.

> into deliberative bodies which exercise the role of custodians of civil good conduct and as the holders of the final word in difficult technical, social and political problems which humanly exceed their professional formation. They run the risk of transferring to their internal life all the germs of tension which afflict the parties and of being converted into just so many "armed political parties" which means internal dissolution.[13]

The Christian Democratic movement has specifically opposed militarism and military dictatorships. The Peruvian group fought the Odría regime and, after the dictator's fall, continually pushed for a full-scale investigation of his government. The Salvadorian group has publicly condemned and refused to cooperate with military men in that nation. In the Dominican Republic, the Partido Revolucionario Social Cristiano opposed the coup that upset the Bosch government and later, during the civil war in 1965, actively fought on the side of the rebel, constitutionalist forces against the military regime. The Argentine party stood against the military dictatorships ruling that nation after the fall of Perón. Indeed, even the Conservative Ecuadorian Movimiento actively opposed the continuation of Ecuador's military regime, which assumed power in 1963 and fell in 1966.[14]

Though the movement has assumed a rather obdurate stance against militarism and military regimes, there seems to be no move among Christian Democrats to completely destroy the armed forces. Instead, the movement looks to reform. One of the particular reforms proposed would probably increase both the size and influence of the military establishment. Many Social Christians think that the military should be utilized in the development process, primarily to undertake special programs of assistance, but also as a basic educative device for thousands who have not had sufficient formal or practical education. A direct result of this project would be obligatory and universal military service; military tenure would prepare the citizen for the responsibilities of civilian life. The Colombian party, for example, has put forth a program of this sort and goes beyond the usual proposals by urging that even those who are physically incapable of serving in the military should be obliged to contribute their

[13] "La Convención Nacional de la Democracia Cristiana Argentina en Rosario," *Política y Espíritu*, XVI (Aug., 1962), 36.

[14] For other examples of Christian Democratic opposition to military dictatorships, see pp. 76–77.

services in other ways.[15] Téfel Vélez has outlined this type of military service.

> The soldiers, recruited without privileges, would receive a fundamental integral education, within which citizenship and patriotism are basically important. Military service would be undertaken on a functional basis, that is, in accord with the personal profession or vocation of the recruit. The campesinos would be housed in farmhouse barracks and attend barracks-schools, assimilating modern farming methods and contributing to agricultural production. The workers would be learning the latest technical advancements and increasing their productive capacity. The students would be formed into brigades for literacy programs or community action.[16]

The position of Latin American Christian Democracy must also be seen against the backdrop of the movement's numerous pleas for disarmament and a cessation of the Latin American arms race. Several of the congresses have called for treaties to limit arms purchases and also a conference for the pacific settlement of disputes. The Social Christians claim that strong military establishments and the increase of armaments serve no useful purpose in Latin America. Neither the economic nor the socio-political situation is strong enough to support large and powerful military establishments. Moreover, military growth favors, as history has proved, the foundation or maintenance of dictatorial government.

CHRISTIAN DEMOCRATS AND THE CHURCH

The relationship of the Christian Democratic movement, Catholicism, and the institutionalized Church is a much-debated and rather clouded issue. Some commentators, identifying the three as one, see Christian Democracy as nothing but organized Catholics actively fighting the Church's battles in the political sphere and the Social Christian political movement as nothing more than an arm of the Black International operating on the orders of the Pope of Rome, who directs the grand strategy of Catholic imperialism. Needless to say, this interpretation is rather naive. On the other hand, some Christian Democratic apologists often depict the relationship be-

[15] Partido Social Demócrata Cristiano de Colombia, *Partido Social Demócrata Cristiano* (Bogotá: Ediciones del Caribe, 1964), p. 23.

[16] Téfel Vélez, *Socialización en la Libertad*, p. 52.

tween the Church and Christian Democracy as being practically non-existent. The apologists admit that Christian Democracy is, or at least has been, partially inspired and guided by the papal social encyclicals but that it is Christian only insofar as it adheres to a social, economic, and political philosophy that has its origins among Christians and that has been fostered by the churches. Both of these interpretations are rather wide of the mark.

Christian Democracy everywhere, and in Latin America specifically, claims practicing members of many major Christian faiths. It also includes nominal Christians, Jews, and lastly, agnostics and other non-believers. Indeed, in Latin America the alienation of progressive Christian Democrats from the Catholic Church is dramatized by the fact that many party members are not conscientious communicants; the Church has not historically been associated with social reform in Latin America and has consequently lost some of its more progressive flock.

Be that as it may, it would be absurd to deny the existence of a fundamental bond among the Church, Catholicism, and Christian Democracy. Certainly, there are many Protestant, Jewish, and non-believers among Social Christian activists, but most are Catholics and many are practicing believers.[17] Similarly, the Christian Democratic electorate is composed of voters other than conscious religious adherents, but not many. Although the papal encyclicals are not the sole inspiration of Christian Democratic ideology, they are an important source rivaled only by other Catholic contributions. Protestant or secular additions make up an inconsequential part.[18] The Christian Democratic movement is more than the Catholic Church's response to revolutionary socialism, although it is partly, and in its middle stages perhaps mostly, Catholic inspired. A *Visión* article, after reviewing the Latin American Christian Democratic claim to aconfessionality, quite correctly asserts: "The reality, however, is

[17] See Luigi Sturzo, "The Philosophic Background of Christian Democracy," *Review of Politics*, IX (Jan., 1947), 5. Sturzo notes that "Christian Democrats have been and are, in their largest majority, faithful Catholics devoted to the Church and attentive to the observance of Christian precepts; they have had the help of Bishops and of Popes, according to time and place. . . ." Sturzo continues that they have frequently been treated very badly by the Church and Catholics, "always according to time and place."

[18] Except in the Netherlands, the beginnings of Christian Democracy were essentially Catholic. See Michael P. Fogarty, *Christian Democracy in Western Europe, 1820–1953* (Notre Dame, Ind.: University of Notre Dame Press, 1957), p. 179.

that, everywhere where it is encountered, Christian Democracy is directed by Catholics, integrated in its almost absolute majority by Catholics and is inspired by the Papal encyclicals."[19] In short, in theory and in practice, in popular conception and in philosophical foundations, for better or for worse, the Christian Democratic movement is inextricably tied to Catholicism and the Roman Catholic Church. It would be foolish as well as unscientific to hold otherwise.

The obvious implication of this conclusion is that Christian Democratic parties are conditioned by and in turn condition the reigning attitudes of the Church. That is, though there may be disagreements between the two, their relationship is both dynamic and intimate. Furthermore, in point of fact, it is theoretically possible to propose, but practically impossible to create, a successful Latin American Christian movement without the support or at least the tacit acceptance of the Church. The movement would suffer from outright Church opposition. This does not mean, of course, that the two are actively working hand in glove. It does import, however, that their positions cannot be diametrically opposed for any long period of time.

Therefore, no description or analysis of the Latin American Christian Democratic movement could claim to be comprehensive without some discussion of Latin American Catholicism and the Latin American Roman Catholic Church. Such is the purpose of this section, specifically to describe the attitudes of Latin American Catholicism toward contemporary problems and the Social Christian political movement. These attitudes may be the crucial factor in the eventual success or failure of the Christian Democratic movement.

THE CATHOLIC CHURCH IN LATIN AMERICA

The evolution of the Latin American Church has been uneven. The early Church, in the words of a Latin American historian, "was a great, noble and creative institution. . . . Yet in the course of time it deteriorated . . . and as economic (as well as spiritual) success accrued to the Church in the Indies, it fell from its original zeal and purity."[20] In the hands of the *peninsulares* the Church generally sided with Spain during the War of Independence. It was the preserve of the rich and well born and lost contact with progressive

[19] "Socialistas que Rezan," *Visión*, XXV (July 26, 1963), 24.

[20] Salvador de Madariaga, *The Rise of the Spanish American Empire* (New York: The Macmillan Company, 1949), p. 143.

forces, becoming instead the defender and apologist of the status quo. As it became more markedly conservative, it wielded its power and influence in behalf of traditionalism and reaction. In this effort, the Church joined with the oligarchy and the military; their joint rule came to be synonymous with dictatorial government. Not until very recent times has it turned from that position. No one could deny the deplorable record of the Church. One commentator notes: "In reality, the consent of the Catholic Church to dictatorial regimes has been clearly visible in the past, and there are sufficient proofs to condemn it for supporting authoritarian regimes which were the very negation of the principles and values which it professed."[21] A Social Christian frankly admits that "Latin American Catholics have neither been distinguished by their intransigency in the defense of political liberty nor by their preoccupation in giving it a concrete base by means of structural reform."[22] The result of this unhappy situation was that the struggle against despotism was inevitably associated with a struggle against the power of the Church and the influence of Catholics.

Indeed, some see the Catholic religion and institutional organization as inherently alien to and incompatible with democratic government. The Church, it is argued, conditions the individual for the acceptance of authoritarianism. Dogmatic thought and paternalism make substantial liberty impossible. These, intensified by Spanish theory and practice, doomed the possibility of democratic regimes in Latin America. Moreover, Conservative Catholicism has all too frequently found a convenient rationalization in equating democracy with the germs of Left totalitarianism. Amoroso Lima recognized the consequences of this brand of Catholicism. "As a result of education, habit or a false view of the permanence of mystic values or of the stability of the Church, one may easily conclude that religion is bound by necessity to everything which constitutes the conservative element in the social order. Hence that confusion, as tragic as frequent, between the religious spirit and the spirit of conservatism."[23]

[21] Federico G. Gil, "Cuatro Tendencias en la Política Latinamericana," *Journal of Inter-American Studies*, I (Oct., 1959), 463.

[22] *Congresos Internacionales Demócrata-Cristianos* (Santiago de Chile: Editorial del Pacífico, 1957), p. 30.

[23] Alceu Amoroso Lima, "The Problem of Labor," *Latin American Social Thought*, ed. Harold E. Davis (Washington: The University Press, 1961), p. 523.

It is incorrect, of course, to paint an entirely black picture of the Church. The standard work on the Latin American Church correctly notes that "so conspicuous was the work of the Catholic Church in the missionary field, in education, the charities and the arts that failure to recognize its constructive achievements would be most unjust."[24] Moreover, contrary to popular opinion, the Catholic Church has never been a unified monolith; both progressive and reactionary factions have always existed in the Church. During the wars for independence, there were revolutionary priests as well as monarchical priests. Indeed, the first call for Latin American independence is credited to the Jesuit, Juan Viscardo y Guzmán.[25] The story of the priest who forged cannon from church bells for San Martín's army is well known in Latin American folklore. It is true that most of the higher clergy opposed independence, but many of the lower clergy fought tenaciously for the Creole forces.

Division into progressive and reactionary factions persists today. There existed both pro- and anti-Perón factions in the Argentine Church; in Cuba there was a Church-Batista side and a Church-Castro side. Explicitly recognizing this sort of political factionalism, a Brazilian bishop has declared that "it is better to see division than injustice in the Church."[26] However, the modern split does differ from the older. The traditional division was almost always horizontal; the lower clergy were often progressive, whereas the ruling churchmen were almost always reactionary. The contemporary split is vertical in nature, encompassing progressive bishops, cardinals, and lower clergy on one side, and a like array on the other.[27]

THE NEW CHURCH AND THE NEW CATHOLICISM

Although two opposing factions still exist within the Church, there seems to be some evidence that the more progressive faction is be-

[24] J. Lloyd Mecham, *Church and State in Latin America* (Chapel Hill: University of North Carolina Press, 1934), p. 49.

[25] Víctor Andrés Belaúnde, *Bolívar and the Political Thought of the Spanish American Revolution* (Baltimore: The Johns Hopkins Press, 1938), p. 83.

[26] Quoted in *Hispanic American Report*, XVII (June, 1964), 381.

[27] See Gil, "Cuatro Tendencias," p. 467. On the same page, the author discusses confidential correspondence passing between Rome and Chile which lends dramatic credence to his point. On the same general theme, see John J. Kennedy, "Dichotomies in the Church," *Annals of the American Academy*, CCCXXXIV (March, 1961), 54–62.

coming dominant in Latin America. All agree, though not always without reservation, that the Latin American Church has taken a decided turn and is now generally to be listed with the forces of progress; therefore, the Church is gaining much of its lost prestige and some of its former influence. Of the three traditionalist groups, the Church has certainly gone furthest in accepting and often taking a leading role in the revolutionary trends of the continent. The old image of the reactionary Latin American clergy is changing. Indeed, the enthusiasm of North Americans concerning this evolution is seemingly unbounded. The literature is filled with comments claiming that the Church is an "important element in the equation of the democratic revolution," that there has been a "new awakening on the part of the Church leaders," or that the "new position of the Church is being interpreted by Latin Americans as having great significance. . . ."[28]

Although some of these observations exaggerate the change in the Church's attitudes, there is little doubt that a noticeable and signficant change has occurred. The Church has begun to regain some of its lost power. With the exception of Cuba, Latin America does not have any major anti-Church movement, and the Church is probably more independent of the state and closer to the masses than it has been for years. It is less pointedly political and more broadly concerned with social and economic problems. These new concerns of the Church obviously have crucial political import, but they are more legitimately the interests of a religious entity than were the political machinations of old. If it is true that the Latin American culture has become more secular, then the Church has seemingly chosen to adapt itself to secular environment, utilizing secular, scientific arguments to tackle secular problems.

There seem to be two basic explanations for the new attitude of the Latin American Church. It may be simply a reaction to the growing strength of revolutionary Socialism, secularism, and Protestantism in Latin America. It may be just another example of an old and

[28] Respectively the quotes are from, Tad Szulc, *The Winds of Revolution: Latin America Today and Tomorrow* (New York: Frederick A. Praeger, 1964), p. 22; Hubert H. Humphrey, "United States Policy in Latin America," *Foreign Affairs*, XLII (July, 1964), 600; Gil, "Cuatro Tendencias," p. 464. For other observations on the same theme, see William Benton, *The Voice of Latin America* (New York: Harper and Brothers, 1961), p. 8 and Eula Kennedy Long, "Catholic Renewal in Brazil," *Christian Century*, LXXVIII (Sept. 21, 1961), 1120–22.

sophisticated political organization's adjusting to the exigencies of the time to insure its continued existence and influence. Certainly the two thousand years of politics that the Roman Church has survived have taught it the merits of adaptation. Gil observes that "we should not be surprised that . . . the Catholic Church has always been more flexible than it appears to be at first glance. Conscious that its vocation is eternal, it tries to adjust itself to the rhythm of history."[29] The warning of Pope Paul VI that the Latin American revolutionary forces were apt to fall under the leadership of secularists if the Church did not respond in this "decisive hour" lends some credence to the charge that the Church's new position is essentially reactionary.[30]

The other explanation of the Church's new departure, and the one most discussed by Christian Democrats, centers on the waxing influence of the "New Catholicism" and the waning of the impact of traditional Spanish Catholic attitudes. Spanish Catholicism has been characterized by a lack of concern with social problems; it is centered on the individual's personal relationship with his God. Frei charges that it evidences a "mental narrowness" and a "poverty of style" in presenting its message in the social sphere.[31] Indeed, the Chilean President has termed Spanish Catholicism a "deviation," stating that "the Spanish stream of spirituality . . . is inconsistent with some of the features of the development ethos."[32] Roger Vekemans, a Belgian Jesuit and one of the outstanding intellectual luminaries of Latin American Catholicism, has also criticized Hispanic Catholicism for not being concerned with man's life in this world. Its other-worldliness is "overly spiritualized" and "overly sentimentalized." It fosters attitudes that clash with modern socio-economic and political necessities.[33]

Christian Democrats, however, hold that Hispanic Catholicism is

[29] Gil, "Cuatro Tendencias."

[30] See *Hispanic American Report*, XVII (June, 1964), 380. See also Gil, "Cuatro Tendencias," especially p. 468, who strongly implies that the new position of the Church is a response to the Communist offensive.

[31] Eduardo Frei Montalva. *La Política y el Espíritu* (Santiago de Chile: Ediciones Ercilla, 1940), p. 196.

[32] Eduardo Frei Montalva, "Notes on the Catholic Church and Development," *Latin America: Evolution or Explosion?* ed. Mildred Adams (New York: Council on World Tensions, Dodd, Mead and Company, 1963), p. 197.

[33] For the analysis, see Roger E. Vekemans, "Is the Church Losing in Latin America?" *Ave Maria*, XCI (Jan. 9, 1960), 5–10.

being replaced in Latin America by a New Catholicism. This development is part and parcel of the contributions emanating from Europe, including the revival of Thomistic thought and the message of political Christian Democracy. It is derived mainly from the Franco-Belgic school. Frei has outlined the characteristics of New Catholicism. First, it is favorably inclined toward change. It is concerned more with the present life than had been Hispanic Catholicism. Moreover, this preoccupation extends to the physical and the material. It shows "resignation only to the inevitable" but "struggles to adapt existence and its structures in order to improve them." The traditional Catholic belief in the imperfectibility of man is, of course, accepted, but the New Catholicism denies that this implies the renunciation of personal responsibility in bringing about change. It merely connotes "a cautious uncertainty concerning the success of endeavor and its real effectiveness in view of the congenital limitation of knowledge and technique, which are always susceptible of improvement." Furthermore, it recognizes the inadequacy of good intention without effective capacity. Finally, New Catholicism asserts that charity must be directed to the common good and toward all mankind, not only to one's family or relatives, which has been the tragically narrow approach in Latin America.[34] These characteristics, then, are part of the New Catholic credo espoused by Social Christians and purported to be gaining influence. Christian Democrats optimistically predict that the growth of New Catholicism will rectify the injustices bred by Hispanic Catholicism.

The new attitudes of the Church have been demonstrated in its growing concern for progressive programs and governments. Perhaps the most dramatic evidence of this new concern is the fact that the Church has voiced increasingly frequent protests against dictatorial regimes and has offered occasional overt assistance in overturning these governments. The most well-known examples are the Church's and Catholics' efforts in unseating Perón in 1955, Rojas Pinilla in 1957, and Pérez Jiménez in 1958. Less well known, but equally significant, has been the stand of the Church and other Catholic organizations against dictatorial governments in Paraguay, Batista's Cuba, Guatemala, Nicaragua, Peru, Haiti, and Honduras. In Paraguay, for instance, the archbishop of Asunción issued a 1958

[34] Frei Montalva, "Notes on the Catholic Church and Development," pp. 198–200.

pastoral condemning the government and calling for progressive participation of the people in politics and for freedom of speech. In Nicaragua, churchmen have actively resisted the government. Although the Church was much too late in officially condemning Batista, Catholic youth groups were a vital force in the struggle against the tyrant. More traditionally, the Church stood against the left-wing dictatorship of Arbenz Guzmán in Guatemala.

Perhaps even more significant than these demonstrations, however, are the numerous, more subtle progressive contributions that are changing the face of Latin American Catholicism and making a decided impact on the continent's masses. Everywhere the Church has gained prestige by favoring land reform. Catholic intellectuals, both lay and cleric, are omnipresent at academic and scholarly conclaves. Priests with advanced social and political ideas are less frequently exiled to mountain parishes or obscure monasteries. The school and university system is growing rapidly and improving steadily. Many of the best secondary schools are Catholic. In ten years the university complex of the Church has increased from 13 to 31 and students from 10,000 to 50,000. The national Catholic universities, particularly those in Lima and Santiago de Chile, rival and sometimes surpass the state schools.[35] The national churches or religious orders have established research centers in several nations. Perhaps the best known of these are the Bellarmine Center in Chile and the Center of Intercultural Formation in Cuernavaca, Mexico.[36]

At the Ecumenical Council the Latin American churchmen consistently backed the most progressive proposals. The Latin American delegates condemned the practice of indiscriminately labeling as Communists all those who favored social reform. A Mexican prelate declared that the Church had endorsed the social goals of the Mexican Revolution. Most memorable, the Brazilian Dom Hélder Câmara called for his colleagues to shed their "fancy vestments which recall the Middle Ages."[37] Indeed, as early as 1955, the Catholic bishops

[35] See Adolf A. Berle, *Latin America: Diplomacy and Reality* (New York: Published for the Council on Foreign Relations by Harper and Row, 1962), p. 71, and Angel del Rio (ed.), *Responsible Freedom in the Americas* (Garden City, N. Y.: Doubleday and Company, 1955), p. 119.

[36] For a description of the Chilean Center, see Hiber Conteris, "La Próxima Disyuntiva de la D. C.," *Marcha*, XXVI (Sept. 18, 1964), 20. The Cuernavaca center publishes the well-known *CIF Reports*.

[37] *Hispanic American Report*, XVII (June, 1964), 380.

of Latin America had officially called for the Church to assume the leadership of social change in Latin America and to inspire Catholics to search for solutions to contemporary social problems.

These general proposals have given birth to numerous revolutionary actions in the practical sphere. The Chilean Church has published studies on several of that nation's problems, including one that contributed to a much-heralded land reform program. The archbishop of La Plata in Argentina has aligned the Church with the Peronista working classes. The archbishop of Caracas has denounced the low wages of the workingman and Venezuela's lack of schooling facilities. The Brazilian Church has formed peasant leagues in the troubled northeast to combat Communist influence. São Paulo's archbishop and eight other clergymen officially declared their support of Goulart's constitutional and agrarian reforms. In Panama, the first native Panamanian has recently been appointed to the country's highest religious office. Even in traditionalist Ecuador, the Church has given its backing to agrarian reform.

LATIN AMERICAN CATHOLIC TRADITION

Underlying and supporting the Church's new position are almost five hundred years of Catholic tradition. Latin American history and politics are inextricably wedded to Catholicism; it is a basic thread in the warp and woof of Latin America. No other large geographic area displays such religious unity. Catholicism and the Church have contributed to its entire history—its colonization, its drive for independence, the education of its leaders, the guidance of its masses, the alienation of its intellectuals, and growth of its basic culture.

Many have strayed from and many have criticized the religion, but few have repudiated it. Latin America is Catholic despite the corruption of the Church, the blind intransigence of her shepherds, the persecution of militant secularists, or the modern challenge of proselytizing Protestantism. The history of the area is replete with examples of the obstinate staying power of the religion and the Church. Even those who personally opposed many of its practices gave public testimony to its importance in Latin American life. Many who repudiated the Church's decadence nonetheless accepted the validity of the Catholic faith. Others who rejected the Church's too-frequent corruption never gave serious thought to denying their own Catholicism.

Perhaps the outstanding example of this kind of thinking is the Liberator, Simón Bolívar. Despite his personal scepticism, as president he felt compelled to attend mass regularly, endow convents, honor bishops, and try to establish relations with the Holy See. Moreover, as Mecham notes, "there is little doubt that the political experiences of the Liberator converted him to Catholicism."[38] Indeed, the foremost study of the revolutionary period claims that the independence movement itself, particularly during its early stages, was informed by "a spirit of religious affirmation. . . . It strengthened itself by its defense of Catholicism in the struggle with French Jacobinism."[39] The same author points up the religious significance of the famous Indian insurrection led by Tupac Amaru. "Not only among the Indians and the cultivated mixed class to which he belonged, but in the masses, the Christian religion and the Catholic liturgy had penetrated deeply. The revolution, in its progress, might have substituted an Inca for the King, but it was not possible to think of the restoration of the cult of the Sun."[40]

Latin American thinkers have been unanimous in emphasizing the importance of religion. Domingo Sarmiento, a militant anti-clerical and a Freemason, repeatedly stressed the "civilizing" contributions of religious adherence. His compatriot, Juan B. Alberdi, also a classic nineteenth-century Liberal, noted that "without religion, man is not a whole man. . . ."[41] Esteban Echeverría also raised his voice in behalf of religion. He noted that religious commitment was an incentive to morality and civilization and decried the Argentine Revolution's lack of religious content. Philosophers may be able to dispense with religion, he warned, but never the people.[42]

Opposition to the Church was directed toward its secular and not its religious activities. The reforms sought to break the Church's hold on education, to weaken its influence by assuming control of some of its huge wealth, to drive it out of practical politics, but not to smother the religion. The great reformers such as Benito Juárez of Mexico, Eloy Afaro of Ecuador, and even José Batlle y Ordóñez of Uruguay considered themselves Catholics. Even in Mexico, where

[38] Mecham, *Church and State in Latin America,* pp. 120, 121.

[39] Belaúnde, *Bolívar,* p. 87.

[40] *Ibid.*, p. 67.

[41] Quoted in William Rex Crawford, *A Century of Latin American Thought* (rev. ed.; Cambridge, Mass.: Harvard University Press, 1961), p. 29.

[42] *Ibid.*, p. 16.

an anti-Church policy was developed into a major plank of revolutionary doctrine, the Church and religion have demonstrated their staying power; neither was destroyed. Scarcely thirty years after the outbreak of the Mexican Revolution, a presidential candidate, Manuel Avila Camacho, was to dramatize this profound truth when he responded to a question on the Church issue with the words, "Yo soy creyente" (I am a Believer).

The Latin American people are Catholic almost by definition. The long history of vociferous anti-clericalism merely attests to the strength of Catholicism. Moreover, an anti-clerical is not necessarily an anti-Christian, and a Latin anti-clerical is most assuredly not. Tannenbaum makes the point succinctly: "The people have remained Catholic, and the Latin American who professes anti-clericalism often is married in church, dies in the faith and his children are baptized as if he had never fallen under the influence of the French philosophers of the eighteenth century or the Marxists of the nineteenth and twentieth centuries."[43]

Superimposed upon this intense adherence to Catholicism among Latin Americans is a relevant political factor: the geographic omnipresence of the Catholic religion throughout Latin America. As the basic texts are fond of reiterating, and rightly so, the Catholic religion and the institutional Church are key unifying factors in Latin America. In an age of rampant nationalism a common religious faith continues to bind together nationalistic Brazilians, proud Argentines, haughty Peruvians, and aggressive Venezuelans. The religion tends to counteract separatist tendencies and to promote continental unity. A common religious devotion has obvious political overtones for parties which claim to be both Christian and strongly internationalist.[44]

THE CHURCH AND THE PARTIES

Theoretically, the Roman Catholic Church neither sponsors nor supports any specific political party or movement. Catholics are able, and in fact are urged, to take an active part in any political party

[43] Frank Tannenbaum, *Ten Keys to Latin America* (New York: Alfred A. Knopf, 1962), p. 63.

[44] For observations on the unifying impact of religion and its importance, see Berle, *Latin America: Diplomacy and Reality*, p. 137, and Eduardo Santos, "Latin American Realities," *Foreign Affairs*, XXXIV (Jan., 1956), 247.

they choose. The Church, supposedly, does not impose upon its communicants a specific opinion in temporal matters. Political parties are within the purview of Caesar, not God. Catholics may and do position themselves along all points of the political spectrum. In the words of a Latin American commentator, the Church "only asks them, and this includes reminding them, to form sane judgments in the light of the faith and of Christian morality."[45]

In sum, the Church sets only two criteria for Catholics, one negative and one positive. The negative forbids the Catholic to support any party whose doctrine and conduct are contrary to the laws of God and the Church. The positive requires the Catholic to choose a party which guarantees that the rights of the person remain inviolate, not only in theory, but also in practice.[46] The two, of course, are really opposite sides of the same religious medal.

In point of fact, however, these conditions are not so bland as they appear. The Church has condemned political movements. The best-known action, of course, is its stand against Communist parties, but similar condemnations have been issued against Action Française and other groups. The point, obviously, is that the theoretical conditions set out by the Church itself do have practical significance and do insert the Church into the political sphere.

The Latin American Church has always been part of the political picture. The Conservative parties have been closely allied with the Church; indeed, "Catholic party" and "Conservative party" have been synonymous terms throughout much of Latin American history. The price for Church support has usually meant that a party must at least oppose divorce and the official separation of Church and state and defend a system of parochial schools. The Church often went beyond these demands, however, to include protection of the Church's land-holdings, opposition to Protestant proselytizing, protection of the oligarchical ruling class, and, generally, maintenance of the status quo.

The relationship between the Christian Democratic parties and the Church has not crystallized to the point where permanent conclusions are possible. The parties are still relatively young, and the traditional Conservative parties, though rapidly declining, still exist in some nations and continue to reap the unofficial blessing of at

[45] Jesús de Orbe y Urquiza, *Acción Católica* (México, D. F.: Editorial Patria, 1950), p. 493.

[46] *Ibid.*, p. 494.

least some sectors of the Church. Moreover, the Church is really not so overtly political as it once was, and patterns are not so obvious. Nevertheless, one Social Christian writing in 1956 listed the Roman Catholic hierarchy among the three main obstacles to the success of the parties, and another writer has said that "after 1954 Christian Socialists have had little in common with the political thesis of the Catholic Church."[47]

It is significant that the parties have achieved greatest success in nations where the Church is either liberal, as in Chile, or weak, as in Venezuela. The Chilean Church has a carefully nurtured reputation for its socially enlightened attitudes. The Venezuelan Church is most noteworthy for its lack of influence; it has not been a real force in politics since the Federal War of the nineteenth century destroyed its wealth and power.

An important factor in its relationship with the Church is the movement's strong aversion to being called a tool of the Church. One conservative Chilean cleric claims that practice "has shown that the Christian Democratic Party has not known how to understand the severe admonishments of the ecclesiastical hierarchy. . . ."[48] The non-confessional nature of the parties is placed high on the list of characteristics in party manifestos and programs. Christian Democrats repeatedly assert that the movement has no official association with the institutionalized Church and that many non-Catholics have supported and joined the Christian Democratic cause. The speeches and writings of the movement seldom mention the institutionalized Church and, in fact, the movement reveals a strong undercurrent of anti-clericalism. This has often been condemned by party leaders. Echoing the words of Lenin on left-wing Communism, one commentator has dubbed Social Christian anti-clericalism as the movement's "infantile disorder."[49]

[47] "Latin America Revisited," *Christian Democratic Review*, VI (May, 1956), 16; "The Enigma of Latin America's Christian Socialists," *CIF Reports*, V (Feb., 1966), 22.

[48] Jorge Iván Hübner Gallo, "Catholic Social Justice, Authoritarianism, and Class Stratification," *The Conflict Between Church and State in Latin America*, ed. Fredrick B. Pike (New York: Alfred A. Knopf, 1964), p. 206.

[49] Arístides Calvani, Lecture at the Instituto de Formación Demócrata Cristiana (Caracas, May 11, 1965). See also Ambrosio Romero Carranza, *¿Qué es la Democracia Cristiana?* (Buenos Aires: Ediciones del Atlántico, 1956), p. 213, who warns that the aconfessional character of the parties should not be permitted to degenerate into crass anti-clericalism.

The Church has never openly supported the Latin American Christian Democratic parties. It is quite impossible, of course, to analyze comprehensively the activities of village priests, many of whom have undoubtedly supported the cause, but official Church pronouncements have not been noticeably effusive. In the two presidential campaigns in which Frei ran, the Church maintained official neutrality, as it had during the campaigns of Caldera in Venezuela and Cornejo Chávez in Peru. No national hierarchy in the continent has ever given its official blessing to the Christian Democratic parties. The Argentine Church, as a matter of fact, issued a special letter, signed by two cardinals and twenty-two bishops, which officially rejected any tie with that nation's Christian Democratic party when it was formed in 1955: "We can declare that the Argentine Episcopate has not accepted, nor can it ever accept, any understanding with any political party to defend the liberties and the rights of the Church. . . . We do not want any other arms or any other force than the force of truth with which Jesus Christ armed us against earthly powers. . . ."[50]

The official stand, of course, does not tell the entire story. In some nations and in some instances parties or individuals have apparently gained the support of the Church and certainly of significant persons or groups within the Church. One source has noted that some Church officials "worked behind the scenes" to gather votes for an expected AD-COPEI candidate in Venezuela before the 1963 presidential elections.[51] Much perturbation resulted when the papal nuncio provided asylum for Caldera when he was being pursued by the Pérez Jiménez government. Indeed, one North American has stated baldly that "the Church has been able to work through COPEI."[52] Moreover, it seems clear that groups within the Salvadorian, Nicaraguan, Paraguayan, and Peruvian Churches have, in varying degrees, favored the Christian Democratic parties of those nations. In addition, it is a well-known fact that many of the more progressive clergy at all levels have shown a marked affinity for Social Christian politics. It may be supposed that Church support of Christian Democracy will increase in the degree that national Conservative parties decline and are not replaced by other Conservative political organizations.

[50] "Prelates Reject Argentine Party," *New York Times*, July 14, 1955, p. 7.

[51] *Hispanic American Report*, XV (Oct., 1962), 726.

[52] Edwin Lieuwen, *Venezuela* (New York: Oxford University Press, 1961), p. 167.

The possibility of overt Church support or approval presents serious problems for Christian Democrats. Church endorsement of the old Conservative parties was a factor in their decline, and even a socially progressive Church might prove to be a practical disadvantage to Christian Democrats. Indeed, even if the parties were to work to maintain their disassociation from the Church, their efforts might be futile if the Church were to insist upon offering its support. The obvious dilemma of the movement is that it must try to reap the benefits of Catholicism without compromising its own independence or political integrity by being popularly associated with the Catholic Church. If the scant data allows any conclusions, the most valid would be that the parties benefit most by a socially conscious or weak Church, which maintains meticulous official neutrality. The possibility of Christian Democratic identification with the Church has been discussed in a recent North American study, which comes to a similar conclusion.

> Will an identity between Catholic and Christian Democrat be established as there was in the past between Conservative and Catholic? A definitive answer is probably not possible at this time, but the indications are to the contrary. Christian Democratic leaders generally profess a personal adherence to the Church, but so do leaders of other groups. Christian Democratic leaders claim the social doctrine of the Church as their particular source of inspiration, but they emphasize the absence of any organizational connection between their parties and the Church. In most countries the movements are of relatively recent origin, and it may be too early to undertake an appraisal of their impact. Their ideological commitments, however, suggest that traditional Christian teachings are adaptable to new situations, and in this connection the movements may reflect the abiding force of the Church.[53]

CHRISTIAN DEMOCRATS AND THE CATHOLIC RIGHT

The Christian Democratic parties have been making steady progress in Catholic circles, but they have by no means won the backing of the entire Catholic community. Some of the most intransigent and vociferous opposition comes from the Latin American Catholic Right. Churchmen have occasionally interceded, but always without

[53] John J. TePaske and Sydney Nettleton Fisher (eds.), *Explosive Forces in Latin America* (Columbus: Ohio State University Press, 1964), p. 54.

success. Conservative Catholics, both lay and cleric, are horror-struck at the progressive tendencies of the parties and accuse them of crypto-Communism. The Christian Democrats have made precious few inroads into this staunchly conservative sector. Even in a few cases where they have been able to benefit from a vacuum on the traditional Right, the support they have won is weak, at best, and ready to bolt the party.[54] The distrust and open hostility of conservative Catholics is demonstrated by the failures of Social Christians in the national Catholic universities in Chile and Venezuela. In Chile, the last university to swing to the Christian Democratic camp was the Catholic University, and in Venezuela the Copeyanos have been frustrated by an independent slate in the Catholic Andrés Bello University.

Before proceeding further, it should be noted that there do remain a few issues on which all Catholics agree. There may be some difference in degree of commitment or some divergence on procedures, but, in the main, both Social Christians and their right-wing brethren staunchly support religious education and adamantly oppose divorce and birth control. In Latin America, as elsewhere, these issues are planks on which both forces "join together against the world."[55] These areas are rather limited, however, and the general atmosphere is one of cold disdain if not vehement hostility.

The Christian Democrats are accused of theological heresy and political Communism. The Peruvian rightist press, for instance, has referred to the Social Christians as "comunistas de sacristía."[56] A Bolivian explains the cries of "Communist" by suggesting that "those interested in maintaining the established order see in every social christian a Communist wolf covered with the skin of a Christian sheep."[57] Christian Democratic planks such as state planning, support of labor unions and the right to strike, recognition of the class struggle, cooperation with Communist parties, and repudiation of

[54] See Mario Einaudi and François Goguel, *Christian Democracy in Italy and France* (Notre Dame, Ind.: University of Notre Dame Press, 1952), p. 220, for a description of a similar situation in post-war France. The Social Christian Popular Republican Movement had reaped a significant number of traditional Catholic votes in 1945 and 1946, but as soon as the Catholic Conservative Gaullist party was formed, the MRP lost these votes and went into decline.

[55] Fogarty, *Christian Democracy in Western Europe*, p. 5.

[56] *Una Tercera Posición . . .* (Lima: Editorial Universitaria, 1960), p. 53.

[57] Remo Di Natale, *América Latina Hoy: Esquemas Populares Demócrata Cristianos* (Caracas: Editorial Nuevo Orden, 1964), p. 11.

the Franco regime are Communistic in the eyes of the Catholic Right. A Chilean has charged that the Christian Democratic party has clearly cut all ties with anything that could be called Catholic.

> In its position of academic leftism, the Falange reveals its impregnation by Marxian socialist value judgments. There is no other explanation for the fact that both the Falangists and the international communists pay primary attention to economic problems. For the Falangist, the most urgent and pressing consideration is the solution of this type of problem. They are willing to postpone consideration of the religious and spiritual needs of the people. The secularism of their policies is characteristic of the attitudes of Leftist Catholics, who object to the traditional values and label them "clerical," who pretend that it is not possible to go back to the status quo of the middle ages, and who maintain that religious questions are no longer uppermost and that the state should concern itself only with providing for the material needs of the workers.[58]

The Christian Democratic response to such attacks is no less vitriolic.[59] One Social Christian calls for the end of "hypocritical holiness," of "unctuous phrases" and the "cheap meekness" which characterize many who display an affinity for clericalism.[60] They accuse the Catholic Right of preoccupation with formal ceremony and external practice and of being unable or unwilling to translate religious faith into religious practice in the social sphere. "Catholicism of the right," says one Social Christian review, "is falsified by prejudices, mental limitations and the defense of special interests. It is a perfect example of how religious and moral sentiments can be subordinated to the economic requirements of one social class."[61] Right-wing Catholics hide their selfish interests behind the cross, say Social Christians, and see physical force as the only possible answer to Communism.

Christian Democrats charge the right-wing groups with finding their greatest support among the Catholic bourgeoisie who expound

[58] Hübner Gallo, "Catholic Social Justice, . . . ," p. 201.

[59] See Romero Carranza, *¿Qué es la Democracia Cristiana?*, p. 107, who cautions his Christian Democratic brethren to be more charitable with their right-wing co-religionists.

[60] Jaime Castillo Velasco, *El Problema Comunista* (Santiago de Chile: Editorial del Pacífico, 1955), p. 163.

[61] An editorial from *Política y Espíritu* quoted in *Christian Democratic Review*, II (Aug. 16, 1952), 7.

Catholic Liberalism. This group, warns a Social Christian, "with their indifference, their elaborate atheism and their religious hypocrisy are much more anti-Christian and much more corrupt . . . than the poor."[62] The Catholic bourgeoisie have always gravitated to the conservative sectors and have always seen the proletariat as a threat to the established social order. Amoroso Lima has explained why: "Industrialists, soldiers, servants, women, the old and devout are most likely to suffer this evil, just because they live more isolated from events, in the world of ideas, of discipline, of the past, of imagination, of the home and of devotion. These are not causes which justify. They merely explain, nothing more. The great task remains to educate, to enlist and to catechise."[63]

Right-wing political parties still attract many Catholics throughout Latin America. In Bolivia, the Socialist Falange advertises its Catholicity and numbers many declared Catholics among its adherents. In Mexico, the rightist, Catholic Partido de Acción Nacional was for many years the semi-official voice of Catholicism and still remains the most powerful of the minor parties. Though clearly on the decline, the Chilean and Ecuadorian Conservative parties still wield some influence. The Colombian Conservative party has shown some progressive evolution, but its right wing includes many of the nation's most reactionary Catholics. After the fall of Perón in Argentina, two right-wing Catholic parties were formed, the Christian Democratic Federal Union and the Blue and White party. The two later merged. The evolution of the old Catholic Civic Union of Uruguay into the Christian Democratic party caused a split and the formation of the right-wing Unión Cívica Católica. In Venezuela, where most Catholics belong to the Social Christian-COPEI, Catholic Conservatives have on several occasions founded new parties, although they have not been successful in maintaining a permanent organization.

In addition to parties organized around traditional Conservative principles, right-wing Latin American Catholics have all too often been attracted to fascist and "integralist" groups. Many Catholics found a home in the Chilean Nazi party during the forties, and the infamous Unión Nacional Sinarquista of Mexico was very attractive to the Catholic right. The contemporary anti-Semitic, fascistic

[62] Castillo Velasco, *El Problema Comunista,* p. 140.
[63] Amoroso Lima, "The Problem of Labor," p. 525.

Tacuara of Argentina advocates a "national, Christian social revolution" and counts many Catholics among its adherents.[64] A Bolivian Social Christian has eloquently explained why his movement repudiates all those who, like fascists, would attempt to destroy democracy.

> And among them are found the representatives of that mixture of politics and religion that is called integralism or Catholic totalitarianism whose champions are the tyrants Franco and the Viet Namese Ngo Dinh Diem. This idea, imported from the continent by a small group of foreign priests, is, like all fascistic movements, a negation of human dignity and of liberty. It constitutes the product of an inferiority complex, of a pathologically pessimistic concept of man, according to which the human intelligence is dangerous and ought to be buried by submitting itself to theology. Projected into the political sphere, this thesis conduces to the implantation of a sectarian, inquisitorial and persecuting government which is against all those who do not profess the official religion.[65]

[64] See *Hispanic American Report*, XVII (June, 1964), 360.
[65] Di Natale, *América Latina Hoy*, p. 92.

Relations with Other Political Forces 9

CHRISTIAN DEMOCRACY—A CENTER MOVEMENT

The Christian Democratic parties call themselves revolutionary; their opponents often dub them communistic or fascistic. But observers correctly typify them as being parties of the Center, their exact position varying from country to country and from time to time. This game of exact placement of parties on the political spectrum is risky, however, for it can give only a rough indication at best and at times can be clearly misleading. A moderately left-wing position in Chile would be absolutely revolutionary in Ecuador. A Nicaraguan revolutionary program would only be moderately progressive in the volatile Dominican Republic. The mere fact that it opposes Stroessner makes the otherwise moderate Paraguayan movement potentially revolutionary. Moreover, the parties are in constant evolution and their positions change.

Two factors complicate the task of accurately characterizing Christian Democracy. First, the adjective "Christian" is often as important in attracting members as is the program or political aim, and consequently the Social Christian parties have traditionally attracted an extremely heterogeneous electorate. This, coupled with the structure which characterizes many of the parties, leads to a diversity of political aims and directions within the parties. A constant balancing is the result, and changes in leadership may alter the position of a party. More often, however, the result is the juxtaposition of contradictory tendencies and seemingly opposed planks in the platform of a single party.

The heterogeneity of the parties is only part of the explanation; the other factor is found in the very basis of the Christian Democratic theory and doctrine. Succinctly stated, the revolutionary means which the Latin Americans espouse are in large part based on conservative premises and have an essentially conservative goal. Make no mistake, however, the Social Christians agree with, and sometimes transcend, other Latin American leftists in their programs and political strategies. Still, as a movement whose very *raison d'être* is in no small part the rejection of Marxian Socialism, Christian Democracy by definition repudiates the reigning and universally accepted concept of a liberal or progressive ideology. The modern political universe has been defined by Marx, and Christian Democracy rejects the Marxist belief in the unlimited perfectibility of man and, concomitantly, unlimited progress in an egalitarian society; it rejects the assertion that the class struggle and the omnipotent state are the only means of resolving the dilemma of the bourgeois society. It repudiates economic determinism and philosophical materialism. In sum, it rejects the philosophical position of the political Left and instead recommends a program of leftist means to achieve essentially conservative ends.

This position does not, of course, imply the maintenance of the status quo; the pursuit of a more just and more individual-oriented society will lead to the achievement of a new stability, which will supersede present instability. Critics have interpreted this goal as a concealed yearning for a return to the Church-dominated Middle Ages; though this is not wholly accurate, it is not totally in error, either. Christians do see naturally evolved hierarchy as being both reasonable and desirable. They do hope for a society in which the influence of the spiritual will again assume an important place in the scheme of things and for the cessation of the idolatrous claims of heretical nationalism. Christian Democrats are conservative because they value stability, but they are liberal and revolutionary because they believe that this stability is to be achieved in the future after the creation of a new synthesis combining the best of both the Middle Ages and modern times. In sum, Christian Democratic parties are difficult to place on the political spectrum because they repudiate the defining criteria.

One writer has stated the problem rather differently: "One cannot tell if they mean to replace semi-feudal structures and Capitalism with Socialism (thus being a true leftist party), or if they are trying to establish governments in which private property, a luxury economy, Socialist structures and effective national sovereignty co-exist (thus being a center party)."[1]

Although the Latin American Christian Democrats have never

[1] Mario Monteforte Toledo, "The Enigma of Latin America's Christian Socialists," *CIF Reports*, V (Feb., 1966), 22.

actually formulated their position as it has been stated here, there is little doubt that they are chary of a facile Right-Left dichotomy. They are fond of proclaiming that they look neither Right nor Left, but *adelante* (straight ahead). To be for social justice, they declare, is not to be disruptive of the society, but is, conversely, the only way to save the values of Christian tradition.

It is nevertheless true, in terms of the generally accepted criteria, that Latin American Christian Democratic parties must be typified as being Center or Center-Left, though their distance from the center varies. The Dominican Partido Revolucionario Social Cristiano leans farther to the Left than most of the parties. Its vociferous condemnation of capitalism and Yankee imperialism is matched nowhere, and its labor affiliate, the Confederación Autónomo de Sindicatos Cristianos (CASC), is the strongest and one of the most vocal members of the Latin American Christian labor union movement. The best example of the party's leftist sympathies was the decision of the majority faction to back the revolutionary, anti-militarist, "constitutional" forces during the 1965 struggle. Among the older groups, the Chilean party has most consistently assumed a leftist position. It opposed the government for almost fifteen years before it came to power in 1964 and often cooperated officially with the Communists. The Social Christian attacks on the class structure of Chile rivaled the Communists in intensity and scope.

Many Christian Democratic parties have had a history of shifting positions. The Venezuelan party began its existence as a moderate party, shifted to the Right, and then demonstrated an increasing tendency to lean to the Left. Three main factors explain the COPEI evolution; its experience during the Pérez Jiménez tyranny, its strong and generally progressive student affiliate, and its present position as opposition to the Leoni government. The Peruvian party has also experienced marked and frequent changes of direction. Its origins were Center, if not Center-Right, but new leadership during the late fifties and early sixties introduced leftist tendencies. When this leadership was overturned, the party assumed a more moderate bent. In the spring of 1965, however, the previous progressive leaders regained power, and the party accordingly moved to the Left again and became probably the most radical of Peru's important political organizations. Under the new leadership, the party moved continually further Left, and internal problems developed between the radical and moderate elements in late 1966 and early 1967.

The Brazilian party has shown the same vicissitudes because

of switches in leadership; it has been called both Socialist and Conservative. The Uruguayan party has demonstrated a steady evolution from a Conservative Catholic to a moderate Social Christian party. The Argentine party moved dramatically toward the Left when new leadership assumed power; its continuing dialogue and cooperation with the Peronistas make it one of the continent's most radical movements. The oppositional attitude of the Bolivian, Mexican, Nicaraguan, and Paraguayan parties makes them revolutionary, although none, with the possible exception of the Bolivian party, has proposed particularly leftist programs.

The Cuban movement's opposition to Castro's Communism and its exile status make it difficult to place, but it seems to be a Center or Center-Right organization. The Guatemalan group began as a Right or Center-Right party but has moved steadily to the Left, and new leadership has hastened its leftward tendency by reorganizing the structure of the party and by purging many of the old Conservatives. The Salvadorian party was originally a group of the moderate Right, but its role as the main opposition of the government has propelled it to the Left. Even the Conservative Ecuadorian Movimiento, which has been refused ODCA recognition because of its rightist stance, assumed a progressively vocal position against that nation's military junta. The other Ecuadorian group, the Partido Demócrata Cristiano, is clearly leftist.

COALITION AND COOPERATION

North Americans see cooperation among democratic sectors as the salvation of Latin America, and they often call for a united front against both traditional autocratic and modern totalitarian challenges. Indeed, Latin American experience illustrates that democratic movements have often joined to overthrow tyrants and have even, though infrequently, cooperated in protecting a democratic regime. Latin American Christian Democratic parties have sometimes cooperated with other political groups even though their theory outlines little positive policy for coalition or cooperation; practice, therefore, has varied. Some of the parties have forsworn any type of cooperation. The Panamanian party, for instance, claims to be the only truly democratic political movement in the nation and claims that cooperation with other forces would dilute its message and be an affront to the Panamanian people. On the other hand, the Guatemalan and Salvadorian parties seem to have accepted the principle of cooperation and have applied it relatively often.

As a general rule, however, the Christian Democratic parties seem more chary than most of participating in electoral, parliamentary, or governmental pacts. This caution is the result of party ideology, which often precludes the possibility of permanent cooperation even with other democratic forces. The wariness is also the consequence of the youth of the movement; it is new enough to the Latin American scene to view alliance with the old parties as a possible source of contamination. The parties, however, have entered into a number of agreements with other groups, and this section will investigate some of those.

Few of the parties have officially outlined their policy on alliances and cooperation. Those that have formulated policies have stated that they will consider compacts only so long as they do not transgress the ideology of the party.[2] Occasionally, the parties have tacitly or explicitly accepted the support of other groups but have rejected formal accords. An international congress of the Latin American movement has formulated a negative policy concerning collaboration: no party should cooperate with a government which had gained power through force except when it had overthrown a previous dictatorship, and even in this situation, there should be popular representation in the government.[3] Caldera has set out two conditions for collaboration with other democratic groups. "One, a clear and concise definition with regard to Communist forces who offer social change, but deny to man the use of representative democracy and the inviolable guarantee of human rights; the other, respect for the spiritual values which inform our movement even when they do not share them as the base of their philosophical position."[4]

The strongest approval of cooperation and the formation of coalitions emanated from the Third World Conference held in Santiago in 1961. The resolution suggested by the Venezuelan COPEI was in-

[2] See, for instance, Movimiento Social Cristiano del Ecuador, *Manifiesto del 13 de Noviembre y Declaración de Principios* (Quito: Editorial Chimborazo, 1951), p. 16, and "Declaración de Principios de la Falange Nacional," *Política y Espíritu*, III (June, 1948), 146.

[3] *Congreso Internacional de la Democracia Cristiana: Anales del quinto . . .* (Lima: Editorial Universitaria, 1960), p. 122.

[4] Rafael Caldera, "Introducción," in Aldo Moro's *La Democracia Cristiana por el Gobierno del País y el Desarrollo Democrático de la Sociedad Italiana* (Roma: A.G.I., 1962), p. 14.

tended to gain approval of COPEI's coalition with Betancourt's Acción Democrática. The resolution said that the conference:

> Considers it commendable that the Christian Democratic parties study, within the possible circumstances of each country and without necessarily evolving agreements of an electoral character, the convenience of collaboration or understanding with those advanced social currents which, even without being founded on a Christian inspiration, are disposed to struggle, respecting the spiritual values which inspire us, for the achievement of social justice within the defense of democracy and of liberty."[5]

Christian Democrats see several advantages to collaboration. They obviously realize that cooperation is a practical method for achieving broad social and political progress, for maintaining political democracy where it already exists, and for realizing social justice. In addition, alliances often serve the interests of the parties. Participation in government gained through collaboration with another group may result in a wider dissemination of Social Christian ideas. Alliances may afford the party an opportunity to enter sectors not previously penetrated; for example, COPEI collaboration with the Acción Democrática before the Venezuelan election of 1958 provided the party with its first solid contact within the labor unions. Christian Democratic cooperation with the Peronistas in Argentina has been justified as a method of penetrating, and eventually winning over, the alienated masses. Last, pacts can clarify the intentions of rival groups: commenting on the Italian *apertura a sinistra* in which the Christian Democrats sought a governmental compact with the Nenni Socialists, Caldera applauds the "generous effort" of the Italian Social Christians and points out that the alliance will be a test of the sincerity of the Socialists. If they do not offer loyal assistance, the Italian people will know that their vocal concern for the populace was a sham.[6]

It is very important, of course, to make a careful distinction between political doctrine and political tactics. Doctrinal considerations might obviate permanent cooperation with Communists, for example, but tactical considerations may occasionally make such alliances advantageous, and even necessary. Both COPEI and the Communists formed part of the united opposition to Pérez Jiménez; rightists and

[5] Quoted in *ibid.*, pp. 13, 14.
[6] *Ibid.*, p. 15.

the Cuban Social Christian movement were united against Castro. Different situations call for and justify varying expedients, and Latin American Christian Democrats have recognized this basic principle of political reality.

CHRISTIAN DEMOCRATS AND COMMUNISTS

The rather conservative *Christian Democratic Review* once noted that several Latin American Christian Democratic parties had occasionally joined with Communists to oppose dictatorships or the traditional parties in Latin America. The journal, published by Central European exiles, was wary of "this peculiar characteristic of Latin American Christian Democracy, this insensitiveness to the Communist danger. . . ."[7]

The appraisal was both right and wrong. Several of the parties have cooperated with Communist or Communist-leaning groups; the most notable example is the Chilean party's long history of cooperation and even parliamentary alliance with Communists. On the other hand, most of the parties clearly reject collaboration with Communism in both theory and practice, perhaps the best example being the repudiation of the Communists by the Cuban Movimiento. The journal's appraisal was clearly wrong in its assertion that Christian Democrats are "insensitive" to Communism. The movement is well aware, indeed sometimes preoccupied, with Communism and emphasizes its role as the main force opposing Communism in the struggle for leadership in Latin America. Often the Christian Democrats seem to forget the existence of other political forces in Latin America and over-simplify the continent's politics by seeing an essentially clear dichotomy—Christians versus Communists. It becomes an "either-or" proposition; either the progressive fraternity of Christian Democracy will save the continent, or it will fall to the godless forces of alien Communism. But the analysis of the *Christian Democratic Review* was correct in its observation that Social Christians do not look upon cooperation with Communists as impossible. One North American publication has said that "Catholic attitudes in Latin America display an exasperating ambivalence toward Communism."[8] Many Christian Democrats are crudely anti-Communist whereas

[7] *Christian Democratic Review*, VI (Jan.-Feb., 1956), 19.

[8] John J. TePaske and Sydney Nettleton Fisher (eds.), *Explosive Forces in Latin America* (Columbus: Ohio State University Press, 1964), p. 56.

others look to the possibility of peaceful co-existence on both international and national levels.

Most of the proclaimed progressive forces of the continent see Communism as a result of the social inequities and economic poverty of Latin America. Communism is depicted as a sickness of the body politic, as an effect and not a cause. The cause is an economically insecure society characterized by low living standards and by gross injustices bred by traditional societal patterns of the Latin American nations. One critic struck close to the mark when he berated the Social Christians for seeing "Communism more as the embodiment of an aspiration for social justice than as a threat of destruction to the Christian world."[9] The response of the Christian who holds this view of Communism is that the cause should be eradicated and that preoccupation with the effect should be avoided. Social revolution and economic growth are the answers; in short, to the Christian Democrat, true anti-Communism implies social activity. "The doctrine of the Catholic Church does not separate the socio-economic question from the 'Communist' struggle. If one is to remain within its spirit, it is not possible to develop 'anti-Communist' action without operating in the area of social transformation."[10] The struggle against Communism, moreover, cannot become a rationalization for the protection of the present order; the order has sown the seeds of Communism and continues to fertilize the soil in which it grows and must, therefore, be ended. Christian Democracy has no intention of battling Communism by defending predatory capitalism. Christian Democrats also believe that it would be a profound error to think that Communism can be defeated by force. "Never in history," notes a Social Christian, "has force been efficacious against ideas."[11]

Christian Democrats deny that anti-Communism is the whole purpose of their movement. They are, assuredly, anti-Communistic but only insofar as this posture is a logical implication of their doctrine.

[9] Jorge Iván Hübner Gallo, "Catholic Social Justice, Authoritarianism, and Class Stratification," Fredrick B. Pike (ed.), *The Conflict Between Church and State in Latin America* (New York: Alfred A. Knopf, 1964), p. 198.

[10] Jaime Castillo Velasco, *El Problema Comunista* (Santiago de Chile: Editorial del Pacífico, 1955), p. 76. In support of the Christian Democratic position *vis à vis* the Communists, Castillo calls in statements made by Presidents Truman and Eisenhower (p. 185).

[11] Eduardo Frei Montalva, *Sentido y Forma de una Política* (Santiago de Chile: Editorial del Pacífico, 1951), p. 60.

If Communism were to pass from the Latin American scene immediately, they hold, the movement would not be substantially affected, for theirs is a complete critique of the modern situation and offers a full-fledged response to the dilemmas of the time. The fear of Communism, say the Social Christians, should not and cannot be the catalyst for their success.

In reality, the actions of the two forces are often parallel and their immediate goals often similar. "This is natural," declares one of the movement's most important contemporary ideologues. Both "are working in a society which is lifting itself up after the fall of capitalism. An enormous number of labor union, political and economic goals, both proximate and distant, can be common. It is possible that these common ends will provoke some affinity in the same vein that peculiar characteristics of each one will impede a sustained understanding."[12] The same author later points out three instances where collaboration is hypothetically possible. The first of these is a situation where contacts between Communists and Social Christians are necessary, where they are imposed by the force of circumstances. An example of such a situation is the labor union. Since both groups are able to operate for the betterment of the working man, means should be sought to avoid differences that would undermine effective militancy. The second area of common activity may be in work presenting an advantage of a general sort. Opposition to dictatorships or authoritarian governments is noted as an example, and is depicted as falling within the definition of political tactics. Could the French Catholics, the commentator asks, have refused to struggle against Hitler because the Communists formed part of the opposition? The third area concerns political strategy or cooperation over the long run. To this third hypothetical proposition, the response must be that long-range alliance is impossible, because the national Communist parties are tools of the Soviet Union and do not share the goals of the Christian Democrats.[13]

THE CHILEAN CHRISTIAN DEMOCRATS AND THE COMMUNISTS

The nation where Communist-Christian Democratic cooperation is best exemplified is Chile. The parties there have often formed parliamentary alliances and occasionally joined in other activities, and

[12] Castillo, *El Problema Comunista*, pp. 173, 174.
[13] *Ibid.*, pp. 172, 207–14.

the programs of the two groups have frequently been similar. The Chilean Communists have maintained a steady opposition to the government in power ever since the breakup of the Chilean Popular Front in 1941; the Christian Democrats have also opposed almost continually both President Ibáñez and President Alessandri. The similar stance of the Communists and Christian Democrats has often resulted in both *de facto* and *de jure* collaboration between the two groups. One example of this cooperation was the parliamentary bloc dubbed "TOCOA," Todas Contra Alessandri (All Against Alessandri), in which both parties operated.

The Communists have occasionally publicly attested to their friendship with the Chilean Christian Democrats. Salvador Allende, the 1964 presidential candidate of the Communist-backed Frente de Acción Popular (FRAP), publicly declared during the electoral campaign that he was ready to join a coalition with the Christian Democrats to initiate immediate reforms in a number of areas. The FRAP, in fact, did ultimately support some Frei initiatives. In 1959, the policy committee of the Communist party issued special orders to the directors of *El Siglo*, the party organ, to cease publishing propaganda of an anti-religious nature and to stop attacking the Christian Democratic party. Later, an editorial noted that the Communists were cognizant of the "valuable support" which the Christians had offered them, especially in abrogating the Defense of Democracy law and in supporting national control of Chilean oil. The Social Christians themselves have called attention to the fact that they are the only Chilean party that has consistently maintained relations with the Communists.[14]

Probably the most striking, and controversial, instance of cooperation with the Communists was the major role played by Christian Democrats in fighting the Defense of Democracy law and in eventually obtaining revocation of the legislation. The Law for Permanent Defense of Democracy was passed by the Chilean legislature in 1948 under President Gabriel González Videla; its practical effect was to outlaw the Communist party. It was repealed under President Carlos Ibáñez del Campo in 1958. The Christian Democrats had opposed the law; indeed, a Conservative critic of the Chilean party holds that it was the "main one responsible" for the repeal of the law.[15]

[14] *Hispanic American Report*, XII (Dec., 1959), 564 and XVI (April, 1963), 162.

[15] Hübner Gallo, "Catholic Social Justice," p. 203.

Christian Democratic explanations for opposing the law ranged from the philosophical to the practical. First, said the party, individual Communists should enjoy the same protection afforded others as long as they undertake no overt activity to overthrow the Chilean state. The more widely discussed rationale, however, centered on the practical results of what the Christian Democrats interpreted as a politically imprudent law. If the law were to be applied vigorously and strictly enforced, it could do nothing but gain sympathy for individual Communists, the Communist party, and the Communist cause. Moreover, the law was responsible for forcing some Communists to act clandestinely, and the Chilean Social Christians said that they preferred to fight the opponent in the open. Furthermore, the party claimed that the law was not effective, that Communists continued to function. It was argued that they had the advantage of political martyrdom without the disadvantage of effective prosecution. Finally, said one Chilean Social Christian, the Chilean Communists do not operate, nor have they proposed to operate, in a revolutionary manner. Therefore, the commentator continues, the best response is to follow the advice of Alcide de Gasperi: as long as the Communist party functions according to the rules of the democracy, it should not be the object of repressive laws.[16]

The Chileans are quick to acknowledge that a democracy has the right to defend itself by taking measures against an overtly revolutionary force; circumstances sometimes oblige a government to suppress a threat to its existence. This, however, is seen as the last resort in a democratic regime and should be pursued only when there is a clear indication that the group is utilizing force to subvert the democratic order. Indeed, Radomiro Tomic echoes a decision of the United States Supreme Court when he draws the distinction between advocacy and activity. The Communists, he says, cannot be persecuted for the first, and care should be exercised in defining the second.[17]

Despite the extraordinary cooperation between Christians and Communists in Chile, it should be clearly emphasized that the fundamental differences between the two groups often explode into outright opposition. The Christian Democratic party has been split on

[16] Castillo, *El Problema Comunista*, p. 204. For a short description of the moderation of the Chilean Communists, see Donald W. Bray, "Chile: The Dark Side of Stability," *Studies on the Left*, IV (Fall, 1964), 90–92.

[17] *Ibid.*, p. 167.

this problem, and some sectors interpret cooperation as a grave ideological and practical error. The party ideologue, for instance, proclaims that "legal tolerance of the Communist Party does not signify a cessation of the doctrinal struggle nor a passive or indifferent attitude before the Party."[18] Chilean Social Christians insist that their collaboration with the Communist party has been merely tactical and stress that they would never relinquish independence of action.

The Communists have frequently charged the Chilean party with clericalism and with trying to court the support of right-wing Catholicism during election campaigns. They have also accused the Christian Democrats of being lackeys of North American imperialism. The Christian Democrats have responded that the Chilean Communists are tools of the Soviet Union and would betray the Chilean nation. They frequently point to examples of religious persecution in Communist countries. They accuse the Communist party of being purposefully vague in its programs. Furthermore, say the Christian Democrats, no Christian who understands his religion could be a member of the Communist party. Frei summed up the position of the Chilean party when he observed that the Christian Democrats know the Communists better than any other party. "We have no illusions. We know that we are, in reality, their worst enemies. . . ."[19]

Relations between the Chilean Christians and Communists during the first year and one-half of the Frei administration seem to have remained unchanged. The Communists, within the FRAP coalition, were a part of the opposition but did lend the Frei government support on several key pieces of legislation. The Communist party is still ideologically opposed to the Frei government, but the party has affirmed several planks of Frei's program. The FRAP coalition, for example, supported the constitutional reform of Article 10, which was necessary for the implementation of Frei's agrarian reform, although the Communists attempted to insert more "advanced" modifications into the legislation. The Left also supported the government's tax reform measures, again complaining, however, that it did not go far enough.

The FRAP did, however, oppose the Frei copper legislation and backed, and perhaps instigated, debilitating strikes in the copper mines which plagued the Chilean government during much of 1965 and early 1966. The coalition charged the government with having

[18] *Ibid.*, p. 206.

[19] Frei Montalva, *Sentido y Forma*, "Semblanza."

"delivered the natural basic wealth of Chile to North American capitalistic imperialism." It called for nationalization and expropriation. Even after the tragic murder of striking miners in 1966, however, the FRAP did not dissolve all support of the government, blaming the incident only on the right wing of the Christian Democratic party.[20] Early in 1967, however, the Communists returned to the offensive and led the opposition in the Senate that prohibited Frei from leaving the country and making a planned visit to the United States.

The Communist attitude before the Frei government seems clearly to be dictated by domestic political considerations—supporting the Christian government's legislative initiatives when absolutely necessary, but opposing the government when it seems politically advantageous.

OTHER CHRISTIAN DEMOCRATS AND THE COMMUNISTS

None of the other Latin American Christian Democratic parties have cooperated as extensively as the Chilean party with the Communists. Although collaboration with Communists in other countries has often been similar, the repudiation of the Communists is usually more pronounced than in the Chilean situation.

In Venezuela both the Communists and the Social Christian-COPEI composed part of the unified opposition to the Pérez Jiménez tyranny. Minimal cooperation continued through the provisional government period, but the Communists vociferously opposed the formation of the three-party coalition when Betancourt assumed power in 1959. Later, when the activities of the Communists and the Movimiento de Izquierda Revolucionaria were suspended, the COPEI officially called for the lifting of the ban so as to be able to fight the Communists openly, but it seems that this move was primarily a formality and that, in reality, the Social Christian party was in substantial agreement with Betancourt's decision to suspend the two revolutionary parties. It officially changed its position later. The Guatemalan party has cooperated with the Partido Revolucionario, which is not Communist, but which had stood with the Communist-leaning Arbenz Guzmán regime during the revolution in 1954. In Brazil, the left-wing and highly controversial Paulo de Tarso had

[20] For a discussion of the copper legislation, see *Noticias de Chile* (Santiago de Chile), No. 6, p. 10; for the strike, see "Huelgas y Política," *Visión*, XXX (April, 1966), 13.

looked for Communist-Christian Democratic collaboration during the regime of Goulart. Tarso reflected a marked tendency among numerous sectors of Brazilian Catholic youth to seek a rapprochement with the Communists.

In other nations, legislation resembling the Chilean Defense of Democracy has usually brought a similar, though perhaps less spirited, retort from Christian Democratic parties. In Argentina, the 1962 national convention of the party announced that it "opposed the dictation of a Law for the Defense of Democracy of the same type which existed in Chile."[21] As early as 1946, the Uruguayan party demonstrated its position when its leader, Regules, opposed a measure directed against the Communist party in that country. The legislation would have impinged upon the Communist press. Regules proclaimed that neither a democratic regime, nor his party, nor "the truth of Jesus" needed the help of government functionaries. The task, rather, was the "vocation of saints," not of the Uruguayan government.[22]

In Peru, the Social Christian organization took a stand in 1961 against a Prado government decree limiting the right of Peruvian citizens to travel to and from Communist countries, including Cuba. The candidate for the vice presidency suggested that the government was promoting the wrong measures to combat Communism; the correct method would be to fight "hunger, illiteracy and demagoguery." In a battle over the repeal of a law that outlawed the Communist party of Peru, the Christian Democrats proposed a change in the loosely worded legislation then on the books. Their revision of the law was more specific and outlined a series of strict procedural protections for the accused party.[23]

Although a number of the parties have cooperated on a minimal level with the national Communist parties, many Social Christians have taken a harder line. The movement in international congress, for example, has proclaimed that "the right of a democracy to defend itself is especially applicable in the case of totalitarianism of Marxist inspiration which is dependent on the Russian government." The

[21] "La Convención Nacional de la Democracia Cristiana Argentina en Rosario," *Política y Espíritu*, XVI (Aug., 1962), 35.

[22] Tomás G. Brena, *La Democracia Cristiana en el Uruguay* (Montevideo: Impresora Zorilla de San Martín, 1946), p. 30.

[23] See, *Hispanic American Report*, XV (June, 1962), 348, and Héctor Cornejo Chávez, *Nuevos Principios para un Nuevo Perú* (Lima: Publicaciones de la Juventud Demócrata Cristiana, 1960), p. 172.

congress did, however, caution that these measures should only be undertaken as a last resort; all efforts must be expended before human rights are limited.[24] Caldera defended the decision of the Betancourt coalition to disavow Communist collaboration by pointing out that the Communists proposed a dictatorship, which was foreign to the Venezuelan concept of human dignity. The Costa Rican party program forswears "understandings" or "alliances of any type" with Communists.[25] The Colombian Partido Social Demócrata Cristiano takes a similar position, noting that the two movements inevitably oppose each other in both doctrine and tactics. "The Christian Democrats," continues a Colombian, "are by vocation and principle on the side of the humble people and we cannot pact . . . with those who exploit them for their political ends and who unscrupulously deceive them."[26] The Cuban movement, understandably, had taken an uncompromising position. It calls for the outlawing of the party, the breaking of relations with the Soviet bloc, and the suppression of the militia. It also looks to a program of "decommunization" patterned after the "denazification" program undertaken in West Germany after World War II.[27]

CHRISTIAN DEMOCRATS AND THE PERONISTAS

Equally as interesting and significant as the long record of Christian Democratic-Communist cooperation in Chile is the much shorter, but markedly more intense, collaboration of the Argentine Christian Democratic party with the Peronistas. The Christian party has officially courted the Peronistas since 1961, but the romance began before then.

Although the Partido Demócrata Cristiano was founded only in

[24] *Congresos Internacionales Demócrata-Cristianos* (Santiago de Chile: Editorial del Pacífico, 1957), pp. 221–23.

[25] Partido Demócrata Cristiano de Costa Rica, *1) Toma de posiciones del Partido Demócrata Cristiano—frente al Comunismo, frente al Capitalismo y frente a los regímenes políticos del país. 2) Declaración de principios del Partido Demócrata Cristiano* (San José, n.d.), p. 2.

[26] Francisco De Paula Jaramillo, *La Democracia Cristiana: Una Nueva Perspectiva para Colombia* (Bogotá: Ediciones del Caribe, 1962), p. 26.

[27] Movimiento Demócrata Cristiano de Cuba, *Movimiento Demócrata Cristiano de Cuba* (Miami, 1961), pp. 3–5. See the anti-Communist stand of the Ecuadorian Movimiento in Movimiento Social Cristiano del Ecuador, *Planteamiento de Reformas Constitucionales Bajo el Signo de la Democracia Cristiana* (Quito: Editorial "Fray Jodoco Ricke," 1963), p. 51.

1955, superseding the Movimiento Social Republicano, Social Christians had been actively organized in Argentina since the second decade of the present century. The original leadership of the modern party was moderate, and the organization assumed an essentially middle-of-the-road stance. Internal conflict troubled the party from the very outset, and in 1961 at the party's annual convention in Rosario, the old, moderate leadership was overthrown, and new, more radical leadership under the direction of Horacio Sueldo assumed control of the party.

At the 1962 convention, the party officially launched a *política de apertura* (an "opening policy," that is, an opening of party policy with the purpose of attracting other sectors), which in practice became an *apertura al peronismo.* The new line was to "serve those excluded from the political, economic and social life of the community," a position, noted a commentator, "profoundly rooted in the popular vocation of Argentine Christian Democracy."[28] The new approach was directed to the "national and popular sectors," the Peronistas. Later, the former, moderate leaders issued an official declaration criticizing the new departure, but they pledged continued support of the party. Their criticism, however, had no practical impact, for their influence had totally waned.

The party's new stance is outlined in its platform, in which strong emphasis is placed on political and economic nationalism. The planks include the cancellation of oil development contracts with foreign companies, an end to relations with the International Monetary Fund, the nationalization of bank deposits, and the institution of exchange control. The party has been vociferous in its condemnations of the United States. It assumes a thinly disguised anti-military posture. It issues frequent pleas for the strengthening of labor organizations and for an end to government intervention in the unions.

The Partido Demócrata Cristiano has succeeded in working out some cooperative projects with the Peronistas, although there has been no permanent cooperation on a nation-wide scale. In late 1962, the Christians joined with the Peronistas, the Intransigent Radicals, and others to put together a National and Popular Front, but the Christians later withdrew from the negotiations. Just before the 1963 presidential elections, the Social Christians offered their presidential candidacy to Raúl Matera, who had previously been the secretary of the coordinating and supervisory council of the Peronist Justicialista

[28] "La Convención Nacional de la Democracia Cristiana Argentina . . . ," p. 35.

movement. The military vetoed the candidacy of Matera, however, and Sueldo carried the party's banner in the elections. There have also been charges that Sueldo has consulted with Perón in Madrid.[29] In 1962, when the Christian Democrats announced their *apertura*, the Peronistas responded with enthusiasm. The party, as a matter of fact, was forced to close its registration books in Jujuy Province because so many Peronistas were joining the party. In La Rioja Province, the collaboration between the two groups for the February, 1962, elections produced the Frente Demócrata Cristiano Justicialista. In early 1966, the Argentine Christian Democrats joined with the Peronistas, Arturo Frondizi's Movimiento de Integración y Desarrollo, the Intransigent Radicals, and the Socialists to discuss common action against the Illia government and the possibility of a Center-Left opposition.

The Christian Democrats offer several explanations for their decision to court the Peronista masses and the old Peronista party leaders. One, of course, is the party's "popular vocation," which is seen as an essential part of Social Christian militancy. The party proclaims that it is out to convince the masses that the material gains which characterized the Perón period can be achieved without the old *Líder*, who brought tyranny and misery as part of his rule. Moreover, the Christian Democrats suggest, the Peronista movement is bound to decay and fragment without the leadership of the dictator, and the party must save the masses from the traditional Communist and Trotskyite parties which are also anxiously courting the Peronistas. In short, the Social Christians claim that they are simply trying to fulfill their declared goal of redeeming the masses.

On a rather more immediate and practical level, the Peronistas compose an extremely large electorate; their support could very well be the means by which Argentine Christian Democracy could rise to the heights of governmental power. Moreover, it would be quite impossible to form a large, successful party representing the masses without at least working with the Peronista electorate, if not with the previous dictator's representatives. Even if the Social Christians do not succeed in weaning away a significant group while the Peronistas continue to function, it is possible that the Peronista party might be outlawed again in the future; in that case, the Christian Democratic party would be the logical home of the former members of the prohibited organizations.

[29] *Hispanic American Report*, XVII (March, 1964), 74.

The Christian Democratic campaign to attract the Peronistas has not been completely successful, although there is little doubt that the party has succeeded in garnering significant numbers of new supporters and militants. In electoral strength as well the Social Christians had made some gains; a Christian Democratic governor was elected in Jujuy Province in 1962. However, these gains were erased in the 1965 elections. That election may not be indicative of Christian Democratic strength, for all of the smaller parties suffered the effects of a polarization in Argentine politics between the Peoples Radicals of ex-President Arturo Illia and the Peronistas. If this polarity is overcome and the Peronista masses lose some of their coherence with the passage of time, it seems possible that the work of the Argentine Social Christians may bear fruit. In fact, one review has insisted that "it is necessary to consider the fact that the major part of the Peronista movement is, really or potentially, a Christian Democratic movement. . . ."[30]

THE VENEZUELAN SOCIAL CHRISTIAN–COPEI AND ACCIÓN DEMOCRÁTICA

Among the coalitions which the Christian Democrats have formed with other parties the most fruitful has been the Venezuelan Social Christian-COPEI collaboration with the Betancourt government and the Acción Democrática party. The two collaborated from 1957 to 1964. Social Christians in other nations have held ministerial posts, and the parties have cooperated with governors and governments, but none of these has lasted for so long, involved such intimate cooperation, or implied such comprehensive commitment. Moreover, the coalition is the symbol of successful cooperation of the two most important democratic forces in Latin America, the established Aprista Social Democrats and the burgeoning Christian Democrats. The great importance of collaboration between these two groups—the twin pillars of the continent's democratic revolution—is constantly emphasized by friends of Latin American democracy.[31]

The coalition grew out of the cooperation between the two groups

[30] "Socialistas que Rezan," *Visión*, XXV (July 26, 1963), 25.

[31] For one of the many observations on this theme, see Robert J. Alexander, *The Venezuelan Democratic Revolution* (New Brunswick, N. J.: Rutgers University Press, 1964), p. 319. Alexander suggests that "upon these two groups of political parties rests most of the burden of bringing about the necessary social changes in a democratic environment."

in their united opposition to the Pérez Jiménez tyranny. This formative period, moreover, saw the practical, if not ideological, transformation of both COPEI's and AD's position, a change which made the coalition possible. When AD was in power between 1945 and 1948, COPEI had, after a short period of alliance, assumed a hostile attitude toward the government, engendered in no small part by the zealous anti-Church attitudes of some elements of AD. In the interim, however, the extreme sectors of the AD party had mellowed and COPEI had shed its more conservative adherents. One observer suggests that the "consensus of values" between the two parties was evoked by a "Christian Democracy traveling leftward and an Aprismo traveling centerward."[32]

The AD, the COPEI, the Unión Republicana Democrática, and the Communists formed the Patriotic Junta in opposition to the dictatorship; the junta operated both in exile and as an underground movement in Venezuela. Later, just after the overthrow of Pérez Jiménez, representatives of AD, COPEI, and URD met in New York to create the Venezuelan Civilian Front. The member parties of the Frente pledged cooperation through the provisional government period in order to insure the establishment of a democratic regime. The original plans called for a single candidate backed by all three parties and the formation of a governmental coalition. The parties were unable to agree on a single candidate, however, and each ran its own nominee, though all three parties agreed to support the eventual victor. AD ran Betancourt, COPEI, Caldera, who was also endorsed by the small Partido Socialista de Trabajadores and the Integración Republicana. The URD selected Admiral Wolfgang Larrazábal, who had been in charge of the provisional government. The Communists supported the URD candidate.

The newly elected President Betancourt assumed power in early 1959 and formed a coalition that included both COPEI and URD. The coalition controlled both chambers of the Venezuelan legislature. From the very beginning, the alliance was racked by dissent. In April, 1960, offshoots of the AD and Communist parties formed the Movimiento de Izquierda Revolucionaria; the URD, a sore spot in the tri-party collaboration from the outset, went into official opposition in November, 1960; and finally, in January, 1962, another faction of the AD, the Acción Democrática-ARS, split with its

[32] Franklin Tugwell, "The Christian Democrats of Venezuela," *Journal of Inter-American Studies*, VII (April, 1965), 265.

parent. By the opening of the congress in March, 1962, the original coalition had lost its majority in the lower house, although it continued to control the Senate. Only the old guard of the AD and COPEI remained in the government. This truncated remainder of the once-powerful three-party government survived until the ascension of President Raúl Leoni in 1964.

COPEI's reasons for entering the government were various. First, there was its genuine commitment to the preservation of the shaky Venezuelan democracy. COPEI deemed it a necessity that the democratic government last out its term of office and successfully achieve its program. The party often emphasized that its cohesion with the Betancourt regime was crucial to the good of Venezuela and Venezuelans. Actually, it might have been more politically advantageous for COPEI to be in opposition. Caldera sketched his personal opinion on the political wisdom of opposition in 1959. "For a party it is not good business to form a part of the coalition in times like these, when the difficulties which face the country are very great and when it is much simpler to be outside the Government, pointing out what the Government has done badly or what the Government has not done instead of being within and having part of the responsibility of a labor which is necessarily unsatisfactory for many people." Adequate credit is never accorded to the junior partners of the coalition for jobs well done, Caldera continued, and little credit is given to either partner in a situation like that in Venezuela. Therefore, the COPEI leader concluded, it would be much easier to be outside the government and thus have absolute liberty to criticize and freedom from the responsibility of governmental activity.[33]

Nonetheless, COPEI chose to back the government for its entire five-year term. Although the basic rationale may have been the heartfelt need to preserve the democratic institutions of the nation, it should be noted that loyalty to the coalition did have its advantages. At the outset of the constitutional period, COPEI was the smallest and least known of the three major parties but was awarded positions out of proportion to its strength and was the recipient of significant amounts of favorable publicity as being part of an essentially popular and well-received government. The very favorable response to Agricultural Minister Giménez Landínez apparently was an important contribution to the fortunes of the party. Moreover, the

[33] Caldera, Jóvito Villalba, and Raúl Leoni, "Desarrollo Democrático y Unidad de las Fuerzas Políticas," *Política*, No. 4, Dec., 1959, pp. 91–92.

party was able to exercise influence out of proportion to its actual strength in government circles, especially after the secession of the other components of the original coalition, and seems to have garnered its share of the praise for government successes without receiving as much of the criticism as might have been expected.

Finally, it must be admitted that COPEI's efforts to preserve the Venezuelan democracy are not entirely selfless. The party is that nation's fastest-growing political force and looks to an electoral victory in the near future. Victory, obviously, depends upon the continued existence of a democratic situation in which COPEI can come to power through the ballot. In short, if COPEI wants to gain an electoral triumph, the protection of a regime that conducts democratic elections is imperative.

The Social Christian contributions to the success of the Betancourt government were considerable. Loyalty to the policies of the government was its basic contribution. Unlike the URD during its period of official collaboration, COPEI sincerely and actively cooperated with its senior partner. There were very few examples of undercutting, sabotage, or overt criticism by those most responsible for COPEI policy. This attitude is exemplified by the party's sponsorship, at the World Congress of Christian Democracy at Santiago de Chile in 1961, of a resolution proposing the cooperation of Christian parties with Aprista parties to further the aims of political democracy and social reform in Latin America.

More specifically, COPEI contributed to the success and stability of the coalition by its particular influence among certain sectors of Venezuelan society. Although both institutions were insistent that there was no official tie, it seems obvious that the Catholic Church, or at least the most numerous parts of it, was more strongly in favor of COPEI than of any other party. Furthermore, there is little doubt that the military looked benignly upon the party, despite its declared anti-militarist stand. Again, despite the official position of the party, it maintained a large following among the industrial and commercial sectors in Venezuela. The adherence of COPEI to the government bred confidence in the government among these groups, who, particularly at the outset, harbored distrust of President Betancourt and the Acción Democrática, which they considered only a little removed from Communism.[34]

Most dramatic and perhaps equally significant was COPEI's

[34] Alexander, *Venezuelan Democratic Revolution*, p. 86.

strength in the student sectors. AD strength in the universities waned markedly after the first breath of success immediately following the overthrow of the tyranny. Conversely, COPEI assumed a growing following in the universities and shortly emerged as the most powerful single force among Venezuelan student political groups. The intensely political students are very important in the nation's politics, and COPEI's contribution in this area cannot be minimized.

Nevertheless, there were instances of discord between COPEI and AD. Especially before the trisection of the AD party, COPEI's spot in the coalition was a bone of contention. The younger and more leftist factions in AD looked upon COPEI as a conservative party which did not represent the authentic aims which the AD sought and felt that COPEI was slowing the pace of the government's program. COPEI's presence in the government was one of the causes contributing to the eventual decision of the Grupo ARS to bolt the party. The ARS was stubbornly against the Social Christians and was incensed at the possibility of Betancourt's backing Caldera as the coalition's candidate for the presidency.[35]

Even at its best, the coalition was occasionally confronted with differences of opinion and minor crises. These differences arose over such issues as the apportionment of positions, tactical methods, and periodically on questions which concerned fundamental ideology. At times these problems were even recorded in the press. A particularly intense crisis concerned the states of Táchira and Mérida; one commentator even blames the argument for the failure of the Río Ghama agrarian reform project. The quarrel raged over supposed discrimination of the AD-controlled Instituto Agrario Nacional in dealing with the COPEI-dominated Peasant Federation local.[36]

Although COPEI continued to participate in the coalition until the assumption of power by Acción Democrática's Raúl Leoni early in 1964, the decisive split had developed when the coalition candidate was selected for the 1963 elections. COPEI favored a joint candidate and was willing to support an independent, a Copeyano, or some specific members of AD. When AD chose Leoni against the advice of COPEI and some influential Adecos, the Social Christians refused to back him in the election. COPEI considered Leoni a party hack and charged the AD with having placed party interests above the good of the Venezuelan nation. COPEI ran Caldera, and the

[35] *Hispanic American Report*, XIV (Feb., 1962), 1105.

[36] Alexander, *Venezuelan Democratic Revolution*, pp. 190, 191.

party emerged from the election stronger than ever; it became the second power in the nation, garnering 589,372 votes or 20.2 percent compared with AD's 957,699 or 32.8 percent.

The election results put COPEI in a stronger bargaining position in negotiations for restoration of the coalition, but the intransigence of both of the former partners made collaboration impossible. AD preferred collaboration with COPEI over any other group, but COPEI stressed that it would demand the acceptance of certain policies which encompassed family subsidies, old age pensions, more emphasis on land reform, and educational and oil legislation.[37] The Leoni government, perhaps embittered at COPEI's trenchant criticism of its standard-bearer, refused to make an authentic attempt at reconciling the differences which separated it from its former partner. It refused to consider the added strength of COPEI as grounds for more voice in the government and even rejected President Betancourt's public entreaty that it enlist COPEI collaboration.

The impasse resulted in Leoni's looking elsewhere for support and in the formation of the Ancha Base ("wide base"), which was a coalition of AD, URD, and the supporters of Uslar Pietri. COPEI assumed an attitude of "Autonomy of Action" rather than a position of outright opposition. Caldera insisted that the party's decision was not attributable to partisan political reasons, but, rather, that its decision was based on the national interest. Nevertheless, the failure to revive the coalition cannot be blamed entirely on Leoni's intransigence. Many think that COPEI's demands were exorbitant. Indeed, it is possible that Caldera purposefully set out to free his party of governmental responsibility; he has said that more freedom to criticize the government could further the cause of COPEI. There are strong elements in the party who think that it should go beyond its present position to one of open opposition. It should be noted, however, that the Social Christian-COPEI is now one of the few examples of a "loyal opposition" in the entire history of Venezuela and, indeed, of the entire continent.

THE PERUVIAN CHRISTIAN DEMOCRATS AND ACCIÓN POPULAR

Peru provides the other example of close and formal Christian Democratic coalition with a governing party. The Peruvian experi-

[37] *Hispanic American Report*, XVII (March, 1964), 50.

ment has some similarities to the Venezuelan experiment, but there are several basic differences. Although both parties were the junior partners in the coalition, the Venezuelan party was more established and stronger than its Peruvian counterpart. There had been a nascent Social Christian organization in Peru since the late forties, but the party itself had existed for only eight years before it entered the government with Acción Popular. Both the Venezuelan Acción Democrática and the Peruvian Acción Popular were and are led by extremely dynamic and popular leaders, Rómulo Betancourt and Fernando Belaúnde Terry, which is noteworthy in view of the fact that Christian Democrats have usually encountered difficulty in producing a figure to match their image, although in Peru the increasing popularity and fame of Luis Bedoya Reyes, the Christian mayor of Lima, have tended to moderate this problem. Moreover, in both nations, the popular presidents seem to have political, and apparently personal, preferences for influential members of the coalitions' junior partners. On several occasions, Betancourt has intimated his support of Caldera's ambitions, and in Peru Belaúnde seems to favor Bedoya Reyes as the next president. Both coalitions had been met with larger opposition groups, in Venezuela by URD and the Left and in Peru by the coalition of convenience that wedded Haya de la Torre's Apristas to Manuel Odría's personalist following. Both COPEI and the Peruvian Christians, as junior partners of the coalition, have molested the unity of the senior group. In Venezuela, the AD party dissidents were composed of those to the left and those who opposed the president's intimate relationship with a leading member of COPEI. A very similar, though perhaps a bit more complex, situation exists in Peru. Many members of Acción Popular are opposed to Belaúnde's fondness for Bedoya Reyes. The AP left, furthermore, favors the policies of the militant Héctor Cornejo Chávez, the president of the Christian party. Finally, both parties probably have and do exert influence out of proportion to their real strength. In Peru, the 5 to 8 percent of the vote which the Christian Democratic party contributed to the coalition's candidate, Belaúnde Terry, was probably the deciding margin in his election. Furthermore, the strength of the Peruvian party is enhanced by a remarkably able, well-prepared, ideologically sophisticated leadership.

In contrast to the Social Christian position in the Venezuelan coalition, the Peruvian Christian party is probably to the Left, rather than the Right, of the major partner. The disagreements which arose between the two parties, therefore, tended to be different from those which occasionally plagued the Venezuelan experiment. Furthermore, the Acción Democrática and the Acción Popular are dissimilar. AD is an old, well-entrenched party by Latin American standards; AP is a brand-new creation. AD is an ideological party based on the indigenous Social Democratic doctrine of the Aprista movement; AP is an amorphous collection of reformers, enlightened bourgeois, peasants, and other groups, and although it shows signs of evolving an ideological foundation, for the most part it is committed to following the leadership of Belaúnde. The party is therefore not radically different from many of the personalist agglomerations that have characterized Latin American political history. Of course, it does differ from the traditional personalist party insofar as it is committed to both social reform and political democracy. The very amorphous nature of Acción Popular has increased the influence of the ideologically coherent Peruvian Christian Democrats.

AP-PDC relations have passed from mutual rejection to relatively harmonious cooperation and lately to increasing discord. The tone of the relationship has been set as much by PDC leadership changes as by the policies of the Belaúnde government. The 1962 elections marked the first efforts at alliance. The Social Christians, at the time, were under the leadership of the party's left wing, and negotiations were very difficult and all too often characterized by recriminations. The Christian Democrats claimed that AP was ideologically vapid and that an alliance with such a group might have catastrophic results for both the party and the nation. The AP, in turn, accused the PDC of unreasonableness. The discussions floundered, and each party decided to run its own nominee. The Christian Democrats chose party leader Héctor Cornejo Chávez, and Acción Popular nominated Belaúnde. The election results were extremely close: Belaúnde and the Apristas' Haya de la Torre both garnered almost 33 percent of the votes; Haya was the victor by less than one percentage point. Odría, the candidate of the Personalist Unión Nacional Odriísta, won about 28 percent of the vote and Cornejo, the Christian Democratic candidate, about 5 percent.[38] The Peruvian army refused to permit the hated Haya to assume the presidency and led a successful coup against the government. The military showed itself uncharacteristically faithful to its promise to set new elections, and actually carried out the election plan in 1963.

The Christian Democrats had not done so well as they had ex-

[38] *Ibid.*, XV (Aug., 1962), 539.

pected and blamed their poor showing on the party's left-wing leaders, who were overthrown. The new leaders were more moderate and favored an agreement with Acción Popular. Javier Correa y Elías assumed the presidency of the party and immediately set out to effect an alliance with AP. Belaúnde was anxious to add to his slim majority the crucial 5 percent of the electorate which the Social Christians controlled. The electoral and governmental coalition was negotiated and officially signed in January, 1963, without further problems.

The document declared that the two parties, "as proof of their patriotic desire to contribute to a democratic solution of the national political problem," would undertake both an electoral and governmental pact for the period 1963–1969, and it outlined two major objectives of the alliance. The parties promised to back the presidential candidate of the alliance, Belaúnde Terry, and, if elected, to "lend him their loyal support in the exercise of his functions so that the country could advance the goals set out in the coalition's program." They also agreed to support one another's legislative initiatives that were part of the previously outlined platform. The parties stipulated that each preserved its liberty in matters not included in the coalition's program, "although, as loyal allies, they should attempt to conciliate their discrepancies."[39]

The coalition functioned rather smoothly for the first two years, although there were occasional differences. The Christian Democrats were faced with the usual problems of being the junior partner in a popular government. It would be difficult to increase their voting force while participating in a government in which they assumed responsibility without being able to claim significant credit for positive accomplishments. Moreover, some factions of the party thought that the government was moving too slowly in its reforms and that it was too friendly with native and North American capitalistic interests. This group, under the leadership of ex-party president Cornejo Chávez, gained strength and re-assumed power when Cornejo was again elected president of the party at its Eighth National Assembly in March, 1965.

The assembly was characterized by a belligerent attitude toward the Belaúnde government. The triumphant faction accused the gov-

[39] Alianza Acción Popular-Demócrata Cristiana, *Bases para el Plan de Gobierno (Texto Preliminar)* (Lima: Librería e Imprenta Hinerva-Miraflores, 1963), pp. 17, 18.

ernment of slowing down promised reforms and called upon it to abide by the alliance's program. The left-wingers charged that the government was too concerned with the opposition and noted that "in such a situation Christian Democracy runs the risk of weakening itself in a government which is sterile from the reformist point of view."[40] Upon assuming the presidency of the party, Cornejo proclaimed that the "climate of peace and quiet which [the government] wants to give the country is costing too much." He added that the Christian Democrats were a revolutionary party and would not accept a "plate of lentils" at the hands of an "unjust and anti-Christian order." Cornejo noted that he believed in the honesty of the President's efforts but that the President's policy of consensus was in error. He called upon the President to mobilize public opinion against the anti-democratic forces of the nation. "The President ought to talk," he declared.[41]

Despite the militantly challenging attitude of the new left-wing leadership, it agreed to soften its line in order to avoid more serious dissension within the party. The official conclusions of the Eighth National Assembly were moderate in tone and expressed the party's faith in the AP-PDC alliance and in the leadership of Belaúnde. The resolutions affirmed the party's determination to "intensify its efforts to execute the program of the Alliance, since the fate of millions of compatriots depends on it" and to combat the reactionary forces of the nation with "energy and resolution."[42]

Even though the March, 1965, crisis was passed without substantially upsetting the coalition, there remains the strong possibility that the hard-liners may prevail and force the party to quit the government. During 1966, for example, the Christians continually badgered the Belaúnde government to nationalize the North American-owned International Petroleum Company. In early 1967, the Christian party split, promising even more problems for the coalition. The Left feels that the President has not used his obvious popularity and power to push basic reforms as rapidly as he should and that the future of the Christian Democratic party will be jeopardized if the crux of the alliance's program is not achieved. Many

[40] "Golpe de Estado en la Democracia Cristiana," *Oiga*, III (March 19, 1965), 7.

[41] *Ibid.*

[42] Partido Demócrata Cristiana del Perú, *Conclusiones de la VIII Asamblea Nacional* (Lima, March, 1965), (mimeographed), pp. 2, 3.

feel that in any event the Partido Demócrata Cristiano would benefit more from opposition than from participation in even the best of governments. The Eighth Assembly, for instance, heard repeated cries of "*solo*" from the delegates for whom, apparently, the example of Chile is important. The Chilean party purposely avoided governmental cooperation for fifteen years before it came to power, and the Peruvians, as well as the other Latin American parties, are much influenced by the Chilean experience. On the Acción Popular side of the ledger, many charge that the Cornejo group was the force that sabotaged the attempt at coalition in 1962, and, at least in some sectors, there is no feeling of friendship for the leaders of the Partido Demócrata Cristiano. Nevertheless, it seems probable that the Christian Democrats will continue to align themselves with Belaúnde's AP, at least for the immediate future. If a break is to come, it will probably be postponed until the next elections are closer.

RELATIONS WITH THE SOCIALISTS

There are two major Socialist groups in Latin America. Although there are minor differences in theory and practice between the two types of Latin American Democratic Socialism, it is both possible and convenient to discuss them within the same section.

The direct heir of European Marxian, evolutionary Socialism was established in Latin America in the last few years of the past century. The parties making up this group exercised some influence during the first thirty or forty years of the century, but, for the most part, have since faded rather rapidly. The movement became overly intellectualized, lost its militancy and, consequently, declined in popular strength and political power. Traditional Socialist parties still maintain some following in Chile, Ecuador, and Argentina, but even in these nations, they are diminishing.

The second and more important group is composed of the indigenous Socialist parties born from the efforts of Haya de la Torre and his Alianza Popular Revolucionario Americana (APRA). The ideology is based on a mixture of Marxian Socialism, indigenous Socialism derived from the practices of the native Indian masses, and continental nationalism. These Aprista parties, which have been and continue to be very important in Latin America, maintain an informal International held together by ideological affinity and personal friendship; the International includes the parent Peruvian

Aprista party, Venezuela's Acción Democrática, Costa Rica's Liberación Nacional, the Dominican Republic's Partido Revolucionario Dominicana, the Paraguayan Febreristas, the old Cuban Auténticos, the Puerto Rican Popular Democratic party, and several smaller and less important factions in other Latin American nations.

The Christian Democrats claim, with some justification, that these parties have passed the height of their influence and are declining. Nevertheless, Aprista Socialism continues to be a strong force in Latin America and undoubtedly will be critically important in the immediate future.

Social Democrats and Christian Democrats are the hope for a democratic Latin America. It is possible that together they could be the crucial weight to tip the balance in favor of social and political reform. Separated, they could do harm to this hope.[43]

Although there is much that separates the Christian and Socialist forces, there is probably even more that unites them, and modern political practice has demonstrated numerous examples of cooperation and coalition. Indeed, as early as 1922, Luigi Sturzo's Popular party set forth a proposal for cooperation with the Italian Socialists in a coalition government. The venture failed because of Socialist obduracy.[44] On the other side of the Atlantic, over twenty years ago both Argentine Catholic Bishop Andrea and Socialist leader Alfredo Palacios could agree upon the need for certain types of social legislation and state their positions in the same book.[45] On the contemporary political scene, Christians and Socialists have been able to fruitfully cooperate in France, Belgium, Germany, Chile, and, most recently, in Italy, Venezuela, and the Dominican Republic.

Political, economic, and social goals of the two movements have gradually become sufficiently close to allow cooperation. The Christian Democrats have assumed an increasingly progressive stance, and the Socialists have moved toward the Center and shed many of their more extreme revolutionary, statist, and anti-clerical postures. The Social Christians themselves have been responsible for a significant decline in Socialist anti-clericalism by proving that Catholics can be interested in political democracy, social reform, and economic

[43] See p. 204 for an observation on this theme in connection with the Venezuelan Acción Democrática-Social Christian-COPEI coalition.

[44] See Malcolm Moos, "Don Luigi Sturzo—Christian Democrat," *American Political Science Review*, XXXIX (April, 1945), 272.

[45] TePaske and Fisher, *Explosive Forces in Latin America*, p. 52.

justice. Moreover, they hold that the Socialists have recognized the wisdom of the Christian politic. In 1935, the Uruguayan Social Christian, Dardo Regules, responded to a proposition that Christians were becoming Socialists: "On the contrary," he noted, "the Socialists have converted themselves into Christians."[46] Another Christian Democrat has echoed this observation; he suggests that "practical experiences" have taught the Socialists the errors of some aspects of the Marxist credo and have forced them to recognize the "essential principles which Catholic philosophy has sustained on the sociological plane."[47]

On the whole, Social Christian-Social Democrat relations in Latin America might be classified as moderately cordial. However, in some instances these relationships have been excellent and in others discordant if not overtly hostile. In Peru, the ideological womb of Latin American Aprista Socialism, the changing relationships between Social Christians and Socialists reflect the evolution of both groups. In the late forties when the Christian Democrats were establishing their initial organization, the Peruvian Apristas were still strongly anti-Church. This, coupled with the rather conservative bent of the Christians, produced a generally reciprocal hostility. Later, however, probably because of the Christian militant opposition to the Odría regime and a generally more progressive tone within the party, relationships improved. One study notes that after 1956 the "Apristas showed considerable sympathy for the PDC . . . because they realized the need for the development of a rival party . . . which, though being anti-Aprista, would constitute a democratic opposition."[48] An important Aprista, however, explained the change differently. He noted that the strong anti-Aprista tendency within the Christian Democratic party had altered because the leadership finally realized that a viable policy must be more than a merely anti-Aprista position.[49] Whatever the cause, the short-lived honeymoon was to end in 1963 when the Peruvian Social Christians coalesced with Acción Popular, and the Apristas almost unbelievably allied with the forces of ex-dictator Odría, who had been their worst

[46] Quoted in Caldera, *Moldes para la Fragua*, (Buenos Aires: Librería "El Ateneo" Editorial, 1962), p. 251.

[47] Eduardo Frei Montalva, *Pensamiento y Acción* (Santiago de Chile: Editorial del Pacífico, 1956), p. 141.

[48] Charles O. Porter and Robert J. Alexander, *The Struggle for Democracy in Latin America* (New York: Macmillan Company, 1961), p. 31.

[49] Carlos Delgado, "Panorama Político Peruano," *Combate*, IV (May-June, 1962), 28.

enemies. The Christian Democrats have looked upon this odd alliance as a betrayal of Peruvian national interest, and scorn and enmity presently characterize the situation. At their Eighth National Assembly, for example, the PDC resolved to: "Particularly caution the people against those ex-revolutionaries who have now been converted into the most solid support of the minorities who unlawfully retain the economic power, and who are trading on the good will of those who continue to sincerely believe in the principles which their leaders have already abandoned."[50]

In Chile, Christian Democrat-Social Democrat relationships have also evidenced some degree of ambiguity, though generally they have been cordial. The Chileans have noted their admiration of and friendship for the Peruvian Apristas[51] and in internal politics have frequently cooperated with the more traditional Chilean Socialist party, both alone and when it was part of a left-wing coalition with the Communists and other smaller parties. Indeed, Frei Montalva's candidacy benefited from ruptures within two Chilean Socialist parties just before the 1964 elections. In 1963 the Partido Democrático Nacional split; an influential faction of the party announced itself as "the new Democratic Left at the service of Chile" and lined up behind the candidacy of Frei.[52] Later, a dissident group of the Socialist party, dubbed the Socialist Peoples party, repudiated the left-wing nomination of Salvador Allende and adhered with "surprising enthusiasm" to Frei.[53] There continues to be a Christian Democratic effort to dislodge the Socialist party from the FRAP opposition, and indications seem to point to the possibility of at least partial success.

Christian Democrats have cooperated with Socialist parties elsewhere in Latin America. The long and creative collaboration between the Venezuelan COPEI and the Socialist Acción Democrática has been discussed in this chapter. Moreover, the more traditional Partido Socialista de Trabajadores (Socialist Workers Party) endorsed the candidacy of Caldera in the 1958 elections. In Guatemala, Christians and Socialists have also cooperated in opposition to the government. The Partido Democracia Cristiana Guatemalteca and

[50] Partido Demócrata Cristiano del Perú, *Conclusiones de la VIII Asamblea Nacional*, p. 2.

[51] Frei Montalva, *Sentido y Forma*, p. 42.

[52] See *Hispanic American Report*, XVI (Sept., 1963), 712.

[53] *Chile*, Estudios de Actualidad, Primera Serie, No. 1 (Montevideo: Instituto de Estudios Políticos para América Latina, 1964), pp. 17, 18.

the Partido Revolucionario collaborated during much of the Ydígoras regime. Close cooperation was particularly effective in the areas of labor and social-welfare legislation, although the parties did differ on international policy and did occasionally disagree over questions of political office.[54]

Finally, the Dominican Republic has been the scene of very close collaboration between the Aprista Partido Revolucionario Dominicana of Juan Bosch and the left-wing Partido Revolucionario Social Cristiano. During the short-lived constitutional regime of President Bosch, the Social Christians formed the main ideological opposition to the government, but it was the only major group to stand in opposition to the military coup which unseated Bosch in 1963. Later, in 1964, the two parties affixed the pact of Río Piedras, which pledged cooperation against the military dictatorship. The two parties were major political forces in the abortive attempt to return Bosch to the presidency in 1965, and both fought on the constitutionalist side during the civil war in 1965. The Social Christians refused to take an active role in any Partido Revolucionario Dominicana government but did promise their support to the government at least until the next elections. Despite some opposition within the party, the Social Christians backed the Bosch candidacy in the elections of 1966. The party had first nominated its own candidate, party leader Antonio Rosario, but Rosario later withdrew his name, supposedly at the insistence of the younger elements of the party.

Despite these numerous examples of collaboration between Christian Democrats and Social Democrats in Latin America, the much-discussed continent-wide alliance between these two forces is still a long way from being a certainty. In addition to the obvious tactical differences which separate the two groups, certain basic doctrinal positions are widely divergent. The Socialists still look with suspicion upon the religious attitudes of the Christian movement. Their positions on education vary widely, and some areas of state activity and foreign policy continue to present obstacles to permanent and comprehensive understanding. Moreover, Social Christian ranks are greatly influenced by the Chilean experience of having repudiated electoral pacts, and many Christian Democrats think that they can win without the assistance of other forces. Many think that the collaboration with the old Aprista parties could be a definite liability

[54] Karl M. Schmitt and David B. Burks, *Evolution or Chaos? Dynamics of Latin American Government and Politics* (New York: Frederick A. Praeger, 1963), p. 209.

because the Apristas are in ideological, political, and perhaps moral, decline. Caldera expressed this widespread doubt when he charged:

> As for Democratic Socialism, its experience in government has generally been characterized by a lack of clear aims and of ambitious solutions. Its internal disintegration is grave. We need only to observe in Peru the profound disillusionment among the people due to the entente between a group such as APRA and the followers of Odría, who once persecuted them, and who represents a rigid conservative position. . . . In Venezuela, this trend is especially noteworthy, since the traditional majority party which won 70 per cent of the popular vote in 1947, fell to 48 per cent in 1958 and 33 per cent in 1963.[55]

RELATIONS WITH THE RADICALS

If the Democratic Socialists are the most logical choice for cooperation to the immediate Left of Latin American Christian Democracy, the Radical parties are the most likely choice for collaboration to the Right. Radical parties are much less numerous in Latin America than are Socialist parties, but they are very strong in the two key nations of Argentina and Chile. Radical-like sectors are found in many of the continent's Socialist parties and some have found a home in the traditional Liberal parties. An analysis of Radical-Christian Democratic relations is useful because it most clearly dramatizes the problem of anti-clericalism which confronts the Social Christians in their relations with many sectors of the Latin American political spectrum.

There are, of course, many similarities between the positions of Social Christians and Radicals. Both are middle parties, Radicals usually being a little to the Right of Center and Christian Democrats a little to the Left. Both groups find their strongest support in the middle class. Both propose programs of political democracy and social reform. Although the classic Liberal suspicion of the omnipotent state is stronger in Radical thought, both Christians and Radicals agree on the desirability of an active, positive state. In sum, at least a marriage of convenience seems possible and practical.

Although cooperation has not been widespread, several examples of collaboration between Social Christians and Radicals in both

[55] Rafael Caldera, *The Growth of Christian Democracy and Its Influence on the Social Reality of Latin America* (New York: Center of Christian Democratic Action, 1965), pp. 17, 18.

Chile and Argentina may be cited. In Chile, the two groups share the political Center; despite Radicalism's serious losses in the 1965 legislative elections, both are very strong and influential. Both the old National Falange and the Conservative Social Christians supported Radical president González Videla during his presidential term. Radical relations were usually better with the Conservative Social Christians than with the more militantly leftist Falange Nacional, but tripartite cooperation did exist for short periods. Moreover, the Social Christian parties joined the Radicals in opposition to President Ibáñez during much of his tenure, and the two groups were often united in opposition against the conservative Alessandri regime. Although the Radicals have generally opposed the Frei government, they did supply precious votes in favor of the copper legislation.

In Argentina, both Intransigent Radical President Arturo Frondizi and People's Radical President Arturo Illia maintained cordial, and occasionally excellent, relations with the Argentine Christian Democrats. The party generally supported Frondizi, who even offered governmental positions to the party, which it refused.[56] Moreover, Frondizi was flexible on the Church issue in direct opposition to traditional Radical theory and practice, even forcing a bill through the Congress allowing for the establishment of Catholic universities. President Illia showed the same attitude toward the Church and occasionally courted Christian Democratic support in both the legislature and during elections. In 1963, Illia's 169 electoral votes fell short of the necessary 239, and the addition of the electoral ballots of the Christian Democrats helped to elect him president.

Despite these examples of cooperation between the Christians and the Radicals, the relationships have not been nearly so close or long-lasting as the concordance of political ideology and practical programs might suggest. The problem is the religious issue. It is understandable, of course, that little accord could be expected on specific issues such as education, birth control, and divorce, but the discord goes deeper than this. Possible cooperation is poisoned by an all-enveloping and intransigent anti-clericalism which often characterizes the Radical position.

Religious questions no longer dominate the continent's politics as they once did, but they are occasionally important. The Chilean

[56] See "La Convención Nacional de la Democracia Cristiana Argentina . . . ," p. 35.

Radicals have summarized their position by noting that they believe that "religion ought to be practiced in its normal place, the Churches, and not in the streets, nor in the schools."[57] Following the Christian Democratic victory in Chile, the Radical party reiterated its stand by pointedly remarking that "it can only consider making agreements with democratic socialists and laic forces. . . ."[58] A study of Chile written just before the 1964 presidential elections suggested that one of the factors militating against a possible Frei victory was some "incident or provocation" that would excite latent Radical anti-clericalism and lose the Radical backing that Frei was expected to muster.[59] Obviously recognizing the explosive nature of this issue even after the elections, President Frei was careful to appoint an education minister known for his independence from the Church. "Before the mere mention of the name Christian Democracy," observes one party leader, "the partisans of old Radical laicism tremble with fear because they see behind it the image of intolerant clericalism of a new mold."[60]

The anti-clerical position is not restricted to the Radical. The Apristas and the traditional Socialists are founded on a rejection of clerical influence, if not actual repudiation of the Church and religion, per se. Indeed, in the 1947 Venezuelan elections, Acción Democrática's Rómulo Gallegos warned against "sinister Jesuit influences" in the COPEI party.[61] The traditional Liberal parties, moreover, are still highly suspicious of Christian Democratic credentials. Latin America has always been sensitive to the religious issue and its history offers numerous examples of violent clericalism and anti-clericalism. The situation has changed for the better; the Church and Christian Democrats have done much to erase the old image, and new bugaboos, economic imperialism, for instance, have taken its place. Nevertheless, anti-clericalism still remains a potentially strong weapon in the hands of the Radicals, Socialists, or Liberals.

If an entente between Christian Democrats and Social Democrats

[57] Quoted in Peter G. Snow, "The Political Party Spectrum in Chile," *South Atlantic Quarterly*, LXII (Autumn, 1963), 479.

[58] "Chile: Convention Reappraisal," *The Latin American Times*, July 1, 1965, p. 3.

[59] *Chile*, p. 16.

[60] Remo Di Natale, *América Latina Hoy: Esquemas Populares Demócrata Cristianos* (Caracas: Editorial Nuevo Orden, 1964), pp. 11, 12.

[61] See Edwin Lieuwen, *Venezuela* (New York: Oxford University Press, 1961), p. 75.

has been heralded as a possible solution to the diseases of Latin American politics, Radical and Christian Democratic collaboration is often prescribed as the proper cure in the southern nations of the continent. The strong Radical parties of Argentina and Chile may hold the key to progress, and cooperation with democratic Social Christian forces may be enough to turn the tide for intelligent reform.[62] There are several factors which may affect such cooperation. First, there is the religious issue. Second, the two forces generally recruit electoral strength from the same socio-economic sectors and, therefore, are natural rivals. The success of one may spell the demise of the other. Evidence of this has already appeared in Chile and Argentina: in Chile, the rise of Christian Democracy has paralleled the weakening of the Radical party, and in Argentina, the 1965 elections witnessed the polarization of Radicalism and Peronism and a marked decline in Christian Democratic strength. Finally, the Chilean Christian Democrats accuse the Radicals of erring in the same way as a triumphant Democratic Socialism—allowing success to bring ideological and practical corruption. Their fate, notes a Chilean, will be the same as that Caldera predicted for the Venezuelan Apristas. "The ornaments of their material situation produces natural contradictions between the situation achieved and the doctrine proposed. Little by little, the contradiction generates disorientation impossible to avoid, fatal oscillation and, finally, the forgetting of the ideal in order to take advantage of the advances. If this is unjust, if it departs from the doctrine, it is not important. . . ."[63]

CHRISTIAN DEMOCRATS AND THE RIGHT

Much Christian Democratic scorn is directed to the parties of the Right: the traditional Conservatives, Liberals, or their variously named brethren. As a rule the Social Christians have been consistent in their refusal to cooperate with parties of the Right. Nevertheless, there have been occasional examples of active cooperation and even

[62] For examples of this analysis, see Robert J. Alexander, "The Emergence of Modern Political Parties in Latin America," *The Politics of Change in Latin America*, ed. Joseph Maier and Richard W. Weatherhead (New York: Frederick A. Praeger, 1964), pp. 109, 110, and Peter G. Snow, "Political Party Spectrum in Chile," p. 468.

[63] Ricardo Boizard, *La Democracia Cristiana en Chile* (3rd ed.; Santiago de Chile: Editorial Orbe, 1963), p. 141.

more of Christian Democratic acceptance of rightist support. Collaboration with Conservative sectors presents special problems for Social Christians. It is no exaggeration to suggest that Christian Democratic parties are on trial with the more progressive sectors of Latin American society, many of whom believe that Social Christians are not solidly committed to social reform. Any suggestion of Social Christian cooperation with the traditional forces tends to reinforce the ingrained prejudices of the Left. Alliance with the Latin American Right can be harmful to any group of the Democratic Left, of course, but it presents particularly difficult problems for Social Christians.

An example of this was the Frei Montalva campaign in Chile. The Social Christians were anxious to avoid any appearance of overt solicitude toward Conservative and Liberal parties. The Communists were quick to condemn Frei for the support he did receive from the Right, charging that the party's revolutionary program had been compromised. One study commented on the Social Christian dilemma by proposing that "it is very important that he [Frei] does not seem to be tied to the political right. . . . Frei, carried to the Presidency, thanks to its support, would immediately be the object of a virulent and intransigent opposition on the parliamentary plane."[64] Since the election, the Conservative forces, which backed Frei as being the lesser of two evils, have defected, and the Liberals and Conservatives have opposed the government on every important piece of reform legislation except the "Chileanization" of the copper industry.

The Cuban Movimiento has drawn criticism for its association with Conservative forces as part of the Democratic Revolutionary Front, which was formed to coordinate activity directed to overthrow Fidel Castro. A leading Christian Democrat has noted that the Movimiento "was compromised, perhaps more than was necessary," by its cooperation with the Front and particularly by its participation in the abortive Bay of Pigs invasion.[65] The Cuban movement bars all collaboration with the followers of ex-dictator Batista but has defended its decision to cooperate with the Frente Revolucionario Democrático in opposition to Castro. The Cubans claim

[64] *Chile*, p. 16.

[65] Tomás Reyes Vicuña, *Planificación en la Libertad* . . . , lecture prepared for El Instituto de Formación Demócrata Cristiana (Caracas, mimeographed), p. 18.

that their cooperation was undertaken only to overthrow the Communist regime on the island and to establish a provisional government. The program of the Frente was carefully framed in the most minimal terms to prevent compromising any of the component groups. Collaboration in this sense did not imply any identification with the history or purposes of any of the participating organizations.[66]

In Paraguay, opposition to an authoritarian government has also resulted in frequent cooperation among the nation's major opposition political parties, the Aprista-lining Febrerista party, the Movimiento Social Demócrata Cristiano (after 1965, the Partido Demócrata Cristiano), and the Partido Liberal. The cooperation has been relatively free of bickering, despite ideological diversity and the acknowledged lack of sophistication which characterizes Paraguayan politics. The groups have worked together and issued several manifestos.[67] Nevertheless, discord occasionally erupts. Both the Social Christians and the Liberals claim that the Febreristas are infiltrated by Communists. The Liberals, moreover, have made the same charge against the Social Christians, claiming that the Social Christians employ Communist techniques and libel the Liberal democracies of Latin America.[68]

Other Latin American Christian Democratic parties that have occasionally allied with right-wing forces include those of Guatemala, El Salvador, and Nicaragua. The Guatemalan Christian Democratic party cooperated with the right-wing Movimiento Liberación Nacional but broke with the group after a younger, more leftist faction assumed control of the Christian party. The Salvadorian organization has made electoral agreements with several conservative groups, including the Partido Social Democrática. The Salvadorian Social Christians defended their decision by noting that the alliance had limited goals and that the program in no way compromised the doctrinal principles of the party. In Nicaragua, a group of Social Christians infiltrated the Conservative party. After failing to effect a change of Conservative policy, however, the group quit the party.

[66] Movimiento Demócrata Cristiano de Cuba, *Movimiento Demócrata Cristiano de Cuba*, p. 47.

[67] See, for instance, Movimiento Social Demócrata Cristiano del Paraguay, *Las Fuerzas Políticas Democráticas del País Frente al Acto Comicial del 10 de Febrero* (Asunción) and *Nota Presentada Por las Fuerzas Políticas de Oposición al Gobierno* (Asunción, Feb. 7, 1962).

[68] See *Hispanic American Report*, XVII (June, 1964), 365.

The more usual practice of the continent's Christian parties, however, has been to eschew any collaboration or alliances with the forces of the political right. In Peru, for example, the party has vehemently opposed all parties of the Right and consistently rejected overtures for electoral, parliamentary, or governmental agreements with the traditional oligarchical political groups. In Bolivia, the beleaguered Partido Demócrata Cristiano has been courted frequently by smaller parties, especially the right-wing Falange. Despite one or two exceptions of very short duration, the party has chosen to stand alone and has rejected countless bids from the Right for cooperation or alliance. Finally, the potentially influential Colombian party has similarly been much-courted and has consistently rejected cooperation with the traditional parties or factions of them—the exception being the Ruiz Novoa adventure.

Latin American Christian Democracy: An Assessment

Handicaps to the Movement 10

A critical analysis of the Latin American Christian Democratic movement reveals many handicaps that may possibly impede Christian Democracy's eventual success. These weaknesses are diverse in both origin and nature; some are intrinsic to the Christian Democratic credo, others are particular to the Latin American branch of Christian Democracy, and still others are imbedded in Latin American politics. And although the movement is barely past its adolescent stage in Latin America, it is conscientiously and energetically grappling with many of the problems that will be discussed here. Solutions are difficult and they will demand considerable time and effort; indeed, some problems may be inherent to the very goals pursued and may call for radical new departures from usual Latin American political practice or Christian Democratic theory.

It would be overly optimistic to suggest that this analysis can pinpoint all the areas of present or future trouble. There are limitations inherent in the scrutiny of any dynamic subject. These limitations are compounded by the fact that the analysis deals with a rapidly changing politic superimposed on a continent in the throes of revolutionary upheaval. Some problems are superseded by newer problems before work on solutions has even begun; others remain latent, waiting only for the proper catalyst to propel them to the forefront of Latin America's most pressing problems. Notwithstanding the myriad obstacles to analysis, several actual and potential weaknesses of the Christian Democratic movement are obvious.

THE MESSIANIC BENT

Fundamental and perhaps causal to many of the specific problems faced by the movement, or yet to be encountered, is Latin American Christian Democracy's messianic zeal and optimistic vitality. There is no denying the contribution this phenomenon could make to the possible triumph of the movement. In the short run, it is decidedly more important than the sophisticated philosophic foundations of the movement. This fervor has attracted a group of party leaders, militants, and auxiliary organizations hell-bent for reform and resolutely laboring to achieve the aims of an aggressive and often pugnacious Christian Democracy. The burgeoning membership lists of the several parties and their increasing influence in Latin America are directly attributable to this fervor.

Christian Democracy is aiming high. Its literature and conversations are studded with allusions to the new society and the new age. Old hatreds, prejudices, hardships, and miseries will be erased; tranquility, fraternity, abundance, and justice will be achieved. The Costa Rican party, for instance, outlines a series of reforms and promises that "all vestiges of exploitation of one class by another and all limitation with respect to the personality will disappear."[1] Discussing the formation of communitarian organizations, the Nicaraguan party predicts that there will be "no discrimination in relation to those who collaborate in the enterprize since it conforms to a new concept, within a Christian social order." The Nicaraguans go on to point out that "all will participate in its benefits, according to their true necessities and capacities."[2] Other party programs, publications, and Christian Democratic spokesmen are equally effusive in their descriptions of the Social Christian community.

The statements have been written off as merely exaggerated campaign promises, but they are really more than that. They reveal a profound faith in the ability of Christian Democracy to transform radically Latin American society and, indeed, human nature. The predictions are infinitely more than the rhetoric of politicians promising the traditional pie in the sky; they are, for the most part, authentically and intensely felt; they are the manifestations of a messianic, revolutionary spirit which permeates the entire movement.

This type of mystique is frequently found in modern, liberal movements, of course, but it is particularly curious in a group that adver-

[1] Partido Demócrata Cristiano de Costa Rica, *1) Toma de posiciones del Partido Demócrata Cristiano—frente al Comunismo, frente al Capitalismo y frente a los regímenes políticos del país. 2) Declaración de principios del Partido Demócrata Cristiano* (San José, n.d.), p. 4.

[2] "ABC de la Democracia Cristiana o Social-Cristianismo," *Combate* (Organo del Partido Social Cristiano Nicaragüense), April, 1964, p. 8.

tises its relationship to the Christian tradition. Modern Christian thought has been characterized by a more moderate tone; its fundamental contribution, and a profoundly important one it is, has been to insist that the temporal world cannot be transformed into a heavenly paradise, and that attempts to make it so often wreak more havoc than positive advances. Indeed, the postulation of heaven on earth is theological heresy as well as bad social and political theory. However, messianic fervor is not limited to Latin American Christian Democracy; a study of Austrian Catholic politics notes: "One is continuously amazed at the confidence Catholics had in the easy and harmonious resolution of the social, economic and political conflicts of a modern industrial society. This Catholic tendency is particularly surprising if one contrasts it with Catholic emphasis on the corrupting influence of original sin."[3]

Latin American Christian Democracy also places great faith in the efficacy of scientific planning and social engineering. The Latin American society, traditionally intensely proud of its humanistic character, has discovered quantitative economics and social planning and now sees them as the solution to the continent's social and political maladies. Difficult political and social problems are depicted as technical problems and written off as easily resolved by technical measures.

The errors inherent in this kind of approach are obvious. The much-heralded Christian society as it is more optimistically described is plainly a pipe dream, and even in a more moderate form will be called upon to solve extremely difficult problems. Its achievement is certainly in the very distant future. The new era is not to be won so readily as the literature proposes. The necessary means involve the very re-structuring of the present system, a far-reaching undertaking that obviously demands infinitely more than the application of scientific planning and technology. Deeply entrenched social, economic, cultural, and political patterns and traditions will have to be modified, if not absolutely overthrown. A moderate Christian Democrat has warned his brethren. "In our ambit there is, unfortunately," he cautions, "a tendency to propitiate with great agility the reform or change of the structures. As you can appreciate, the change of the structures is a very serious thing. I prefer to believe

[3] Alfred Diamant, *Austrian Catholics and the First Republic* (Princeton, N. J.: Princeton University Press, 1960), p. 173.

that this initiative is caused by immature enthusiasm, a lack of profound reflection or perhaps mistaking the structural for what is really merely functional or accessory."[4]

All this does not mean, of course, that the entire Christian Democratic movement has gone off half-cocked in pursuit of the patently impossible. On the contrary, there are Christian Democrats at all levels who are realistic, prudent, and all too cognizant of the dilemmas that characterize Latin American politics. However, the very dynamic and messianic quality that is most important to the strength of the movement in the short run is, in the long run, a weakness, for it involves an unrealistic evaluation of the potentials of political action or of the opportunities for significant advance in the near future. Although many Christian Democrats do recognize that their goals are realizable only in the distant future, the fervor and optimism nonetheless predominate.

The practical consequences are obvious. The Latin American people have been interminably harangued by promises of socio-economic reform and have become skeptical of the politicians. If Christian Democracy does not produce significant reform, the people may—and undoubtedly will—reject it, relegating it to the political junkheap of unfulfilled promises and unrealized proposals. The tragic truth may be that the movement has created an atmosphere in which it will be impossible to meet the expectations that it has encouraged, purposely or accidentally. If this be true, the Latin American people may well look elsewhere for their salvation, specifically to the Communist or Jacobin Left.

IDEOLOGICAL LACUNAE

THE STATE AND PLURALISM

A number of specific weaknesses are implicit in the ideological stance and political program of the movement. One of the most obvious is the practical problem of organizing an authentically pluralistic society by means that place strong emphasis on state planning and leadership in socio-economic spheres. There is no absolute or necessary contradiction between a planned economy administered by a

[4] Iván Vila Echague, *Cuestiones Disputadas en la Democracia Cristiana* (Buenos Aires: Ediciones del Atlántico, 1960), p. 19.

strong state and a pluralistic society, but there seems little doubt that an emphasis on one does mean serious problems for the maintenance of the other, and the situation becomes more serious as the degree of state leadership increases. Christian Democrats believe economic planning is necessary if the defects of under-development and the anti-social activity of predatory capitalism are to be overcome, but at the same time believe it equally important to encourage the formation of workers' councils, labor unions, local government, professional organizations, and other groups. It may be that successful state planning will vitiate the strength of the independent groups. It is difficult to see exactly how strong, independent groups can achieve full maturity in a society with a penchant for dynamic, active central government, which has been so characteristic of Latin America. Achieving a workable harmony between the two will be a great challenge to Christian Democracy.

The Christian Democratic answer is that each group will spontaneously seek its proper sphere in the society where it will function harmoniously with the other groups. Christian Democrats are inclined to view the interaction of individuals and societal structures as naturally compatible. One Latin American critic sees this as evidence of the Catholic thinking that incorrectly transfers the supposed religious and philosophic harmony of the Middle Ages to modern Latin America.

> That society, if it once existed, does not exist any more. Latin America has definitely entered upon a process of secularization. The Christian faith has been converted into a strictly individual phenomenon; the Christian has become . . . a solitary believer; his community is not the Church, but a skeptical society; his field of action is not circumscribed by an orbit where Christian values obtain, but is fixed by the much wider limits of the modern society and life in its social, cultural and political expressions.[5]

The interconnectedness of social, economic, and political phenomena and the vibrant activity of competing bodies are hallmarks of modern industrial society. Within such a context spheres of competence inevitably clash; it is unrealistic and politically unwise to view it otherwise. It seems correct, moreover, to propose that the Christian Democratic faith in natural harmony is the direct result of

[5] Hiber Conteris, "La Próxima Disyuntiva de la D.C.," *Marcha*, XXVI (Sept. 18, 1964), 20, 21.

Christian Democratic belief in the possibility of an organic society, which leads many Catholic thinkers to view the solution of social problems as merely a matter of adjusting a substantially symmetrical phenomenon.

The strong state and effective pluralism do pull in opposite directions. Either the state predominates and the intermediate bodies become mere agencies of an omnipotent, centralized government, or the intermediate organs predominate, becoming jealous of their own autonomy and creating an ungovernable, chaotic situation. These, of course, are the extreme alternatives, and neither is inevitable, but Christian Democratic failure to recognize the very real dangers here is unsound. Indeed, one student sees this problem as being characteristic of Catholic social thought in general: he suggests that its inadequacy "lies in its inability to devise a set of concepts applicable to the modern, complex multi-group society."[6] It must be admitted that the charge is relevant to Latin American Christian Democracy.

CORPORATISM AND COMMUNITARIANISM

Associated with this weakness is the insufficiency of corporative theory, which the movement has revived and made a central part of its political program. Although many of the Latin American Christian Democrats would deny it, their theory is essentially traditional, Catholic corporatism. As such, it is vulnerable to all of the criticism generally leveled at corporative theory.

Corporatism is based on the proposition that each man is naturally affiliated with his economic endeavor, and that the economic community ought to be encouraged through legal and political recognition. That is, each economic group should be given the authority to set its own standards, resolve its own internal conflicts, and send its own delegates to the policy-making agencies of the state. These agencies have the authority only to set out general guide lines within which the various corporations operate. The system theoretically places a stress on the internal self-government of the various communities; it can be democratic.

In Italy and Austria, however, where the system was tried, it became an instrument of dictatorial, if not totalitarian, oppression. Latin American Christian Democrats hold that the Italian experience was a perversion of corporatism and cannot be used to refute the

[6] Diamant, *Austrian Catholics and the First Republic*, p. 287.

validity of corporative theory. It is reasonable to argue that two experiences should not condemn the possibility of eventual success. It is not proved that dictatorial government is inherent in the movement. The key consideration, as the Latin American Social Christians suggest, is the nature of the relationship between the state and the communities. If the communities evolve naturally and if they are subject only to legal recognition and general governmental guidance, then the system could function according to theory. However, if the communities are created by the state and are totally subject to state supervision, then the system is indeed corrupted. One student makes the pessimistic observation that "in a modern complex industrial society a corporative system either dissolves into anarchy or becomes dominated completely by a political authority—the experience of Austria after 1934 proved that only the second alternative was a realistic one in the twentieth century."[7]

Other factors also seem to militate against the success of a corporative system. The system ignores class consciousness, which does, in fact, exist and is a fundamental part of modern society. One can foresee that even in a corporative society there could be more rapport between those in positions of hierarchical responsibility, be they representatives of labor or management, than between labor leaders and labor rank and file. Certainly, man has a natural affiliation to his economic endeavor, but the ties that bind him to his economic class are also of basic consequence. It is foolish to ignore the existence of class antagonism. The basic question is whether this antagonism negates the possibility of the development of vertical communities based upon economic endeavor.

Even more fundamentally, the Christian Democratic critique of liberal capitalism may miss a basic point. Scholars suggest that the Marxist critique of capitalism is in reality an examination of large-scale industrialism, per se, and not of any particular organization of the industrial complex. The alienation of man is not necessarily the result of capitalism but of the bigness that the modern industrial system necessarily implies. The same observation may be applied to the Christian Democratic theory. It is the complexity of the system that lies at the root of the modern dilemma, and insofar as the corporative or communitarian state retains large-scale industrial organi-

[7] *Ibid.*, p. 151. For another observation of this dilemma, see John Clark Adams, "Some Antecedents of the Theory of the Corporate System," *Journal of the History of Ideas*, III (April, 1942), 182.

zation, it will be characterized by a similar problem of alienation. This is not to say that beneficial modifications cannot be achieved through communitarian reforms; it does suggest that modern man must nonetheless pay the price of industrialization, involving at least a partial loss of community. The critics are correct when they warn the Christian Democrats that it is quite impossible to return to the idealized community of the Middle Ages, no matter what reforms are undertaken.

The same problem of integration applies on the national political level. Economic parliaments may not provide the cohesive factor that the theory proposes. Indeed, the very specialized expertise of these various groups creates the need for a political agency representing the nation as a whole. The official representation of economic and social interests may tend to divide more than it unifies the various sectors of the society. Traditional political party representation, which cuts across economic and social lines, seems to achieve more effective cooperation and consensus. Corporative legislative bodies may only accentuate the already serious divisions of Latin American society.[8]

In addition to these weaknesses of theory, there are practical social and economic problems involved in the Latin American Christian Democratic corporate, or communitarian, program. The fundamental question is whether or not the program can make a significant practical contribution to the solution of the problems facing Latin American society. A conservative Social Christian expresses doubt on this point. "I think that communitarian enterprises like joint associations of labor and capital and cooperatives . . . are plausible, desirable and merit assistance and promotion by means of adequate legislation. I do not believe, however, that these undertakings can seriously be offered as a solution for the recuperation and economic development of this country."[9] The social benefits of communitarianism will not necessarily have the economic effects that many optimistic Christian Democrats envision. Christian Democratic economic literature has not devoted adequate space to these problems. The practical problems inherent in the administration of any enterprise would seem to be compounded in a corporative communitarian situation, at least until a penetrating sense of community develops. One commentator

[8] See Sigmund Neumann (ed.), *Modern Political Parties* (Chicago: University of Chicago Press, 1956), p. 413.

[9] Vila Echague, *Cuestiones Disputadas*, p. 50.

echoes a criticism voiced earlier in this chapter when he concludes that "the communitarian enterprise demands in its collaborators and directors spiritual and moral conditions which are rarely encountered."[10]

It should be noted parenthetically that none of the Latin American parties has ever proposed a full-fledged corporative system with the legislative branch completely in the hands of corporate representation. Usually it is proposed either that one house in a bicameral legislature be formed on a corporate basis or that economic and social councils be established as advisory organs. Nevertheless, corporate thinking is an important strain in Latin American Christian Democracy, and the movement is clearly in danger of falling heir to the traditional fallacies of corporatism.

One final point merits attention. Commenting on his own nation's social Catholic program, an Austrian, Ernst Karl Winter, made this statement about corporative theory: "The idea of the corporative state is a metaphysical goal performing the same heuristic functions as the eschatology of the classless society. Playing the role of transcendent goals, both are legitimate bases for a concrete set of social policies. . . . It is quite clear that every political ideology needs a set of more or less similar goals for the spiritual basis of its action program."[11] If indeed, the concepts of corporate state or communitarian society are employed in this sense by Latin American Christian Democrats, a more moderate and realistic tone is set. If this functional postulation is not corrupted into crass demagogic deception or opportunism but remains an authentically felt aspiration and a model to be vigorously sought and practically approximated, then a felicitous balance of messianic idealism and hard-headed realism can be achieved. The Christian Democratic revolution can be achieved and maintained only by an artful blending of messianic zeal and realistic practicality.

THE LACK OF MIDDLE PRINCIPLES

Much of the vagueness of Latin American Christian Democratic programs might be attributed to their relative youth. The parties simply have not had the time and experience to compile more detailed and sophisticated programs. Another explanation is the

[10] *Ibid.*, p. 49.

[11] Diamant, *Austrian Catholics and the First Republic*, p. 238.

immaturity of Latin American politics as a whole; the lack of comprehensive platforms and well-constructed plans is not peculiar to Christian Democracy. It may be stated with some confidence that Christian Democrats are, on the whole, rather more concerned than most with filling in the lacunae of their programs. Nevertheless, all but the most advanced of the Latin American parties lack the time, money, experience, and expertise to construct well-prepared and internally consistent programs. Commenting on this problem in 1951, Frei Montalva admitted that "until now Christian Democracy has lacked an efficacious technology and generally has remained in the easy terrain of general principles."[12] He specifically set out to remedy the situation. It cannot be said, in all honesty, that he was very successful. Furthermore, even in those few instances where technical experts are to be found in sufficient numbers in Social Christian ranks, it is these very experts who are the most ideologically naive; the wedding of theory and program is still a difficult undertaking.

All Christian Democratic parties, both European and Latin American, have demonstrated a weakness in the development of what the movement refers to as "middle principles." Christian Democrats themselves call attention to this characteristic flaw and deplore their inability to work out a set of principles to link their well-developed philosophical ideas to day-to-day tactical considerations. A Latin American Christian Democrat, speaking of Christian Democratic communitarianism, demonstrates this concern. He asks these "classic questions: What goods are to be produced? For whom will they be produced?" They are not original questions, he admits, but they are an integral part of any political program.[13] A less friendly critic hits the same point. He charges that Christian Democratic efforts have been "scarcely superior to a diagnosis." "Christian Democracy postulates modification of the enterprise so that the worker will actively participate in the profits and administration. It does not explain 'how' this is to be achieved. My personal suspicion is that Christian Democracy has not found the 'how' or is not animated to pronounce on it, which is, in the last analysis, the same thing."[14]

There are several explanations for this weakness. One, the heterogeneity of the parties impedes agreement on solid measures. Two, the

[12] Eduardo Frei Montalva, *Sentido y Forma de una Política* (Santiago de Chile: Editorial del Pacífico, 1951), p. 66.

[13] Vila Echague, *Cuestiones Disputadas*, p. 42.

[14] Conteris, "La Próxima Disyuntiva de la D.C.," p. 20.

important religious implications of Christian Democratic thought are very difficult to reduce to plans of action and political programs. Three, the practical problems the parties face change rapidly, and permanent middle principles are therefore difficult to devise. Though this last point may often be used as an excuse for the weakness of party programs, the conditions inviting the ploy are quite real. In this vein, a Brazilian party leader emphasizes the necessity of recognizing the fundamental distinction between "ideology" and "program." Programs are concrete measures proposed for the solution of particular problems, which occur in determined times and places. Social doctrine is founded on reason and cannot be interpreted as being applicable to all times and all places. "Therefore, in the measure in which reality is transformed, programs vary and change." The ideology of the movement, on the other hand, is fixed and unalterable. "It can be made more profound and enriched by new perspectives, but cannot be substituted." An example of an unalterable dictum of "ideology" is the Social Christian belief in the fundamental equality of all human persons. One means to this end in modern Latin America is agrarian reform, an important cog of the Christian Democratic program.[15]

The vagueness and incompleteness of their programs limit the Christian Democrats to negative activity, to simply responding to initiatives emanating from other political groups or governments. Criticism or opposition tends to be too general in nature and concentrates on broad issues rather than centering on immediate problems. Seldom do Christian Democratic critiques include a technical evaluation, and even less often do they offer a well-prepared alternative. The unhappy result is that the parties are unable to point out next year's program with the same facility that they describe tomorrow's tactics or the Christian millennium's bountiful goodness. The older parties, such as those of Chile and Venezuela, suffer from this malady less than do the younger and weaker ones. Even at best, however, the programs lack sufficient clarity for really effective militancy or productive government.

Moreover, the lack of solid middle principles would seem to imply the danger of over-intellectualization and, therefore, a decreasing ability to meet the practical challenges of political reality. The history of the traditional Socialist parties in Latin America provides a dra-

[15] Andrés Franco Montoro, "Tarea de los Demócrata Cristianos," *Política y Espíritu*, XV (May, 1960), 11, 12.

matic example of just this problem. The well-known Latin American affinity for the philosophical and abstract makes very clear and present the danger of losing contact with the realities of politics. Neither Christ nor Maritain, sadly enough, offer concrete programs to solve concrete problems: over-reliance on either in the political arena can spell disaster. A large dose of political and intellectual discipline is necessary to an effective politic in Latin America, and Christian Democracy's ideological sophistication, its very strong point, could contain the germ of its destruction. The lessons of European Christian Democracy, valid or not for the Latin American scene, show that those parties which have been least ideological and most technologically prepared are the ones that have achieved success. Perhaps one of the reasons for the decline of the French party was its failure to devise a set of middle principles;[16] the successful German party, on the other hand, has had a sophisticated practical program and a relative dearth of philosophy.

However, the very fact that the middle principles of the movement are nebulous may be an advantage; the parties can benefit from their consequent flexibility. Christian Democrats are not regulated by arid and untimely pronouncements emanating from Moscow or Peking. Moreover, those who criticize the nebulous principles and the failure to construct a coherent program miss an important point. Victory and success, in the short run, are bred by the dynamics of a mystique, which the Christian Democratic movement has assuredly created. The cry of "Peace, Land and Bread," for instance, was not a sophisticated program, and yet it caught the spirit of the times and penetrated the masses.

INTERNAL PROBLEMS

A viable democratic system requires willingness to compromise and to cooperate, both with other parties or groups in a national society and within the group itself. Unbending ideological stances by political parties can create insurmountable difficulties for the society; rigid adherence to factions within a political organization can be equally deleterious to its effectiveness. Diversity and conflict are inevitable.

[16] See Michael P. Fogarty, *Christian Democracy in Western Europe, 1820–1953* (Notre Dame, Ind.: University of Notre Dame Press, 1957), pp. 338, 339, and Mario Einaudi and François Goguel, *Christian Democracy in Italy and France* (Notre Dame, Ind.: University of Notre Dame Press, 1952), pp. 123, 124.

Of course, differences vary in their degree. Still, a test of Christian Democracy in Latin America will be how well it succeeds in handling the internal struggles it will inevitably face.

The volatile and incoherent nature of Latin American politics is well known. The traditional parties were constantly plagued by dissident factions. The Personalist agglomerations divided and redivided at the whim of the leader or counter-leader. The ideological parties of the twentieth century have had to deal with this same problem; the Radicals, traditional Socialists, Aprista Socialists, and even the Communists have been troubled with internal division which has frequently erupted into complete party splits. A mere listing of prominent Latin American political parties dramatizes this point. Among them are Peoples Radicals, Intransigent Radicals; Acción Democrática, Acción Democrática-ARS; Red Communist, Black Communist; Auténticos, Ortodoxos; and Social Christian Conservative, Traditional Conservative.

In such a context of division and defection, it is perfectly natural that the Christian Democrats also would have experienced internal difficulties. Generalization is rather difficult, but an investigation of the Social Christian parties seems to indicate that they have suffered less than most from internal disintegration. On the nineteenth anniversary of the founding of the Venezuelan Social Christian-COPEI, for instance, the Caracas daily, *La Esfera*, editorialized that the "magnificent cohesion," and "internal unity" of the COPEI "merits careful study and understanding."[17]

The COPEI experience is unusual even for Christian Democratic ranks, however; few of the parties have been so fortunate. The splits among Social Christians are of two types: division within a formally unified Christian Democratic party, and, in a few countries, division between two or more competing parties. Often the more Conservative of the Christian parties is not a Social Christian entity at all, but a traditional Catholic party.[18] These Catholic parties often include numerous authentic Social Christians among their militants and adherents, weakening the effectiveness of the Christian Democratic party's activity. Conversely, especially in nations having no traditional Conservative parties, the internal problems of the Christian Democratic groups are frequently the result of the inclusion of tra-

[17] Quoted in Prensa Nacional, *Los 19 Años de COPEI* ("Publicaciones de la Fracción Parlamentaria de COPEI," No. 28 [Caracas, 1965]), p. 746.

[18] See pp. 9–12 for the distinction.

ditional, conservative Catholics in Social Christian organizations.

In addition to the conservative Catholic middle class, which usually provides the opposition from the Right, the various youth affiliates and Christian labor union organizations often draw the parties to the Left. The labor groups are not so obdurate as the youth organizations, however, and usually learn the realistic lessons of political militancy more readily than their younger brethren.[19] Other common divisive factors are the personal ambitions of some Social Christians and the frequent lack of effective leadership.

Even when the parties are blessed with able leadership, the very immaturity of Latin American politics can create disciplinary problems. The much-discussed Latin individualism and ingrained distrust of regimentation augurs ill for internal discipline. A Chilean, whose party has been relatively free of acute internal problems, suggests that the Social Christian parties have suffered an "excess of tolerance, a congenital good faith" and that they "lack a sense of discipline and permit a prejudicial dispersion between the . . . national directorates and the local or specialized agencies."[20] Moreover, coordination has been impeded by numerical growth within the parties. As the parties come closer to actually gaining governmental power, they often acquiesce to pressure from one faction or another in order to increase their electoral strength.[21]

Furthermore, as has been noted, the Christian Democrats often fall victim to their own heterogeneity. Latin American Christian Democratic parties usually encompass a less comprehensive vertical slice of the society than do their European cousins, and yet they still include a more varied electorate than do any of the other major forces in Latin America. The problem is less severe for those parties in nations having relatively strong Conservative parties that can provide a home for conservative Catholics, thus reducing the diversity in Christian Democratic party membership. The corporate structure of Christian Democratic parties intensifies this problem, for it tends to

[19] Enrique Pérez Olivares and Néstor Coll Blasini, interview (Caracas, May 18, 19, 1965).

[20] Jaime Castillo Velasco, "El Partido Social Cristiano, Instrumento de una Política Popular," *Política y Espíritu*, X (Aug. 15, 1954), 17.

[21] Pedro Pablo Aguilar, *Los Partidos Demócrata Cristianos*, lecture prepared for El Instituto de Formación Demócrata Cristiana (Caracas, mimeographed, n.d.), p. 13. Aguilar posits the Italian party as an example.

encourage separate policies, and reconciliation and compromise are made more troublesome. A Venezuelan Social Christian observes this tendency among Christian Democratic parties and warns that "there must be great care that it does not encroach upon the unity of the party or impede the efficacy of partisan activity.'[22]

Each party faction exercises some degree of influence on programs and policies, and Social Christians consequently cannot approach the homogeneity or unity of action demonstrated by some of their rivals, particularly the Communists. The chasms separating "Socialists who pray," middle-class reformers, and those who are allied to the cause as the least of several evils are sometimes impossible to bridge. The result is either vagueness or internal inconsistency in party programs and pronouncements. Duverger sees this problem as being characteristic of all Center parties.

> Every Center is divided against itself and remains separated into two halves. For the Center is nothing more than the artificial grouping of the right wing of the Left and left wing of the Right. The fate of the Center is to be torn asunder, buffeted and annihilated: torn asunder when one of its halves votes Right and the other Left, buffeted when it votes as a group first Right then Left, annihilated when it abstains from voting. The dream of the Center is to achieve a synthesis of contradictory aspirations; but synthesis is a power only of the mind. Action involves choice and politics involves action. The history of Center parties would provide examples in support of this abstract argument: take for example the fortunes of the Radical Party under the Third French Republic, the fortunes of the Socialists or the MRP [i.e., Christian Democratic party] under the Fourth. There are no true Centers, only superimposed dualisms.[23]

Another problem, particularly acute in countries without vital rightist political groups, is the difference that can prevail between the attitudes of the leaders and those of less progressive electors. The leaders have been drawn from the ranks of genuine Social Christians who were often nurtured in their university days on the papal encyclicals and the teachings of liberal European Social Christian thinkers. Much of the electorate, however, is still recruited from the ranks

[22] *Ibid.*

[23] Maurice Duverger, *Political Parties: Their Organization and Activity in the Modern State* trans. Barbara and Robert North (New York: John Wiley and Sons, Inc., 1963), p. 215.

of the traditional Catholic Right. The growing social consciousness of Catholic parties throughout the world has exacerbated this tension between Christian Democrats and Conservative Catholics. It is a problem facing Christian Democrats in Europe as well as in Latin America.

Convincing would-be party members that Christian Democracy implies more than regular attendance at mass is a constant problem. Many join for religious reasons and have no idea of the political and social implications of the connection. One recent study of Latin American politics has noted:

> A problem faced by all the parties of Christian Social orientation is that of maintaining equilibrium between the terms at the two ends of the Hyphen, as it were, and especially of not allowing the party's proclerical predilection to eclipse its stand for social progress. The problem arises in this form because many supporters are attracted to an avowedly Christian party, for reasons of conscience, who do not share its progressive orientation on social questions. The more devout are still likely, in Latin America as elsewhere, to be the more conservative; and the party's leaders have to maintain constant vigilance lest the party's political position begin to drift Rightward in response to opinion among the rank and file.[24]

In the same vein, Frei Montalva has cautioned that one of the "great dangers" for the future of Christian Democracy is the "tendency to falsify it. There are those who simultaneously want to applaud De Gasperi, Bidault and Franco."[25]

Since President Frei's electoral triumph in Chile, this peril has become more immediate. Christian Democracy has become a vogue in Latin America, and everyone declares himself a Christian Democrat. It has been correctly noted that "Christian Democracy can suffer from semantic confusion and can easily become a cloak with which discredited Right wing parties hide their nakedness."[26] Amoroso Lima issued a similar warning much before the Frei victory. The infiltration and predominance of traditional "conservative and proprietary" forces within social Catholic ranks, he cautioned, would mean that "the only prospect for the future is bloody conflict, the

[24] Martin C. Needler, *Latin American Politics in Perspective* (Princeton, N. J.: D. Van Nostrand Company, 1963), pp. 97, 98.

[25] Frei Montalva, *Sentido y Forma*, p. 86.

[26] Alistair Hennessy, "The Bolivian Coup d'etat," *The World Today*, XXI (Feb., 1965), 53.

dictatorship of the proletariat, Soviet imperialism and the indefinite postponement of the more human and rational society . . . to which we aspire."[27]

It should be noted, in conclusion, that despite these problems and dangers, the Latin American Christian Democrats have built relatively close-knit and effective organizations. There may be several explanations for the relative solidarity of the Christian Democratic parties. They are still rather young, and many have simply not had the time to develop serious internal problems. Moreover, except in a few instances, the parties have not assumed the reigns of government; they have not encountered the problems of reconciling ideals to reality, always a crucial confrontation for political parties. Most important, however, seems to be the quasi-religious nature of Social Christian organizations and the pronounced mystique which the Latin American parties have developed and nurtured. This bond has replaced the traditional one of rationalized mutual self-interest,[28] and, up to now, has sufficed. The parties have not been inordinately troubled with internal splits or ideological deviation. The test, however, will come when the parties attain power and are forced to activate a practical program. Then the internal inconsistencies may create much more serious difficulties.

DISSENSION IN THE LATIN AMERICAN PARTIES

The intensity of internal dissension in the several Latin American Christian Democratic parties varies. Several of the parties—perhaps the Chilean Partido Demócrata Cristiano and the Venezuelan Social Christian-COPEI are the best examples—have displayed a strong and very un-Latin American unity. Other parties have not fared so well.

The Brazilian party has been traditionally plagued by vociferous, and often petty, internal differences. The party is divided into three wings. The Right is composed of traditional Conservatives, Catholic Conservatives, and some military men. It is led by ex-Marshall Juarez Tavora and is strongest in the south. One of the faction's outstanding spokesmen, Ney Braga, has held the gubernatorial post in Paraná state. The Right controlled the party machinery when Braga

[27] Alceu Amoroso Lima, "The Problem of Labor," *Latin American Social Thought*, ed. Harold E. Davis (Washington: The University Press, 1961), p. 524.

[28] For an observation on this point, see Duverger, *Political Parties*, p. 27.

was president and Juaréz Tavora the secretary-general, from 1963 until 1965. The Right was overthrown at the party's 1965 national convention and the Center faction, led by Franco Montoro, took power.[29] The Center assumes a moderate Left position characteristic of most Latin American Christian Democratic parties. The Center leadership formally rejected cooperation with the ruling military government established in 1964 despite the fact that most of the party's national representatives voted with government forces. The left wing of the Brazilian party has been led by the dynamic, disputatious, and controversial Paulo de Tarso Santos. Its greatest strength is in the north of Brazil. The left wing supports radical reforms in internal affairs and a policy of nationalism and neutralism in foreign affairs.[30] De Tarso and the left wing are very strong among the radical Social Christian student element which operates in the Acção Popular. De Tarso held the post of education minister under the Goulart regime and was on the first of the 1964 revolution's proscription lists. He was arrested by the Castello Branco military government and jailed. Several Social Christian parties and labor organizations of other Latin American countries formally protested the arrest of De Tarso by the Brazilian government. He eventually went into exile in Chile.

Although the Brazilian group grew rather rapidly during the late fifties and early sixties, its internal dissensions have crippled its ability to take full advantage of the ideological vapidity of the traditional Brazilian parties and the seemingly fruitful terrain for growth. Internal problems have never resulted in a serious split within the party or even in numerous desertions; differences are usually compromised. Nevertheless, the Christian Democrats are in danger of falling into the same mold as the rest of the nation's parties; programs are vague if they are published at all, party discipline is practically non-existent, leadership is weak, and party militants vacillate between support and rejection of the party's so-called official line. Indeed, the organization has been racked with opportunism and shows clear signs of already having crested in strength and importance.

There are three explanations for the extreme ideological vagueness and undisciplined activity. First, there is no Catholic right-wing

[29] See "¡Derrotado Ney Braga en Elección del PDC!" *DECE*, I (April, 1965), 4.

[30] See *Hispanic American Report*, XVI (Dec., 1963), 1015.

party in Brazil. Consequently, some of the Catholic Right has gravitated to the Christian Democratic party and formed its most conservative sector. In some other nations, the battle between Social Christians and conservative Catholics has crystallized around two identifiable parties, but in Brazil the struggle is within the party. Moreover, the right wing is, on the whole, more tightly organized than the other party factions and exercises a strong influence in party circles. Second, the internal struggle has sapped the energies and diverted the attention of the more progressive sectors and resulted in ideological incoherence. Finally, no strong leader has emerged to unite the disparate factions. Both the Left and the Right lack the strength to guide the party, and the Center has been vacillating and indecisive, if not opportunistic.

All this, of course, must be seen in the context of Brazilian politics. All major parties in Brazil are marked by internal dissension, diverse wings, and lack of clear programs. Certainly, much of the explanation is to be found in the geographic complexity and intense regionalism of Brazil. In addition, Brazilian political history displays more pragmatism than is found elsewhere on the continent. There is, in fact, some similarity between Brazilian and North American politics in their lack of ideological commitment, regionalism, and essentially pragmatic content.

Of all Latin American Christian Democratic parties the Argentine party has surely exhibited the most dramatic change of direction during its history. In 1955, the Argentine party was formed as a moderate Center organization; but after splits and leadership changes it has shifted to the Left, if not the Jacobin Left, in pursuit of the Peronist electorate. Moreover, the Christian Democratic or Catholic effort has been split among competing forces in Argentina. This split comes as no surprise in a nation which has numbered two Radical parties, two Socialist parties, and two Communist groups. One Social Christian observer sees the problems of the Christian Democratic movement as being but a part of the post-Perón adjustment period "which reflects the radical changes in the political and economic system. . . ."[31] After the fall of Perón, the Christian Democratic party, the Christian Democratic Federal Union, and the Blue and White party were formed. The last two of these organizations were more nationalistic and Catholic than the Partido Demócrata

[31] "CD Crystallizes in Argentina," *Christian Democratic Review*, IX (June-July, 1959), 17.

Cristiano. The opportunity for a broadly based Christian Democratic party was obviated by the rivalry among the three groups. The impossibility of expansion to the Right undoubtedly played a role in the eventual decision of the party to seek support from the Left when its policy changed under new leadership in 1961.

The change of leadership has not resolved the Christian Democratic party's internal problems. In 1964 the party was still plagued by dissension. A former vice-president of the party flaunted the line of the group, resigned, and accepted an ambassadorial post.[32] The party has not fully enacted its policy of courting the Peronist masses because of strong opposition from within the party ranks. The entire history of the Argentine party displays numerous splits and an inconsistent policy, for it has never been completely unified.

The movement in the Dominican Republic has suffered the same problems as in Argentina: the Catholic and Christian Democratic forces have been divided among three parties, and the strongest, the ODCA-blessed Partido Revolucionario Social Cristiano (PRSC), has itself been troubled by internal dissension. After the fall of Trujillo, three parties utilizing the Social Christian name were formed: the Partido Demócrata Cristiano, the Partido Progresista Demócrata Cristiano and the Partido Revolucionario Social Cristiano; the first two were conservative and much smaller than the third. The PRSC has been rent by internal division almost from the beginning. The international Christian Democratic movement sent missions to mediate the problems of the potentially powerful party and refused to accept students at the Caracas leadership school until the PRSC had reunited. During the military struggle in the spring of 1965, the two factions became even more widely separated. The minority group of the party, led by Guido D'Alessandro, refused to support either the military junta or the constitutionalists. The other faction, under the leadership of Antonio Rosario and Caonabo Javier Castillo, was a major component of the Caamaño constitutionalist forces. This more progressive group also had the support of the strong Dominican Social Christian labor movement. The crisis was finally resolved at an ODCA executive meeting in August, 1965, but internal problems again plagued the party during the presidential elections in 1966.

The Uruguayan party has suffered the classic crisis of a Christian Democratic organization evolving from a conservative Catholic

[32] See *Hispanic American Report*, XVII (June, 1964), 358.

party. The internal schisms are basically ideological in nature but tend to be reinforced by the confrontation of different generations. The party, after a series of internal splits, defections, and purges throughout the early sixties, is now in the process of achieving unity. The younger, more advanced sectors of the party have been gaining increasing strength. In 1961, internal problems resulted in the suspension of some of the younger members of the party who were Castro sympathizers.[33] Three years later, however, similar doctrinal differences resulted in the defection of a significant sector of the party's old guard and the formation of the Unión Cívica Católica. To be sure, some of the party's more radical youth bolted the group in that same year, but the progressive younger factions have slowly been achieving ascendency over the traditional leadership of the party. The party's internal problems are intensified by a division between Montevideans and the provincials of Uruguay. Furthermore, the neighboring Argentine *apertura al Peronismo* has attracted the attention of some sectors of the Uruguayan party, and a similar radical departure is often discussed among the more advanced groups within the Partido Demócrata Cristiano.

The growth of Christian Democracy in Mexico, and the attempt of several groups to capitalize on the increasing prestige of the Social Christian label, has produced many self-styled Christian Democratic parties and movements. The old Partido de Acción Nacional, the Unión Nacional Sinarquista, the Partido Demócrata Cristiano, and the Movimiento Social Demócrata Cristiano have, with varying degrees of enthusiasm and credibility, called themselves Christian Democratic or Social Christian movements. ODCA recognized the Movimiento, and it benefited from defections from the other parties, especially the large and politically significant Partido de Acción Nacional. Indeed, the PAN traditionally harbored a left-wing Social Christian movement. There are no strong divisions within the Movimiento, although some regionalism has caused minor problems.

The internal division of the Cuban exile movement is an interesting variation on the theme of dissension. There are ideological differences centering on the usual Liberal-Conservative dichotomy, but the Cuban problems revolved around a split within the Movimiento over the policy appropriate to a party in exile. The two factions are those that favor putting an emphasis on the military overthrow of

[33] See *ibid.*, XIV (Sept., 1961), 646.

Castro and those that see ideological formation, study, political training, and preparation for eventual return as most important. The party has been criticized by other Latin American Social Christians for over-emphasizing the importance of Communism to the detriment of the formation of coherent doctrine.[34]

The Peruvian party has been clearly divided into leftist and conservative sectors. Until early 1967, however, the party had been successful in containing the frequently intense differences that separated the two wings. Both groups had controlled the party, and neither attempted to destroy the other. In point of fact, both had been ready to make important concessions in the interests of party unity and effective action. At the party's Eighth National Congress in 1965, the factions demonstrated their ability to compromise. The left-wing faction controlled the conclave and elected its leadership. Despite its obvious dissatisfaction with previous policy, the new leadership compromised its differences with the conservative wing, toned down its critique of the government, and awarded several important posts to the conservatives. The party had been controlled by the conservative wing from 1962 to 1965 and managed to resolve its internal problems. The long-smoldering internal dissension finally broke the bonds of compromise early in 1967, however, when the conservative wing bolted the party and formed a new group, the Partido Popular Cristiano. The new group counts all of the old guard and is led by Senator Mario Polar Ugarteche and Bedoya Reyes. The Partido Demócrata Cristiano, led by the militant Cornejo Chávez, managed to retain about two-thirds of the party membership and is very strong among the youth.[35]

It is no surprise, of course, that the strongest of the Latin American Christian Democratic parties are precisely those that have most successfully used compromise to contain or resolve their internal differences. There are, it seems, mutually reinforcing factors at work. Success implies possible advantages from party membership and encourages unity; on the other hand, unity has made success at the polls possible. The continent's two most successful parties, the Chil-

[34] See, for instance, Tomás Reyes Vicuña, *Planificación en la Libertad . . .*, lecture prepared for El Instituto de Formación Demócrata Cristiana (Caracas, mimeographed), p. 19.

[35] On the party split, see "Gatos de Dos Tipos," *Vision*, XXXII (Jan. 20, 1967), pp. 113–14. For a description of the 1965 party convention, see "Golpe de Estado en la Democracia Cristiana," *Oiga*, III (March 19, 1965), pp. 6–8.

ean and Venezuelan, have been successful in resolving internal differences and forming unified policy and doctrine.

Moderation has characterized the factions within the strong Chilean party. Factions representing Left, Right, and Center exist in the party, and all three have controlled the party's presidency without sabotaging its unity. Frei Montalva leads the party's Center. His commanding personality has been an important cohesive factor, but even at their most extreme the Left and Right are not far removed from the Center position. The Left is led by the dynamic and able Radomiro Tomic, clearly the second figure in the party. The Left's program differs more in degree than in substance from the Center; no unbridgeable chasms separate them. The long-time rallying point of the Left, an opening of the party to Chilean Socialists and Communists, has proved unnecessary; the Christian Democrats elected both a president and congressional majority without the electoral assistance of the Chilean Left.[36]

The Venezuelan Social Christian-COPEI is another example of a close-knit Latin American party. The success of the party is certainly one of the explanations; its leadership has guided the organization well. COPEI is Venezuela's fastest growing party and has an excellent chance of coming to power in 1969. Party leader, Rafael Caldera, is highly respected even among the aggressive, more advanced leadership of the party, who sometimes strain against the tight reins of moderation. This group, led by Luís Herrera Campins, Rodolfo J. Cárdenas, and Hugo Briceño Salas, seems to display a rather more pugnacious bent than does Caldera, but there are no glimmerings of overt rebellion. The party has suffered no serious ideological deviations, and occasional examples of opportunism are handled swiftly and efficiently, providing strong evidence of the organization's effective discipline.[37]

THE REVOLUTION

Latin American Christian Democracy has set a high goal for itself: the fundamental transformation of the Latin American society. Such a revolution involves basic social and economic reforms. Moreover,

[36] For a dissenting opinion on the coherence of the Chilean party, see Conteris, "La Próxima Disyuntiva de la D.C.," p. 20.

[37] See Romualdo Ventura, "Los 19 Años de COPEI," *Bohemia*, Jan. 24, 1965, pp. 14A–15A.

the revolution is to be achieved within a democratic system. The movement, in sum, seeks a *Revolución en Libertad.* It is, even in its most moderate form, a very far-reaching proposal.

Many have noted that Latin Americans may be growing disenchanted with political democracy. One of the causes is the presence of demagogues who have promised much and delivered little. The Christian Democratic movement has not been demagogic, but it has at least given the impression that a Christian Democratic government can and will live up to the promise of the good society. Furthermore, the literature makes reasonably clear the belief that measurable progress can be achieved within a relatively short time; it insists that changing the structure of society is politically feasible. Much of the campaign rhetoric is, naturally, effusive, but the sobering questions must be asked: Is the revolution possible and is it possible under Christian Democratic aegis? The success of the programs, obviously, depends upon the efficiency, imagination, power, and good fortune of the movement.

Christian Democracy will encounter grave problems in delivering the messianic dream to the people of Latin America. One astute student of Latin American politics has pointed to the fundamental problem:

> The social and cultural matrix within which Latin America's political leaders operate at present is such that effective and representative popular democracy is, with few exceptions, not a feasible alternative. The only really responsible question that a democratically minded observer can ask of a politician in Latin America today is whether his conduct is conducive toward increasing the prospect of popular and representative democracy.[38]

Another study points up other problems.

> Politics is the art of the possible. Latin America differs fundamentally from many of the new nations of Africa and Asia in that the traditional power holders have not withdrawn, but remain a vital part of the political system. The new leaders, the fervent interpreters of the revolution of rising expectations in this area, have a fundamental choice to make. To make their program effective, they must either destroy their political competitors when their policies come in conflict with the interest of the dominant groups, as seems

[38] Frank Tannenbaum, *Ten Keys to Latin America* (New York: Alfred A. Knopf, 1962), p. 144.

to be the case in Cuba, or seek to accommodate and reconcile the interests of those dominant groups within their programs.[39]

The task of reconciling the demands of political office, and the undeniable corrupting influence of power with the promised democratic means and the revolution, is destined to be the greatest challenge to Christian Democrats. The decline of the Aprista Socialists is in no small part attributable to this very same quandary. The hopes engendered by Betancourt, Haya de la Torre, Figueres, and Bosch were simply impossible to fulfill; even the best of circumstances coupled with the most effective policies would have fallen short.

The debilitating influences of political struggle and of governmental responsibility are all too obvious to need detailed description. One commentator on Latin American politics has already predicted the possible effects on Christian Democracy. Commenting on the Argentine party's courting of the Peronistas, he notes pungently: "It may be too early to say, but it seems that . . . Christian Democracy in Latin America will condemn itself to being just another crab in the basket." The Argentine example was seen as a generally applicable indication of the plight of Latin American Christian Democracy.

> Christian Democracy seems to be failing in Latin America. It appealed to many because it offered something more satisfying than material progress. . . . Yet this mirage seems to be little more than a glimmer on arid sands. The sorry plight of the Christian Democratic movement in Argentina shows its essential weakness. The brute struggle for political power, which is a basic fact of life everywhere and especially in Latin America, has destroyed the dream of Christian brotherhood.[40]

Although this observation was elicited by the internal power struggle in the Argentine party, it nonetheless dramatized the fact that a Christian effort is often not possible in the unredeemed world of practical politics. The messianic crusade proposed by the Social Christians is an over-simplification and all too frequently creates more problems than it solves.

The corrosiveness of governmental responsibility is omnipresent. Power necessarily tends to diminish the following of a governing

[39] Charles W. Anderson, "Politics and Development Policy in Central America," *Midwest Journal of Political Science*, V (Nov., 1961), 349.

[40] "Commentary," *Hispanic American Report*, XVII (March, 1964), 6.

party. A party is forced to modify its program and cannot always fulfill the promises that brought it to power. Furthermore, power tends to accentuate the diversities within the ruling party and draws out previously compromised differences. This dilemma will be faced by the Christian Democratic parties as they gain control of government, and it will be exaggerated to the degree that they have created unrealizable expectations.

The brief experience of the Christian Democratic government in Chile provides a concrete example. "The Government of Frei," as one Latin American commentator notes, "is loyally and skillfully leading Chile toward the goals announced by this Christian Socialist Party during the election."[41] The statement is probably correct. The Frei government has been rather successful in translating the *Revolución en Libertad* into concrete legislation. The dynamic president has done amazingly well, and the party has maintained good, although not perfect, discipline. A North American student surveyed the Chilean situation after the first year or so of Frei's presidency and arrived at a cautiously optimistic conclusion. He first warned that the program is "too ambitious" and that "the government is not likely to produce the money required to finance the public investments that Frei called for during his campaign." Be that as it may: "the government's prospects of achieving sufficient economic gains and social reform to keep totalitarian forces at bay are good, and they compare favorably with the hopes of democratic forces elsewhere in the hemisphere."[42]

Nevertheless, the government experienced very serious labor problems during 1965, and ominous signs appeared which possibly indicate more of the same for the future. Admittedly, much of the blame may be placed on political manipulation by the left-wing FRAP. This explanation, however, is quite beside the point. The fact is that the government has entered upon a very dangerous course which has, at least temporarily, cost it popularity and support. A Chilean writes that "the President and his collaborators, nevertheless, have remained firm. They recall that the country was offered three or four hard years along a difficult, and perhaps painful, path. In order to attain the fixed goals, they say, it is necessary to inflexibly maintain

[41] "The Enigma of Latin America's Christian Socialists," *CIF Reports*, V (Feb., 1966), 23.

[42] Cole Blasier, *Chile in Transition* (Washington: Public Affairs Press, 1966), p. 14.

themselves within the planned route, although it may be at the cost of a loss of popularity."[43]

It is, of course, easy to sympathize with the Frei government and wave a righteous finger at the intemperate and shortsighted masses. Again, sadly enough, this retort is beside the point. The *Revolución en Libertad* demands, indeed, presupposes, popular support. A revolution without popular support is first a corruption of the ideology and, more relevantly, perhaps practically impossible. Frei himself has proclaimed that his election must be considered a mandate. What the Chilean people have given, however, the Chilean people may take away. The author quoted above has outlined the response of at least one sector of these people: "They have—they say—many immediate problems to resolve. They are not able to wait."[44] Thus far this attitude has not cost the Frei government the backing of the majority of the people, but it would be foolish to fail to see the possible problems of the future. The Chilean union movement is still dominated by the Socialist and Communist Left, and it is abundantly clear that the opposition will make trouble for the Frei government at every conceivable opportunity.

Moreover, the ideological purity and practical zeal of Christian Democracy is sure to be compromised by the infiltration of opportunistic elements, especially prevalent in developing nations where governmental position is both highly regarded and relatively lucrative. The amazing growth of Latin American Christian Democracy has already attracted these groups. This is not to charge that consciously evil men are working to upset the plans of the movement but only to recognize that successful political groups naturally attract the previously lukewarm. Commenting on the Frei government, a Chilean Radical has pointed up this danger. "Christian Democracy will wilt and wither away simply because it is in power," he warns. "Its ranks have changed from an elite class of technicians to a heterogeneous mass which has been infiltrated by displaced Marxist-Socialists, ultranationalists and others."[45]

More fundamental than these debilitating practical problems is the question of the practicality of the ideological postulates. The

[43] Alejandro Cabrera Ferrada, "1965: Año del Desafío para Frei," *Ercilla*, No. 1.595, Dec. 29, 1965, p. 11.

[44] *Ibid.*, p. 12.

[45] "Chile: Convention Reappraisal," *The Latin American Times*, July 1, 1965, p. 3.

movement continually reiterates the need to work within the democratic system, utilizing democratic measures and respecting the human personality. Christian Democrats insist that authoritarian and totalitarian methods are self-defeating and unproductive. The important question, however, centers on whether or not democratic measures can achieve the radical aims which the movement seeks. Can a movement which operates in an even minimally democratic atmosphere hope to achieve reforms which are sure to mean recalcitrant opposition from strongly entrenched sectors of Latin American society? The lessons of Latin American experience in the past, as well as present indications, demonstrate the difficulties involved. Major reform movements in Latin America, including those in Mexico, Bolivia, Argentina, and Cuba, have resulted in authoritarianism and violence. Perhaps Uruguay has been the only nation to undertake significant economic reforms without a major upheaval, and even there the reforms have not reached the entire society.

In a study on *The Venezuelan Democratic Revolution* one scholar concludes: "It has not been shown that economic development sufficiently rapid to bring measurable benefits to sizable segments of the population in a short time is possible in Latin America through democratic processes."[46] The Venezuelan experiment counted the advantages of popular, honest, hardworking, and relatively able leadership, adequate financial resources, a receptive populace, and outside assistance. It was still unable to achieve the projected economic goals in the democratic environment which was so hopefully predicted. Moreover, the situation appears to be growing worse rather than better. The increasing restlessness of the Latin American masses inflamed by Cuban, Russian, and Chinese propaganda, coupled with the growing obduracy of the right-wing forces, seems to presage even more difficulty for democratic movements. In short, the *Revolución en Libertad* is but a slim hope; social revolution in tandem with political democracy is a noble but probably overly hopeful proposition.

A critic has framed the dilemma rather differently, but he has hit on the essential problem. Discussing the Chilean Christian Democratic government, he asks: "How long will it be able to maintain the illusion of simultaneously remaining faithful to its Christian prin-

[46] Robert J. Alexander, *The Venezuelan Democratic Revolution* (New Brunswick, N. J.: Rutgers University Press, 1964), p. 314.

ciples, to a procedure chained to the individual rights which only through an error of historical perspective or a lack of theological clarity have been made consubstantial with the Christian faith?"[47] The same observer elucidates what he thinks are the inherent limitations of Christian Democracy. The movement considers the problem of Chilean copper but it does not arrive at the only "natural resolution, nationalization." It talks much about agrarian reform but is unable to propose the "viable and immediate" solution of expropriation because Christian Democracy is wedded to the principles of private property and total indemnification. In conclusion, the commentator predicts a "grave and not very distant dilemma" for the movement. Chilean Christian Democracy will either have to renounce its goals and utilize the smoke screen of postponement and patience because it cannot solve the basic problems certain to be encountered, or it will have to align with the forces of the Chilean Left, the Socialists and Communists, and "make use of methods which are not only repugnant to its conscience but are also those which it had harshly criticized during the campaign."[48]

This interpretation would seem to be substantially valid. If the descriptions and predictions of much of the recent literature be correct, then the movement will be forced to make a fundamental decision. Either it will choose to abide by the Christian and democratic methods which it has outlined, and probably be relegated to the impotent position of middle-class reformers, or it will forsake the much-heralded means in favor of radical reforms that create basic tensions in the society if not overt violence, repression, and authoritarianism. Either alternative is a corruption of the optimistic Christian Democratic politic and a failure to attain the promises of *Revolución en Libertad.*

Moreover, either decision would probably spell profound internal dissension within the parties and within the supporting electorate. Despite the existence of left and right wings, the movement is essentially in the Center, and a failure to succeed in its promised line will no doubt play havoc with discipline and electoral strength. In-

[47] Conteris, "La Próxima Disyuntiva de la D.C.," p. 21.

[48] *Ibid.*, pp. 20, 21. This article was written before the legislative elections of March, 1965, in which the Christian Democrats gained an absolute majority in the lower chamber and improved their position in the Senate. The increased strength of the party might modify this interpretation, although, it must be admitted, it does not substantially alter the essential critique.

deed, the middle position of the parties hits at the very core of the problem. A revolution, with or without liberty, implies dynamic activity and tight discipline, and a middle party may not be capable of such an undertaking. European experience indicates that Christian Democratic parties have not been innovators and revolutionaries at all but, instead, constructive rebuilders and effective adapters. European Christian Democracy has been conservatively pragmatic, not revolutionary.[49] There is, admittedly, a difference between the Latin American and European movements, but it is not fundamental. Neither their theory nor their practice indicates that the Latin American Christian Democrats will be successful revolutionaries.

THE CHRISTIAN ELECTORATE

If European experience serves as any indication, the Latin American Christian Democratic parties will eventually face the problem of expanding beyond the bedrock base of conscious believers. This assumes the proportions of a dilemma if Christian Democratic parties are indeed restricted by their identification with the Christian religion and the Catholic Church.[50] Of course, this is not a problem to the parties until they have been successful in completely absorbing their natural electorate; few of the groups have yet to achieve this much success at the polls, although the rapid growth of most of the Latin American parties seems to indicate that it is a distinct possibility.

The European parties have found their Christian identification very advantageous, but they have also discovered that it has limitations. European Christian Democracy, especially in its earlier years, achieved little success in garnering support in non-Christian strata; more recently there has been a concerted effort to transcend the image of narrowly religious politics. Commenting on the European situation, one student has said:

> The fact that some at least of the Christian Democratic movements, in such important fields as politics or the labor movement, have expanded to, or within striking distance of, the natural limits of their recruitment, obviously poses a question. Where next? If their

[49] See Arnold J. Heidenheimer, *Adenauer and the CDU* (The Hague: Martinus Nijhoff, 1960), pp. 16, 17.

[50] For the link between the parties and the Church, see pp. 167–169, 178–182.

> influence is to go on growing, are new sources of membership to be tapped, or is it enough to strengthen the various movements within their existing limits and add to their alliances outside? Should the existing structure of Christian parties and social movements, recruiting in fact if not in theory overwhelmingly from Christian believers, be "broken through"?[51]

There is good reason to believe that a similar situation will plague the Latin American branch of the Christian Democratic movement. As Latin America becomes increasingly modernized, it will also become more receptive to the messages of competing ideologies, cultural patterns, and political doctrines. The result, of course, will be that the Social Christians will have to expand their electoral strength beyond the scope of Christian adherents; the word of Christ and the village priest will not suffice. The decline of the traditional Conservative parties has already borne witness to this development; the Catholic atmosphere and the Catholic Church will not be enough to carry the parties.

Some European Social Christians have suggested that the ecumenical movement has adversely affected political Christian Democracy. Cooperation among the several sects and the much-publicized attempts at dialogue between Catholics and Socialists and Communists have broken down some of the old prejudices, erasing the stigma against Catholics' seeking other political allegiances. Catholics now feel free to join or vote for Liberal, Socialist, and Communist parties.

One student, writing on "The Future of Christianity in Latin America," notes that "Latin America today is already a pluralistic world, even if some 90 per cent of the population in most countries has been baptized." "Each man has many ideologies in front of him, . . . and he can choose the one he likes."[52] Although the census figures in Latin America perennially report that well over 90 percent of the continent is Catholic, one recent study estimates that only 20 or 30 percent may be active communicants.[53] Even this figure may be exaggerated. Not all Catholics are sure to be Christian Democratic supporters, but it is reasonable to suspect that the movement has and

[51] Fogarty, *Christian Democracy in Western Europe*, p. 377.

[52] R. Segundo, "The Future of Christianity in Latin America," *Crosscurrents*, Summer, 1963 (reprint), pp. 275, 276.

[53] John J. TePaske and Sydney Nettleton Fisher (eds.), *Explosive Forces in Latin America* (Columbus: Ohio State University Press, 1964), p. 52.

will find most of its electoral strength in this area; 20 or 30 percent is not enough.

Finding the solution to this problem will be difficult. It will involve choosing between the relatively assured support that a religious politic implies or repudiating the Christian character of the movement in search of wider electoral strength. Theoretically, these two alternatives are not mutually exclusive. The parties in either case would surely retain much of their previous support. There may be a perfect point at which the parties would not even suffer a temporary loss of strength.

It is possible that the image of the party could evolve without a conscious change in its position. The German Christian Democratic Union, for example, has slowly shed some of its original Christian identification and assumed the mantle of a more pragmatic political organization. Its assumption of the responsibilities of government explains much of this transformation, but the change may also reflect a general feeling among Christian Democrats everywhere that a "breakthrough" is necessary. The French Christian Democratic labor union movement was the first to take practical steps in this direction by dropping the adjective "Christian" from its official name. The union was recruiting among Moslem and Protestant sectors and felt compelled to modify its position. Other world groups have been affected by the French union's leadership, and a general debate is now underway concerning the wisdom of the move.[54]

Indeed, it may be proposed that the practical approach of Christian Democratic parties has been mainly that of a holding operation against the chaos and Communism that threatened Europe after World War II. The Christian message formulated by the parties has injected stability into the body politic. As stability increases in the several nations, and this would apply to both Europe and Latin America, the parties will become less "Christian" and assume a more traditional image; the parties will de-emphasize the Christian message and stress the more pragmatic political and economic postulates of their position. In this sense, Christian Democratic parties become vehicles of transition for a society progressing from the unstable, unpredictable, and revolutionary to a more predictable politic where

[54] See, for example, "The CSC Congress: Problems of the Providence State," *Labor* (Official Journal of the International Federation of Christian Trade Unions), No. 6, 1964, pp. 247, 248.

the applicability of the religious base becomes less crucial to either political success or national well-being. This interpretation would seem to support the arguments of those who see the Social Christian movement as essentially a response to revolutionary Socialism. This interpretation is partly correct, but a fuller extrapolation of the argument sees Christian Democratic politics as applying to all chaos-producing phenomena. In Europe, the response was not only to the threat of Communism, but to the ravages of war and the bankruptcy of the traditional forces. In Latin America, a Christian Democratic transitional politic confronts not only Communism, but North American imperialism, and, most importantly, the dislocations of economic development and, perhaps, of international organization. One writer has proposed that one contribution of the Argentine Christian Democratic party might have been to "provide a 'moral prop' in the insecure state of mind in which the Argentine people collectively find themselves."[55] Commenting on the Portuguese political situation, another writer makes a similar point:

> . . . the Catholic vote or, in other words, a Christian Democracy, offers the only hope of providing an adequate instrument for the solidification of a democratic regime; in short, only it could guarantee government stability in the initial years and re-establish regional equilibrium over the long haul. Postwar Italy, whose condition seems much like that of present-day Portugal, is the example toward which everyone looks; and the success of Frei in Chile provides a strong confirmation.[56]

NATIONALISM

Latin American nationalism and Christian Democratic internationalism could possibly present another problem for the movement. The Christian Democratic call for continental unity, a key plank in the movement's program, could fall on deaf ears in a period when militant nationalism is growing in Latin America. It is, indeed, a poignant paradox that the objective necessity of union may clash with the subjective reality of rampant nationalism. As is true of Asia

[55] John J. Johnson, *Political Change in Latin America: The Emergence of the Middle Sectors* (Stanford, Cal.: Stanford University Press, 1958), p. 127.

[56] Janio Nubuco, "Dead End in Portugal," *Commonweal*, LXXXIII (Nov. 26, 1965), 242.

and Africa, the cult of nationalism is burgeoning in Latin America. One student pronounces unequivocally that "the predominant ideology of Latin America for the last generation has been nationalism."[57]

Although Christian Democratic theory strongly condemns the excesses of nationalism, the Latin American parties have reflected the tremendous influence of nationalism in varying degrees; the Argentine, Dominican, and Panamanian parties are intensely nationalistic, and although the parties in Venezuela and Chile show a less vociferous chauvinism, even in these countries the nationalistic issue is important. The Chilean Partido Demócrata Cristiano, for example, has traditionally been critical of the practices of the Anaconda and Kennecott copper companies, and the Frei government has set out to "Chileanize" the nation's copper industry. The move includes more state ownership and stipulations which encourage the foreign companies to refine more of the mineral in Chile.[58] In the same vein, the Venezuelan Social Christian-COPEI has perennially been concerned with the development of more national participation in the nation's oil industry. A plank of the 1958 party program, for example, called for a "constant effort for economic liberation as an indispensable complement and solid support of political independence."[59] Caldera has noted that petroleum must be dominated by the nation. He also asserts that the development of the contributory and derivative industries should be controlled by Venezuelans.[60]

The increasing fervor of Latin American nationalism, reflected in even the most moderate of the Social Christian movements, will make it difficult for Christian Democracy to achieve its goal of a united Latin American continent. If anything, it seems reasonable to predict that nationalism will become even stronger in Latin America. Another handicap facing Christian Democracy in a Latin America of burgeoning nationalism is the movement's foreign origin; it is not home-grown as is the Mexican Revolution or the Aprista movement. It has been imported from Europe, and although Euro-

[57] Robert J. Alexander, "Nationalism: Latin America's Predominant Ideology," *Journal of International Affairs*, XV (1961), 108.

[58] See "Chile Rescata su Requeza No. 1 El Cobre," *DECE*, I (Jan., 1965), 3.

[59] Partido Social Cristiano-COPEI, *Programa* (Caracas: Secretaría Nacional de Propaganda, 1958), p. 31.

[60] See, for instance, Rafael Caldera, "Contestación del Académico," in Arturo Uslar Pietri, *El Petróleo en Venezuela* (Caracas: Empresa el Cojo, 1955), pp. 47–49.

pean thought has had great prestige and influence in Latin America, this factor probably will become a distinct disadvantage to Latin American Christian Democracy in the future.

One last factor deserves attention. Despite the growing intensity of nationalism, there remains a strong "continentalism" in Latin America. There is a Chilean or Brazilian or Dominican nationalism, but superimposed and intertwined with this narrow particularism is a genuine Latin American nationalism which encompasses the entire continent and feeds upon the rejection of North American and Soviet imperialism.[61] As long as this trans-national commitment continues, the Christian Democratic movement may benefit from its existence. No other Latin American political movement has the geographic comprehensiveness of Christian Democracy, nor have any of the other political forces evolved the concern for Latin American internationalism which the Social Christian movement displays.

61 Alexander, "Nationalism . . . ," p. 110.

Assets of the Movement 11

IDEOLOGY AND NON-TRADITIONALISM

Although Latin American Christian Democratic parties must meet and overcome numerous problems to insure their eventual success, there exists an equally impressive array of advantages that favor the growth and political prosperity of the movement. These positive factors vary widely. Some are an intrinsic part of the general Christian Democratic credo, others are features of the message which the Latin American branch in particular has developed and still others are the result of the interaction of the Latin American political environment with Social Christian ideology.

An important asset to the Latin American movement is its strong ideological bent, which is remarkably appropriate to a continent assiduously seeking an answer to its myriad problems of economic development, industrialization, imperialism, and the attractiveness of the Communist critique. Indeed, the mere fact of being ideological is advantageous to any party existing in a cultural environment long recognized as being unusually interested in ideas and philosophical constructs. One student notes that Latin Americans have a "consuming interest in ideas and sentiments."[1] Concepts, words, and forms are important in Latin America: ideas eloquently stated are valued for their own sake. The rise of the mass parties of the twentieth century demonstrates the advantages of even minimally formal ideological systems. The traditional Socialists and the Radical parties that were founded or gained momentum in the early part of this century were the first organizations to formulate a critique of the Latin American situation and to offer a solution. Later, the even more successful Aprista Socialists offered the masses an ideological

[1] John P. Gillin, *Social Change in Latin America Today* (New York: Vintage Books, 1960), p. 43.

answer to the inquietudes of the times and became the major vehicles of political activity among the discontented sectors.

Personalist politics are clearly on the wane in Latin America; no movement can hope to win and hold support on the basis of personalistic *macho*. Any movement, be it democratic or authoritarian, must offer an ideological program.[2] In most recent times, the successful Latin American political movements have been ideological or at least pseudo-ideological. Even a partial listing is proof of this point—the Apristas, the Christian Democrats, Perón, Castro, Vargas.[3]

The two fastest-growing political movements in Latin America at the present time, Communism and Christian Democracy, are both intensely ideological in nature. In many nations they are the only coherent groups which challenge personalist or traditional oligarchical parties. Christian Democrats emphasize their ideology, recognizing its importance for effective militancy and deriding those who have no philosophical basis.[4] The importance of this in Peruvian politics, for example, is exemplified in the comment of an influential Aprista, who says that the Peruvian Partido Demócrata Cristiano "constitutes a distinct political phenomenon" because it has "an ideology and a doctrine." Despite its periodic defeats, its ideological stance makes the party a viable organization and is the basis for its growth in the future.[5]

Another, and related, asset of the Christian Democratic parties is their newness and non-traditional character. In a continent weary of the bankruptcy of traditional forces and the fading Aprista Socialists and Radicals, the parties seem to be bright, new alternatives. The parties are, on the whole, ideologically pure and morally clean. In an atmosphere in which the entire value system is threatened, the Christian Democrats offer another hope for salvation. They have not yet been forced by political circumstances to corrupt their programs or to compromise their goals. The European Christian Demo-

[2] On this point, see Eduardo Frei Montalva, *La Verdad Tiene su Hora* (Santiago de Chile: Editorial del Pacífico, 1955), p. 74.

[3] See Russell H. Fitzgibbon, "The Party Potpourri in Latin America," *Western Political Quarterly*, X (March, 1957), 11. Fitzgibbon suggests that a distinction between ideological and non-ideological parties is the key factor in the typology of Latin American parties.

[4] See, for example, Ambrosio Romero Carranza, *¿Qué es la Democracia Cristiana?* (Buenos Aires: Ediciones del Atlántico, 1956), pp. 189, 190.

[5] Carlos Delgado, "Panorama Político Peruano," *Combate*, IV (May-June, 1962), 27, 28.

cratic parties emerged and achieved success, it is proposed, because of the collapse of the traditional political forces after World War II. It may be that a similar situation is now overtaking Latin America, and the Latin American Christian parties may very well be able to profit from it.

The parties constantly call attention to their non-traditional position. The Panamanian party, for example, officially suggests that its youthfulness and lack of ties with the past are assets it should exploit fully.[6] The Colombian party declares that its leadership is composed of "new people" who "have no connection with the policies or militancy of the old Liberal and Conservative parties." The party further notes that its prospects are "frankly favorable" because "the Colombian people are disgusted with the promises, tactics and conduct of the traditional parties. All seek something new, different. . . ."[7] In another instance the party declares that "Christian Democracy is the only party sector which has not sinned against Colombia."[8]

HERITAGE OF THE PARTIES

More important than the form of the Christian Democratic message is its content. The entire history of Latin America demonstrates the attraction of new ideologies which set out to solve the problems of the continent, but all of these panaceas, obviously, have proved wanting. Domingo Sarmiento and others dreamed of North Americanizing Latin America; Vallenilla Lanz proposed Democratic Caesarism; the Communists have tried to import the proletariat revolution, the Radicals looked to Solidarist thought and Perón concocted an entirely new mixture which proposed the essential harmony of the materialistic and spiritual and of the individualistic and collectivistic. Much of the explanation for the failure of these schemes must be found in the fact that the Latin Americans have attempted to import alien philosophies, ideals, institutions, and practices too rapidly and without discrimination. Success might have been at-

[6] Partido Demócrata Cristiano de Panamá, *El Partido Demócrata Cristiano de Panamá: Historia, Principios, Programa, Estructura* (Panamá, 1964), p. 29.

[7] Partido Social Demócrata Cristiano de Colombia, *Partido Social Demócrata Cristiano* (Bogotá: Ediciones del Caribe, 1964), pp. 5, 6.

[8] "La DC es Hoy el Unico Partido que no Ha Pecado Contra Colombia," *Pueblo y Libertad*, III (Aug., 1964), 3.

tained if parts had been carefully chosen for their appropriateness to Latin American cultural and political traditions. Instead, the carelessly chosen foreign theories have merely imposed other disruptive factors on an already confused society. Clearly, the only intelligent answer is to build on the Spanish heritage as it has developed in Latin America. Christian Democracy seems ideally suited to this task.

If Latin America is looking for an ideology and a program of action, Christian Democracy, unlike Marxism and other imported responses, does not imply a break with the Catholic, humanistic value system of the Latin American cultural tradition. Christian Democratic ideologues and propagandists are aware of this fact; the movement accuses those whom it opposes, to the Right or Left, of materialism and draws around itself the prestigious cloak of humanism and spiritualism. Latin American culture is "humanist rather than materialist . . . , compassionate rather than egalitarian, authoritarian rather than democratic,"[9] and Christian Democracy embodies this tradition more completely than any other major political force.

The materialism and cold efficiency of modern industrialism are usually seen as threats to the Latin value system, and the Social Christians have promulgated a doctrine which supposedly reaps the benefits of development without sacrificing deeply ingrained values. Moreover, in a continent where society is becoming more secularized, where politics is gaining ascendency over religion, Christian Democracy has the unique advantage of combining religion with politics. One student lists the highest values of the rising middle sectors in Latin America; they include: "Personalism, kinship, hierarchy or stratification, materialism of a special kind, transcendentalism or interest in 'spiritual values,' the high worth of inner states and emotional expression and fatalism."[10] It is uncanny how closely most of these values parallel the traditional doctrinal values of philosophical and political Christian Democracy.

Much of the Latin American value system is closely tied with and influenced by Catholicism and the Church, the same influences that have molded the Christian Democratic message. The Social Christian political movement need not sow the seeds of a new message in

[9] Frank Tannenbaum, *Ten Keys to Latin America* (New York: Alfred A. Knopf, 1962), p. 128.

[10] Gillin, *Social Change in Latin America Today*, p. 28.

Latin America; it needs only to reap the fruits of a society and culture long established. A North American student makes the point.

> The Catholic faith has been the greatest single unifying or integrating element in the Latin American scene. It has penetrated more widely than the Spanish language and, in any event, is a positive force making for oneness. . . . We often do not realize what a tremendous influence the Catholic faith and ecclesiastical organization have had in inducing a like-minded outlook in matters social and political, and even economic.[11]

The Christian base of the Latin American society offers a ready-made recruiting ground for the movement. Indeed, the parties publicize their Christian nature with just this in mind. One ideologue of Social Christianity notes the value of its Christian heritage when he suggests that "the existence of God and the call to fraternity, at least with his immediate neighbor, are things which the people can understand."[12]

Specific Christian Democratic doctrines provide numerous examples of the affinity of Christian Democratic and traditional Latin American values. Certainly, no example is more vivid than the identity of Christian Democratic and Latin American theories concerning personality and the interpretation of the individual. A recent study outlines the accepted Latin American definition. "The underlying emphasis is upon the inherent uniqueness of each person. The individual is valued precisely because he is not exactly 'like' anyone else. Each individual merits respect because of his unique inner worth, regardless of the social form it may take." In further describing the *dignidad de la persona* so intrinsic to the Latin American value system, the same commentator notes: "Originally, no doubt, the influence of the Catholic Church, with its strong emphasis upon the soul, contributed heavily to the definition of this value."[13] Originally, no doubt, the Catholic Church contributed to exactly the same concept in Christian Democratic philosophy.

Equally close to Latin American custom and tradition is the Social Christian emphasis on the importance of communal organization and intermediate groups. Although this may be more marked in the

[11] Russell H. Fitzgibbon, "Pathology of Democracy in Latin America: A Political Scientist's Point of View," *American Political Science Review*, XLIV (March, 1950), 121.

[12] Jaime Castillo Velasco, *El Problema Comunista* (Santiago de Chile: Editorial del Pacífico, 1955), p. 133.

[13] Gillin, *Social Change in Latin America Today*, pp. 29, 30.

rural areas, the concept of social organization in Latin America is centered on family and community rather than on the individual. The Social Christian concept of the family, the professional organization, or the *municipio* is fundamentally in tune with these attitudes. Christian Democracy has placed more stress in this area than any other important political force on the continent.

Even the concept of naturally evolved hierarchy is characteristic of both the Latin American culture and Christian Democratic theory. The universal order, including human society, is hierarchical in nature. Communistic egalitarianism is foreign to the Latin American psyche. Christian Democratic emphasis on harmonious hierarchical organization, however, strikes a responsive chord. Despite the negative implications inherent in hierarchical theory and its practical corruption in Latin America, the concept is still deeply imbedded in the value system.[14]

The more specific planks of the Christian Democratic platform also follow closely the Hispanic tradition. Positive state leadership in economic planning, for instance, is a traditional part of Spanish political theory and practice. The state has always been the integrating factor, and its competence properly includes all areas of endeavor. Any Latin American political program must take this entrenched concept into consideration. "The fact that Spanish America is by tradition accustomed and by economic necessity forced to rely heavily on official planning, intervention and protection has on occasion led its statesmen to a 'total view' (to be distinguished carefully in nature and content from a totalitarian view)."[15]

The various Christian Democratic plans for corporative representation also fit closely into the Latin American mold. Many of the nations have or have had stipulations for such representation in their constitutions. The Argentine Constitution of 1819, for example, outlined a senate which was to consist of one member from each province, plus representatives of the army, the Church, and the universities. The Ecuadorian Constitution of 1929 allotted seats to several sectors of the society on the basis of functional representation as does the present 1946 Constitution. In 1951, Perón imposed a constitution on a newly created province which outlined that half of the legislature was to be composed of functional representatives. Indeed,

[14] See *ibid.*, pp. 34, 35, and John P. Gillin, "Changing Depths in Latin America," *Journal of Inter-American Studies*, II (Oct., 1960), 388.

[15] Richard M. Morse, "Toward a Theory of Spanish-American Government," *Journal of the History of Ideas*, XV (Jan., 1954), 89.

even the internal organization of the Mexican governmental party indicates a strong corporative inclination.

In sum, the parallel between Christian Democratic theory and programs and traditional Latin American cultural attitudes is almost perfect. From Christian thinking on the nature of man to various facets of the practical programs, Christian Democracy goes hand in glove with Latin America. In fact, Christian Democracy may be the only strong political movement in the entire history of the continent which so closely adheres to the deeply entrenched cultural and philosophic substructure of Latin America. Christian Democratic theory, in short, is Latin American theory.

The careful observer, of course, will not be surprised at this. Both theories have the same roots; Catholicism has molded and conditioned the Latin American society, and it has also exercised a fundamental influence on the development of Christian Democratic theory. Catholic personalism is the basis of both, Catholic rejection of the class struggle informs both, Catholic stress on intermediate societal structures conditions both. Christian Democracy and Latin America are both Catholic—that is a simple, but profoundly important, truth.

Lest this interpretation be misconstrued, it seems imperative to re-emphasize one further point. If Christian Democracy is Catholic, it is also more than Catholic. The movement is progressive Social Christianity, attempting to synthesize traditionalism and permanency with a program of progress based upon a critical analysis of modern problems. It combines a streak of idealistic philosophy which has always been so attractive to the Latin psyche with a common-sense critique of the Latin American malady. It joins a religious appeal with the politics of economic development and social welfare.

Commenting on the establishment of the National Falange in Chile, one observer has described the ideal form of the movement. The solution of the "Spanish tragedy" must be found by political groups which are: "At the same time, conservative and renovating, which know how to distinguish accidental forms from permanent values, which can strive toward progress without forgetting tradition, which can renounce the prejudice of thinking all that is new is necessarily excellent and, at the same time, the prejudice of thinking all that is old ought to be conserved. . . ."[16] The Falange, the author concludes, can achieve in Chile what has been lacking in Spain.

[16] Ricardo Boizard, *La Democracia Cristiana en Chile* (3rd ed.; Santiago de Chile: Editorial Orbe, 1963), p. 248.

The actual achievement of this tremendous task will be difficult. It is, obviously, quite true that the two aspects are not always perfectly compatible. It does seem valid, nevertheless, to suggest that no other Latin American political movement is so theoretically well equipped to meet successfully this gargantuan challenge.

REPUTATION OF THE PARTIES

Much of the sophisticated analysis of Latin American politics misses a fundamental point. Perhaps the most heartfelt desire of the masses is for honest, conscientious government. Those who make a sincere effort to supply this type of government may be able to secure the support of the populace despite the strength, or weakness, or absence of political philosophy.

The motives and sincerity of men are, of course, always very difficult to gauge. Its Christian name does not protect the movement from the curse of incompetents, opportunists, demagogues, or scoundrels. Christian Democracy is a political movement and liable to the weaknesses of any political group. Nevertheless, thus far the parties have maintained a fairly good record. They have managed to attract able and relatively honest militants. In a continent literally racked with corruption, the Christian Democratic movement has compiled a rather enviable record. There is no doubt that this has been important to the growth of the various parties. Indeed, one Christian Democrat has noted that "the Christian Democratic movement is gaining its main strength less because of its economic theories than by the integrity of its men."

The Latin American Christian Democratic parties have attracted or developed rather able and sophisticated leadership. One writer explains, "Christian Socialists have been very careful in the selection of their leaders. They have abstained from breaking the discipline of their ideals and their hierarchies to attract fly-by-night disciples."[17] Indeed, Christian Democratic and Catholic parties all over the world have been fortunate in this area. In Europe, the names of De Gasperi, Adenauer, and Schumann are among the most illustrious of the present century. In Latin America, Frei Montalva has become the

[17] Quoted in Frank Bonilla, "The Student Federation of Chile: 50 years of Political Action," *Journal of Inter-American Studies*, II (July, 1960), 324, and in Mario Monteforte Toledo, "The Enigma of Latin America's Christian Socialists," *CIF Reports*, V (Feb., 1966), 23.

best-known contemporary figure on the continent; he has emerged as the spokesman for Latin America in international circles and his 1965 European tour established him as the recognized leader of the continent.

A recent North American study says of Christian Democratic parties that "the quality of their leadership is generally high. They include among their ranks some of the outstanding intellectuals of the region, particularly those of the younger generation."[18] The same author has noted elsewhere that the leadership of the Chilean party "is of particularly high intellectual quality. . . ."[19] Another observer has described the Chilean party as being composed of "widely respected young men of sincerity and intellect."[20] Among others, the small but ideologically mature Peruvian party has also been praised for the high caliber of its members. One journal has characterized the Christian Democratic party as Peru's "most enlightened parliamentary group" and proposed that the party has "managed to congregate a substantial number of followers because of its efficient organization and the intellectual stature of its leaders."[21] Effective leadership is by no means limited to the Peruvian and Chilean groups. The strong Venezuelan and smaller Colombian parties are blessed with particularly strong, able, and responsible leaders, and many of the leaders of the other parties are clearly above average in quality.

Many of the party leaders and several of the movements also enjoy the prestige of political martyrdom. By having persecuted Christian Democrats, authoritarian governments have often increased the strength of the parties. "The Christian Socialists are now promoting independence for their nations," observes a writer, "and have adopted a line calling for progress. With this ideology they have won persecution from dictators, attacks from right-wing groups and excommunication in many Bishoprics."[22] In Venezuela, COPEI members

[18] Robert J. Alexander, "The Emergence of Modern Political Parties in Latin America," *The Politics of Change in Latin America*, ed. Joseph Maier and Richard W. Weatherhead (New York: Frederick A. Praeger, 1964), p. 111.

[19] Robert J. Alexander, *Today's Latin America* (Garden City, N. Y.: Anchor Books, Doubleday and Company, 1962), p. 153.

[20] Roger S. Abbott, "The Role of Contemporary Political Parties in Chile," *American Political Science Review*, XLV (June, 1951), 453.

[21] *Hispanic American Report*, XV (Aug., 1962), 540 and (April, 1962), 157.

[22] "The Enigma of Latin America's Christian Socialists," p. 22.

suffered imprisonment and persecution throughout the Pérez Jiménez regime. In 1953, 80 members of the party were imprisoned, including long-time party leader Rafael Caldera and the party president Pedro del Corral. Later, in 1957, Caldera was again incarcerated by the government and spent five months in jail before being released. On January 1, 1958, another group of Copeyanos was imprisoned, including del Corral and agricultural expert, Giménez Landínez. The Argentine party benefited from its persecution by the Perón regime. Numerous Christian Democrats were hounded by the Perón security police. Party leader Manuel Ordóñez was jailed for a short time. Sectors of the Guatemalan, Brazilian, and Salvadorian groups have been persecuted by authoritarian governments and have been able to point to their sacrifices in fighting for the cause of representative government. Christian Democrats are actively engaged in combating the dictatorships in Paraguay, Nicaragua, and Cuba, and the parties will undoubtedly benefit from this activity when unrestricted political activity is again possible.

Finally, the potentially powerful Dominican Partido Revolucionario Social Cristiano will assuredly reap the advantages of having actively fought on the constitutionalist, rebel side during the 1965 civil war. The Social Christians were probably the best-organized non-Marxist opposition group and assumed important positions on the barricades as well as in the constitutionalist government. Indeed, many continental Christian Democrats propose that the Dominican party will become the major political movement in that nation within a relatively short time.

ORGANIZATION AND TRAINING

One of the explanations for Christian Democratic success in developing an effective leadership is the emphasis it places on political formation and training. Christian Democrats were quick to establish schools in Europe, and the Latin American branch of the movement has also placed a high priority on the foundation of special schools and institutes to develop both a sophisticated doctrine and the ability of its leaders. The Organización Demócrata Cristiana de América maintains a leadership school, the Instituto de Formación Demócrata Cristiana, in Caracas, and many of the national parties have established similar facilities. In addition, Christian Democracy has reaped the benefits of similar agencies established by traditional Catholic Action groups and the Christian Democratic labor union movement in Latin America.[23]

Latin American Christian Democracy has also stressed the importance of developing modern political techniques. Greatly influenced by the expert management of the 1960 Kennedy presidential campaign, the movement has increasingly stressed strong organization and scientific methods of activity. Public opinion research is utilized. The Venezuelan COPEI has a close working agreement with the Center of Public Opinion in Caracas, and the Uruguayan and Argentine parties have also developed working associations with similar institutions in their nations. Communication methods are studied and analyzed, and the parties make a concerted effort to spread their message through the effective use of publicity media. An "eminent" Chilean Radical, for example, noted that "Christian Democracy won the election because it was equipped with good publicity" and "used modern language."[24]

Furthermore, all of the parties give primary importance to studying the problems of the nation and to the development of comprehensive programs. Although most of the efforts are still very rudimentary, several of the groups have made measurable progress. A survey of the Chilean election noted that "for the first time in Latin American history a new party will take power with adequate advanced planning."[25]

Beyond the considerations of internal cohesion, the parties often increase their impact by taking advantage of their position at the center of the political spectrum, a position that implies an importance disproportionate to their actual numerical strength. It puts them in a key position for the formation of governmental or opposition alliances, which are almost always necessary in a continent characterized for the most part by a multi-party system. Christian Democrats can coalesce with the major democratic forces in Latin America—with

[23] For a short list and description of Christian Democratic leadership resources, see David Spencer, "Leadership Training: Catholic Action and Christian Democratic Methods," *Student Politics in Latin America*, prepared by David Spencer (United States National Student Association, mimeographed, 1965), pp. 78–90.

[24] "Chile: Convention Reappraisal," *The Latin American Times*, July 1, 1965, p. 3.

[25] Donald W. Bray, "Chile: The Dark Side of Stability," *Studies on the Left*, IV (Fall, 1964), 87.

traditional and Aprista Socialists on the Left or Radicals and some Neo-Liberal parties on the Right.

ELECTORAL APPEAL AND SUPPORT

Underlying the assets discussed thus far is one other profoundly important consideration. An analysis of the various components of Latin American society reveals that Christian Democracy is strongest in exactly those sectors of the electorate that can be expected to exercise more political influence and cast more ballots in the future. Those areas include the women, the youth, the peasantry, and the middle sectors. All these groups have been receptive to the Social Christian message; all will play an increasingly vocal part in Latin American politics.

Fourteen of the twenty Latin American nations have enacted women suffrage only since World War II. Organizations similar to the North American League of Women Voters have appeared in most of the continent's nations. A recent study of social change in Latin America highlighted the developing role of women in areas previously dominated by men. "Middle-status women work in clerical positions, as teachers, as trained nurses and hygiene experts, as physicians and lawyers, and in a variety of other callings. And many middle-status housewives who are not gainfully employed take part in activities of women's clubs. . . ."[26] Women are casting more ballots, both comparatively and absolutely, in every succeeding election. They are already an influential political force in several of the nations. One observer notes that "one of the most startling of the modern changes has been the recent recognition of women's rights and their emergence as an important, even powerful, factor in public life."[27] The number of feminine deputies, senators, ministers, and other politicos is increasing rapidly. Both San Juan, Puerto Rico, and Santiago de Chile have had women mayors in recent years, for example.

There is little doubt that the emergence of women as a significant political force in Latin America implies modification, if not profound change, in the continent's political life. It is safe to assume that the Catholicism popularly associated with the Christian Democratic par-

[26] Gillin, *Social Change in Latin America Today*, pp. 49, 50.
[27] Gillin, "Changing Depths in Latin America," p. 382.

ties will attract many of the new women voters; the strong hold which the Roman Catholic Church has over women of all economic levels is well known and indisputable. Indeed, one of the principle reasons for denying the women the vote in Latin America until very recently was the fear that the measure might increase the temporal power of the Church. Women were thought to be overly receptive to clerical influence.

Christian Democracy is, of course, aware of this vast storehouse of feminine votes. The Panamanian party states officially that it sees the women of the nation as a source of votes.[28] Most of the parties seek to nurture and exploit this reservoir of ballots; women's rights and the importance of women in the nation's life are reiterated in all of the formal programs and manifestos. When women were granted the vote in Paraguay, for instance, the nation's Social Christian movement gave special attention to the development: "Christian Democracy rejoices at the promotion of women to the exercise of civil and political rights. It knows that in this difficult hour, women will bring forth, with their good sense and prudence, that inexhaustible wealth of abnegation and sacrifice with which they have played such an outstanding role in Paraguayan history."[29]

Latin American Christian Democratic parties have been quick to offer concrete evidence of their regard for women. Christian Democratic women hold important political posts in several of the nations. Perhaps the outstanding example was the Dominican Partido Revolucionario Social Cristiano's nomination of Josefina Padilla de Sánchez as vice-presidential candidate in the 1962 elections. This was the first time in Latin American history that a female had seriously run for such an exalted post.

Although comprehensive statistics are not readily available, there is evidence of the ability of Catholic and Christian Democratic political parties to garner a significant bloc of the feminine vote. In Mexico, for example, the granting of the vote to women during the Rúiz Cortines regime (1952–1958) coincided with a marked increase in electoral strength for the Catholic Partido de Acción Nacional. The slow demise of the laic Chilean Radical party began at about the

[28] Partido Demócrata Cristiano de Panamá, *El Partido Demócrata Cristiano de Panamá . . .*, p. 29.

[29] Movimiento Social Demócrata Cristiano del Paraguay, *Mensaje de Navidad del Movimiento Social Demócrata Cristiano al Pueblo del Paraguay* (Asunción, Dec. 25, 1961), p. 4.

same time that women were granted the vote in Chile, and the rise of the Chilean Christian Democratic party dates from the same time.

Chilean elections afford more specific indications that the women are attracted to the Chilean Christian Democratic party and that they reject Marxist parties. In 1958, Socialist Salvador Allende won 600,000 votes, but only 100,000 of them from women.[30] A fundamental explanation for Christian Democratic gains in the 1963 municipal elections, which marked the first time that the party emerged in first place, was the fact that the rival Marxist Frente de Acción Popular received the votes of 40 percent of the men voters, but only 15 percent of the women.[31] Finally, in the 1964 presidential election, Frei received a total of 1,418,101 votes of which 744,423 were cast by women.[32]

The 1957 Argentine elections attest to the strength of the Christian Democratic party among women voters in that nation. In the Federal Capital, 63,553 women but only 25,072 men cast Christian Democratic ballots. Elsewhere in Argentina, women accounted for 66 percent of Social Christian electoral strength in the Old Provinces and 56 percent in the New Provinces.[33]

The explanation is obvious. Women are clearly attracted to a party characterized by a religious mystique, and the Christian Democratic movement, correctly or no, is looked upon as a religious movement having ties with the Roman Catholic Church. Women have cast and will continue to cast at least for the foreseeable future a religious vote for the Christian Democratic party, and Latin American women will be voting in increasing numbers. The several Social Christian groups will almost assuredly benefit.

The second sector of Latin American society which is growing in political importance and which may add to the electoral strength of Christian Democrats is the peasantry. Christian Democratic parties have traditionally been significantly fortified by the rural vote, and growth of the *campesino* electorate in Latin America would seem to augur well for the Christian Democratic future.

Christian Democratic platforms and programs have placed agrar-

[30] Donald D. Ranstead, "Chile Turns Left," *Commonweal*, LXXX (Sept. 4, 1964), 596.

[31] *Hispanic American Report*, XVI (Aug., 1963), 604.

[32] "Resultado Final de la Eleción," *DECE*, I (Oct., 1964), 4, 5.

[33] Eduardo Zolvendo, *Geografía Electoral de la Argentina* (Buenos Aires: Ediciones Ancora, 1958), pp. 58, 80, 81.

ian reform high on the list of priorities, and the parties have successfully campaigned among the rural populations of Latin America. The strong Catholic attitudes of the rural sectors is, of course, also a factor in the success of Christian Democracy in this area. Even in the more developed nations of Latin America—Chile, Venezuela, Uruguay, and Argentina—a large percentage of the Christian Democratic electorate continues to be centered in the *campo*, and opportunities for growth are good. The Frei government has centered much of its attention on this area. A study undertaken after the Christian Democratic assumption of power in Chile notes:

> Recognizing that both the Right and Left have always neglected the peasants, Frei hopes to make them the bastion of his political power. In campaigning for a more equitable distribution of income, Frei asserts that peasant income should increase more rapidly than that of any other social group. He also insists that social welfare legislation be fully implemented in the countryside where it has often been ignored, and encourages peasants to organize their own trade unions freely. In fact, the Christian Democrats have a commanding lead in the peasant syndical movement. Frei has frequently referred to himself as "President of the Peasants."[34]

In the less developed nations, of course, the *campesino* vote is of basic importance. Although the Social Christian parties have not, on the whole, developed so well in these nations, the work of the party in rural areas in Nicaragua, Guatemala, El Salvador, and Panama is on the increase. The Guatemalan party, for instance, notes that the *campesino* sectors are receiving the Social Christian message "with true enthusiasm," and the party claims to have been very successful in the organization of peasant leagues and cooperatives.[35]

The strength of Christian Democratic parties among the youthful sectors of Latin American society has been outlined in Chapter 2. Although some of the parties have not been as successful as others, the movement generally has achieved significant success in the secondary schools, universities, and youth organizations.

Support from the student sector is important for two reasons.

[34] Cole Blasier, *Chile in Transition* (Washington: Public Affairs Press, 1966), p. 6.

[35] Partido Democracia Cristiana Guatemalteca, *Projecto de la Campaña Nacional del Partido Democracia Cristiana Guatemalteca para Lograr su Reconocimiento como Institución Política de Derecho Pública* (Guatemala, mimeographed, Aug. 15, 1964), pages not numbered.

Young people become voters and many of them can be expected to retain their political affiliation. Several parties already control university politics in their respective nations and several others are growing rapidly; the obvious result should be an increase in Social Christian strength in coming years. Also, the universities and other organized youth groups are a good source for militant and well-trained leaders. Youthful leaders have frequently assumed positions of responsibility in the parties already, demonstrating the importance of this factor.

The middle sectors of Latin American society are also increasing rapidly in numbers and influence. These groups already occupy an important position in Argentina, Brazil, Chile, Mexico, and Uruguay —nations that comprise about 65 percent of the total Latin American population and turn out more than two-thirds of the continent's gross national product. The parties' strength among these groups is not documented but apparently is fairly solid. One of Christian Democracy's attractions for them, probably, is its position at the center of the political spectrum. Moreover, in several of the nations the Christian Democrats are thought to be the only viable alternative to much more radical groups, and this factor should be of considerable benefit at the polls. Despite COPEI's trend to the Left, for instance, the party still retains favor among middle and upper classes. The mature Chilean party also seems to do well in these sectors. A study has estimated that about 55 percent of small businessmen, and an even greater percentage of those higher on the socio-economic scale, supported Frei.[36]

ANTI-COMMUNIST BENT

The Prologue to this book alluded to the image of Frei Montalva's Christian Democratic party in North America as the alternative to a Communist victory in Chile. The movement as a whole is usually identified as a viable anti-Communist force. The popular press, of course, tends to depict all political movements in their relation to the Communist threat in Latin America, and the Catholic heritage of the movement and the European experience of Christian Democracy have added credence to this interpretation.

[36] *Chile*, Estudios de Actualidad, Primera Serie, No. 1 (Montevideo: Instituto de Estudios Políticos para América Latina, 1964), p. 15.

The Christian Democratic movement is more than anti-Communist. Nevertheless, this aspect of Social Christian strength must not be underestimated. The Latin American parties insist that their position must not be construed as sterile anti-Communism, and these claims are substantially correct. Be that as it may, it is equally true that the movement has garnered, and will continue to garner, significant electoral support because of its association with the anti-Communist crusade in Latin America.

Much of the early success of the European branch of Christian Democracy can be attributed to the fact that it presented itself as the only major anti-Communist force. The movement often received votes that were anti-Soviet and not necessarily pro-Christian Democratic. Europe is not Latin America, and the preoccupation with Communist strength and Soviet imperialism is not nearly so widespread in contemporary Latin America as it was in post-war Europe. Nevertheless, particularly since the corruption of the Cuban Revolution by Soviet intervention, the Communist threat is more widely recognized in Latin America, and the Christian Democratic parties may expect to benefit from this growing fear.

Atheistic Communism has become a minor issue in Latin America. Despite the official denials, examples of cheap anti-Communistic demagoguery have occasionally crept into Social Christian campaigns. Cuban and Soviet persecution of the Catholic faith has been publicized, Cuban regimentation of the peasantry is broadcast, and Cuban and Soviet expropriation of property is well known. The Latin American Christian Democrats cannot expect to ride to power on the crest of an anti-Communism wave as did the Italian party following World War II.[37] Nevertheless, the anti-Communism of the parties must not be disregarded in an analysis of their strength. The parties themselves are assuredly not forgetting it as part of their strategy.

Finally, Christian Democratic anti-Communism may prove to be a mixed blessing to the parties. It could lead to support from the United States, true, but this support might very well suffocate the movement.

Aprista Socialism has had the support of official and non-official

[37] For a statement on the inability of Communism to act as a catalyst of political growth, see Alfredo Galletti, *La Política y los Partidos* (México: Fondo de Cultura Económica, 1961), pp. 241–42.

circles in the United States for the last several decades. The Apristas produced some progress and brought forth men of real character and ability such as Betancourt and Figueres, but there seems to be some indication that the movement is in decline. In its search for another strong anti-Communist and anti-Russian force to replace the Apristas, the United States is showing interest in Christian Democracy. Indeed, Frei has pointed out that the Chilean Christian Democrats count on increasing aid from the United States, even if the movement's policies are not all that Uncle Sam seeks. Frei can nonetheless hold on to United States aid, because if Christian Democracy fails in Chile, goes the analysis, then the Communist-dominated FRAP would assume power.[38]

THE FUTURE

How much Frei's experience in Chile will influence other countries in Latin America is, in 1967, still a matter of conjecture, but a Social Christian sweep of the continent seems clearly beyond realization. Several Christian Democratic parties are making significant progress, however. The Venezuelan Social Christian-COPEI, which, as might be expected, often chafes at its relegation to the "second" position among Latin American Christian Democratic groups, has been long-established and was well on the way to success before the 1964 Frei victory. The Copeyanos have made steady strides in Venezuela and look optimistically to the 1968 presidential elections. It is doubtful that the COPEI will enjoy an electoral victory to match Frei's 1964 triumph, but indications are that it may succeed in emerging as the largest in a four party contest composed of the Acción Democrática, the Unión Republicana Democrática, the Uslar Pietri group, and COPEI. The early 1967 split in the Peruvian party may have endangered the hopes of the popular Bedoya Reyes for presidential victory in 1969, but it seemed possible as this was written that he might become the candidate of the Acción Popular government party in coalition with the rump of the Partido Demócrata

[38] See Stanley Rothman, "The Choice for Chile: Left or Far Left," *The Reporter*, XXXI (July 2, 1964), 26–29. On this same point, see Luís Vitale, *Esencia y Apariencia de la Democracia Cristiana* (Santiago de Chile: Arancibia Hnos., 1964), p. 104, for a crude left-wing analysis which sees the Latin American movement as the newest agent of Yankee imperialism.

Cristiano. Victory in such circumstances would place a Christian Democrat at the head of a coalition in which Christian Democrats would be in the minority—a victory more personal than party-based.

Among other Latin American Christian Democratic parties, the prospects are more difficult to ascertain. The large, but amorphous, Salvadorian group continues united and offers some hope for future victory. Latin American Christian Democrats have pointed to the Dominican and the Guatemalan groups as parties of the future, and some have expressed optimism concerning the Panamanian group. For many years, the Social Christians have looked to the Argentine party to blossom, but predictions are very difficult to apply to that volatile nation.

In conclusion, although the Frei victory may not have introduced a continent-wide trend toward Christian Democratic governments, it is nonetheless true that the victory signalled a period of sustained growth for the movement which may well produce several other Social Christian triumphs within the next decade.

Bibliography

LATIN AMERICAN CHRISTIAN DEMOCRACY

Books

Ahumada C., Jorge. *En Vez de la Miseria.* 3rd ed. Santiago de Chile: Editorial del Pacífico, 1960.

Amoroso Lima, Alceu, *et al. Integracão Econômica, Social e Política da América Latina.* Rio de Janeiro: Livaria Agir Editôra, 1958.

Belaúnde, Víctor Andrés, *et al. Política, Deber Cristiano.* Lima: Editorial Universitaria, 1963.

Benites, Tulio, *Meditaciones de un Católico ante la Reforma Agraria.* Guatemala: Editorial del Ministerio de Educación Pública, 1952.

Blasier, Cole. *Chile in Transition.* Washington: Public Affairs Press, 1966.

Boizard, Ricardo. *Cuatro Retratos en Profundidad: Ibáñez, Lafertte, Leighton y Walker.* Santiago de Chile: Editorial del Pacífico, 1950.

———. *La Democracia Cristiana en Chile.* 3rd ed. Santiago de Chile: Editorial Orbe, 1963.

———. *Voces de la Política, el Púlpito y la Calle.* Santiago de Chile: Editorial del Pacífico, 1948.

Brena, Tomás G. *Democracia Cristiana en el Uruguay.* Montevideo: Impresora Zorilla de San Martín, 1946.

Caldera, Rafael. *El Bloque Latinoamericano.* Santiago de Chile: Editorial del Pacífico, 1961.

———. *Democracia Cristiana y Desarollo.* "Colección Desarrollo y Libertad," No. 2. Caracas, 1964.

———. *Derecho del Trabajo.* Caracas: Tipografía la Nación, 1939.

———. *La Idea de Justicia Social Internacional y El Bloque Latinoamericano.* Caracas: Editorial Sucre, 1962.

———. *Idea de una Sociología Venezolano.* Caracas: Empresa "El Cojo," 1953.

———. *Moldes para la Fragua.* Buenos Aires: Librería "El Ateneo" Editorial, 1962.

Castillo Velasco, Jaime. *Las Fuentes de la Democracia Cristiana.* Santiago de Chile: Editorial del Pacífico, 1963.

———. *El Problema Comunista.* Santiago de Chile: Editorial del Pacífico, 1955.

Chi-yi Chen, J. *Desarrollo y Planificación.* "Colección Desarrollo y Libertad," No. 1. Caracas, 1964.

II Congreso Internacional de Democracia Cristã. São Paulo: mimeographed, 1957.

Congreso Internacional de la Democracia Cristiana: Anales del quinto . . . Lima: Editorial Universitaria, 1960.
Congresos Internacionales Demócrata-Cristianos. Santiago de Chile: Editorial del Pacífico, 1957.
Cornejo Chávez, Héctor. *Nuevos Principios para un Nuevo Perú.* Lima: Publicaciones de la Juventud Demócrata Cristiana, 1960.
———. *Que Se Propone la Democracia Cristiana.* Lima: Ediciones del Sol, 1962.
Democracia Cristiana en Acción: Cuenta Parlamentaria de la Unión Cívica, 1946–1950. Montevideo: Ediciones de la Unión Cívica, 1950.
Foyaca de la Concha, Manuel. *Democracia Social Cristiana. Conferencias, Discursos, Ensayos.* Habana: Agrupación Católica Universitaria, 1948.
Franceschi, Gustavo Juan. *La Democracia Cristiana.* Buenos Aires: Ediciones Criterio, 1955.
Frei Montalva, Eduardo. *Aun es el Tiempo. . . .* Santiago de Chile: Talleres Gráficos "El Chileno," 1942.
———. *Chile Desconocido.* Santiago de Chile: Ediciones Ercilla, 1937.
———. *Pensamiento y Acción.* Santiago de Chile: Editorial del Pacífico, 1956.
———. *La Política y el Espíritu.* Prólogo de Gabriela Mistral. Santiago de Chile: Ediciones Ercilla, 1940.
———. *El Regime del Salarido y su Posible Abolición.* Santiago de Chile: Editorial del Pacífico, 1933.
———. *Sentido y Forma de una Política.* Santiago de Chile: Editorial del Pacífico, 1951.
———. *La Verdad Tiene su Hora.* Santiago de Chile: Editorial del Pacífico, 1955.
Giménez Landínez, Víctor M. *Agricultura, Reforma Agraria y Desarrollo.* Caracas: Editorial Arte, 1962.
———. *Una Nueva Política de Conservación.* Caracas: República de Venezuela, Ministerio de Agricultura y Cría, 1962.
———. *Política de Producción Agropecuria.* Caracas: República de Venezuela, Ministerio de Agricultura y Cría, 1961.
Gonzales Ruiz, Fernando. *Chile en la Balanza; el dilema de la industria y del comercio.* Santiago de Chile: Editorial del Pacífico, 1960.
———. *La Reforma Tributaria Frente a la Economía Chilena.* Santiago de Chile: Editorial del Pacífico, 1962.
Larraín Errázuriz, Manuel. *La Hora de la Acción Católica.* Santiago de Chile: Editorial del Pacífico, 1956.
———. *Redención Proletaria.* "Colección Estudios Sociales." Santiago de Chile: Club de Lectores, 1948.
Lozano Gutiérrez, Gustavo. *El Sindicalismo Colombiano Ante la Doctrina Social de Iglesia.* Bogotá: Pontifica Universidad Católica Javeriana, 1960.
Martínez Candía, Marcelo. *Ni Marxismo ni Liberalismo: Social Cristianismo.* Santiago de Chile: Editorial del Pacífico, 1952.
———. *El Pensamiento Social-Cristiano en la Economía.* (Memoria de Prueba.) Santiago de Chile: Imp. "America," 1947.
Di Natale, Remo. *América Latina Hoy: Esquemas Populares Demócrata Cristianos.* Caracas: Editorial Nuevo Orden, 1964.
———. *Revolución Agraria en Bolivia.* Cochabamba: Imprenta Universitaria, 1953.

Organización Demócrata Cristiano de América. *VI Congreso Latinoamericano de la Democracia Cristiana: Informe Final.* Caracas, May 15–18, 1964.
Pacheco Gómez, Máximo. *Política, Economía y Cristianismo.* Con prólogo por Eduardo Frei. Santiago de Chile: Editorial del Pacífico, 1947.
———. *Principios Fundamentales de la Doctrina Social Cristiana.* Santiago de Chile: Impr. Universitaria, 1947.
Palacios Silva, Bartolomé. *Por los Fueros de la Verdad Tradicionalistas y Social-Cristianos.* Santiago de Chile: "Gutenberg" Impresores, 1948.
De Paula Jaramillo, Francisco. *La Democracia Cristiana: Una Nueva Perspectiva para Colombia.* Bogotá: Ediciones del Caribe, 1962.
Plá Rodríguez, Américo. *Los Principios de la Democracia Cristiana.* Bogotá: Ediciones del Caribe, 1962.
Rasco, José Ignacio. *Cuba 1959: Artículos de Combate.* 2nd ed. Buenos Aires: Incograf Impresores, 1962.
Rodríguez-Arias Bustamante, Lino. *La Democracia Cristiana y América Latina.* Lima: Editorial Universitaria, 1961.
Romero Carranza, Ambrosio. *Del Precursor al Propulsor de la Democracia Cristiana.* Buenos Aires: Talleres Gráficos San Pablo SRL, 1953.
———. *¿Qué es la Democracia Cristiana?* Buenos Aires: Ediciones del Atlántico, 1956.
Secco Illa, Joaquín. *Historia de la Unión Cívica.* Montevideo: Impresora Zorrilla de San Martín, 1946.
Silva Bascuñán, Alejandro. *Una Experiencia Social Cristiana.* Santiago de Chile: Editorial del Pacífico, 1949.
Silvani, Maurilio. *Diplomatica et Sacra.* Santiago de Chile: Imprenta Chile, 1946.
Téfel Vélez, Reinaldo Antonio. *Socialización en la Libertad.* Managua: Editorial Nicaragüense, 1964.
Una Tercera Posición. Selección de discursos demócrata cristianos pronunciados entre 1956 y 1960. Lima: Editorial Universitaria, 1960.
Tomic, Radomiro, *et al. Con los Probres de América.* Lima: Fela Ediciones, 1962.
Vila Echague, Iván. *Cuestiones Disputadas en la Democracia Cristiana.* Buenos Aires: Ediciones del Atlántico, 1960.
Vitale, Luis. *Esencia y Apariencia de la Democracia Cristiana.* Santiago de Chile: Arancibia Hnos., 1964.

Periodicals, Articles in Collections, and Speeches

Amoroso Lima, Alceu. "Discussion and Commentaries," on William S. Stokes' "Catholicism and Democracy in Latin America," *Responsible Freedom in the Americas*, ed. Angel del Rio. Garden City, N. Y.: Doubleday and Company, 1955, pp. 380–83.
———. "An Interpretation of Brazilian Politics," *Social Science*, XXVI (Oct., 1951), 202–14.
———. "Men, Ideas and Institutions," *Atlantic Monthly* (supplement), CXCVII (1956), 152.
———. "The Problem of Labor," *Latin American Social Thought*, ed. Harold E. Davis. Washington, D. C.: The University Press, 1961, pp. 520–29.

Cabrera Ferrada, Alejandro. "1965: Año del Desafío para Frei," *Ercilla*, No. 1595, Dec. 29, 1965, pp. 10–12.

Caldera, Rafael. "The Christian Democrat Idea," *America*, CVII (April, 1962), 12–15.

———. "Contestación del Académico," in Arturo Uslar Pietri, *El Petróleo en Venezuela*. Caracas: Empresa el Cojo, 1955.

———. "Crucial Test for Christian Civilization," *The Alliance for Progress: A Critical Appraisal*, ed. William Manger. Washington: Public Affairs Press, 1963, pp. 23–28.

———. *The Growth of Christian Democracy and Its Influence on the Social Reality of Latin America*. New York: Center of Christian Democratic Action, 1965.

———. "Introducción," Aldo Moro, *La Democracia Cristiana por el Gobierno del País y el Desarrollo Democrático de la Sociedad Italiana*. Roma: A.G.I., 1962.

———. "Una Nueva Constitución para Venezuela," *Política*, No. 2, Oct., 1959, pp. 38–49.

———. "[Speech] At the Closing Session," *Report of the Second Inter-American Congress of the Inter-American Association for Democracy and Freedom*. 1961, pp. 24–33.

———. "Venezuela on Election Eve," *Commonweal*, XLIV (Oct. 4, 1946), 590–92.

———, Jovito Villalba, and Raúl Leoni. "Desarrollo Democrático y Unidad del las Fuerzas Políticas," *Política*, No. 4, Dec., 1959, pp. 91–96.

"Christian Democrats Undercut Communists," *Report*, II (July, 1965), 9–12.

Conteris, Hiber. "La Próxima Disyuntiva de la D.C.," *Marcha*, XXVI (Sept. 18, 1964), 20ff.

"Cornejo Chávez Pide: Dar la Batalla por la Transformación," *El Comercio* [Lima], April 25, 1965.

"Cornejo Chávez Rechaza una Superconvivencia," *El Comercio* [Lima], April 25, 1965.

Corvalán Vera, Manuel. "Un Año de Lucha Contra la Inflación," *Ercilla*, No. 1595, Dec. 29, 1965, p. 17.

Culhane, Eugene K. "Congress in Caracas," *America*, CVII (June 9, 1962), 370.

Frei Montalva, Eduardo. "The Aims of Christian Democracy," *Commonweal*, LXXXI (Oct. 9, 1964), 63–66.

———. "Current Trends and Prospects in Latin America," *Journal of International Affairs*, XII (1958), 107–17.

———. "Notes on the Catholic Church and Development," *Latin America: Evolution or Explosion?* ed. Mildred Adams. New York: Council on World Tensions, Dodd, Mead and Company, 1963, pp. 191–200.

———. "President Frei on United States' Capitalism," *America*, Sept., 1964.

———. "The Road to Follow," *Latin American Social Thought*, ed. Harold E. Davis. Washington: The University Press, 1961, pp. 541–49.

Giménez Landínez, Víctor. "Reforma Agraria Integral: Bases Jurídicas de su Planificación," *Política*, III (Dec., 1963), 13–36.

Godoy, Horacio H. "Planificación y Sociedad," *Temas del BID*, II (Feb., 1965), 31–39.

"Golpe de Estado en la Democracia Cristiana," *Oiga*, III (March 19, 1965), 6–8.
"La Internacional Demócrata Cristiano," *SP* (Madrid), IX (April 1, 1965), 15–18.
Javier Castillo, Caonabo. "El Socialcristianismo y La Propiedad Privada," *Eistín Diario* [Santo Domingo], Aug. 4, 1964.
Magnet, Alejandro. "Armamentismo y desarme en América Latina," *Política*, No. 6, Feb., 1960, pp. 56–73.
Miller, Nathan. "A New Force in Latin America? The Rise of Christian Democracy," Baltimore *Sun*, Sept. 9, 1963.
Monteforte Toledo, Mario. "The Enigma of Latin America's Christian Socialists," *CIF Reports*, V (Feb., 1966), 22–23 (translated from *Siempre*, Dec. 29, 1965, México, D.F.).
"Un Nuevo Partido Político en Bolivia," *Estudios Americanos*, VIII (Aug.-Sept., 1954), 213–14.
Read Vitini, Mario. "Hacia una Economía Humana," *Eistín Diario* [Santo Domingo], Aug. 4, 1964.
Rodríguez-Arias B., Lino. "Presente y Futuro de la Democracia Cristiana," *Escena Nacional*, I (June, 1964), 11–12.
Silvert, Kalman. "Interview with a Candidate" [Eduardo Frei Montalva], *American Universities Field Staff: Reports Service*, West Coast South America Series, Vol. 4, No. 10 (New York, Aug., 1957).
"Socialistas que Rezan," *Visión*, XXV (July 26, 1963), 24–26.
Tugwell, Franklin. "The Christian Democrats of Venezuela," *Journal of Inter-American Studies*, VII (April, 1965), 245–68.
Ventura, Romualdo. "Los 19 Años de COPEI," *Bohemia*, Jan. 24, 1965, pp. 14ff.

Party Programs, Manifestos, and Statutes

Alianza Acción Popular-Demócrata Cristiano. *Bases para el Plan de Gobierno (Texto Preliminar)*. Lima: Librería e Imprenta Minerva-Miraflores, 1963.
———. *Plan de Gobierno Municipal: Miraflores*. Lima, 1963.
Comité Organizador del Partido Demócrata Cristiano. "Manifiesto," *La Prensa Gráfica* [El Salvador], Dec. 5, 1960, p. 13.
Movimiento Demócrata Cristiano de Cuba. *Ideario*. Miami.
———. *Movimiento Demócrata Cristiano de Cuba*. Miami, 1961.
———. *Nuestra Postura*. Miami, II Congreso Nacional en el Exilio, 1962.
———. *Reglamento*. Miami, mimeographed, 1964.
———. *Reglamento de Disciplina*. Miami, mimeographed, 1964.
———. *Reglamento Para Delegaciones*. Miami, mimeographed, 1963.
———. *Tesis Sindical*. Mimeographed.
Movimiento Social Cristiano del Ecuador. *Manifiesto del 13 de Noviembre y Declaración de Principios*. Quito: Editorial Chimborazo, 1951.
———. *Planteamiento de Reformas Constitucionales Bajo el Signo de la Democracia Cristiana*. Quito: Editorial "Fray Jodoco Ricke," 1963.
———. *Principios Doctrinarios de la Democracia Cristiana Ecuatoriana*. Quito: Editorial Victoria, 1964.
Movimiento Social Demócrata Cristiano de México. *Bases Ideológicas*. Folleto Numero 1. México, D. F., March 28, 1963.

Movimiento Social Demócrata Cristiano del Paraguay. *Acta Fundacional y Declaración de Principios.* Asunción, 1960.
———. *Manifiesto del Movimiento Social Demócrata Cristiano del Paraguay a la Ciudadania.* Asunción, May 31, 1960.
———. *Manifiesto del Movimiento Social Demócrata Cristiano del Paraguay a la Ciudadania.* Asunción, Oct. 12, 1960.
———. *Mensaje del Movimiento Social Demócrata Cristiano al Pueblo del Paraguay.* Asunción, Dec. 25, 1960.
———. *Mensaje de Navidad del Movimiento Social Demócrata Cristiano al Pueblo del Paraguay.* Asunción, Dec. 25, 1961.
———. *Mensaje a Los Trabajodores.* Asunción, May 1, 1964.
———. *Nota Presentada Por las Fuerzas Políticas de Oposición al Gobierno.* Asunción, Feb. 7, 1962.
———. Partido Liberal, Partido Revolucionario Febrerista. *Las Fuerzas Políticas Democráticas del País Frente al Acto Comicial del 10 de Febrero.* Asunción.
Partido Demócrata Cristiano de Chile. *Estatutos.* Santiago de Chile: Editorial del Pacífico, 1962.
Partido Demócrata Cristiano de Costa Rica. *1) Toma de posiciones del Partido Demócrata Cristiano–frente al Comunismo, frente al Capitalismo y frente a los regimenes políticos del país. 2) Declaración de principios del Partido Demócrata Cristiano.* San José.
Partido Demócrata Cristiano de Panamá. *El Partido Demócrata Cristiano de Panamá: Historia, Principios, Programa, Estructura.* Panamá, 1964.
Partido Demócrata Cristiano del Perú. *Conclusiones de la VIII Asamblea Nacional.* Lima: mimeographed, March, 1965.
———. *Partido Demócrata Cristiano: IV Asamblea Nacional Arequipa, 1959.* Publicación hecha por el Comité Distrital de San Isidro. Lima: Editorial Ausonía, 1959.
———. *Programa de Gobierno.* Una publicación de la Secretaría Nacional de Estudios. Lima: Imp. "El Cóndor," 1962.
Partido Revolucionario Social Cristiano de la República Dominicana. *Declaración de Principios y el Programa de Gobierno de Partido Revolucionario Social Cristiano.* Mimeographed.
———. *Democracia Cristiana: Principios e Ideas Fundamentales.* Mimeographed.
———. *Programa del Partido Revolucionario Social Cristiano.* Mimeographed.
Partido Social Cristiano-COPEI. *Estatutos.* Caracas, 1961.
———. *Programa.* Caracas: Secretaría Nacional de Propaganda, 1958.
———. *Programa.* 3rd ed. Caracas: Secretaría Nacional de Propaganda, 1961.
Partido Social Cristiano de Nicaragua. *¿Que es el Partido Social-Cristiano Nicaragüense?* Managua, 1961.
Partido Social Demócrata Cristiano de Colombia. *Partido Social Demócrata Cristiano.* Bogotá: Ediciones del Caribe, 1964.

PARTY PUBLICATIONS AND PAMPHLETS

"ABC de la Democracia Cristiana o Social-Cristianismo," *Combate* [Organo del Partido Social Cristiano Nicaragüense], April, 1964, pp. 2–10.
El ABC del Movimiento Revolucionario Social Cristiano. [Dominican Republic]: Imp. de L. H. Cruz, 1964.

Acevedo Amaya, Valmore. *Regiones Pobres y Regiones Ricas.* Publicaciones de la Fracción Parlamentaria de COPEI, No. 10. Caracas, 1963.

Bolaños Ramírez, Jorge, Juan Hurdano, and Enrique Arguedas Ibáñez. *El ABC de la Democracia Cristiana.* Lima: Editorial Universitaria, 1960.

Briceño Salas, Hugo. *Sobre el Desarrollo Industria y Agrícola.* Publicaciones de la Fracción Parlamentaria de COPEI, No. 13. Caracas, 1963.

Caldera, Rafael. *Defensa de la Constitucionalidad.* Publicaciones de la Fracción Parlamentaria de COPEI, No. 4. Caracas, 1962.

———. *Lucha Constante por la Libertad.* Ediciones "Hercamdi," Colección "Palabras y Problemas," No. 1. Caracas: Empresa El Cojo, 1958.

———. *El Mito del Andinismo.* Caracas: Empresa El Cojo, 1958.

———. *Políticos y Técnicos.* Publicaciones de la Fracción Parlamentaria de COPEI, No. 14. Caracas, 1963.

Calderon Berti, Humberto. *Petróleo y Desarrollo Económico.* Publicaciones de la Fracción Parlamentaria de COPEI, No. 2. Caracas, 1964.

Calvani, Arístides. *En El Congreso Técnico.* Publicaciones de la Fracción Parlamentaria de COPEI, No. 15. Caracas, 1963.

———. *Sobre la Immunidad Parlamentaria.* Publicaciones de la Fracción Parlamentaria de COPEI, No. 19. Caracas, 1964.

Cárdenas, Rodolfo José. *La Candidatura Presidencial.* Caracas: Ediciones "Hercamdi," 1958.

Cardozo, Hilarión. *Sobre la Autonomía Universitaria.* Publicaciones de la Fracción Parlamentaria de COPEI, No. 20. Caracas, 1964.

Castillo Velasco, Jaime. *Allende y los Comunistas.* Santiago de Chile: Editorial del Pacífico, 1964.

I Congreso Nacional de Profesionales y Técnicos de COPEI y Independientes Socialcristianos. *Acta Final.* Rev. ed. Publicación de Secretaría Nacional de Organismos Profesionales del Partido Socialcristiano-COPEI, No. 2. Caracas, 1963.

———. *100,000 Viviendas por Año para Venezuela (Plan Caldera).* Publicación de la Secretaría Nacional de Organismos Profesionales del Partido Socialcristiano-COPEI, No. 1. Caracas, 1963.

Dario Gonzales, Rubén. *Estructuras Sindicales.* Publicaciones de la Fracción Parlamentaria de COPEI, No. 1. Caracas, 1964.

Datos Referentes al Movimiento Social Cristiano (Democracia Cristiana) del Ecuador. Mimeographed.

Definición de las Estructuras Económico-Sociales proprias de la Democracia Cristiana. Folleto No. 1. México, D.F.: Juventud Popular Social Cristiana, 1962.

Fernández, Rafael. *Jacques Maritain.* Publicaciones de la Fracción Parlamentaria de COPEI, No. 8. Caracas, 1963.

———. *Sobre Política Educativa.* Publicaciones de la Fracción Parlamentaria de COPEI, No. 18. Caracas, 1964.

Flores, Eduardo. *Principios para una Sociedad Demócrata Cristiana: Un Nuevo Orden Social en Busca de Puerto Rico.* San Juan, 1964.

Frei Montalva, Eduardo. *Chile, 1964–1970: Dos Discursos.* Santiago de Chile: Editorial del Pacífico, 1964.

———. *Soy Categoricamente Partidario de Reforma la Constitución: Posición del*

Senador don Eduardo Frei ante las ideas de reforma de la Constitución. Santiago de Chile: Editorial del Pacífico, 1964.

———. *360,000 Nuevos Habitaciones se Construirán en el Gobierno de Frei.* Santiago de Chile: Sopech Impresores, 1964.

Fuentealba, Renán. *Tercera Declaración de Millahue y Cuenta Política del Presidente Nacional de la D.C.* Santiago de Chile: Impresores El Imparcial, 1964.

González, Godofredo. *Venezuela y la Intergración Latino-americana.* Caracas, May 15, 1964.

de Guzmán Polanco, Manuel. *El Movimiento Social-Cristiano del Ecuador.* Quito: Editorial "Prensa Católica," 1959.

Herrera Campins, Luis. *La Victoria de Eduardo Frei.* Publicaciones de la Fracción Parlamentaria de COPEI, No. 24. Caracas, 1964.

———, and Dagoberto González. *El "Informe Confidencial."* Publicaciones de la Fracción Parlamentaria de COPEI, No. 11. Caracas, 1963.

Instituto Nacional de Estudios Sindicales. *Carácteres del Sindicalismo Cristiano.* Publicaciones de la Fracción Parlamentaria de COPEI, No. 7. Caracas, 1963.

Instituto Nacional de Estudios Sociales. *Sobre Libertad Sindical.* Publicaciones de la Fracción Parlamentaria de COPEI, No. 17. Caracas, 1964.

Juventud Demócrata Cristiano de Cuba. *Una Respuesta.* Miami, 1964.

Lara Velado, Roberto. *Hacia Donde Queremos Ir.* San Salvador: Publicación del Partido Demócrata Cristiano, 1964.

López Luque, Jesús. *Ley Moderna para la Agricultura.* Publicaciones de la Fracción Parlamentaria de COPEI, No. 23. Caracas, 1964.

López Meléndez, Teodulo. *Puntos de Vista sobre la Universidad.* Publicaciones de la Fracción Parlamentaria de COPEI, No. 4. Caracas, 1964.

Maspero, Emilio. *Revolución en Latinoamérica.* Folleto No. 2. México, D.F.: Juventud Popular Social Cristiana, 1962.

Molina Camacho, Carlos. *Cooperativismo Agrario.* Publicaciones de la Fracción Parlamentaria de COPEI, No. 16. Caracas, 1963.

Movimiento Social Demócrata Cristiano de México. *Primer Seminario Nacional de Extensión Social Universitaria para el Desarrollo de la Comunidad.* Guadalajara, México, Jan. 25–29, 1965.

Partido Democracia Cristiana Guatemalteca. *Projecto de la Campaña Nacional del Partido Democracia Cristiana Guatemalteca para Lograr su Reconocimiento como Institución Política de Derecho Público.* Guatemala: mimeographed, Aug. 15, 1964.

Partido Demócrata Cristiano de Costa Rica. *Fundamentos de la Democracia Cristiana.* San José: Series de divulgación doctrinaria, 1965.

Partido Demócrata Cristiano del Ecuador. *ABC de la Democracia Cristiana.* Quayaquil: Editorial Aldo Manuzio, 1965.

Partido Social-Cristiano-COPEI. *Carta Fundamental del Magisterio Social Cristiano de Venezuela.* Caracas: Publicaciones de la Secretaría Nacional de Educación, 1958.

Partido Social Demócrata Cristiano de Colombia. *Revolución en Libertad.* Bogotá, 1965.

Pilonieta, Luis Guillermo. *Sobre la Ley de Seguro Social.* Publicaciones de la Fracción Parlamentaria de COPEI, No. 30. Caracas, 1965.

Ponce Enríquez, Camilo. *El Pensamiento de Camilo Ponce.* Quito: Editorial "La Unión," 1962.
Prensa Nacional, *Los 19 Años de COPEI.* Publicaciones de la Fracción Parlamentaria de COPEI, No. 28. Caracas, 1965.
La Riva, Edecio. *Sobre la Ley de Conmutación de Penas.* Publicaciones de la Fracción Parlamentaria de COPEI, No. 27. Caracas, 1965.
Téfel Vélez, Reinaldo Antonio. *El Partido Social Cristiano de Nicaragua.* Mimeographed.
Tomic, Radomiro. *Unidad y Diversidad de la Democracia Cristiana en el Mundo.* Santiago de Chile: Imprenta del Pacífico, 1962.
Los Trabajadores y la Unidad de América Latina. Carta de Rio de Janeiro aprobada en el VII consejo Latino Americano de Trabajadores, March 9, 10, 11, 1964.

Lectures
Prepared for El Instituto de Formación Demócrata Cristiana,
Caracas, Venezuela (mimeographed)

Acevedo Amaya, Valmore. *Geografía Socio-Económica y Política de América Latina.*
Allo Georges. *La Doctrina Social de la Iglesia.*
Althammer, Walter. *Historia de Los Partidos Políticos en Alemania.*
Aguilar, Pedro Pablo. *Los Partidos Demócrata Cristianos.*
Castillo Velasco, Jaime. *La Democracia Cristiana.*
Chélini, Jean. *Introducción a la Democracia.*
Haberl, Fridolino. *Doctrina Social Cristiana.*
Herrera Campins, Luis. *La Democracia Cristiana: Orientaciones Generales en su Acción Política.*
Plá Rodríguez, Américo. *Democracia Cristiana.*
Reyes Vicuña, Tomás. *Planificación en la Libertad . . . .*
Tindemans, Leo. *Doctrina Política Cristiana.*

LATIN AMERICAN POLITICAL PARTIES

Books

Carmo, J. A. Pinto da. *Diretrizes Partidarias. UDN-PRD . . . PDC . . . .* Rio de Janeiro: Pongetti, 1948.
Cope, Orville G. "Politics in Chile: A Study of Political Parties and Election Procedures." Unpublished Ph.D. dissertation, Claremont Graduate School, Claremont, Cal., 1964.
Edwards Vives, Alberto, and Eduardo Frei Montalva. *Historia de los Partidos Políticos Chilenos.* Santiago de Chile: Editorial del Pacífico, 1949.
Galletti, Alfredo. *La Política y los Partidos.* México: Fondo de Cultura Económica, 1961.
Gil, Federico G. *Genesis and Modernization of Political Parties in Chile.* Latin American Monographs. Gainesville: University of Florida Press, 1962.

González, Ariosto Domingo. *Los Partidos Tradicionales*, ed. José María Serrano. Montevideo: Librería Cervantes, 1922.

Guilisasti Tagle, Sergio (ed.). *Caminos de la Política: Un Enfoque de Cinco Doctrinos.* Santiago de Chile: Editorial Universitaria, 1960.

Hernández Urbina, Alfredo. *Nueva Política Nacional.* Trujillo, Perú: Ediciones Raíz, 1962.

———. *Los Partidos Políticos y la Crisis del APRA.* Lima: Ediciones Raíz, 1956.

Institute for the Comparative Study of Political Systems. *Argentina: Election Factbook.* Washington: Operations and Policy Research, Inc., 1963.

———. *Brazil: Election Factbook.* Washington: Operations and Policy Research, Inc., 1962.

———. *Chile: Election Factbook.* Washington: Operations and Policy Research, Inc., 1963.

———. *Venezuela: Election Factbook.* Washington: Operations and Policy Research, Inc., 1963.

Magellanes, M. V. *Partidos Políticos Venezolanos.* Caracas: Tip. Vargos, 1959.

Manual del Elector. Lima: Editorial Juan Mejía Baca, 1962.

Mirando Ramírez, Hugo. *Los Partidos Políticos en la Derecho Constitucional Chileno.* Santiago de Chile: Impresiones Senda, 1947.

Miró-Quesada Láos, Carlos. *Autopsia de los Partidos Políticos.* Lima: Ediciones "Paginas Peruanas," 1961.

Montecinos Rozas, Edmundo. *Apuntaciones para el estudio de la evolución de los partidos políticos Chilenos y de su proyección jurídica.* Santiago de Chile: Dirección General de Presiones, Imp., 1942.

Orfila Reynal, Arnoldo. *Crisis de los Partidos Políticos Argentinos.* México: Universidad Nacional Autónoma de México, 1960.

Terán Gómez, Luis. *Los Partidos Políticos y su Acción Democrática.* La Paz: Editorial "La Paz," 1942.

Zolvendo, Eduardo. *Geografía Electoral de la Argentina.* Buenos Aires: Ediciones Ancora, 1958.

ARTICLES

Abbott, Roger S. "The Role of Contemporary Political Parties in Chile," *American Political Science Review*, XLV (June, 1951), 450–63.

Anderson, Charles W. "Central American Political Parties: A Functional Approach," *Western Political Quarterly*, XV (March, 1962), 125–39.

Busey, James L. "Our Political Gap in Latin America," *Midwest Quarterly*, III (April, 1962), 219–29.

Delgado, Carlos. "Panorama Político Peruano," *Combate*, IV (May-June, 1962), 23–30.

Díaz, Antonio. "Los Partidos Políticos del Ecuador," *Política*, III (Nov., 1963), 105–16.

Fitzgibbon, Russell H. "The Party Potpourri in Latin America," *Western Political Quarterly*, X (March, 1957), 3–22.

Freyre, Gilberto. "Personalities versus Parties for the Presidency of Brazil," *Reporter*, XXI (July 23, 1959), 28–30.

Gil, Federico G. "Responsible Parties in Latin America," *Journal of Politics*, XV (Aug., 1953), 333–48.
Potash, Robert A. "Argentine Political Parties, 1957–58," *Journal of Inter-American Studies*, I (Oct., 1959), 515–24.
"Que Piensan los Partidos en Materia Económica," *Camoatí*, XVII (May, 1957), 158–63.
Snow, Peter G. "The Political Party Spectrum in Chile," *South Atlantic Quarterly*, LXII (Autumn, 1963), 474–87.
Taylor, Philip B. "Interparty Co-operation and Uruguay's 1952 Constitution," *Western Political Quarterly*, VII (Sept., 1954), 391–400.
Townsend Ezcurra, Andrés. "Panorama Preelectoral en el Perú," *Política*, No. 10, June, 1960, pp. 95–99.
Wyckoff, Theodore. "Brazilian Political Parties," *South Atlantic Quarterly*, LVI (Summer, 1957), 281–98.

GENERAL

Books

Adams, Mildred (ed.). *Latin America: Evolution or Explosion?* New York: Dodd, Mead and Company, Council on World Tensions, 1963.
Alexander, Robert J. *The Venezuelan Democratic Revolution.* New Brunswick, N. J.: Rutgers University Press, 1964.
Almond, Gabriel A., and James S. Coleman (eds.). *The Politics of Developing Areas.* Princeton, N. J.: Princeton University Press, 1960.
Belaúnde, Víctor Andrés. *Bolívar and the Political Thought of the Spanish American Revolution.* Baltimore: The Johns Hopkins Press, 1938.
Chile. Estudios de Actualidad, Primera Serie, No. 1. Montevideo: Instituto de Estudios Políticos para América Latina, 1964.
Colombia. Estudios de Actualidad, Primera Serie, No. 4. Montevideo: Instituto de Estudios Políticos para América Latina, 1964.
Council on Foreign Relations. *Social Change in Latin America Today.* New York: Published for the Council on Foreign Relations by Harper and Brothers, 1960.
Crawford, William Rex. *A Century of Latin American Thought.* Revised edition. Cambridge, Mass.: Harvard University Press, 1961.
Davis, Harold Eugene (ed.). *Government and Politics in Latin America.* New York: The Ronald Press, 1958.
——— (ed.). *Latin American Social Thought.* Washington: The University Press, 1961.
Dewart, Leslie. *Christianity and Revolution: The Lesson of Cuba.* New York: Herder and Herder, 1963.
Diamant, Alfred. *Austrian Catholics and the First Republic.* Princeton, N. J.: Princeton University Press, 1960.
Duverger, Maurice. *Political Parties: Their Organization and Activity in the Modern State,* trans. Barbara and Robert North. Foreword by D. W. Brogan. New York: John Wiley and Sons, 1963.

Ecuador. Estudios de Actualidad, Primera Serie, No. 3. Montevideo: Instituto de Estudios Políticos para América Latina, 1964.

Einaudi, Mario, and François Goguel. *Christian Democracy in Italy and France.* Notre Dame, Ind.: University of Notre Dame Press, 1952.

Fogarty, Michael P. *Christian Democracy in Western Europe, 1820–1953.* Notre Dame, Ind.: University of Notre Dame Press, 1957.

Johnson, John J. *The Military and Society in Latin America.* Stanford, Cal.: Stanford University Press, 1964.

———. *Political Change in Latin America: The Emergence of the Middle Sectors.* Stanford, Cal.: Stanford University Press, 1958.

Kennedy, John J. *Catholicism, Nationalism and Democracy in Argentina.* Notre Dame, Ind.: University of Notre Dame Press, 1958.

Lieuwen, Edwin. *Arms and Politics in Latin America.* New York: Published for the Council on Foreign Relations by Frederick A. Praeger, Inc., 1960.

———. *Venezuela.* New York: Oxford University Press, 1961.

Maier, Joseph, and Richard W. Weatherhead (eds.). *The Politics of Change in Latin America.* New York: Frederick A. Praeger, 1964.

Needler, Martin C. *Latin American Politics in Perspective.* Princeton, N. J.: D. Van Nostrand Company, 1963.

Neumann, Sigmund (ed.). *Modern Political Parties.* Chicago: University of Chicago Press, 1956.

Orbe y Urquiza, Jesús de. *Acción Católica.* México, D.F.: Editorial Patria, 1950.

Paraguay. Estudios de Actualidad, Primera Serie, No. 8. Montevideo: Instituto de Estudios Políticos para América Latina, 1964.

Perú. Estudios de Actualidad, Primera Serie, No. 2. Montevideo: Instituto de Estudios Políticos para América Latina, 1964.

Pike, Fredrick B. *Chile and the United States. The Emergence of Chile's Social Crisis and the Challenge to United States' Diplomacy.* Notre Dame, Ind.: University of Notre Dame Press, 1963.

——— (ed.). *The Conflict Between Church and State in Latin America.* New York: Alfred A. Knopf, 1964.

———, and William V. D'Antonio (eds.). *Religion, Revolution and Reform.* New York: Frederick A. Praeger, Inc., 1964.

Porter, Charles O., and Robert J. Alexander. *The Struggle for Democracy in Latin America.* New York: Macmillan Company, 1961.

del Rio, Angel (ed.). *Responsible Freedom in the Americas.* Garden City, N. Y.: Doubleday and Co., 1955.

Schmitt, Karl M., and David B. Burks. *Evolution or Chaos? Dynamics of Latin American Government and Politics.* New York: Frederick A. Praeger, 1963.

Tannenbaum, Frank. *Ten Keys to Latin America.* New York: Alfred A. Knopf, 1962.

TePaske, John J., and Sydney Nettleton Fisher (eds.). *Explosive Forces in Latin America.* Columbus: Ohio State University Press, 1964.

Venezuela. Estudios de Actualidad, Primera Serie, No. 5. Montevideo: Instituto de Estudios Políticos para América Latina, 1964.

Whitaker, Arthur P. *Argentine Upheaval.* New York: Frederick A. Praeger, 1956.

Articles

Alexander, Robert J. "Nationalism, Latin America's Predominant Ideology," *Journal of International Affairs,* XV (1961), 108–14.

Bagú, Sergio. "Diagramo político de la Argentina de hoy," *Cuadernos Americanos,* XV (Nov.-Dec., 1956), 38–57.

Betancourt, Rómulo, *et al.* "Discursos pronunciados en el acto de Promulgación de la Ley de Reforma Agrarian en Venezuela," *Política,* VII (March, 1960), 99–112.

Blanksten, George I. "Political Groups in Latin America," *American Political Science Review,* LIII (March, 1959), 106–27.

Bonilla, Frank. "The Student Federation of Chile: 50 Years of Political Action," *Journal of Inter-American Studies,* II (July, 1960), 311–34.

Cardozo, Manoel. "The Brazilian Church and the New Left," *Journal of Inter-American Studies,* VI (July, 1964), 313–21.

Davis, Harold Eugene. "Trends in Social Thought in Twentieth Century Latin America," *Journal of Inter-American Studies,* I (Jan., 1959), 57–71.

Fitzgibbon, Russell H. "The Political Impact on Religious Development in Uruguay," *Church History,* XX (March, 1953), 21–32.

Gil, Federico G. "Cuatro Tendencias en la Política Latinamericana," *Journal of Inter-American Studies,* I (Oct., 1959), 459–75.

Gillin, John P. "Changing Depths in Latin America," *Journal of Inter-American Studies,* II (Oct., 1960), 379–89.

Kennedy, John J. "Dichotomies in the Church," *Annals of the American Academy,* CCCXXXIV (March, 1961), 54–62.

Kling, Merle. "Political Instability in Latin America," *Comparative Politics, Notes and Readings,* ed. Roy C. Macridis and Bernard E. Brown. Homewood, Ill.: The Dorsey Press, Inc., 1961, pp. 499–510.

Lieuwen, Edwin. "The Changing Role of the Military in Latin America," *Journal of Inter-American Studies,* III (Oct., 1961), 559–69.

Morse, Richard M. "Toward a Theory of Spanish-American Government," *Journal of the History of Ideas,* XV (Jan., 1954), 71–93.

Pierson, W. W. (ed.). "Pathology of Democracy in Latin America: A Symposium," *American Political Science Review,* XLIV (March, 1950), 100–150.

Segundo, R. "The Future of Christianity in Latin America," *Crosscurrents,* Summer, 1963, pp. 273–81. (Reprint.)

Sturzo, Luigi. "The Philosophic Background of Christian Democracy," *Review of Politics,* IX (Jan., 1947), 3–15.

Tannenbaum, Frank. "The Future of Democracy in Latin America," *Foreign Affairs,* XXXIII (April, 1955), 429–44.

Trenary, Don C. "Brazil's Curitiba Has Big Plans For Future," *The Milwaukee Journal,* March 17, 1966, Part I, p. 26.

Washington, S. Walter. "Student Politics in Latin America: The Venezuelan Example," *Foreign Affairs,* XXXVII (April, 1959), 463–73.

Weigel, Gustave, S.J. "A Theologian Looks at Latin America," *Review of Politics,* XX (Oct., 1958), 419–30.

Whitaker, A. P. "Problems of Representative Democracy in Latin America," *Social Science*, XXVIII (Oct., 1953), 211–15.

Young, Jordan M. "Some Permanent Political Characteristics of Contemporary Brazil," *Journal of Inter-American Studies*, VI (July, 1964), 287–301.

Index

Acção Popular, 90, 246
Acción Cubana, 15
Acción Democrática (AD), 21, 22, 108, 163, 192, 203–211, 221
AD-ARS, 205, 206, 208
AD-Social Cristiano-COPEI Coalition, 204–209
Influence on COPEI, 21–22, 188
See also Betancourt, Rómulo
Acción Nacional (Venezuela), 15
Acción Popular (Peru), 23, 209–214, 216, 281. *See also* Belaúnde Terry, Fernando
Acción Social Demócrata (Panama), 17
Adenauer, Konrad, 271
Afaro, Eloy, 177
Agrarian Reform, 105–108, 123–124, 130, 175, 198, 209, 239
Agrupación Demócrata Cristiana (Peru), 14
Aguilar, Pedro Pablo, 22n, 88n, 170n
Alayza Grundy, Ernesto, 65
Alberdi, Juan B., 177
Alessandri, Jorge, 196
Allende Gossens, Salvador, 3, 196, 217, 277. *See also* Frente de Acción Popular
Alliance for Progress, 148, 151–152. *See also* Punta del Este; United States
Amoroso Lima, Alceu, 14, 32, 40, 41n, 56, 140, 170, 185, 244
Andrea, Miguel de, 13, 215
Anti-Clericalism, 74, 172, 178, 180, 184, 215–216, 219, 220, 221, 222
Aprista Parties, 3, 4, 6, 107n, 163, 204–209, 210, 214–219, 224, 241, 253, 264, 265, 275, 280–281. *See also* Aprista Party; Haya de la Torre, Víctor Raúl; Socialism
Aprista Party (Peru), 163, 210, 216, 217. *See also* Aprista Parties; Haya de la Torre, Víctor Raúl; Socialism
Arbenz Guzmán, Jocobo, 76, 175, 199
Argentina, Revolution of *1955*, 65
Asociación Nacional de Obreros Campesinos (Chile), 93
Avila Bastos, Fernando, 34
Avila Camacho, Manuel, 178

Barrientos, René, 137, 163
Batlle y Ordóñez, José, 12, 177, 256
Bedoya Reyes, Luis, 24, 210, 251, 281
Belaúnde Terry, Fernando, 23, 99, 209–214. *See also* Acción Popular
Belaúnde, Víctor Andrés, 10
Bellarmine Center, 175
Betancourt, Rómulo, 22, 23, 76, 143, 155, 163, 192, 199, 201, 203–209, 210, 253, 281. *See also* Acción Democrática
Birth Control, 95–97, 183, 220. *See also* Latin American Christian Democracy
Bloque Revolucionario Universitario Cristiano, 76, 90. *See also* Youth Groups
Bolaños Ramírez, Jorge, 51
Bolívar, Simón, 177
Bosch, Juan, 25, 166, 218, 253. *See also* Partido Revolucionario Dominicana
Braga, Ney, 24, 129, 245

Briceño Salas, Hugo, 251
Bustamante y Rivero, José Luis, 15
Bustos, Ismael, 34, 119

Caldera, Rafael, 15, 18, 21, 23, 32, 33, 34, 39, 55, 73, 76, 96, 97, 102, 105, 129, 137, 138, 146, 147, 149, 158, 181, 191, 192, 201, 205, 206, 208, 209, 210, 217, 219, 222, 251, 262, 273
Calderón Guardia, Rafael Angel, 16
Calvani, Arístides, 105
Câmara, Hélder, 175
Capitalism, 41–47, 97, 115, 116, 127–129, 147, 148, 149, 188, 194, 195, 199, 212, 233, 234–237. *See also* Latin American Christian Democracy, Third Position; Liberalism
Caribbean Congress. *See* International Congress, Caribbean
Castello Branco, Humberto, 24, 246
Castillo Velasco, Jaime, 27, 34, 41n, 42n, 75n, 175n, 194n, 195n, 197n, 198n, 242n
Castro, Fidel, 3, 15, 22, 33, 34, 88, 144, 158, 159, 171, 193, 223, 265. *See also* Cuban Revolution
Catholic Action, 13, 274
Catholic Electoral League (Brazil), 14
Catholicism, 11, 26–28, 71–74, 138, 161–169, 192, 216, 231, 233–234, 244, 258–261, 266–270, 275–276, 279, 280, 281. *See also* Anti-Clericalism; Roman Catholic Church
Catholic Liberalism, 182–185. *See also* Liberalism
Catholic Parties, 9–12, 244, 246, 247. *See also* Conservative Parties
Center of Intercultural Formation, 175
Center of Public Opinion, 274
Central American Christian Democratic Federation, 142
Central American Common Market, 45, 142
Central University (Venezuela), 90
Chávez, Federico, 14
Christian Democracy, Africa and Asia, 137–138
Christian Democracy, Europe, 10, 17, 20, 27, 28, 29, 30, 38, 44, 47, 48, 56, 81, 87, 94, 135, 137, 138, 139, 183n, 192, 195, 215, 231, 240, 242, 243, 244, 257, 258, 259, 260, 261, 265, 271, 272, 273, 280
Christian Democratic Congresses. *See* International Congresses
Christian Democratic Federal Union (Argentina), 185, 247
Christian Democratic Parties, General, 9–12. *See also* Christian Democracy, Africa and Asia, Europe; Latin American Christian Democracy; Latin American Christian Democratic Parties
Christian Democratic Party. *See* Christian Democracy, Africa and Asia, Europe; Movimiento; Partido
Christian Democratic Review, 193
Christian Democratic Union of Central Europe, 137
Christian Socialism, 118–119, 121
Church and State, 63–65, 178–182
Civic Union (Uruguay). *See* Unión Cívica
Civil Service Reform, 108
Class Struggle. *See* Latin American Christian Democracy; Marxism
Coalition Government, 71, 190–193, 196, 197, 204–214, 218, 274–275
Co-determination, 117. *See also* Communitarianism
Colombia, National Front, 45–46
Colonialism, 45, 156–158
Colorado Party, 4, 12. *See also* Batlle y Ordóñez, José
Combate (Organo del Partido Social Cristiano Nicaragüense), 12n, 39n
Comisión Económica para América Latina (CEPAL). *See* United Nations Economic Commission for Latin America
Commodity Price Stabilization Programs, 146, 148–149
Common Market, Europe, 45, 107, 139, 141
Communism, 6, 21, 40, 46–50, 62, 71, 77, 80, 81, 82, 89, 90, 91, 104, 114, 115, 134, 148, 153–156, 159, 160, 179, 183, 187, 189, 191, 192–201, 224, 231, 241, 243, 247, 250, 255, 257, 259, 260, 265, 266, 269, 279–281. *See also* Latin American

Communism (*Continued*)
Christian Democracy, Third Position; Marxism
Communisto Manifesto, 27
Communist Parties. *See* Communism
Communitarianism, 104, 111, 115, 116–123, 127, 128, 230, 231, 234–237, 238, 268–269. *See also* Cooperativism; Corporatism
Concha Subercaseaux, Enrique, 13
Confederación Autónoma de Sindicatos Cristianos (CASC), 91, 189
Confederación Latino Americana de Sindicalistas Cristianos (CLASC), 91, 92, 157n
Conservative Parties, 4, 6, 10, 16, 17, 18, 19, 20, 33, 79, 169, 179, 181, 182–185, 222–225, 241, 242, 259, 266. *See also* Catholic Parties; Latin American Christian Democratic Parties
Convivió (Cuba), 15
Cooperativism, 30–31, 107, 121, 122. *See also* Communitarianism
Co-ownership. *See* Communitarianism
Co-participation. *See* Communitarianism
COPEI. *See* Partido Social Cristiano-COPEI
Cornejo Chávez, Héctor, 14, 34, 37n, 39, 42n, 45, 49, 62n, 75, 76, 79, 125, 132, 181, 210, 211, 212, 213, 251
Corporatism, 82, 110, 111, 119, 120, 122, 232–238, 269. *See also* Communitarianism; Legislative Reform
Corral, Pedro del, 273
Correa y Elías, Javier, 63, 212
Cruz Coke, Eduardo, 19
Cuban Revolution, 33, 64, 158–160, 172, 256, 280. *See also* Castro, Fidel

D'Alessandro, Guido, 248
Defense of Democracy Law, 74, 77, 196–197, 199, 200
Democracia Social Cristiana (Cuba), 15
Democratic Christian Union of Argentina, 13
Democratic Party (Argentina), 20
Democratic Socialism. *See* Socialism
Derisi, Nicolás, 32
DiNatale, Remo, 31, 96, 118, 122n, 186n
Discipline, Party. *See* Latin American Christian Democratic Parties
Divorce, 95, 179, 183, 220. *See also* Latin American Christian Democracy
Duvalier, François, 65, 144

Echeverría, Esteban, 177
Economic Planning, 61–62, 123–126, 131, 233, 269
Education, 100–102, 218. *See also* Roman Catholic Church
Eisenhower, Dwight D., 47, 194
Elections
Argentina, *1957*, 24, 25, 277; *1962*, 25, 77, 203, 204; *1963*, 25, 202, 203, 220; *1965*, 204
Brazil, *1945*, 24; *1948*, 24
Chile, *1949*, 33; *1958*, 277; *1964*, 3, 23, 33–34, 81, 86, 91, 217, 244, 277, 279; *1965*, 3n, 23, 33, 257n
Ecuador, *1956*, 25
El Salvador, *1964*, 22
Italy, *1948*, 3
Peru, *1962*, 211; *1963*, 23, 99, 163, 181, 211, 212; *1969*, 213
United States, *1960*, 82, 274
Venezuela, *1948*, 219; *1958*, 108, 181, 217, 219; *1968*, 207
Electoral Reform, 111
El Siglo, 196
Esfera, La, 241
European Christian Democratic Parties. *See* Christian Democracy, Europe
European Common Market. *See* Common Market, Europe
Expropriation. *See* Private Property

Falange Nacional, 3, 14, 18, 19, 20, 23, 33, 74, 91, 115, 144, 184, 220, 270. *See also* Partido Demócrata Cristiano (Chile)
Family Allowance Laws, 94
Fascism, 120, 185–186, 187

Federación de Estudiantes Social Cristianos de Centro América y Panamá (FESCAP) 90, 142
Figueres, José, 16, 253, 281. *See also* Liberación Nacional
Fogarty, Michael P., 10n, 17
Foreign Investment, 147–151
Foyaca, Manuel, 15
Franceschi, Gustavo, 45
Franco Montoro, Andrés, 24, 75, 94, 239, 246
Frei Government, 33, 34, 96, 100, 102, 104n, 113, 129, 131, 132, 150, 158, 198, 199, 220, 223, 262, 264, 278
Frei Montalva, Eduardo, 3, 23, 29, 30, 32, 33, 34, 36, 37, 40, 44n, 45, 50n, 54n, 57, 59, 60, 61, 62n, 71, 72n, 77, 88, 91, 97, 99, 100, 101, 102, 104, 109, 110, 111n, 113, 114, 119, 120, 123, 125, 126, 134n, 137, 141, 142, 148, 152, 156, 163, 173, 181, 198, 216n, 217, 221, 223, 238, 244, 251, 261, 271, 272, 281. *See also* Elections, Chile; Falange Nacional; Frei Government; Partido Demócrata Cristiano (Chile)
Frente Campesino (Venezuela), 93
Frente de Acción Popular (FRAP), 3, 196, 198, 217, 254, 277, 281
Frente Revolucionario Democrático (Cuba), 22, 223, 224
Freyre, Gilberto, 7
Frondizi, Arturo, 77, 203, 220
Functional Representation. *See* Corporatism

Gallegos, Rómulo, 221
Gasperi, Alcide de, 197, 244, 271
Gil, Federico G., 5, 172
Giménez Landínez, Víctor, 23, 78, 106n, 107, 108, 126, 206, 207, 273
Goldsack, José, 157n
Gómez, Juan Vicente, 15
González Ruiz, Fernando, 34
González Videla, Gabriel, 196, 220
Grupo ARS. *See* Acción Democrática, AD-ARS
Gumucio, Rafael L., 18

Haya de la Torre, Víctor Raúl, 163, 210, 211, 214, 253. *See also* Aprista Parties; Aprista Party
Heidenheimer, Arnold J., 10n, 139
Herrera Campins, Luis, 251
Hispanic American Report, 11n
Housing Policy, 97–98, 130
Hurtado, Patricio, 88

Ibáñez del Campo, Carlos, 18, 196, 220
Ideological Development, 6–9, 69, 72, 264–266. *See also* Latin American Christian Democratic Parties
Illia, Arturo, 25, 142, 204, 220
Imperialism. *See* Colonialism
Instituto de Formación Demócrata Cristiana, 86, 134, 273
Integralism. *See* Fascism
Inter-American Peace Force, 146
International Congresses of Latin American Christian Democracy
  Caribbean, 65n, 144, 154, 155, 156, 159
  Fifth, 30, 33, 63, 73, 97, 99, 102, 115, 123, 143, 151, 156–157, 191
  First, 32, 73, 122, 133
  Fourth, 142, 152
  General, 133–138, 167
  Second, 47, 48n, 61, 77, 121
  Seventh, 123, 155, 159
  Sixth, 142–143
  Third, 115, 124n, 126n, 130, 143, 144, 200
  See also Organización Demócrata Cristiana de América (ODCA)
International Union of Christian Democratic Youth, 90

Javier Castillo, Caonabo, 114n, 248
John XXIII, Pope, 26, 119
Juárez, Benito, 177
Judicial Reform, 109
Junta Promotora Nacional (Argentina), 21
Juventud Demócrata Cristiana de América, 90. *See also* Youth Groups

Kennedy, John F., 151

Labor Unions, 59, 77, 79, 80, 82, 90–92, 102–105, 111, 150, 183, 192, 233, 242, 248, 254, 260. *See also* Confederación Latino Americana de Sindicalistas Cristianos

Land Reform. *See* Agrarian Reform
Larrazábal, Wolfgang, 205
Latin American Christian Democracy, Theory of
 Christian Democratic Era, 36–37
 Class Struggle, 102, 103, 104, 115–117, 183, 188, 189, 235
 Man, Nature of, 51–54, 112–115, 267–269
 Pluralism, 56–60. *See also* Pluralism
 Political Authority, 61, 62, 64, 65
 Politics, Primacy of, 80–81
 Revolution, the, 37–41. *See also* Revolución en Libertad; Revolution, the
 State, the Positive, 60–64, 104, 122–132, 232–235
 State, Limitations on the, 64–65, 101
 Third Position, 41–51
 See also Birth Control; Christian Democratic Parties; Divorce; Latin American Christian Democratic Parties; Pluralism; Rebellion
Latin American Christian Democratic Parties
 As Opposition, 20–23, 76, 77, 166, 195, 206
 Conservative Parties in Foundation of, 19–20
 Discipline, 83, 84, 87, 240–251, 258
 European Influences, 28–31
 Heterogeneity of, 81–82, 187, 238, 239, 241, 242, 246
 Indigenous Contributions, 31–35
 Leadership, 81–87, 240–251, 271–273
 Organization, 30, 81–93, 187, 188, 240–251, 273, 274
 Publications, 22, 34, 79, 85, 86, 193
 Roman Catholic Church as Influence, 26–28
 Youth Movements in Foundation of, 17–19
 See also Christian Democratic Parties; Ideological Development; Latin American Christian Democracy
Latin American Free Trade Association, 141
Latin American Integration, 138–143, 261, 262, 263
Legislative Reform, 109–110. *See also* Corporatism
Leo XIII, Pope, 13, 26, 28
Leoni, Raúl, 22, 189, 206, 208, 209
Liberación Nacional (Costa Rica), 16n. *See also* Figueres, José
Liberalism, 11, 12, 26, 37, 38, 44–47, 49, 51, 52, 56, 62, 147, 219, 222–225, 235, 259. *See also* Capitalism; Latin American Christian Democracy
Liberal Parties, 4, 6, 50, 79, 222–225, 266, 275

Madariaga, Salvador de, 5
Maritain, Jacques, 28, 29, 32, 37, 55, 56, 239
Marxism, 27, 28, 32, 41, 47–50n, 52, 71, 121–122, 177, 188, 214, 216, 235, 267. *See also* Communism; Socialism
Mater et Magistra, 26, 119
Medina Angarita, Isaías, 15
Mexican Revolution, 144, 175, 178, 256, 262
Middle Principles, 237–240
Middle Sectors, 207, 219, 275, 279
Monroe Doctrine, 152
Montevideo Movement. *See* International Congresses
Mosquera Garces, Manuel, 16
Movimiento de Estudiantes Conservadores (Chile), 18
Movimiento de Izquierda Revolucionaria (Venezuela), 89, 199, 205
Movimiento Demócrata Cristiano (Cuba), 15, 22, 53, 59, 71, 72, 82–85, 103, 125, 127, 129, 134, 135, 136, 154, 155, 190, 192, 193, 201, 223, 249, 273
Movimiento Demócrata Cristiano de Tucumán, 15
Movimiento Democrático (Peru), 14
Movimiento Popular Cristiano (Bolivia), 135
Movimiento Social Cristiano (Ecuador), 16, 19, 20, 25, 65, 95, 110, 130, 134, 136, 155, 166, 190
Movimiento Social Demócrata Cristiano (Mexico), 14, 19, 33, 41, 43, 104, 118, 119, 123n, 135, 136, 249
Movimiento Social Demócrata Cristiano (Paraguay), 22, 38, 64, 77, 81, 95, 100, 164, 224, 273, 276
Movimiento Social Republicano (Argentina), 15, 201

National Falange (Chile). *See* Falange Nacional (Chile)
National Institute of Trade Union Research (Venezuela), 86
National Liberation Party (Costa Rica). *See* Liberación Nacional
National Party (Curaçao), 136
National Students Union (Venezuela), 18
National Union of Popular Action (Nicaragua). *See* Unión Nacional de Acción Popular (Nicaragua)
Neo-Thomism, 31–32, 61, 65, 174
Neumann, Sigmund, 69
New Catholicism. *See* Roman Catholic Church
Nouvelles Equipes Internationales (NEI), 137

Odría, Manuel, 15, 21, 166, 210, 211, 216, 217
Oligarchy, 4, 78, 79, 161, 169, 170, 179, 252
Ordóñez, Manuel, 144, 273
Organización Demócrata Cristiana de América (ODCA), 16n, 97, 133–138, 151, 156, 159–160, 190, 248, 273. *See also* International Congresses
Organización Regional Interamericana de Trabajadores (ORIT), 92
Organization, Party. *See* Latin American Christian Democratic Parties
Organization of American States, 145–146

Pacem in Terris, 26
Padilla de Sánchez, Josefina, 276
Palacios, Alfredo, 215
Panama Canal, 153
Participation, Political. *See* Pluralism
Partido Acción Cristiana (Puerto Rico), 135
Partido Corporativo Popular (Chile), 14
Partido de Acción Nacional (Mexico), 14, 185, 249, 276
Partido Democracia Cristiana Guatemalteca, 17, 76, 86, 88, 190, 199, 217–218, 224, 273, 278, 282
Partido Demócrata Cristão (Brazil), 22, 24, 32, 86, 94, 129, 134, 189, 190, 245–247, 273
Partido Demócrata Cristiano (Argentina), 20, 21, 24, 34, 64, 77, 86, 95, 101, 105, 114, 124, 125, 128, 165, 166, 181, 190, 200, 201–204, 220, 247, 248, 253, 261, 262, 273, 274, 277, 282
Partido Demócrata Cristiano (Bolivia), 16, 99, 137, 225
Partido Demócrata Cristiano (Chile), 3, 17–18, 20, 33, 78, 82–87, 127, 151, 158, 164, 180, 189, 196, 214, 217, 218, 219–222, 239, 242, 245, 250, 251, 254, 255, 256, 257, 262, 277, 279. *See also* Falange Nacional (Chile)
Partido Demócrata Cristiano (Costa Rica), 16, 36, 101, 136, 201, 230
Partido Demócrata Cristiano (Dominican Republic), 136, 248, 282
Partido Demócrata Cristiano (Ecuador), 16, 19, 136, 190
Partido Demócrata Cristiano (El Salvador), 17, 22, 25, 73, 113, 128, 134n, 166, 190, 191, 224, 273, 282
Partido Demócrata Cristiano (Panama), 17, 26, 48, 64, 65, 70, 71, 78, 80, 81, 83, 86, 111, 131, 153, 159, 190, 262, 266, 276, 282. *See also* Acción Social Demócrata; Unión Cívica Nacional
Partido Demócrata Cristiano (Paraguay). *See* Movimiento Social Demócrata Cristiano (Paraguay)
Partido Demócrata Cristiano (Peru), 23, 50, 58, 61, 70, 77n, 86, 98, 106, 109, 110, 127, 128, 129, 146, 151, 166, 189, 200, 209–214, 216, 217, 225, 250, 251, 265, 272, 281
Partido Demócrata Cristiano (Uruguay). *See* Unión Cívica (Uruguay)
Partido Popular (Chile), 14
Partido Progresista Demócrata Cristiano (Dominican Republic), 136, 248
Partido Revolucionario Dominicana, 218
Partido Revolucionario (Guatemala), 199, 218
Partido Revolucionario Social Cristiano (Dominican Republic), 17, 26, 44, 46n, 72, 76, 80, 84, 95, 110, 111, 136, 150, 151, 166, 189, 218, 228, 248, 262, 273, 276

Partido Social Cristiano (Bolivia). *See* Partido Demócrata Cristiano (Bolivia)
Partido Social Cristiano-COPEI (Venezuela), 15, 21, 23, 34, 72, 76, 78, 83–88, 91, 94, 108, 135, 141, 142, 144, 155, 163, 164, 181, 185, 189, 191, 192, 199, 204–209, 210, 221, 239, 241, 245, 251, 262, 272, 273, 274, 279, 281
Partido Social Cristiano (Nicaragua), 16, 20, 22, 39, 43n, 63, 103n, 104n, 113, 117n, 224, 230, 273. *See also* Unión Nacional de Acción Popular
Partido Social Demócrata Cristiano (Colombia), 16, 37, 45, 64, 79, 95, 98, 111, 131, 141, 163, 166, 201, 224, 266, 272
Partito Populare (Italy), 29, 30, 74, 215. *See also* Sturzo, Luigi
Party Discipline. *See* Latin American Christian Democratic Parties
Paula Jaramillo, Francisco de, 46, 73, 113n
Paul VI, Pope, 173
Paz Estenssoro, Víctor, 16, 79, 144, 256
Peasant Groups, 78, 88, 93, 120, 208, 277, 278
Peoples Radicals (Argentina). *See* Radical Parties
Peralta, Enrique, 76
Pérez Jiménez, Marcos, 21, 76, 88, 144, 145, 163, 164, 174, 176, 181, 189, 192, 199, 205, 273
Peronism. *See* Perón
Perón, Juan Domingo, 3, 4, 15, 20, 21, 25, 29, 36, 77, 144, 166, 171, 174, 201–204, 248, 249, 253, 256, 265, 266, 269, 273
Personalism, 51–52, 55, 56, 75, 103, 114, 139–140
Personalist Politics, 6, 7, 210, 211, 241, 265, 268
Philosophy of Movement. *See* Latin American Christian Democracy
Pike, Fredrick B., 19n
Pius XI, Pope, 26
Plá Rodríguez, Américo, 55, 59, 60, 70, 112n, 116n, 139, 140
Pluralism, 56–60, 81–82, 84, 101, 119, 232–237, 267–268. *See also* Latin American Christian Democracy
Polar Ugarteche, Mario, 251
Political Parties, Latin America, 4–12, 162
Política y Espíritu, 86
Ponce Enríquez, Camilo, 20, 25, 136
Popular Party (Italy). *See* Partito Populare
Population Problems. *See* Birth Control
Presidential Power, 104, 106, 108–109
Private Property, 113–115, 119, 123, 127–132. *See also* Latin American Christian Democracy
Promoción Popular, 98, 125–126
Protestantism, 63, 73, 168, 172, 176, 179, 260
Puerto Rico, 157
Public Opinion Studies, 82
Punta del Esta Conference, 146n. *See also* Alliance for Progress

Quadragesimo Anno, 26
Quadros, Jânio, 24, 45

Radical Parties, 4, 6, 51, 202, 203, 204, 219–222, 241, 247, 264, 266, 275
  Argentina, 4, 20, 25, 203, 204, 220
  Chile, 4, 74, 219–220, 255, 274, 276
Rasco, José, 15, 154
Read Vitini, Mario, 47n
Rebellion, Legitimacy of, 23, 64, 65, 66n
Regules, Dardo, 32, 38, 75, 133, 137, 145, 200, 216
Rerum Novarum, 13, 26, 103
"Revolución en Libertad," 34, 39, 230, 251–258. *See also* Latin American Christian Democracy
Revolution, the, 37–41, 115, 118, 230, 251–258. *See also* Latin American Christian Democracy
Reyes Vicuña, Tomás, 38n, 137, 145n, 151n, 153, 156n, 157
Rivera Concha, Alvaro, 79
Robles, Aswaldo, 32
Rodríguez-Arias, Lino B., 34, 46n, 110, 111, 120n, 121n
Rojas Pinilla, Gustavo, 174
Roman Catholic Church, 11, 21, 26, 27, 63, 73, 74, 113, 161, 167–181, 194, 207, 221, 258, 268, 272, 276, 277
  Education, 18, 30, 90, 99–102, 175, 179, 220

Roman Catholic Church (*Continued*)
New Catholicism, 28, 29, 171–175
See also Anti-Clericalism; Catholicism; Latin American Christian Democracy; Latin American Christian Democratic Parties
Romero Carranza, Ambrosio, 9, 64n, 73n, 75n, 78n, 127n
Rosario, Antonio, 218, 248

Sarmiento, Domingo, 100, 266
Scandinavia, 28, 30. *See also* Socialism
Scholasticism. *See* Neo-Thomism
Schumann, Robert, 271
Secco-Illa, Joaquín, 12n
Social Christian Federation (Chile), 19
Social Christian Party. *See* Movimiento; Partido
Social Democracy. *See* Socialism
Social Democratic Party (Bolivia), 16
Socialism, 26–28, 30n, 41–49, 81, 82, 127, 134, 168, 172, 188, 203, 214–219, 221, 222, 241, 259, 261, 264
Aprista, 204–209, 214–219, 253, 262, 280–281. *See also* Aprista Parties
Scandinavia, 28, 30–31
Yugoslavia, 31
Socialist Falange (Bolivia), 136–137, 185, 225
Socialist Parties (Latin America), 219–222, 239–240, 247, 255, 257
Somozas, 15, 16, 22, 64, 144
Sovereignty, 61–62, 141
Soviet Union. *See* Communism
Spain, 169, 170, 183, 186, 244, 267, 270
Spanish Catholicism, 173, 174
Spanish Character, 5
Stroessner, Alfredo, 22, 65, 144, 175, 187
Students. *See* Youth Groups
Sturzo, Luigi, 14, 29, 30, 56, 74, 86, 168n, 215. *See also* Partito Popolare (Italy)
Subsidiarity, 58, 64
Sueldo, Horacio, 202, 203

Tacuara, 185
Tannenbaum, Frank, 62n, 252n
Tarso Santos, Paulo de, 90, 199, 200, 246
Tavora, Juárez, 245, 246
Téfel Vélez, Reinaldo Antonio, 18, 19n, 40, 45n, 113, 142n, 165n, 167
Testimonio, 16, 92
Theoretical Positions. *See* Latin American Christian Democracy
Thomism. *See* Neo-Thomism
Tiempo, 14
Tomic, Radomiro, 138, 140, 197, 251
Trujillo, Rafael, 65, 76, 95, 135
Truman, Harry, 144n

Underdeveloped World. *See* Colonialism
Unión Cívica Católica, 185, 249
Unión Cívica Nacional (Panama), 17, 95
Unión de Campesinos Cristianos (Chile), 93
Unión Cívica (Uruguay) 3, 11–12, 13, 25, 32, 50, 62, 70, 74, 78, 86, 94, 99, 105, 107, 108, 131, 154–55, 185, 190, 200, 248, 249, 274
Unión Demócrata Cristiana de Córdoba (Argentina), 15
Unión Nacional de Acción Popular (Nicaragua), 16, 19
Unión Nacional Sinarquista, 184, 250, 251, 285
Unión Popular Demócrata Cristiano (Bolivia), 136
Unión Republicana Democrática (Venezuela), 21, 108, 205, 207, 209
United Nations Economic Commission for Latin America, 33, 35
United States, 3, 102, 145, 146, 154, 155, 156, 158, 159, 196, 202, 212, 247, 281. *See also* Alliance for Progress; Foreign Investment
University Groups. *See* Youth Groups

Vekemans, Roger, 173
Venezuelan Revolution of *1958*, 65
Venezuelan Students' Federation, 18
Vergara, Hernan, 16
Vila Echague, Iván, 232n

War of the Pacific, 45
Wars of Independence, 10, 65, 169, 170, 176
Winter, Ernst Karl, 237
Women's Groups, 88, 93, 95, 275–77
Women's Rights, 94–97, 275
World Congress of Christian Democracy, 135, 138, 191, 207
World Union of Christian Democracy, 135, 137, 138
World War I, 13
World War II, 31, 152, 201, 261, 266, 275

Ydigoras, Miguel, 76
Youth Groups, 9, 17–19, 79, 82, 89, 90, 142, 242, 279
  Brazil, 90, 199
  Chile, 47, 49, 89, 183
  Dominican Republic, 90
  Guatemala, 88
  Nicaragua, 90
  Venezuela, 89, 183, 207–208

EDWARD J. WILLIAMS is thoroughly familiar with the Christian Democratic movement, having conducted research at the Instituto de Formación Demócrata Cristiana in Caracas, Venezuela, and having worked also with the movement's New York office, the Center of Christian Democratic Action. His interest in political theory and in Latin American politics was developed during undergraduate and master's degree studies at Duquesne University and at Johns Hopkins University, where he received his doctorate. He has taught at St. Francis College, and is currently a member of the political science faculty of Marquette University.

Latin American Christian Democratic Parties

was set on the Linotype in ten-point Caledonia, a clean twentieth-century typeface designed by W. A. Dwiggins, the well-known American typographer. Dwiggins intended to adapt an early nineteenth-century modern face, Scotch Roman, but in part Caledonia was finally based as well on one of William Martin's roman faces of the same period. Hugh Bailey, who designed this book, chose a Monotype "grotesque" face, Standard, for display lines.

Heritage Printers, Charlotte, North Carolina, composed the book and printed it on Warren's Olde Style Antique Wove. Carolina Ruling and Binding Company, Charlotte, bound it in a cloth manufactured by Arkwright-Interlaken.

THE UNIVERSITY OF TENNESSEE PRESS